Dr Palmer held a College Lecturership at University College, Oxford, from 1978 to 1980, and was a Junior Research Fellow at St Hilda's College, Oxford, from 1980 to 1982.

OXFORD CLASSICAL MONOGRAPHS

*Published under the supervision of a Committee of the
Faculty of Literae Humaniores in the University of Oxford*

To Andrew

PRUDENTIUS
ON THE
MARTYRS

ANNE-MARIE PALMER

CLARENDON PRESS · OXFORD
1989

Oxford University Press, Walton Street, Oxford OX2 6DP

Oxford New York Toronto
Delhi Bombay Calcutta Madras Karachi
Petaling Jaya Singapore Hong Kong Tokyo
Nairobi Dar es Salaam Cape Town
Melbourne Auckland

and associated companies in
Berlin Ibadan

Oxford is a trade mark of Oxford University Press

Published in the United States
by Oxford University Press, New York

British Library Cataloguing in Publication Data

Palmer, Anne-Marie
Prudentius on the martyrs
1. Poetry in Latin. Prudentius clemens,
Aurelius 348– ca. 405
I. Title II. Series
871'.01

ISBN 0-19-814721-X

Library of Congress Cataloging in Publication Data

Palmer, Anne-Marie.
Prudentius on the martyrs.
(Oxford classical monographs)
Bibliography: p.
Includes index.
1. Prudentius, b. 348. Peristephanon. 2. Christian
poetry, Latin—History and criticism. 3. Christian
martyrs in literature.   I. Title. II. Series.
PA6648.P6P477 1989 874'.01 88–12473

ISBN 0-19-814721-X

Filmset by Eta Services (Typesetters) Ltd, Beccles, Suffolk

Printed in Great Britain
at the University Printing House, Oxford
by David Stanford
Printer to the University

Acknowledgements

I⊤ would be difficult to enumerate all those who have con-
tributed towards the conception and completion of this
book. I could go back to the Reverend Mother of my first
convent school, who successfully encouraged us all to read
and reread the stories of the saints and martyrs. However, I
must at least record my gratitude to the supervisor of the
doctoral thesis (Oxford, 1983) from which this book de-
veloped, Dr John Matthews, who put his great knowledge
of the period at my disposal and whose advice and criticism
were always invaluable. I would also like to pay tribute to
the late Colin Macleod, who kindly looked over the more
literary sections of my work in their early stages, and whose
comments were extremely helpful. My examiners, Mr A. S.
Hollis and Dr E. D. Hunt, contributed some constructive
criticisms. I am grateful also to the Principal and Fellows of
St Hilda's College, Oxford: the encouragement of Dr
Barbara Levick and Dr Doreen Innes during Greats made
the idea of research attractive to me, and a Junior Research
Fellowship at that college made its completion possible and
pleasant.

The last year of work on the book was spent very much
on the move, in Germany, Israel, and finally Holland. In
each country my thanks are due to those who made me wel-
come in their libraries. In Munich Dr Peter Flury and Dr
Ursula Keudel encouraged me to work in the wonderfully
well-stocked library of the *Thesaurus Linguae Latinae* and Dr
Kai Brodersen made me welcome in the Institute for
Ancient History. Kai Brodersen also gave invaluable help
with the book's bibliography. In Jerusalem, by the kindness
of the Director, Père Vesco, I was able to make use of the
facilities of the École Biblique et Archéologique Française.
In Groningen, Dr F. Akkerman both welcomed me to the
Library of the Classical Institute and introduced me to the
University Library and its most helpful staff.

I must also register my heartfelt thanks to my family.
First, to my parents, who were endlessly encouraging and

enthusiastic about my work. It was thanks to them that I was originally able to visit the Christian sites of Rome. Then to my husband, Dr Andrew Palmer, who inevitably lived with and shared all the strain of completing this work. His advice, sympathy, and general support were always freely given, and much appreciated. I must also thank Miss Ria Schepel and Miss Moira Allan, whose help with the children during the last stages of work was indispensable. Last but not least, special thanks are due to the children themselves: only the patience and adaptability of Rebecca, Molly, Thomas, and little Rosie made the completion of the book possible.

A.-M.P.

Contents

	Abbreviations	ix
	Introduction	I
1.	The Man and his Poetry	6
2.	*Curiositas* and Credulity	32
3.	The Form and Purpose of the *Peristephanon*	57
4.	Prudentian *Imitatio* and Christian 'Augustanism'	98
5.	'Egregiae Animae'	140
6.	Prudentius and the Imperial Poets	180
7.	The Martyrdom of Bishop Fructuosus and his Deacons	205
8.	The *Peristephanon* and its Sources	227
	Epilogue	278
	Bibliography	281
	General Index	313
	Index of Passages and Works Discussed	320

Abbreviations

AASS	*Acta Sanctorum quae collegit J. Bollandus* (1643–)
BHG	*Bibliotheca Hagiographica Graeca*, 3 vols. (1957³)
BHL	*Bibliotheca Hagiographica Latina Antiquae et Mediae Aetatis*, 2 vols. (1889–1901)
BSS	Bibliotheca Sanctorum
CCL	Corpus Christianorum, Series Latina (1954–)
CIL	*Corpus Inscriptionum Latinarum*, 16 vols. (1863–)
CSEL	Corpus Scriptorum Ecclesiasticorum Latinorum (1866–)
CTh	Codex Theodosianus, ed. Th. Mommsen and P. M. Meyer (1905)
DACL	*Dictionnaire d'archéologie chrétienne et de liturgie* (1907–)
Dessau	*Prosopographia Imperii Romani, Saec. I, II, III* (1897)
EC	*Enciclopedia cattolica* (1948–54)
GCS	*Die griechischen christlichen Schriftsteller der ersten Jahrhunderte* (1897–)
ILCV	*Inscriptiones Latinae Christianae Veteres*, ed. E. Diehl (1924–31)
ILS	*Inscriptiones Latinae Selectae*, ed. H. Diehl (1892–1916)
LRE	A. H. M. Jones, *The Later Roman Empire: A Social, Economic and Administrative Survey (284–602)*, 3 vols. and maps (1964)
Lewis and Short	*A Latin Dictionary* (1879)
Mansi	*Sacrorum Consiliorum Nova et Amplissima Collectio*, ed. G. D. Mansi (1759–98)
MGH Auct. Ant.	*Monumenta Germaniae Historica: Auctores Antiquissimi* (1826–)
NOHM	*New Oxford History of Music*, ed. A. Hughes (1955; repr. 1969)
OCD	*The Oxford Classical Dictionary*, ed. N. G. L. Hammond and H. H. Scullard (1978²)
ODCC	*The Oxford Dictionary of the Christian Church*, ed. F. L. Cross, and E. A. Livingstone (1974²)
PG	*Patrologiae Cursus Completus, series Graeca*, ed. J.-P. Migne (1844–)
Pe.	*Peristephanon Liber* (Prudentius)
PL	*Patrologiae Cursus Completus, series Latina*, ed. J.-P. Migne (1844–)

PLRE i, ii	A. H. M. Jones, J. R. Martindale, J. Morris, and (vol. ii) J. R. Martindale, *The Prosopography of the Later Roman Empire*, i, *A.D. 260–395* (1971); ii, *A.D. 395–527* (1980).
RE	*Real-Encylopädie der classischen Altertumswissenschaft,* ed. Pauly–Wissowa–Kroll (1893–)
SC	*Sources chrétiennes* (1940–)
TLL	*Thesaurus Linguae Latinae* (1900–)

Titles of periodicals are abbreviated as in *L'Année philologique*.

Introduction

PRUDENTIUS is a major poet. This is obvious from the very scope and quality of his poetry. He is also the greatest Christian poet of the Late Antique period, writing in an age of transition from the world of classical, pagan Rome to the new Christian Roman Empire, which had lately come to complete fruition under Theodosius. Prudentius' poetry is written at a climax and also at a turning-point in the history of the Western Empire. As the poet recognizes and celebrates in his poetry, Theodosius' reign marks a new Golden Age for Rome. Prudentius does not seem to have lived to know of the sack of Rome in AD 410, and he ignores the signs of the dark age to come. Instead, his poetry gives expression to the new confidence felt by contemporary Christians, by accepting implicitly many aspects of secular poetry and combining them with the new ideals and forms of expression provided by Christianity and its growing literature. The synthesis is deep and complete, resulting in poetry which is highly sophisticated, but also alive with freshness and novelty.

It is, therefore, astonishing that so few full studies of Prudentius' poetry exist to do him justice with modern readers. The work produced in the last century reflected most critics' low opinion of this 'late' poet: to them, his work was tasteless, overblown, and derivative, deserving analysis only in the form of bald lists of parallel texts which revealed his slavish reliance on classical 'sources'. Otherwise, the poetry was neglected in favour of examination of its theological content. Only Puech attempted anything like an extensive study,[1] and Prudentius continued to be treated elsewhere in brief entries in large-scale studies of Latin literature. The picture has improved this century, with the work of Bergman and Lavarenne, for instance, but most major studies have concentrated on the *Psychomachia*, with its obvious importance for medieval allegory and iconography, and on the *Cathemerinon*, whose freshness of lyrical form gives it an immediate appeal for modern audiences.[2] The didactic poems are slowly gaining the

---

[1] Puech (1888).
[2] See e.g. the work of Smith (1976) and Charlet (1982).

attention they deserve as poems, and not only as theological trea-
tises.[3]

The *Peristephanon* has suffered most from this neglect. A
number of articles have been written on various aspects of the
poems, and several editions with translation and brief comment-
ary appeared in the first half of this century (see the bibliography).
However, none of this work has gone far enough towards produ-
cing a thorough study of the poems. This lack is partly the result
of the very nature of the poems. Of all Prudentius' works, these
are, in many ways, the most inaccessible for modern readers, who
find it difficult to identify with, and understand, a genuine enthu-
siasm for martyr-cult and for stories that concentrate on, and
glory in, the lurid details of torture and death, and the startling
operation of the supernatural. An effort of historical imagination
is required. Yet an understanding of this background is vital for
any evaluation of the *Peristephanon*. Without it, it is all too easy to
dismiss various features of the poems as tedious and unnecessary.

The only way to arrive at a more far-reaching and balanced
judgement of the poems is to set them in their complete cultural
context. They should be related to the general tastes and outlook
of their contemporary audience, since poetry in Prudentius' day
still kept its immediate audience very much in view. Due weight
must be given to consideration of their varied background both in
classical Latin literature and in the more popular forms of Chris-
tian literature and oral tradition. The religious preoccupations of
his time must not be undervalued for their influence on the form,
as well as on the contents, of the *Peristephanon*, which can also, in
turn, be used as a source of information concerning cult practices,
particularly for those in Rome and Spain. Recognition of all these
factors makes it easier to appreciate both the form and the purpose
of the poems, and also their striking novelty. In many ways they
are the most arresting compositions in the whole Prudentian cor-
pus, with their daring (if sometimes uneven) combination of clas-
sical and Christian elements.

In this book, I have attempted to supply the need for such a
study. I examine various aspects of the poet's life and the society
in which he moved (Chapters 1 and 2), the relation of the *Peri-
stephanon* to the heritage of classical literature (Chapters 4–6), and

[3] This development is well exemplified by Palla (1981), whose edition of the *Hamarti-
genia* is supported by a full commentary. See my review in *CR*, NS 32 (1981) 175–6.

(equally important), its sources in contemporary martyr-literature (Chapters 7 and 8). I reopen the question of the poems' primary purpose by a close examination of their form, coming to the conclusion that the poems were not, as it has often been assumed, intended in the first place as liturgical hymns (Chapter 3). They provided devotional reading-matter for a cultured audience outside a church context. This realization contributes towards painting as clear a picture as possible of the poems' first audience, which has been one of the aims of this book. Consideration of the poet's likely biography (Chapter 1), is not intended to find facts where none exists, but to place the poet firmly in his general social milieu. This makes it possible to define the range of influences affecting his poetry. Living and moving for some time in the profoundly Christian atmosphere of the imperial court, he experienced the influence on court circles of the Christian (and, significantly, Spanish) emperor Theodosius, and the remarkable figure of Ambrose. International experience of martyr-cult, particularly in the Western centres, Milan and Rome, must have been formative for the conception and composition of at least part of the *Peristephanon*. The poet's background in upper-class Christian circles in Spain and at a predominantly Spanish imperial court, indicates the sort of friends and contacts who would have provided an important stimulus for the composition of the individual poems of the collection, which seems to have evolved gradually, rather than being conceived from the outset as a unity. The different requirements of each recipient may partially explain the poems' varied approach and treatment in dealing with the uniting theme of martyrdom.

Such an audience not only was steeped in classical literature as the result of its traditional Roman education (Chapter 4), but also participated fully (and inevitably) in the general culture of the period, influenced as this was by so many elements which were un-Roman and un-classical (Chapter 2). The events and sights of fourth-century society were the living proof of a distinctive and individual culture resulting from an often quite hectic degree of social mobility. Christianity played its part: Christian literature alone (the Bible, apocryphal writings, and martyr-literature), with its roots in popular experience and self-expression, provided a vigorous new influence which helped to reshape reading tastes and aesthetic sensibilities. With all this in mind, it becomes easier to understand the popularity of the *Peristephanon* with an upper-class audience. It was this *mélange* of influences that worked on Prudentius' poetic imagination for the composition of the *Peristephanon*. The result was what amounts to a new genre, the lyrical ballad (that is, Christianized epic set in lyric form). The popular background in martyr-literature seems to have freed the poet from the more conventional and restricting conceptions of poetic genre.

However, Christianity did not influence the poet from the stylistic point of view alone. It must never be overlooked that the *Peristephanon* is firmly rooted in profound religious feelings and impulses focused on the cult of the martyrs. The element of prayer in the poems is not simply a matter of form: it is a vital part of the poems' purpose, as the basis for private religious devotions and spiritual meditations. Something of the flavour and forms of devotion to the martyrs emerges from the poems, and this must be recognized to have been stimulated by the realities of cult practices, and the deep involvement in them of Prudentius' Christian contemporaries. The piety of the Spanish court under Theodosius has often been related to his public activities. The *Peristephanon*, together with the rest of Prudentius' poetry, illustrates this piety at work in the more private sphere: even 'leisure reading' must be supplied with a wholly Christian literature. Abroad, pious Spaniards undertook the rigours of pilgrimage. At home, they had in the *Peristephanon* a literary recreation of their experiences on which to meditate in peace.

There are other threads, too, binding the *Peristephanon* together. Strong feelings of patriotism run through the poems: patriotism for the triumph of a now fully Christian Rome (*Pe.* 2, 11, and 12), or a more local *campanilismo*, which proudly celebrates the possession of a local hero, a town's 'resident' martyr and heavenly *patronus* (*Pe.* 1, 3, 4, 5, and 6). Such feelings blend well with the lyric celebration and prayers in the poems. At a deeper level, the very stylistic texture of the poems celebrates the Christian heroes in terms recalling those used of their non-Christian ancestors, the traditional Roman heroes who figure in Augustan poetry, particularly in the *Aeneid*. This is not merely a matter of literary ornamentation, but it relates Prudentius' conception of Christian patriotism and heroism, as exemplified by the martyrs, to Rome's non-Christian past. By expressing these Christianized ideals in language reminiscent of Virgil or Horace, Prudentius demonstrates a new assimilation of the old ideals, as well as an implicit acceptance of previously rejected pagan literature. The new Christian Golden Age finds appropriate expression in references to the values and the language of the chief poets of the Augustan Golden Age. Prudentius sees and expresses in this way an essential continuity with the Roman past at a time when Christians feel secure in their position in fourth-century culture. Just as pagan statues can be accepted and preserved as works of art (*CTh* 16. 10. 8, AD 382), so Prudentius can fearlessly absorb and reuse the best aspects of pagan literature for Christian ends.

This is the background against which the *Peristephanon* can be most fully appreciated and evaluated for its contribution to our understanding of fourth-century culture and society. In undertaking to paint it in, I have had to be selective in the areas chosen for study. The *Peristephanon* is a large collection (over three and a half thousand lines), and it is difficult to do all the poems equal justice. Thus I have omitted a detailed study of *Pe.* 10. My justification is that, as the manuscripts show, this long poem was originally treated as a separate book and not included in the collection. It is long enough (over a thousand lines) to merit a separate study—one in fact already undertaken by Henke,[4] who has covered the main points of interest in *Pe.* 10. As for the biblical influence on the *Peristephanon*, preliminary work suggests that it is small in comparison with the influence of martyr-literature. The influence on Prudentius of his contemporary, Ausonius, has already been examined—in the study of Charlet.[5] In conclusion, I can only hope that my study of the *Peristephanon* gives some idea of the character and balance of the collection.

> Sum mutus ipse, sed potens facundiae
> mea lingua Christus luculente disseret.

---

4 Henke (1983); I review this work in *CR*, NS 34. 2 (1984) 327–8.
5 Charlet (1980*a*).

I

The Man and his Poetry

'THE least egotistical of the Christian latin poets'[1] is brief and allusive in writing about himself; yet there is no better source for his biography.[2] To attempt a detailed reconstruction of his life is pointless. But the *Praefatio*, which was intended as a general introduction to his poetry,[3] is the obvious starting-point for the vital task of investigating the poet's social background and his conception of the purpose and usefulness of purely Christian poetry. The *Peristephanon* (*Pe.*) itself contains some important autobiographical information, though it is scattered and often indirect.

The first necessity is to discover the exact relationship of literary and personal elements in the *Praefatio*, an expression of the Christian vocation of a poet which is both original and mature. A correct evaluation of this document,[4] including the autobiographical material in it, is only possible in the light of an investigation of its background and intention. Then we may be in a position to study the *Peristephanon* 'in the round', giving proper place to the formative influence of Prudentius' social environment and to the relationship between his career in the imperial administration and his decision to abandon that and become a poet.

---

[1] Waddell (1930) 297.

[2] Sidonius Apollinaris (*Ep.* 2. 9), Avitus (*De laude castitatis*, 375 ff.), Gregory of Tours (*De gloria martyrum*, 1, 41, 93, 106; *De gloria confessorum*, 112), Fortunatus (*De uita S. Martini*, 1. 19), and Isidore of Seville (*Carmen* 9) gives no biographical information; the late-5th-century reference to Prudentius in Gennadius' continuation of Jerome's *De uiris illustribus* will be discussed below (nn. 40 and 82, and chap. 3, p. 87), but contains no more information than the *Praefatio* itself, on which it is obviously based.

[3] It seems unlikely, on grounds of content, that the *Praefatio* was written as an introduction to the *Cathemerinon liber* alone, as Lana suggests (1962: 34–5). For a full bibliography on this question see van Assendelft (1976) 6–7. That the earliest surviving MS of Prudentius, the 6th-century Puteanus (BN 8084), does not contain the *Praefatio* proves nothing, since it probably represents a private collection of the poems made before the composition of the *Praefatio*, AD 404–5. Bergman (1921: 36) posited the loss of pages at the beginning of this MS, but my own examination of the codex supports Cunningham's statement (1958: 32–7) that the *Praefatio* was never part of this collection.

[4] For a fully literary evaluation of the *Praefatio* see Witke (1968) 509–25. Also Brožek (1967–8) 149–56 and Rapisarda (1948) 51–61.

The *Praefatio*: Literary Background

Per quinquennia iam decem,
ni fallor, fuimus; septimus insuper
annum cardo rotat, dum fruimur sole uolubili.

Instat terminus, et diem
uicinum senio iam Deus adplicat: 5
quid nos utile spatio temporis egimus?

Aetas prima crepantibus
fleuit sub ferulis; mox docuit toga
infectum uitiis falsa loqui, non sine crimine.

Tum lasciua proteruitas   10
et luxus petulans (heu pudet ac piget!)
foedauit iuuenem nequitiae sordibus et luto.

Exim iurgia turbidos
armarunt animos, et male pertinax
uincendi studium subiacuit casibus asperis.   15

Bis legum moderamine
frenos nobilium reximus urbium
ius ciuile bonis reddidimus, terruimus reos.

Tandem militiae gradu
euectum pietas principis extulit,   20
adsumptum propius stare iubens ordine proximo.

Haec dum uita uolans agit,
inrepsit subito canities seni,
oblitum ueteris me Saliae consulis arguens,

sub quo prima dies mihi.   25
Quam multas hiemes uoluerit et rosas
pratis post glaciem reddiderit, nix capitis probat.

Numquid talia proderunt
carnis post obitum uel bona uel mala,
cum iam, quidquid id est, quod fueram, mors aboleuerit?   30

Dicendum mihi: 'quisquis es,
mundum, quem coluit, mens tua perdidit;
non sunt illa Dei, quae studuit, cuius habeberis.'

Atqui fine sub ultimo
peccatrix anima stultitiam exuat;   35
saltem uoce Deum concelebret, si meritis nequit.

Hymnis continuet dies,
nec nox ulla uacet, quin Dominum canat;
pugnet contra hereses, catholicam discutiat fidem;

conculcet sacra gentium,   40
labem, Roma, tuis inferat idolis;
carmen martyribus deuoueat, laudet apostolos.

    Haec dum scribo uel eloquor,
uinclis o utinam corporis emicem
liber, quo tulerit lingua sono mobilis ultimo!   45

Prudentius, now in his fifty-seventh year (1–3), stops to review
the usefulness of his life, which is drawing to a close (4–6). He
speaks briefly of each stage in his career, from his 'aetas prima' (8)
and his schooldays, through his periods of office as provincial
governor (16–18), until his final promotion by the emperor to a
high position in the court (19–21). The realization of his advanc-
ing years (22–7) then overwhelms him as he considers that all his
achievements are nothing in the face of death. It is now time for
his sinful soul to put off the foolishness of wordly involvement in
order to celebrate God with its poetic voice, since his own wordly
achievements are unworthy to do this. He outlines (37–42) the
sorts of poetry his soul could sing in its new, wholly Christian vo-
cation. He ends with a prayer that he might die in the act of writ-
ing or reciting his verse and so be freed from his body to go
heavenward, whither his tongue had been carrying him with its
last utterance (43–5).

    The poet's awareness of his obligations as an orthodox Chris-
tian (39) have led him to review his past life in a negative way. It is
as if he were making his last confession and resolving to repent by
devoting his remaining years to the composition of poetry writ-
ten exclusively for the glorification of God. His poetic career is
represented as the result of a spiritual conversion which is spoken
of as if it were happening in the course of writing the *Praefatio*
itself. This explains the present tenses of the first two stanzas,
which are not contradicted by the perfect tense of line 22: the poet
returns to the present realization of old age with 'nix capitis
probat' (27).[5] Prudentius brings his state of mind vividly before
the reader, who relives with the poet this spiritual reawakening.
The sense of a new beginning, starting from now—that is, the
dramatic present of the *Praefatio*—is reinforced by the forceful
way in which the poet encourages himself to fulfil this new form

---

[5] Witke (1968: 513) compares Prudentian and Horatian imagery of old age, referring to
Horace, *Odes*, 1. 9. 17–18 'sperne puer neque tu choreas/donec uirenti canities abest
morosa' and 4. 13. 12 'capitis niues'.

of Christian vocation: Prudentius uses the series of jussive sub-junctives ('uacet', 'canat', 'pugnet', 'discutiat', 'conculcet', 'inferat', 'deuoueat', 'laudet') to exhort himself to begin his self-imposed task, as a Christian poet.

How original is such a 'confessional' *Praefatio* in the history of Latin literature and how does it relate to the rest of Prudentius' poetry? If the poet feels he is near the end of his life, can it be true that he is only now setting out to write what is to become a size-able and varied corpus of poetry? It seems more probable that the *Praefatio* was written as an introduction to an already existing cor-pus, the bare outlines of which are reflected in the types of poetry listed (37–42). But is there not a discrepancy between the poet's Christian honesty in laying bare his past faults and his aspirations for the future, and his literary deception in post-dating his vo-cation as a Christian poet? To answer such questions we must probe the subtlety and elusiveness of the *Praefatio* in order to analyse its complex literary debt. Prudentius draws freely on the classical tradition; indeed, he is steeped in it. But his attitude to tradition is profoundly affected by the Christian revolution, and his literary inheritance includes Augustine's *Confessions*. In Pru-dentius, the Christianization of classical poetry achieves its matur-ity.

Classical conventions and the new Christian morality are com-bined by Prudentius with freedom and sensitivity in the *Praefatio*. His adaptation of the commonplaces of the classical *exordium*,[6] for example, informs the husk of rhetorical prescription with the rich meaning of Christian intentions.[7] It was conventional for the poet to obtain the reader's sympathy (*captatio benevolentiae*) by a profes-sion of modesty,[8] and to explain his undertaking (*causa scribendi*). The latter regularly became a dedication to God in the Christian poets. The effect of 'spiritualization' is seen even better in the sub-stitution of humility for false modesty (*modestia affectata*) in the *captatio benevolentiae*; this produces a mixture of rhetorical vocabulary and moral intent. Classical *exordia* often express the poet's sense of daring (e.g. Virgil, *Georgics*, 2. 175; Propertius, 2. 10. 5), followed by a profession of inadequacy which was *de rigeur*; Prudentius translates this into a feeling of awe and a con-

---

[6] Junod-Ammerbauer (1975) 13–54.
[7] Junod-Ammerbauer (1975) 15–16; Thraede (1965) 26.
[8] Cicero, *De inuentione*, 1. 16.

sciousness of sin in the face of his heavenly dedicatee. In pagan
imperial panegyric we find the poetic creation formally assimil-
ated to a sacrifice on the altar of the divinized emperor; *carmina
pro muneribus*;[9] for Prudentius, the praise of God is a true spiritual
panegyric which gives life to the insincere themes of secular
rhetoric. Thus, in the *Praefatio*, the poet's not inconsiderable
worldly achievements are quite discounted in the context of his
divine undertaking: 'saltem voce Deum concelebret, si meritis
nequit' (35).[10]

The confessional and self-analytical side of the *Praefatio* marks it
out from its non-Christian counterparts. Autobiographical intro-
ductions and conclusions to a poet's writing had a history going
back to the Hellenistic period,[11] when, however, such prefaces
were brief, factual, and impersonal, in spite of the frequent use of
the first person singular and of the poet's name. It was the Roman
poets of the Augustan age who injected a more personal note into
such introductory or concluding autobiography. Thus Horace
'took over the scholastic style of those Alexandrine biographies of
the classics in delicate miniature in order to spice the expression of
his sense of poetic individuality'.[12] At *Ep.* 1. 20. 19ff. Horace
gives his biography according to the scholastic scheme, including
descent, career and achievements, appearance, character, and age.
The fullest example of such an autobiographical poem concludes
the fourth book of Ovid's *Tristia* (4. 10), where Ovid tells of his
home, his descent, and his education. He gives the year and day of
his birth, he mentions the equestrian rank of his family, and tells
about his brother and his early death. He depicts himself as a born
poet and tells of his withdrawal from an official career which
would have brought him to the Senate. The topics covered by
Horace and Ovid have an obvious bearing on Prudentius' auto-
biographical statements in the *Praefatio*,[13] but neither of the pagan

[9] Junod-Ammerbauer (1975) 18–22 and Thraede (1965) 42. Examples from classical
poetry are: Propertius, 2. 10. 23 ff.; Ovid, *Tristia*, 2. 73–7 and *Pont.* 4. 8. 33; Statius, *Siluae*,
1. 4. 31 ff. In the Christian sphere, Paulinus of Nola compares his poem to the widow's
mite (Luke 21: 2; Mark 12: 41–4) at *C.* 18. 46–61 and 213–18.

[10] Curtius (1979) has an interesting discussion of rhetorical topics, particularly the exor-
dium (79 ff.) and affected modesty (83–4).

[11] Misch (1973) 1. 295–306: 'The literary practice of self-revelation among poets'. Also
Kranz (1961) 3–46 and Curtius (1979) 90 (topics of the conclusion).

[12] Misch (1973) 1. 301, with reference to Horace, *Ep.* 1. 20. 19 ff. and the autobio-
graphical passages in the *Sermones*.

[13] Horace, *Ep.* 2. 1. 70; also *Serm.* 1. 3. 120; cf. Juvenal, *Sat.* 1. 15; Martial, 10. 62. 10;
Ausonius, *Ep.* 12. 1. 1; *Lib. protrepticus*, 24 ff.; Quintilian, *Inst. or.* 1. 2. 16 ff.

poets reviews his past life with the self-analytical preoccupation of the Christian. They are still nearer to the Hellenistic tradition. The novelty of Prudentius' style of *praefatio* in the light of this tradition becomes clearest on comparison with the *praefatio* of a near contemporary (and fellow Christian), Ausonius. Ausonius' form of autobiographical introduction covers the traditional topics, but leaves no room for doubt, and is written with pride in his achievements, rather than with humility.

> qui sim, qua stirpe, lare et patria,
> adscripsi, ut nosses, bone vir, quicumque fuisses,
> et notum memori me coleres animo.
>
> (*Praef.* I. 2–4)

While Prudentius' *Praefatio* has close parallels with the traditional biographical scheme exemplified by Ovid and Ausonius, it also contains elements which must be explained in terms of the poet's Christianity.

The autobiographical structure of the *Praefatio* provides Prudentius with a fresh way of presenting a *causa scribendi*, here set in terms of 'conversion' from a worldly career to a single-mindedly Christian way of life. Personal statements of conversion had a double background, Christian and non-Christian. The theme of conversion to philosophy as the conversion to a higher, better life was not unknown in pagan Rome and had found literary expression in autobiographical form.[14] This form of literary expression was not necessarily an accurate account of a conversion, which may turn out in reality to have been a slow adoption or exchange of ideas.[15] In Roman poetry there existed one famous model of a statement of conversion to the more serious pursuit of philosophy: the first poem of Horace's first book of *Epistles*.[16] Horace's claim to sudden conversion obscures his earlier interest in philosophy, attested elsewhere in his writings. Prudentius can hardly have been unaware of this example of the theme of conversion in the introduction to a book of poetry. But in the *Praefatio* he may also have had in mind the first poem of Horace's first book of

---

[14] Nock (1933) 164 ff.: 'Conversion to philosophy'. Courcelle (1963: 92) shows how the idea of describing in autobiographical form the author's approach to the truth is not specifically Christian. He uses the example of Dio Chrysostom, *Or.* 13 (and elsewhere), which describes his turning away from the frivolity of eloquence towards philosophy.

[15] See Moles (1978) on the 'conversion' of Dio Chrysostom.

[16] Macleod (1979).

Odes, where poetry is set above the other careers open to men and
seen as a vocation to withdraw from the majority (*Odes*, I. I. 29–
32). The thought of these two prefatory poems is combined in
Prudentius' claim to the new vocation of Christian poet. For
whereas Horace had seemed to reject the frivolity of poetry in
favour of the wholehearted pursuit of philosophy, Prudentius
frankly identifies his new seriousness of purpose as a Christian
with a resolve to write poetry dedicated to God. In *Odes*, I. I.
poetry is presented as the highest pursuit and one through which
the poet is immortalized; this thought forms the climax of the
poem. Likewise, in Prudentius' *Praefatio*, the writing of Christian
poetry is valued far above the poet's past experience of a worldly
career. In Horace's poem, withdrawal from the world is seen as
necessary for the poet. Prudentius, too, sees his adoption of Chris-
tian poetry as a mark of his withdrawal from wordly affairs in a
Christian sense.[17] In Prudentius, a new emphasis is laid on the
content of the poetry, which must be Christian. Only in this way
can poetry become the means of a truer form of immortality, the
Christian poet's own salvation.

The *Praefatio* also derives much of its force from a strictly
Christian theme of 'conversion' to a deeper religious conviction
and of withdrawal from the world. Prudentius is not talking
about conversion to Christianity from paganism, which he could
have exploited in a different way in the *Praefatio*.[18] Here he speaks
of his experience in terms reminiscent of the contemporary
phenomenon exemplified by the withdrawal from the world of
Paulinus of Nola, whose 'conversion' was a decision to live out a
fuller commitment to Christianity.

In the late fourth century the general taste for biography found
its Christian expression in enthusiasm for Lives of saints, initiated
by the popular *Life of St Anthony*, which was soon brought to the
West in Latin translation.[19] This, along with the Christian habit
of self-examination for the confession of sins,[20] forms the back-

---

[17] On withdrawal in the 4th century and its pagan background see Fontaine (1972).

[18] Cf. Commodian's explicit statement about this sort of conversion, *Praef. instruc-
tionum*, I. 4–9.

[19] For the general popularity of biography in this period, see the comments of Ammia-
nus Marcellinus, 14. 6 and 28. 4. Augustine, *Conf.* 8. 6 gives Ponticianus' account of the
deep impact made by the Latin translation of the *Life of Antony* (see n. 42 below).

[20] Misch (1973) 2. 580–4 traces the connection between penitential practice and con-
fession as a literary form, as in the writings of Ephraim the Syrian and Gregory of Nazian-

ground to a new development of the autobiographical theme: spiritual self-analysis. Prudentius' *Praefatio* is a concise example of this and it seems that its literary history lies in the recent Christian past. Jerome in *De uiris illustribus*, 91 seems to give a tantalizing glimpse of such a work by a fellow Spaniard, one Acilius Severus, who 'composuit uolumen quasi ὁδοιπορικόν totius uitae suae, statim continuens tam prosa quam uersibus, quod uocauit καταστροφήν sive πεῖραν, et sub Valentiniano principe obiit'. Acilius Severus told some of his life in verse, and the words καταστροφή and πεῖρα seem to contain a hint of spiritual conversion.

Acilius' work is lost. More important is the survival of Augustine's *Confessions*. The early books of this work involve an analysis of the author's youth from the perspective of his mature, Christian outlook. Courcelle (1963) pursues the literary antecedents of Augustine's spiritual autobiography back to the early Fathers. However, in spite of a recurrence of autobiographical *schemata*, he concludes that the idea of an autobiography in the form of a confession of sins is not a western one. As parallels he cites the preface to Commodian's *Instructions*, 1–2 and 4–9, and his *Carmen apologeticum*, 3–9, and Prudentius' *Praefatio*. The *Confessions* may have influenced at least the Prudentian example.[21]

Late in his life, Augustine noted the widespread popularity of the *Confessions*,[22] whereas he shows no knowledge of Prudentius' poetry. The probable date of the *Praefatio*[23] comes after the early books of the *Confessions*, which were written in the late 390s.[24] Lines 7–15 of the *Praefatio* seem to encapsulate the matter of these books, using similar terms to describe the same phases. If lines 7–8 recall Horace's picture of 'plagosus Orbilius' and other classical

zus, which preceded Augustine's *Confessions*. On penance see Michel (1933) and the *Dictionnaire de spiritualité ascétique et mystique, doctrine et histoire* 12. 1 (1984) 943 ff. On examination of conscience see Jaeger (1959), Lagarde (1925), and Fredriksen (1986), who is especially interesting on the subject of the 'retrospective self'.

[21] Commodian's date is problematical: 3rd or 5th century? See *ODCC* s.v. Commodian, with bibliography. Courcelle (1946: 227–46) argued for the 5th century, but Salvatore (1960: 161 ff.; see also 1977: 1–2) uses passages from Prudentius' didactic poems to prove that Commodian was earlier than these.

[22] *De dono perseuerentiae*, 20 (AD 428 or 429).

[23] AD 404–5, calculated from the birth-year given in the *Praefatio* and Prudentius' statement there that he is in his 57th year.

[24] On the purpose and form of the *Confessions*, see Brown (1967) 158–81 and Courcelle (1950). In his chronological table Brown dates the *Confessions* to AD 397–401.

models (see n. 13 above), they evoke equally strongly the vivid
description of Augustine's schooldays from *Confessions* 1. 9 ff.
Prudentius might draw on Horatian vocabulary in lines 10–12,[25]
but with the expression of disgust, 'heu pudet ac piget!', the word
of implied rejection, 'foedavit' and the summing up of such ado-
lescent immorality in 'nequitiae sordibus et luto', Prudentius
surely imitates the censorious tone of the *Confessions*. The next
stanza, too, recalls Augustine's rejection of rhetoric (for example,
Confessions, 3). Where the poet's career diverges from that of
Augustine, he is noticeably more neutral in tone. The central
position of the phrase 'pietas principis' in line 20 covers a carefully
muted note of pride in his service of the 'Servant of God'. This is,
however, quickly dispelled by the realization of the next three
stanzas: life flies rapidly past, old age creeps up suddenly, and only
the 'nix capitis' makes him aware of its advance. Here once again
Augustine's outlook, and even his language, may be at the back of
the poet's mind: 'uita misera est, mors incerta est; subito
obrepat—quomodo hinc exibimus? et ubi nouis discenda sunt
quae hinc negleximus?' (*Confessions*, 6. 11). This passage seems to
be recalled by 'inrepsit subito', *Praefatio*, 23. The similarity seems
striking, although it is true that expressions of such realizations
did already exist in Christian literature—in the Psalms, for in-
stance, where remorseful self-analysis was also to be found.[26]
Repentence for sins committed at a time of less spiritual awareness
might find expression in exaggeration of such sins. So, in Jerome's
epitaph for Paula, he notes, 'In qua fontes crederes lachrymarum.
Ita leuia peccata plangebat, ut illam grauissimorum criminum
crederes reum.'[27] Rejection of the past self, of past sinfulness is the
sine qua non of full commitment for the convert. This idea had its
roots in the Gospels in the call to give up everything and follow
Christ (e.g. John 17: 1–11), and was familiar from St Paul's writ-
ings: 'Put off your old nature which belongs to your former man-

---

[25] *Odes*, 1. 19. 3 and 7: 'lasciua licentia' and 'grata proteruitas'.

[26] See e.g. Ps. 39, expressing the insignificance of man before God and the brevity of his
divinely determined lifespan. Ps. 42, touching the grey hairs of old age, has parallels with
the *Praefatio*. Cf. Paulinus of Nola in his letter to Ausonius: 'breue, quidquid homo est,
homo corporis aegri,/temporis occidui est sine Christo puluis et umbra'.

[27] Jerome's epitaph for Paula, *Ep.* 108. 15. Cf. the comments of the priest Macarius on
monastic conversion (Wilmart (1920) 72): 'In primis quidem, si coeperit homo semetipsum
agnoscere quur creatus sit, et exquisierit factorem suum Deum, tunc incipiet paenitere
super his quae commisit in tempore neglegentiae suae. Sic demum benignius Deus dat illi
tristitiam pro peccatis.'

ner of life and is corrupt through sinful lusts and be renewed in
the spirit of your mind ...'[28] So Paulinus of Nola notes that 'se
enim ipsum mutat et superat, qui renuntiat moribus suis et se
abdicat sibi' (*Ep.* 40. 11).

Thus the 'uel bona uel mala' of Prudentius' secular career are, in
this Christian perspective, useless for the gaining of salvation. He
talks of himself as already dead: 'quidquid id est, quod fueram', in
language reminiscent of the common Roman epitaph,[29] as well as
the Gospels and the Epistles of St Paul. Such sentiments are re-
peated by contemporary Christians: 'When we turn to Him, we
turn away from the world, when we live in Him, we are dead to
the elements of this world'; Gregory of Nazianzus refers to him-
self in this *Carmen de se ipso* as 'dead in life': αὐτὰρ ἐγὼ τέθνηκα
βίῳ.[30]

With 'peccatrix anima stultitiam exuat' (*Praefatio*, 35), Pruden-
tius draws once again on Pauline thought in a reminiscence of the
'stultitia mundi': 'I will destroy the wisdom of the wise and the
cleverness of the clever I will thwart. ... Has not God made
foolish the wisdom of the world?' (1 Cor. 1: 19.) This realization
of past stupidity finds a place in Augustine's *Confessions*: 'Garrie-
bam plane quasi peritus ... iam enim coeperam uelle uideri
sapiens ... insuper autem inflabar scientia' (20. 26). Prudentius'
final image of the 'uincula corporis' has more than one parallel in
Augustine, who speaks of 'sarcina saeculi', 'uincula mea', and 'ori-
ginalis peccati uinculum'.[31] Some of these similarities may admit-
tedly come from the common stock of Christian attitudes; but
Prudentius' treatment of his past life in the light of his conversion
to a more fully Christian activity may owe much to Augustine's
literary innovation.

The Roman poets had hoped to gain immortality from the last-
ing qualities of their poetry (cf. Horace, *Odes*, 1. 1. 35–6 and 3. 30;
Ovid, *Tristia*, 4. 10. 129–30). The Christian poet also hopes for
immortality, but his hopes are not based on the survival of his
poetry, but on his own personal salvation, gained as the reward
for the very act of writing poetry dedicated to the glorification of

[28] Eph. 4: 22–4; cf. Col. 3: 9 and Rom. 6: 6–11. Paul also exhorts men to keep a constant
watch on themselves: 1 Cor. 9: 27; 2 Cor. 13: 5.

[29] Armstrong (1901); also Lattimore (1942) 266 ff.

[30] Paulinus of Nola, *Ep.* 45. 5; Gregory of Nazianzus, *C.* 45. 131–9.

[31] *Conf.* 8. 5, 8; 1, 5. 9; cf. Paulinus of Nola, *C.* 24. 925–6: 'iamque expediti sarcinis
angentibus, laxate uinculis pedes'.

God. Thus at *Praefatio*, 35 ff. Prudentius sees his new and wholly
Christian life as completely absorbed in the writing of poetry,
which is to be the expression of his love for God and of his dedi-
cation of the rest of his life to Him. He even prays (43 ff.) that
death will come upon him in the act of composition. The poet's
soul, his 'anima' (35), seems to be identified with his *ingenium*, his
genius for poetry.[32] This is appropriate, since that poetry is to be
devoted exclusively to Christian prayer and praise, the highest
function of the soul. Here again Prudentius transforms the classi-
cal tradition by using its conventions to convey a Christian idea:
the well-worn theme of the poet's immortality gains a striking
and unexpected significance and becomes a fitting climax to his
Christianized exordium.

The *Praefatio* as an Introduction to Prudentius' poetry

Prudentius' other major concern in the *Praefatio* is to give the
reader some idea of the scope of the poetry for which this intro-
duction is written.[33] This 'list of contents' (37–42) has caused
some difficulty to those who ask how a truly Christian poet can
pretend that works are yet to be written when they already
exist.[34] The poet's 'character' is hardly 'redeemed' by the conjec-
ture that at least some of the works to which he refers were pro-
jected for the future at the time of writing; nor does this theory
find any support in the language of Prudentius, who uses the same
subjunctive throughout. If such scrupulousness were carried to its
logical extremes, the strangeness of a Christian vocation lived out
purely through the composition of poetry would have to be ad-
mitted. Prudentius' renewed sense of Christian vocation is syn-
onymous with his vocation as poet. His turning to each in his old
age can be described as a single experience of conversion. This
surely has a basis in Prudentius' own spiritual history, however re-
mote or recent. But he chooses, by poetic licence, to situate the
experience in the dramatic time of the *Praefatio*. Hence the
repeated present tense and the sequence of tenses in the pivotal
self-examination of 28–34. Prudentius did not expect the reader to

---

[32] Thraede (1965) 32.
[33] Most critics have recognized this; Lana (1962: 39–40) gives a full bibliography.
[34] Lana (1962) 35 ff.

envisage his conversion literally occurring as he writes the *Praefatio*, any more than Catullus, for instance, for all the immediacy of his 'Lesbia' poems, expected the reader to imagine him living his love affair directly through them. Prudentius here uses a poetic convention to enliven with immediacy, vividness, and the true fervour of religious enthusiasm the literary expression of his resolution to hymn God with his last breath. There is certainly artifice at work here; it would be inappropriate to expect a statement corresponding exactly with the historical reality. The poet is not untruthful about the experience itself; he is only vague about the chronology.

In the *Praefatio*, the poet artfully combines a sketch of his spiritual autobiography with an outline of his poetic programme. That this programme did not lie entirely in the future at the time of writing the *Praefatio* (AD 404–5) is shown by the secure dating of the *Contra Symmachum* to the year AD 402–3.[35] Moreover, the lack of any reference to the sack of Rome in AD 410 suggests strongly that the entire corpus was completed before that date, which would seem unlikely if it was begun only after the *Praefatio*. In fact, it may already have been finished when Prudentius wrote the *Praefatio*; the already completed *Contra Symmachum* is described in lines 40–1,[36] and, in the same way, 37–42 may be taken to refer to all the poems in the corpus. Much effort has been expended on identifying the individual poems.[37] The didactic poems, in particular the *Psychomachia*, have seemed to cause the

[35] *Contra Symmachum*, 2. 696 ff. refers to the battle of Pollentia, which took place on Easter Sunday, 6 Apr., AD 402 (Orosius, 7. 37. 2). There is no reference to the battle at Verona, which probably took place the following year, according to Barnes (1976) followed by Vanderspoel (1986: 253); Cameron (1970: 181, 471) supports the traditional date, AD 402.

[36] Bergman (1926: xii–xiii) thinks that line 40 refers to *Pe.* 10, which appears separately from the *Pe.* in the MSS. In the 7th-century Ambrosian MS D. Supp. 36, *Pe.* 10 is given the title 'sancti Romani martyris contra gentiles dicta'. On this MS, see Winstedt (1905). However, *Pe.* 10 could certainly be covered by 'carmen martyribus deuoueat' (line 42). A major work in two books like the *Contra Symmachum* might easily merit a two-line introduction and its subject certainly answers the description given in lines 40–1.

[37] In the controversy surrounding line 39, Hoefer (1895: 49) sees only a reference to the *Apotheosis* and suggests (58–9) that the *Hamartigenia* and the *Psychomachia* had yet to be written. Among the others who understands Prudentius to mean here the *Apotheosis* and the *Hamartigenia* are Allard (1884) 358, Rösler (1886) 22, Puech (1888) 56, Dressel (1860) 3, Schmitz (1889) 8, Ebert (1889) 1. 2, Bardenhewer (1923) 3. 441, de Labriolle (1947) 2. 699, Peebles (1951) 22, Lavarenne (1955) 1. 2, n. 2, Kurfess (1957) 1041, Schanz–Hosius–Krüger (1914) 4. 1. 236. A few critics think that the *Psychomachia* is included here: Puech (1888) 56–8, Weyman (1926) 65, Rodríguez-Herrera (1936) 14, Pellegrino (1963) 74–5.

greatest problems.[38] A minor work, the *Dittochaeon*, which may
have been intended to supply the legends for a series of church
paintings,[39] is certainly not referred to in the *Praefatio*. This may
be because of its genre, or because it did not form part of the col-
lection which the *Praefatio* was intended to introduce.[40] As for the
Epilogue, it forms a counterpoise to the *Praefatio*, and therefore
need not be mentioned in the latter.

The dramatic and spiritual framework of the *Praefatio* is vital
for a true understanding of the vagueness of the list at lines 37–42.
A line-by-line correspondence with the already completed works
of the poet would not fit in with the context of the list, in the

[38] Some, with Bergman (1926: xiii), date the *Psychomachia* after AD 404–5 on the
grounds that it is not alluded to in lines 39–42. Peebles (1951: 23) points out that the *Ditto-
chaeon* is so different from the other poems that the absence of an allusion to it here is not
surprising, and argues that the same applies to the *Psychomachia*. But there is reason to sup-
pose that the three didactic poems, the *Psychomachia*, the *Hamartigenia*, and the *Apotheosis*,
were treated from an early date as a group and numbered accordingly as successive books,
whether in a separate publication, or in the 'complete works' which seems to lie behind
one family of manuscripts; on this 'omnibus' edition, see Bergman (1908) 8–9, 24 ff. and
Lavarenne (1955) xxviii, and for the piecemeal publication of even short poems, see
Dziatzko (1897) 965 ff., Birt (1882) 118, and Newmyer (1979) 45 ff. This numbering of the
three poems first appears in the Codex Puteanus, though the hand is secondary and ident-
ical with that of the marginal glosses and of the 'subscription' of Vettius Agorius Basilius
Mavortius, consul in AD 527: Winstedt (1904) 177; Bergman (1926) xxv n. 2. In MS Monte
Cassino 374 and in the 9th-century Cambridge MS. C. Chr. 223 the same headings are
found, but in the Ambrosian MS the *Apotheosis* is unnumbered: James (1909–11) 523. If
indeed the three poems already formed a unity at the time of writing the *Praefatio*, lines 39–
42 may after all contain a general allusion to the *Psychomachia* together with the *Apotheosis*
and the *Hamartigenia*. Winstedt (1903) and Brožek (1970) speculate that the Puteanus re-
flects a collection of the poems predating the 'omnibus' edition for which the *Praefatio* was
composed (cf. n. 3 above), which supports my interpretation of these lines.
[39] Mannelli (1947) suggests that the stanzas were not intended as a commentary, but as
suggestions for an artistic interpretation. Charlet (1975) however, in demonstrating that
the *Dittochaeon* shows the influence of Paulinus of Nola on Prudentius, confirms that the
stanzas were intended as subscriptions for existing paintings, as argued independently by
Pillinger (1980: 18).
[40] Puech (1888: 229–301), Schanz–Hosius–Krüger (1914: 4. 1. 250–2), and Lavarenne
(1933: 624) think that the *Dittochaeon* was included in the collection but not mentioned in
the *Praefatio*; Bergman (1908) supposes that it was added later. He notes that the Greek title
is not original, but was coined by Gennadius. Henriksson (1956: 82–9), in a thorough dis-
cussion of Prudentius' knowledge of Greek, thinks the Greek titles of the didactic poems
are original to the author. After all, the Latin poets of the Golden Age had also used Greek
titles. But the poems of the *Pe.* and of the *Cathemerinon* were transmitted under their indi-
vidual titles for centuries, which explains their variable order and position in the MSS; the
collections do not appear under their Greek titles in Gennadius' list, so these must have
been invented by a later editor on the analogy of the didactic poems. The MSS may also
give a clue about the late date of composition of the *Dittochaeon*, or at least about its late
inclusion in the Prudentian corpus: in many MSS it appears after the Epilogue. Details in
Lavarenne (1955): xxvii–xxix.

midst of the poet's 'conversion', his admission of his past sinful-
ness, and his resolution to turn 'now' to a life of new Christian
commitment in his vocation as a Christian poet. The range of
poetry, already in fact written, is thus best described in vividly
enthusiastic potential terms. The list is deliberately set in the
subjunctive mood, to avoid the definite time scheme which
would be expressed by the future indicative. Instead, the sort of
poetry which Prudentius *might* write is set in the form of a prayer,
which forms a climax within the vague dramatic time scheme im-
plied in the *Praefatio*. The prayer is then immediately realized in
the corpus which follows. This should not be regarded as proof of
the poet's dishonesty, nor of the late realization of an as yet
unstarted programme, but as a confirmation of Prudentius' role as
Christian poet. He sincerely believes that his poetic achievement is
the answer to his prayers. It is God-given, as well as given to God.
This is the basic personal truth behind the *Praefatio*, in which
the poet imaginatively reconstructs, in dramatic terms, the spir-
itual mainspring for his poetry. To miss this artistic reshaping in
the *Praefatio* is to deny the truth implicit in Prudentius' under-
taking: poetry, with all its techniques for encapsulating realities
in imaginery terms, can legitimately be put at the service of
Christ.

The *Praefatio* is therefore a far more subtle literary composition
than its personal tone suggests at first reading. This does not call
into question Prudentius' basic honesty as a Christian poet, but
should encourage caution in the reconstruction of a detailed bio-
graphy on the basis of its information. In fact, only Prudentius'
age at the time of writing is clearly stated. The suppression of per-
sonal detail is deliberate; with self-conscious Christian humility he
is playing down the importance and worth of his worldly in-
volvement. His modesty throws into relief that part of the *Prae-
fatio* that is given clear expression: his 'conversion' and his new-
found vocation as a Christian poet. The poet is aware of the
daring novelty of announcing a Christian vocation in terms of a
poetic career and wants to make this point the climax of his *Prae-
fatio*. He puts a new emphasis on retrospective self-analysis and
penitence, and goes one stage further in introducing the idea of
full Christian commitment lived out through the writing of
Christian poetry. This idea shows a new openness to the potential
of poetry in Christian life; it had been regarded with suspicion by

Christian authors for its association with the pagan tradition.[41]
Prudentius wastes no time in justifying the adaptation of poetry
to Christian ends. Instead, he boldly maps out a renewed Chris-
tian commitment in terms of a career as poet.

•

Prudentius' Origins

The *Praefatio* should not be taken too literally. It is the poetic
expression of Prudentius' conviction that Christian hope, not
worldly ambition, gives purpose to life. In the course of a success-
ful career in the imperial service, the question had dawned on
him: 'cuius rei causa militamus?'[42] But, unlike the young man in
Augustine's *Confessions*, it was a poetic, not an ascetic, vocation
that seems to him the valid alternative. Perhaps he was already on
the verge of retirement and had written the bulk of his poetry
before he formulated this re-evaluation of his life; but the *Praefatio*
expresses in terms of dramatic truth a genuine shift in his values. It
may be a commonplace among Christians today that a good edu-
cation should not be squandered, but used to the glory of God,
but the dilemma of an educated Christian was a real one for Pru-
dentius' generation. His poetic vocation integrated his back-
ground with his beliefs, instead of making a radical break with
classical civilization.

The lyric form of the *Praefatio*, like that of the *Peristephanon*,
invites the intrusion of the poet's person, even if this is marked by
a rare modesty, which contrasts strongly with the traditional self-
advertisement of Prudentius' older contemporary, Ausonius.[43]
The unworldly theme of Prudentius' *Praefatio* made excessive em-
phasis on the facts about his origins and his career inappropriate.

[41] Cf. Tertullian, *Praescr.* 7 and Jerome, *Ep.* 22. 30, 'Ad Eustochium': 'What have
Horace and the Psalms, Virgil and the Evangelists, Cicero and the Apostles in common?'
On such agonizings, also experienced by Augustine, see Marrou (1958) 339–56 and
Bartelink (1986). Rodríguez-Herrera (1936) notes the novelty of Prudentius' expression of
his Christian vocation as a poetic vocation.

[42] Augustine, *Conf.* 8. 6 (Ponticianus' report of the comments of a young man on read-
ing the *Life of St Antony*): 'tum subito repletus amore sancto, et sobrio pudore iratus sibi,
coniecit oculos in amicum et ait illi: "dic, quaeso te, omnibus istis laboribus nostris quo
ambimus peruenire? quid quaerimus? cuius rei causa militamus? maiorne esse poterit spes
nostra in palatio, quam ut amici imperatoris simus? et ibi quid non fragili plerumque
periculis?"'

[43] Ausonius is quite clear about his origins: 'Vasates patria est, gens Haedua matri/de
patre Tarbellis et genetrix ab Aquis,/ipse ego Burdigalae genitus' (*Praef.* 1. 5–7).

Hence the tantalizing vagueness of his autobiographical state-
ments. But for us, the self-effacing poet must be dragged into the
light, if we are to place his work in its social context. Our concern
is with the *Peristephanon* and this happens to be the main source
for information about Prudentius' life.

To begin with, it is clear that he came from the north-eastern
province of Hispania Tarraconensis, and probably from Calagur-
ris, which is modern Calahorra. Suggestively, the collection
begins with six poems, all but one of which are dedicated to
Spanish saints. The first has a special connection with Calagurris.
But it is the second, dedicated to the Roman St Lawrence,[44]
which contains the decisive passage:

> Nos Vasco Hiberus diuidit
> binis remotos Alpibus
> trans Cottianorum iuga
> trans et Pyrenas ninguidos

Prudentius places himself on the Spanish side of the Pyrenees—
which, incidentally, can be sighted from Calahorra[45]—beyond
the River Ebro. Of the three Spanish cities which he calls his own
('nostra' no doubt because all are in the province of Tarraconen-
sis).[46] only Calagurris and Caesaraugusta (Saragossa) match this
description, Tarraco itself (the modern Tarragona) being north of
the Ebro. Caesaraugusta was not cut off by the river so much as
Calagurris was, since it commanded a Roman bridge.[47] More-
over, the term 'Vasconian' (or 'Basque') for the Ebro, if it is more
than a poetic epithet, seems to point upstream from Caesarau-
gusta, which was situated in the region of the Editani;[48] Calagur-
ris, on the other hand, is described as a city of the Vascones (*Pe. 1.*
194).[49] This conclusion fits with the prominence of the first

[44] Later versions of Lawrence's martyrdom claim that he was of Spanish origin. This
may be the result of the popularity of *Pe.* 2, written by a Spaniard for Spaniards. See *AASS*
Aug. 3. 511 and Lavarenne (1963*b*) 29. The Spanish pope Damasus may also be associated
with *Pe.* 2 (see n. 62 below).

[45] Guillén and Rodríguez (1950) 14. For a possible Ausonian model for the phrase
'Pyrenas ninguidos', see Charlet (1908*a*) 65.

[46] For ancient statements see Gennadius (AD 480–500). Also the *Chronicon* (*ps.-*)*Dextri*
ad ann. 388, which claims that Prudentius had a Caesaraugustan father and a Calagurritan
mother. See further Messenger (1962) and van Assendelft (1976) 2 ff.

[47] Hübner (1897*a*).

[48] Pliny, *NH* 3. 3. 24.

[49] Lana (1962) 6–9; Cirac (1951) 109 ff.; Guillén and Rodríguez (1950) 4–9. On Cala-
gurris, Hübner (1897*b*).

hymn,[50] which is dedicated to the two Calahorran martyrs,[51] and
with the conspicuous use of the word 'nostra' to qualify Calagur-
ris in *Pe.* 4. 31–2, as distinct from the rest of the cities listed
there.[52]

   The poet's full nomenclature, as attested by the manuscripts
and ancient authors,[53] was Aurelius Prudentius Clemens; he him-
self gives us only the name Prudentius at *Pe.* 2. 582, where he calls
himself 'Christi reum Prudentium'. Numismatic evidence has
been adduced to show that the name Clemens was connected
with an ancient line in Caesaraugusta, but the case seems slight.[54]
The most that can be said is that the name Clemens may indicate
the Christian religion of the bearer.[55] This matter seems hardly in
question for Prudentius on the basis of the evidence of the *Praefa-
tio* itself, where he makes not even an oblique reference to pagan
origins, by complete contrast, for example, with Commodian's
Instructiones, which begin with a dramatic statement of his con-
version to Christianity.

   Prudentius was born in the consulate of Salia in AD 348 (*Praefa-
tio*, 24: 'consulis . . . Saliae'[56]): he had boyhood memories of the
reign of Julian (AD 360–3).[57] His education followed a familiar
pattern for a son of good family: grammar, rhetoric, law, and

   [50] Bergman (1908) 14–23, (1926) ix–x; Ludwig (1976); Guillén and Rodríguez (1950)
14–16. Cf. *Pe.* 8, probably the dedication for a baptistery at the burial place of Emeterius
and Chelidonius. In some of the oldest MSS it closes the first half of the book, which may
also be significant; details in Bergman (1908) 14–18. Prudentius may have been writing for
an audience (in Calagurris?) so familiar with the saints that they did not need to be named.

   [51] Gregory of Tours, *De gloria martyrum*, 1. 93 confirms the connection of Emeterius
and Chelidonius with Calagurris.

   [52] Cf. *Pe.* 11. 237–8 (the addressee is a certain Bishop Valerianus): 'Inter sollemnes
Cypriani vel Chelidoni/Eulaliaeque dies currat et iste tibi.' Álamo (1939) thought he had
discovered a connection between Bishop Valerianus and Calagurris, but the bishop-lists for
that city begin too late to confirm this. Nevertheless, there may have been a bishop there in
Prudentius' time, since *Pe.* 8 attests a baptistery; but this is hardly a proof that Calagurris
was Prudentius' birthplace.

   [53] Guillén and Rodríguez (1950) 3 n. 1: Prudentius is the *nomen* in all MSS, Aurelius is
frequently the *praenomen*; Clemens as *cognomen* appears less frequently, e.g. in the Puteanus
and in Gregory of Tours, *De gloria martyrum*, 92. PLRE 1. 214 correctly favours the order
Aurelius Prudentius Clemens. No weight here attaches to the 16th-century *Chronicon* (*ps.-
)Dextri*, which gives the *praenomen* Flavius.

   [54] Flórez (1757) 1. 240 refers to a coin with an inscription for the *duouiri* Lucretius and
Clemens. Dressel (1860): iii and Bergman (1926): x connect this with Prudentius.

   [55] It appears in Phil. 4: 3; cf. Guillén and Rodríguez (1950) 4 n. 47.

   [56] Bergman's emendation in line 24 has been generally accepted. Fl. Salia was *consul
ordinarius* with Fl. Philippus: Degrassi (1952) 81.

   [57] *Apotheosis*, 449–50; the emperor Julian is clearly intended.

legal practice (*Praefatio*, 7–15).[58] Augustine and Ausonius went through much the same stages; but, while they became teachers of rhetoric,[59] Prudentius proceeded to enter the service of the state. Ausonius and Paulinus were educated at Bordeaux and Prudentius may have crossed the Pyrenees to follow in their footsteps.[60] On the other hand, rhetoric was very well taught at Caesaraugusta in the middle years of the fourth century, as we learn from an addition to Jerome's *Chronicle*.[61]

When did Prudentius begin to compose poetry? Only two of his poems can be firmly dated:[62] the *Praefatio* was written in his fifty-seventh year (AD 404–5), as is stated in the first stanza; and the *Contra Symmachum* can be dated two years earlier, to AD 402–3.[63] This is established at the end of the poem by an invitation to Honorius to have no gladiatorial spectacles during the triumph which he is to celebrate in Rome (this occurred in January 404),[64] and by the fact that the battle of Pollentia (Easter 402), but not the battle of Verona (summer 403), is mentioned in the second book. As for the rest of the poems, they are unlikely to have been widely published[65] much before AD 392, when Jerome drew up a comprehensive list of Christian writers, including even his contemporary Bishop Ambrose, and the controversial

---

[58] Marrou (1965) 400 ff., 451 ff.

[59] Augustine, *Conf.* 2. 2; Ausonius, *Praefatiunculae*, 1. 17–18. Cf. Ovid, *Tristia*, 4. 10. They omitted the period of training in the law-courts.

[60] See Matthews (1975) 149–50, 151–2, 161, 168, on the links between Aquitania and north-eastern Spain attested by Paulinus of Nola's retirement to this region; cf. Fontaine (1974*b*).

[61] *PLRE* I. 691: 'Petrus I'. This teacher figures in a 5th-century addition to Jerome's *Chronicle*, under the year 355: 'Petrus, Caesaraugustae orator insignis, docet'.

[62] The *Psychomachia* and several of the *Pe.* poems can be given an approximate date: on the *Psychomachia* see n. 38 above; Harries (1984: 73) argues that *Pe.* 2 was probably written during the lifetime of Theodosius I and before Prudentius' visit to Rome; referring to Chastagnol (1966), Harries shows that *Pe.* 12 is likely to have been written after the dedication of St Paul's-without-the-Walls in AD 391 and before Theodosius' death in 395; Harries also suggests an association between the pope Damasus' interest in the martyrs and the genesis of the poems on Lawrence and Agnes, who were martyred at Rome (*Pe.* 2 and 14), which would suggest an early date for these.

[63] See n. 35 above.

[64] *Contra Symmachum*, 2. 1114–32. Gladiatorial shows (cf. Theodoret, *Hist. Eccl.* 5. 26) were in fact abolished by Honorius (i.e. before AD 423), though whether in 404 as a response to this appeal of 402 or later is not known: Solmsen (1965) esp. 239. The imperial decision may even, assuming a literary conceit in the *Contra Symmachum*, 2. 1128–9, have preceded the poetic appeal: Ward-Perkins (1984) 92 ff., 111–13. See chap. 7, nn. 25–7.

[65] See n. 38 above.

Spaniard, Priscillian,[66] but excluding Prudentius. If this *argumen-
tum e silentio* is valid, it restores a measure of credibility to Pruden-
tius' claim, in the *Praefatio*, to have begun writing poetry in his
old age. But the first six poems of the *Peristephanon* are liberal in
their references to Spanish martyr-cults and encourage the
opinion that they might have been written in the first place for
natives of the cities mentioned. There were, of course, Spaniards
elsewhere than in Spain, especially under the Spanish emperor
Theodosius I; but the passage quoted above from *Pe.* 2 suggests
that Prudentius was actually south of the Pyrenees when he wrote
it:

> Blessed the inhabitant of the City [Rome], who is near enough to vener-
> ate you and the resting-place of your bones! [...] We [however] are
> divided [from Rome] by the Basque [river] Ebro and separated by two
> high mountain chains [...] It is hardly [even] known [among us] by
> rumour, how full of entombed saints Rome is.

If these poems were composed in Spain, they may have preceded
the final stage of Prudentius' career at the imperial court at Milan.
Certainly, the passage quoted seems to imply that he had not yet
visited Rome. That career and Prudentius' acquaintance with
Rome now claim our attention.

Prudentius' career

Prudentius was propelled, largely by his own talent, into the
highest levels of government. A careful study of the evidence
should enable us to identify some people and places that may have
influenced and formed the author of the *Peristephanon* during his
career. The basic text is *Praefatio*, 16–21, the two concluding stan-
zas which lead up to the climax of this autobiographical section.
The three preceding stanzas have a confessional tone: as a child he
was beaten, later he learned to lie, then he indulged in sex and
devoted himself with malicious obstinacy to winning thorny cases
at law. What follows has a more neutral tenor, with perhaps a
touch of pride.[67] Yet Prudentius could hardly have given less
space to his distinguished career in comparison with his wasted

---

[66] Jerome, *De uir. ill.* 121 and 124; Kelly (1975: 174–7) dates this work to AD 392–3.

[67] Pride is expressed by 'reximus' and by the alliteration and the climactic positioning
of the allusion to the emperor. 'Tandem' shows that the promotion had been long and
intensely desired.

youth. In one stanza he records his two appointments as provincial governor, without identifying the provinces concerned or his precise title: in the other, he manages to convey, with elegant brevity, his promotion through the civil service to a position in the vicinity of the Emperor, without telling us who the Emperor was[68] or exactly what rank he gave to Prudentius. He does not boast: his success speaks for itself.

Prudentius' deliberate vagueness in 16–21 has led to much pointless conjecture. 'Reximus' cannot be pressed to show that Prudentius was technically *corrector* of a province, for in his time *consulares*, *correctores*, and *praesides* exercised the same power.[69] The poem about the bishop of Siscia (*Pe.* 7) cannot be used to argue that Prudentius governed the Pannonian province of Savia. Indeed, had he done so, he would certainly have enlivened the narrative with local detail and have given some hint of his personal connection with the cult of the martyred bishop Quirinus. Besides, he claims that Quirinus was buried in Siscia, which was not the case.[70] The existence of *Pe.* 7 is better explained by reference to Theodosius' victory at Siscia in AD 388;[71] the poem was an indirect tribute to the Emperor, who may well have adopted the local cult of Quirinus.

Prudentius puts considerable emphasis on the word 'bis'. It was indeed unusual to hold two such appointments, as appears from an anecdote retailed by Ammianus Marcellinus (29. 3. 6): Africanus was the governor of a province, who had begun his career, like Prudentius, as an advocate. Encouraged by the father of the future Emperor Theodosius, he applied to the Emperor Valentinian for transference to another governorship. Instead of

[68] In spite of Seager's objection (1983: 160) that it was simply stock attribute of emperors, 'pietas' seems to have been applied to contemporaries more especially to Theodosius I, under whom the empire was 'fully' christianized: Ambrose, *De obitu Theodosii*, 12, *Ep.* 51; Augustine, *De ciu. dei*, 5. 26 ('De fide ac pietate Theodosii Augusti'); Paulinus of Nola, *Ep.* 28. 6 (referring to a lost panegyric).

[69] Ensslin (1956: 608) on the office of *praeses*; Kübler (1900: 1140) on that of *consularis*; Premerstein (1901) on that of *corrector*. Also Ensslin (1929: 1556) on the title *spectabilis* and Wesenberg (1957: 1015) on *provincia*. The governorship in Prudentius' time is discussed by Lana (1962: 19).

[70] See chap. 8, pp. 236–7. The translation of the relics to Rome probably occurred after Prudentius' time, so that would not have been the occasion of his first-hand acquaintance with the cult: *AASS* Junii 1. 372; *BHL* 2. 1023; Ferrua (1942) no. 64, 235 ff. It is significant that Prudentius gives no details about the feast-day of Quirinus or about his mausoleum on the Via Appia, on which see Lana (1962) 20.

[71] On Theodosius' victory at Siscia: Pacatus, *Paneg.* 2. 34. 1; Piganiol (1972) 280.

exchanging his province, the unstable emperor snapped, 'Go, count, and change his head for him!'; and Africanus was executed for his ambition.

Prudentius is much more likely to have been governor in Spain,[72] Italy, or Gaul. Perhaps it was during a governorship in Spain that he had the chance to make contact with the future emperor during his years of enforced retirement on his family estates at Cauca, in Gallaecia (AD 376–8).[73] In any case, the unnamed emperor who noticed and elevated him is surely Theodosius I, whose reign began when Prudentius was thirty-one, the right age to contemplate a new step in his career by joining the Spanish emperor's predominantly Spanish entourage.[74] There is no evidence to suggest that Prudentius accompanied the emperor on his eastern campaigns in a military capacity.[75] Probably he joined the western-based court at Milan, perhaps thanks to the influence of another Spaniard in the court circle. If Prudentius had already achieved some local renown for his poems on Spanish martyrs, someone with an interest in Christian writers may have introduced him to Theodosius. Nummius Aemilianus Dexter, Jerome's addressee in his *De viris illustribus*, springs to mind here. The emperor himself might have known his compatriot's earlier work and realized the potential usefulness of a Christian poet in the struggle to promote orthodox Christianity in the face of resurgent paganism and recurrent heresy.[76] The Emperor was not

[72] There were four *praesides* in Spain (*Notitia dignitatum, Occ.* 1. 24), but Chastagnol (1965: 286–7) shows how little evidence there is for the governorship in Spain at that time, on which see also Puech (1888) 48–9; Kurfess (1957) 1041; and Sündwall (1915) 64 n. 102.

[73] Matthews (1975) 93–4. Theodosius was born at Cauca: Zosimus, *Historia nova*, 4. 24. 4; *Consularia Constantinopolitana*, s.a. 379. His retirement to Spain is recorded by Pacatus, *Paneg.* 9.

[74] Ancient sources refer frequently to Theodosius' often ill-considered generosity in promoting Spanish friends and relations: Eunapius, frr. 53 and 60; Zosimus, *Historia nova*, 4. 27; John Lydus, *De magistratibus populi romani*, 3. 35, 123–4; Themistius, *Or.* 16. 203d; Aurelius Victor, *Epitome de Caesaribus*, 48. 18. Legislation for these years attests overstaffing in the Civil Service (*CTh* 1. 15. 12, AD 386) and corruption of officials (*CTh* 1. 5. 9, AD 389), on which see Matthews (1971) and (1975) 109–13.

[75] As suggested by Rösler (1886: 18–9). The lack of references to the East in Prudentius' poetry, except for those to the Holy Land in the *Dittochaeon*, which were, as Harries observes (1984: 69), taken from the store of common knowledge, suggests that he may have joined the court only when Theodosius came to the West in AD 389–91. *Pe.* 7 indicates ignorance rather than first-hand knowledge of the East (see p. 237 below).

[76] Thus Bergman (1921: 27): 'Seine Religionspolitik ist es, die im Liede seines Landsmannes Prudentius Ausdruck findet'. By analogy with Horace and Virgil Prudentius is 'der religionspolitische Dichter … des christlichen Augustus', which distinguishes him from Claudian, 'der unkritische lobsingende Hofpoet'.

slow, for instance, to express admiration for Ausonius' poetry, as the letter preserved in the poet's *Praefatiunculae* proves,[77] and he could not fail to have been impressed by Prudentius' Christian exploitation of his poetic talent.

The reference to 'militia' in line 19 need have no connection with service in the army.[78] This was the usual word for service of the state, even in the imperial offices.[79] 'Militia litterata' was distinguished from 'militia armata',[80] although the two kinds of service were assimilated in the uniforms prescribed and in the grant of *castrense peculium*.[81] Prudentius was indeed a 'Palatinus miles',[82] but his combat was with the word, not with the sword. This seems to be implied by the use of the term 'proximus' in line 21: the second in command of one of the imperial *scrinia*[83] was called 'proximus scriniorum'. Those 'qui in sacris scriniis militantes' are described as 'having frequent access' to the *consistorium*,[84] the closest council of the Emperor. It is this standing council that is referred to in line 21: 'propius stare iubens ordine proximo'. Prudentius' career as advocate and judge fitted him for the *scrinium libellorum*, but his literary accomplishments might equally have won him a place in the *scrinium memoriae*.[85]

The growth of the *scrinia* in the fourth century made them either a career for the humbler *litterati* or a valuable starting-point for those with higher ambitions. The post of *magister memoriae*[87] was given to men outside the *scrinia*, who were being shown imperial favour, and like that of *quaestor palatii*, provided its

---

[77] *Praef.* 3: *epistula Theodosii Augusti*; cf. *Praef.* 4 (Ausonius' reply): 'Domino meo et omnium Theodosio Augusto Ausonius tuus'. Theodosius' literary interests extended to history: he was 'multumque diligens ad noscenda maiorum gesta' (Aurelius Victor, *Epitome de Caesaribus*, 48. 11). On his deathbed he advised his son to do the same (Claudian, *De IV. cons. Honorii*, 400).

[78] Dressel (1860) 4 n. 8. Cf. Sixt (1889).

[79] *CTh* 6. 26. 5: 'qui in sacris scriniis militant'. Cf. *CTh* 6. 26. 8.

[80] *Cod. Just.* 12. 9. 8, AD 444.

[81] *CTh* 6. 36, AD 326.

[82] Gennadius, *C.* 13, where Prudentius is also called 'uir saeculari litteratura eruditus'; see Richardson (1896) 57 ff. and Bergman (1926) viii.

[83] Seeck (1921) 897.

[84] *CTh* 6. 26. 5.

[85] Seeck (1921).

[86] *CTh* 6. 26; *LRE* 2. 575–8.

[87] On *magistri scriniorum* see Seeck (1921) 896; *magistri* were *perfectissimi* until AD 355, when they were put on an equal footing with *uicarii* (*CIL* 6. 510, Dessau 4152), and in 372 they were promoted even further (*CTh* 6. 11) to become, eventually, the equals of *proconsules*, before whom they are placed in the *Notitia dignitatum*, Or. 19, Occ. 17.

holder with a position of power and proximity to the Emperor which could lead to even higher promotion. The letters of Symmachus show what sort of men reached these positions and tell of their subsequent advancement.[88] Prudentius should not perhaps be considered as the political equal of figures whose careers advanced far beyond the *scrinia*. He can be compared rather with the poets who won entry to political life and the *sacra scrinia* in particular by means of their poetic talents.[89] Perhaps Paulinus of Nola originally hoped for similar advancement when he composed his now lost panegyric of Theodosius.[90] Or perhaps Prudentius can be compared with the author of the *Querolus*,[91] for whom 'paruas ... litterulas non paruus indulsit labor'. This man also reached the post of *proximus*, and then retired to his lands in Gaul for the 'honorata quies' granted to those who had served a full term in the *scrinia*.[92] Prudentius may have remained in service at court for twenty years with gradual advancement, and having reached the post of *proximus*, may have been granted his 'honorata quies'. Fifteen or twenty years' service was certainly not unknown for the *scrinia* in this period,[93] and Prudentius' own words at lines 19–21 imply a long wait for the climactic promotion. According to contemporary legislation, his tenure of this post may have been restricted to two years or even one,[94] after which time he would have attained the rank of *spectabilis* on retirement.[95]

[88] Seeck (1883): *Ep.* 9. 1, for instance, is a request to advance Palladius, a protégé of Symmachus (Seeck ccii); this man was the son of a famous Athenian rhetorician, who was recommended to Ausonius, then praetorian prefect, for his ability in public declamation (*PLRE* 1. 660: Palladius 12). By AD 381 he was *comes sacrarum largitionum* (*CTh* 4. 13. 8; 10. 23. 2 and 3) and in 382 he became magister officiorum (*CTh* 6. 27. 4), residing subsequently at Constantinople (Gregory of Nazianzus, *Ep.* 103 and 107). A pagan counterpart to the Christian Palladius also appears in Symmachus' correspondence: Macrobius Longinianus, the addressee of *Ep.* 7. 93. 101 (Longinianus 2 in *PLRE* 1. 685–7).

[89] Cameron (1970) 1–29.

[90] *Ep.* 28. 6: 'fateor autem idcirco me libenter hunc ab amico laborem recepisse, ut in Theodosio non tam imperatorem quam Christi seruum, non dominandi superbia sed humilitate famulandi potentem, nec regno sed fide principem praedicarem.'

[91] Lana (1979) notes that this is the only surviving text from late Latin theatre. The Rutilius of the dedication is probably the poet, Rutilius Namatianus.

[92] *CTh* 6. 26. 7 and 8, AD 396.

[93] *CTh* 6. 26. 1, AD 362: 15 years; *CTh* 6. 26. 7, AD 396: 20 years.

[94] *CTh* 6. 26. 6, AD 396: two years; *CTh* 6. 26. 11, AD 397: one year.

[95] *CTh* 6. 26. 11; by this edict, retired *proximi* with the title *spectabilis* were put on a level with *uicarii* in the full sense, that is, as if they had actually served as *uicarius*, not just in an honorary capacity, such as had been awarded to them in the West in AD 381 (*CTh* 6. 26. 2) and in the East in AD 386 (*CTh* 6. 26. 4).

There is no reason to suppose that Prudentius returned immediately to Spain on retirement, although it seems clear from several points in the *Peristephanon* that he did eventually do so.[96] An edict of AD 412 suggests that it was common practice for retired *proximi* to remain with the court, or at least pay it frequent visits;[97] the Emperors 'grant the unrestrained and perpetual right to come to the Imperial court', and 'command that in the case of those persons it shall not be necessary to await our August Command'. It may be to such a period of semi-retirement that Prudentius' pilgrimages in Italy belong.

On at least one occasion the poet visited Rome. He draws on this experience in *Pe.* 9, 11, and 12, particularly in the striking description of the commemoration of the martyrs at the end of *Pe.* 11 and in *Pe.* 12. A great deal of effort has been expended on the conjectural reconstruction from supposed autobiographical data in these three poems of an 'episode' from Prudentius' life: his 'journey to Rome'.[98] In fact, there is no reason why they should all be taken to refer to a single journey, although they resemble one another in style and subject-matter.[99] The adoption of a variety of *personae* warns against such a literal interpretation. The poet's personal experience is not unimportant, but supplies material for his identification with others of his kind. Thus, when the narrator in *Pe.* 9 describes his 'uulnera' and 'dolorum acumina', he indicates the normal emotional state of the typical pilgrim,[100] as well as supplying the spiritual counterpart to the wounds inflicted on the martyr's body by the 'acumina ferrea' (line 51) of the vengeful schoolboys.

In *Pe.* 12, Prudentius describes St Paul's and the new Vatican baptistery of St Peter's with the fresh perceptions of an eyewitness, but his observations are not intended as a diary entry, let alone an archaeological report. Observation and spiritual experience are inextricably tangled together.[101]

[96] *Pe.* 9. 106: 'domum reuertor, Cassianum praedico.'; *Pe.* 11. 179–80: 'Quod laetor reditu, quod te, uenerande sacerdos,/complecti licitum est, scribo quod haec eadem ...'; *Pe.* 12. 65–6 (although Prudentius never explicitly identifies the curious visitor to Rome as himself): '... tu domum reuersus/diem bifestum sic colas memento.'

[97] *CTh* 6. 26. 14, AD 412. This point eludes Lana.

[98] Dressel (1860) xiv n. 29; cf. Messenger (1962) 96–9. Lana (1962: 24–5) takes *Pe.* 9, 11 and 12 to refer to a single journey, which supposes too literal an interpretation of these poems.

[99] They often follow each other in the MSS: Bergman (1908) 14 ff.

[100] Bardy (1949) 224 ff.

[101] See Fontaine's sensitive article (1964b).

Where the question of the effect of Rome on Prudentius can more fruitfully pursued is in the indications that the inspiration for the *Peristephanon* may have come partly from the monuments and the verse-inscriptions erected in honour of the martyrs by another famous Spaniard of the time: Pope Damasus (d. 384).[102] It is not difficult to see the influence of Damasus' epigraphic celebration of Agnes in Prudentius' treatment of Agnes and Eulalia in *Pe.* 3 and 14 (see pp. 240 ff. and 250 ff. below). In describing St Peter's in *Pe.* 12, Prudentius focuses significantly on the baptistery built by Damasus, while, in the same poem, he describes St Paul's-without-the-Walls, a basilica at least begun under the Spanish Pope.[103] Both poets celebrated St Lawrence, for whom Damasus had erected a new basilica.[104] Damasus had promoted the cult of the Apostles of Rome and encouraged Roman pride in such forebears;[105] Prudentius in his Roman poems invites comparison between the martyrs and the traditional heroes of the Roman past.

Theodosius, Damasus, Ambrose: the Spanish emperor, the Spanish Pope and the Bishop of Milan all in some way promoted the cult of martyrs.[106] Two of them wrote poetry about it.[107] Through his career in Milan and his experience of Rome Prudentius came under their influence. This can be perceived in the dedications of the *Peristephanon* poems and in the treatment of some of them.[108] Nor can the social and ideological background of the court of Theodosius be ignored as a formative influence. Clearly the investigation of Prudentius' life is a worthwhile task, though it is difficult working from the text of the poems. What he chooses to tell about himself in the *Praefatio* and the *Peristephanon* must be considered in its context. A narrow path must be found between overworking the data and discounting significant allu-

---

[102] That Prudentius had himself seen these inscriptions is indicated by *Pe.* 11. 7–8: 'Plurima litterulis signata sepulcra loquuntur/martyris aut nomen aut epigramma aliquod'; On Damasus see Marique (1962) 13–80.

[103] As noted by Ruysschaert (1966).

[104] See chap. 3, p. 95, and chap. 8, pp. 243 ff. and p. 258.

[105] Bardy (1949) and Piétri (1961).

[106] On the dramatic *inuentio* of the martyrs Gervasius and Protasius, see Augustine, *Conf.* 9. 7. 16; *Retractationes*, 1. 19. On Ambrose and the martyrs, see Homes Dudden (1935) 1. 298–320.

[107] On Ambrose as hymnographer, see pp. 62 ff. below.

[108] The influence of St Ambrose on the *Cathemerinon* and the *Contra Symmachum* was also very important, but falls outside the area under discussion.

sions. Enough can be inferred to justify the following summary of
his life.

As an educated provincial from an upper-class Christian family
in north-east Spain, Prudentius underwent the traditional educa-
tion of his period. His training as an advocate fitted him for the
governorship of two provinces, probably in Gaul, Italy, or Spain.
He then received promotion to a position at court, either as the
result of personal contact with Theodosius during the latter's re-
tirement in Spain, or through an influential Spanish contact at
court. He spent a long period at court workig in one of the *scrinia*,
where his services and perhaps his known literary talent won him
final promotion to the post of *proximus*. During this period of his
career, he must have experienced the staunchly Christian attitudes
of the members of the court at Milan, and in particular, of Bishop
Ambrose, whose hymns are reflected in Prudentius' own poetry.
At this time he also had ample opportunity to visit Imola and
Rome itself, and this experience was translated into the terms of
Pe. 9, 11, and 12. After retirement from his post, the poet made
his way back to Spain, perhaps after a period of less formal attach-
ment to the court, during which he could certainly have made a
(second?) pilgrimage to Rome. The date of his death is unknown,
although it may have occurred before or not long after the down-
fall and death of Stilicho in AD 408 and the sack of Rome in AD
410, since neither of these important events finds a place in the
poems.

2

Curiositas and Credulity

MODERN studies of fourth-century martyr-literature influenced by contemporary reactions to what seems the absurd and the incredible, find it difficult to explain its evident popularity among all classes of early Christians. Refuge has been sought in a two-tier view of Christian society which supposes that increased enthusiasm for the cult of martyrs and saints was somehow the result of a 'landslide conversion' of the lower classes of the Empire.[1] Their simple faith in the powers of a multiplicity of martyrs represents a Christianized form of popular religious belief, which, by sheer weight of numbers, the lower-class converts imposed on the upper end of Christian society, which would otherwise have remained secure in its own intellectual world and impervious to such vulgar nonsense. Thus Gibbon sees, in the cult of the martyrs, a form of popular mythology which he associates with the 'reign of polytheism'.[2] Some comfort for holders of this split view of Christian society can be found in the use of Martyr-Acts, *Passiones*, and Panegyrics in the celebration of a martyr's feast-day: various comments from the intellectual leaders of the Church seem to confirm the idea that these compositions catered for the lowest common denominator in congregational tastes. Jerome, in apologizing for the appearance of incorrect but colloquial words in his translation of the Bible, answers by pointing out that he is matching his style to the simplicity of what he calls 'the simple uneducated folk who form the majority in Church congregations'.[3] Augustine also has no illusions about the mental capacities of his congregation at Hippo, whose short memory

---

[1] Brown (1981).

[2] Gibbon (1909–14) 3. 225.

[3] Jerome, *In Ezechielem prophetam*, 14. 47. 1–5: 'simplices quoque et indoctos quorum in congregatione ecclesiae maior est numerus'; cf. *Ep.* 53. 10: 'nolo offendaris in scripturis sanctis simplicitate et quasi utilitate uerborum, quae uel uitio interpretum uel de industria sic prolatae sunt, ut rusticam contionem facilius instruerent et in una eademque sententia aliter doctus, aliter audiret indoctus.' On Jerome as a biblical translator, see Kelly (1975) 159 ff.

concerning local miracles needs the help supplied by regular read-
ings from the specially instituted *libelli miraculorum*.[4] Gregory of
Tours in the sixth century notes the needs of 'homines rustici'
when he speaks of the need for a written version of the martyr
Patroclus' history to act as an *aide-mémoire* for congregations.[5]

It is, however, often assumed by modern critics that what was
acceptable to the Christian 'rustici' could surely not have been
accepted by their educated contemporaries who, with us, would
have brought a more sceptical attitude to bear on these often
incredible Christianized folk-tales. On the basis of these assump-
tions, there seems to be a contradiction in the *Peristephanon*: on
one side, here are high-quality literary compositions, classicizing
in language and metre, and so evidently aimed at an audience of at
least the average literary culture of their day; on the other, the
poems' content is firmly based on the popular versions of the
martyrdoms with which they deal. The same features recur: the
prominent position given to the miraculous, the detailed treat-
ment of violence and death, the stereotype martyr-figure, and the
tendency to expand and embroider the basic account. Yet Pru-
dentius was not so involved in gaining his own salvation by the
writing of Christian poetry that he was not aware of writing for a
definite earthly audience. This audience presumably appreciated
all aspects of the *Peristephanon*: their Horatian-style metres, their
Virgilian echoes, their use of Christian apologetic in poetic form,
and the more basic matter of martyrdom-narratives.

These poems were intended for the sort of Gallic aristocrat in
whose sitting-room they appear in the fifth century, according to
the report of Sidonius Apollinaris (*Ep.* 2. 9, quoted below p. 91).
In this setting, they correspond significantly on the Christian side
to the works of Horace found in the profane section of a private
library. It must be considered then, in what sense the contents of
such poems would have been acceptable to an audience of this
level of literary culture, which represented the highest form of
education in the period. How far would their credulity have been
strained, and on what grounds did they accept it?

By the beginning of the fifth century, the later versions of the
martyrdom accounts were so generally accepted within the

---

[4] Augustine, *De ciu. dei*, 22. 8.

[5] Gregory of Tours, *De gloria martyrum*, 64. The people of Troyes need to hear the story
of Patroclus (*PL* 71. 763).

Church that they began to be admitted in abbreviated and stylist-
ically elevated form into the solemn 'praefationes' or prayers pre-
ceding the Sanctus and Offertory within the Mass itself. Tension
between the popular and the more cultured elements has been
seen here;[6] with reference to an apparent discrepancy between the
simple popular content of the martyr-stories and the sophisticated
literary style and form of the prayers. In the context of the
liturgy, this 'tension' may, of course, be explained by the accept-
ability and even desirability of both a more elevated and even ob-
scure style[7] and a celebration of the Church's acknowledged
champions. But this still does not fully explain how the so-called
'popular' aspect of the content of the martyr-stories could appeal
to an intellectually more sophisticated section of a congregation.
Recourse can be had to the 'eye of faith', Jerome's 'oculi fidei' (*Ep.*
108. 10. 2), but this involves positing a form of Christian double-
think by means of which men of culture could accept for the sake
of its spiritual value what they would normally reject in a secular
context.

While this sort of explanation might just work in an ecclesiasti-
cal context, it is less easy to impose on a work like the *Peristepha-
non*, which stands outside the liturgy and which is written for a
narrower and more cultured class of Christians than that repre-
sented by a mixed church congregation. The poems are indeed
written with reference to the liturgical use of hymns, but their
purpose is different, since they are intended for private devotional
reading, as I shall demonstrate in the next chapter. In the light of
this, it must be considered whether or not it is correct to talk in
terms of a discrepancy between content and form in these poems,
since this entails the supposition that even outside the church ser-
vice, Christians had to adopt an outlook untypical of the intellec-
tual norms of their class and period. It is, of course, true that
educated Christians had had to adjust their standards of literary
decorum in order to be able to accept the 'sermo humilis' of the
Bible.[8] But the reader's attitude towards the contents of the *Peri-
stephanon* strikes more deeply at the question of general intellec-
tual standpoint. Are educated Christians who accept the contents

---

[6] See Lazzati (1956b: 36) for 'la tensione'.

[7] Mohrmann (1957) chap. 1.

[8] Auerbach (1965) 25–66. See Augustine's reaction to the low style of the Bible at *Conf.*
3. 5.

of the *Peristephanon* along with its setting consciously submerging their higher intellectual standards for religious reasons and thus diverging from the intellectual outlook of the day? Do they exemplify by their acceptance an unusual level of unconscious credulity? Or is their acceptance simply a further illustration of what can be proved to be current intellectual standards and outlook?

In fact, a survey of the literary and historical interests of the period as a whole, outside as well as within the strictly Christian sphere, shows that the *Peristephanon* can be fitted into a general pattern of ideas and taste for the period. There is no real contradiction at work, either in the liturgy or in the *Peristephanon*. In attempting such a survey here, I shall restrict at least the first part to sources uninfected by the Christian outlook, since the truest results can only be gained by making the non-Christian side of the picture clear as the necessary control and complement to the Christian. At the same time, the importance of *fides* for the Christian outlook cannot be completely ignored. If it was such a real force that it could overcome and even reform the aesthetic sensibilities and tastes of educated Christians, it might also be brought into play in the acceptance of martyr-accounts in which the heroes strain credulity by, for instance, continuing to float when attached to heavy stones, or speaking at length after their tongues have been removed (see *Pe.* 7 and 10). As Hilary of Poitiers says at the beginning of his hymn of the Trinity, 'Ante saecula qui manes',

> felix qui potuit *fide*
> res tantas penitus credulus assequi.[9]

Jerome, in the preface of his *Vita Pauli*, appeals to his readers' Christian *fides* for the narrative to follow, with a reference to St Mark's Gospel: 'I know of course', he says, 'that all this will seem incredible to those who will not admit that "All things are possible to them that believe."'[10] Sulpicius Severus, in his *Life of St Martin*, and in the *Dialogues*, goes so far as to label as sin lack of belief in the deeds of Martin: 'si qui haec infideliter legerit, ipse peccabit.'[11] A control for gauging the importance of Christian

---

[9] Hilary, *Hymn* 1. 21–2.
[10] Jerome, *Vita Pauli* 6 = *PL* 23. 13 ff., with reference to Mark 9: 23.
[11] Sulpicius Severus, *Vita Martini*, *Epil.* 27.

fides to the credulity of the educated in the case of martyr-literature must therefore be established outside the realm of Christian literature.

A more general warning is also needed by way of a preface: carefully to be avoided in such a survey is what has been termed an 'anachronistic rationalism'.[12] It is all too easy to apply modern standards to a judgement of ancient reactions to the material represented by the *Peristephanon*. On these terms, the poems can easily be dismissed as written for people blinkered, under pressure from the expectations of the new religion, into a child-like gullibility, people consciously suppressing their normally rational twentieth-century-style outlook in order to make sure of their place in the New Jerusalem. The poems and the audience they assume must, of course, rather be placed firmly within their own complete cultural context, and this must entail reference to contemporary secular, pagan outlooks and standards on the same or similar subjects.

In fact, the *Peristephanon* provides the perfect test case and starting-point for reaching a fuller appreciation of what has been termed the *naïveté commune* of the period.[13] This *naïveté* of taste for material assuming a high level of credulity in its audience was characteristic of the culture of the period as a whole, and can be seen not only among the lower classes of the Late Empire, where it has appeared acceptable to modern commentators, but also, more surprisingly, as the poems of the *Peristephanon* themselves suggest in the strictly Christian sphere, among the educated classes in general. By the level of credulity which they assume in their audience, the poems do not represent an awkward case to be explained away purely in terms of Christian *fides* or 'unresolved tension'. This view suggests too harsh a division of fourth-century culture, both horizontally and vertically. Either this results in a picture of educated Christians within the Church being forced to accept a distinct and alien primitive culture, artificially imposed from below by the majority of lower-class Christians, or else it encourages an Augustinian 'City of God' view of the period, by

---

[12] MacMullen (1968); cf. Momigliano, (1977) 155: 'In the fourth and fifth centuries there were of course plenty of beliefs which we historians of the twentieth century would gladly call popular, but the historians of the fourth and fifth centuries never treated any belief as characteristic of the masses and consequently discredited among the élite.'

[13] Fontaine (1975a) 758 and 771.

which Christians of all classes shared in splendid isolation a fully Christianized culture distinct from contemporary pagan culture. This schematized view simply does not work in the face of the continuing cultural unity of Western society: the Ambroses, Symmachuses, Augustines, and Prudentiuses of the period shared the same basic education and the outlook and attitudes which this formed; they moved in the same social circles, spoke the same language, and were preoccupied with many of the same problems, both spiritual and temporal. In the realms of education alone, for example, the idealistic rejection of pagan literature had finally had to be abandoned through the practical impossibility of formulating a purely Christian curriculum. Jerome's work in Bethlehem and Augustine's ideas in his *De doctrina christiana* give proof of this. Prudentius too falls back to a large extent on classical forms in his Christian poetry.

In this period the pagan and Christian should be seen as two facets of the same society and culture, features of which are shared, exchanged and assimilated slowly in these years to make a new whole. Both pagan and Christian authors of the period must be studied with close reference to each other, since they both conform to unified canon of taste which belongs peculiarly to Late Antiquity.[14] This is the line which will be followed here in an attempt to show that the poems of the *Peristephanon* do not represent an isolated Christian phenomenon standing outside the overall culture of the period, but rather exemplify, in the Christian sphere, tendencies of taste and interest which were generally prevalent.

Secular Reading in the Fourth Century

A 'marked revival of interest in the classical authors'[15] has often been noted for the fourth century. It was demonstrated in the emendation and editing of a wider range of classical writers than that commonly in use in the schools. Ammianus Marcellinus, however, in a well-known passage of his *Res gestae* sets the literary culture of the majority of Roman senators of his day much lower.

[14] Cf. Brown's comment (1972: 138–9) that the Later Empire is 'a period ... in which men worked (and most creatively) on an unbroken ancient legacy, and which is not to be reduced to a prelude to the Middle Ages.'

[15] Cameron (1964*a*).

He gives a rather biassed but not wholly unreliable view of the
reading-matter of the whole class in a judgement which presum-
ably stands good for Christians and pagans alike. He tells us that
the literary interests of the Roman senators are so limited that they
hate learning like poison; the Roman libraries are 'shut up like
tombs' and senators' leisure-hours are spent in reading only
Juvenal and Marius Maximus.[16] Juvenal, it is true, represents one
of the latest 'classical' rediscoveries of the day,[17] but his associa-
tion in a context of contempt, with the disreputable writer of
scurrilous imperial biographies gives some indication of the level
of interest in the satirist. Perhaps it is worth noting that Marius
Maximus gets his only other mention outside the *Historia Augusta*
in the *Scholia* of Juvenal.[18] The passage of Ammianus at any rate
makes clear the sort of thing which senators are reading 'curatiore
studio'. The audience of Marius Maximus is thus limited by the
historian to the idle and frivolous in Rome, those who in a crisis
preferred dancing-girls and musicians to 'sectatores disciplinarum
liberalium' like himself.[19] Interest in this rather shadowy author
was, however, typical of an age in which biography was tremen-
dously popular.[20] A closer look at the characteristic features and
aims of this genre, a favourite, too, of educated circles, throws im-
portant light on the historical sensibilities and expectations of the
age.

It must be noted, in the first place, that the large-scale works of
the classical historians had gone out of fashion several centuries
earlier: abridgements of Livy were already replacing his full-
length work in the age of Hadrian. After Tacitus, Latin historical
writings were either epitomes, brief surveys, or collections of bio-
graphies. 'It was Suetonius, not Livy or Tacitus who most pro-
foundly influenced succeeding generations ... historical epitomes
and short surveys had a strongly biographical cast.'[21] Aurelius
Victor's *Caesares* and the *Breviaria* of Eutropius and Festus were
the best that the fourth century, for the most part, could produce,
or perhaps, rather, wanted to produce in the way of history. The
interest of Symmachus and of three generations of Nicomachi

---

[16] Ammianus Marcellinus, *Res gestae* (*RG*), 28. 4. 14 and 14. 6. 18.
[17] Cameron (1964a). Servius' pupil Nicaeus edited Juvenal.
[18] *Scholia ad Juvenalem*, 4. 53.
[19] Ammianus Marcellinus, *RG* 14. 6. 19.
[20] Syme (1968) 89.
[21] Laistner (1957) 19.

Flaviani in the text of Livy might suggest a return of interest in the classical forms of history among the educated classes, but whether or not Symmachus' enthusiasm for Livy stretched to an intimate knowledge of the whole text, there is no surviving major historical work written by these men. It is true that Symmachus' friend Protadius was interested at least in writing a Gallic history, while another friend Naucellius seems to have translated a history of the 'prisca res publica' from the Greek; Nicomachus Flavianus the elder, too, was praised in a commemorative inscription with the epithet 'disertissimus' for his historical writings.[22] But whatever the scale and nature of these works, insofar as the age in general was interested in historical facts, it wanted them in an easily accessible form; handbooks to the Roman heritage which would help all (provincials, perhaps, in particular), to the minimum background-knowledge and cultural qualification necessary for inclusion within the ruling class of the Empire.[23]

The latest obsession was, however, Marius Maximus,[24] whose continuation of Suetonius' *Lives of the Emperors* from Nerva to Elagabalus seems to have had a revival of popularity in the late fourth century. His work has not in fact survived, and the only insight into its nature (apart from the one brief and condemnatory remark already mentioned) is provided by the references to him in the notoriously problematical writings of the so-called *Scriptores Historiae Augustae*. The authors, or rather probably the author, of this work, claims to use the biographies of Marius Maximus at many points as a source for his own collection of imperial biographies. From the numerous citations of the biographer in the *Historia Augusta*, it can be gathered that Marius Maximus was given to retailing the more unverifiable and scandalous anecdotes about figures at the imperial court, and seems to have included lengthy direct quotations from what purported to be genuine speeches, letters, and sections of the *acta urbis*.[25] The

---

[22] Symmachus, *Ep.* 4. 18. 5 (Protadius), *Ep.* 3. 11. 3 (Naucellius). For Nicomachus Flavianus see *CIL* 6. 1782–3 'historico disertissimo'. It is possible that Symmachus in fact gained some of his knowledge of Livy from the epitome of Valerius Maximus. See Cameron (1964*b*) 27.

[23] Momigliano (1963*c*).

[24] For Marius Maximus see Townend (1967) and Birley (1967). See too *OCD* 649. For his probable biography, see *ILS* 2935 and Dessau 346–7.

[25] Marius Maximus, *Historia Augusta* (*HA*) quotes *speeches*: Marcus Antoninus 25. 10, Commodus 18. 2; *adclamationes* on the death of the emperor, Pertinax 2. 8; *letters*, Avidius

Historia Augusta condemns its model as 'Homo omnium uerbosis-simus', 'qui et mythistoricis se uoluminibus implicauit'.[26] This judgement of verbosity in combination with some degree of inac-curacy or even untruthfulness is confirmed both by the nature of the *Historia Augusta* itself, which is at least based on the example of Marius Maximus, and by the contempt of a contemporary his-torian of somewhat higher aspirations.

Thus brevity, viewed as desirable in the more serious kind of history, is balanced by an apparently inexhaustible interest in the less-easily verified details of historical lives. In the latter the true and the fictitious can be thrown together without scruple and even be given explicit confirmation as the whole truth. Research was not felt to be necessary and hearsay—whether retailed as such or not—was evidence enough. Historical standards had slipped somewhat since the days of the classical historians, or rather had developed those features of their histories less conducive to the highest standards of accuracy: the composition of speeches, for in-stance, and the inclusion of only marginally relevant material for the sake of its own interest. Then, in the later period, the standard histories and collections of information presented in writing by earlier centuries became a ready fixed source of material making further research unnecessary for those of an almost exclusively literary culture. The eye might in theory be acknowledged to be more trustworthy than the ear, in an attractively antithetical topos,[27] but the historical scruples implicit in such a statement could hardly carry much weight in an age of unrest, when travel was a huge and dangerous undertaking and systematic scientific research, even of the most primitive variety, was a phenomenon of the distant past. Erudition was measured only in terms of familiarity with a static and exclusively literary culture. Historical accuracy was to be measured in general not so much by an object-

---

Cassius 9. 9; *acta urbis*, Commodus 15. 5. He quotes at excessive length: Commodus 18. 2, Pertinax 15. 8. He records the less public aspects of court intrigues, for example, Hadrian 2. 10, on Hadrian's marriage—it pleased Plotina, but not Trajan; Hadrian 20. 3, the cruelty of Hadrian was only modified so that he might escape Domitian's fate; Avidius Cassius 9. 9, he wishes to defame Faustina; Hadrian 21. 4, Hadrian's favourite mixture of sow's udders, peacock, ham in pastry, and wild boar.

[26] *HA*, Firmus 1. 1.

[27] Lucian, *De conscr. hist.* 29, where the topos 'the ears are less trustworthy than the eyes' is used by the charlatan historian; cf. Eusebius, *Martyrs of Palestine*, 4. 14. 15: 'men naturally trust their ears less than their eyes'.

ive reality hard to verify at first hand, as by the level of credulity of the audience.

This was the sort of atmosphere in which the *Historia Augusta* could be sure of finding a wide and appreciative audience, perhaps at more than one level of sophistication.[28] The work parodies its own genre and the audience-tastes for which this catered; its author is a humorous deutero-Suetonius, who delights in presenting to his reader, with all appearance of research in imperial libraries and with references to other bogus authorities and even epigraphic evidence, a set of biographies which can be described for the most part as no better than romantic fiction, or, at best, historical fiction. The very traits criticized by the author in Marius Maximus and other biographers find their reflection in exaggerated form in the writer's own practice. One Junius Cordus, for example, comes under fire for giving too many trivial details;[29] yet the author comments about his own practice that 'nil curiositas recusat'. The work is 'munus ... quod ego ... non eloquentiae causa sed curiositatis in lumen edidi'. He is, by his own account, 'unus ex curiosis' and his criticizes those who write 'multa incuriose, multa breuiter'.[30]

It is this concept of *curiositas* which could be said to characterize the intellectual outlook of the period, and certainly its attitude towards what is considered to be the historical and factual. *Curiositas* forms the complement and in part the explanation for the high level of credulity assumed in their audience by the fourth-century biographers and historians. H.-I. Marrou has noticed[31] that it represents an important 'orientation de pensée', which for him is well-exemplified by Augustine. A brief glance at the entry for *curiositas* in the *TLL* soon confirms the peculiarity of the concept to the later period, by the relatively late appearance of the abstract noun: it makes a single appearance in the correspondance of Cicero, and is then forgotten until it is taken up by Apuleius in his *Metamorphoses* in the second century and Tertullian in the third. The word's floruit belongs to the late period and, in particular, to the fourth century.

---

[28] Syme (1971) 287.

[29] *HA*, Opellius Macrinus 1. 3–5.

[30] *HA*, Aurelianus 10. 1; Carus et Carinus et Numerianus 21. 2; Probus 2. 8. Criticism of Pollio's carelessness and brevity: Aurelianus 2. 1.

[31] Marrou (1958) 131 ff.

In the *Metamorphoses* both the older adjective and the abstract
noun are used repeatedly to point a basic theme, the 'spirit of re-
search' of Lucius the hero, which, however, turns out to be a
negative form of *curiositas* in the religious context of prying into
cult secrets. This bad sense of *curiosus* had a long history, going
back as far as Roman comedy and the well-known 'curiosi' of
Catullus' seventh poem.[32] To look ahead to the fourth century,
this sense of *curiosus* finds official recognition in the Theodosian
Code for the year AD 355. An edict for this year (6. 29. 1) recog-
nizes the term *curiosi* as provincial terminology for *agentes in rebus*
on the job. The *curiosus* feels a compulsion to seek out knowledge
which lies outside his legitimate sphere of interest, perhaps to the
detriment of those whom it does concern. Cicero goes some way
towards expressing a more Aristotelian concept of disinterested
knowledge, but this more intellectual appreciation of research for
its own sake is counterbalanced by his equal involvement in the
Roman ideal of utility, even in intellectual pursuits, and the close
connection of this with Stoic moral diatribe against man's
audacity. Thus a negative moral view of *curiositas* was current
even in classical times, and it is the tension set up by the presence
of this which leads directly to its condemnation in a more nar-
rowly religious context, first in Apuleius and then, of course,
among Christian writers.

Tertullian has no difficulty in connecting *curiositas* with heresy,
magic, and vice in general.[33] Augustine, an intellectual before he
was a Christian, provides a more interesting case. He recognizes
the end of *curiositas* in knowledge as representing a 'studium scien-
tiae' (*Confessions*, 2. 13) and the pleasure that this can bring: 'et
omnis illa quae appellatur curiositas, quid aliud quaerit quam de
rerum cognitione laetitiam?';[34] since 'quid … appetit curiositas
nisi cognitionem?'[35] He tells how this passion for knowledge
spread in his own time: 'et eunt homines mirari alta montium, et
ingentes fluctus maris, et latissimos lapsus fluminum, et Oceani
ambitum, et gyros siderum.'[36] In the Christian context of pilgri-

<hr/>

[32] Plautus, *Aulularia*, 562; L. Afranius fr. from *Incendium*, 190, with sceleratus; Catullus
7.

[33] Tertullian, *Ad nationes*, 1. 1. 3; *De praescriptione*, 8. 1.

[34] Augustine, *De uera religione*, 49 (94).

[35] Ibid., 52 (101).

[36] Augustine, *Conf.* 10. 8. 15.

mage to the Holy Places, this more positive side of *curiositas* might find expression through the 'sanctorum locorum desiderium' experienced by the pilgrim. The Spanish pilgrim Egeria, for instance, describes herself as 'curiosa' (*Itinerarium Egeriae*, 16. 3) and can only find satisfaction in actually seeing the Holy Places with her own eyes. Augustine, the rigidly spiritual Christian, however, must ultimately view the aims and effects of *curiositas* in moral terms: it can become an unhealthy 'libido scientiae', a 'uenenum curiositatis',[37] distracting us away from proper spiritual awareness and introspection, and encouraging a corrupting concentration on the things of the world. It becomes part of a triad of vices together with *superbia* and *uoluptas*, and can be paralleled with the *concupiscentia* warned against in St John's first Epistle.[38]

Viewed from outside the period the intellectual results of *curiositas* have been seen more positively to represent something of a reaction against the tyranny over learning exercised by the fixed corpus of knowledge received from Classical Antiquity and carefully preserved in the predominantly literary education of the later period. Augustine's experiment to test the incorruptibility of peacock's flesh, or the verification in fact sought by the pilgrim,[39] were a move in the right direction, but this practical approach was unfortunately the exception not the rule, and in any case had mixed results. On one side, the mentality implied in *curiositas* encouraged a haphazard collection of, at best, half-understood facts, valued purely for their interest as individual 'curiosities' or collector's pieces, with no attempt to categorize or formulate a scientific system governed by laws; on the other, even this collector's enthusiasm for new and striking facts could fall back on a literary tradition represented for the West by, for instance, Pliny's *Natural History*. The result was a move away from scientific research and the Aristotelian empirical outlook towards an enthusiasm for the weird and wonderful, whatever its source or credentials. Hence works like the probably third-century collection of *Mirabilia* by Solinus—mainly plagiarized, in fact, from Pliny. In his preface, this author even explicitly states the difficulty of telling anything new in the face of the omniscience of the

[37] Ibid., 13. 21.
[38] Ibid., 10. 35: 1 John. 2: 15–17.
[39] *De ciu. dei* 21. 7 (the peacock's flesh). The importance of first-hand experience to the pilgrim is emphasized by Hunt (1982) 86 ff.

authors of antiquity.[40] Other works of the late period confirm this tendency and illustrate the domination of *curiositas* over more strictly disciplined intellectual interests: the commentaries of Servius, the *Saturnalia* of Macrobius and the work of Martianus Capella provide good examples of the 'compendia' to which the indulgence of *curiositas* could lead.

Curiositas was condemned on moral grounds by the Christian Augustine: where information was lacking to satisfy the *curiosus*, little scruple was felt in fabricating a likely substitute for the real thing, as anyone who has sampled the commentaries of the fourth and fifth centuries on classical authors will know. There was a marked interest in pseudepigrapha, that is, forged documents and inscriptions, written not necessarily to deceive by supporting bogus historical claims, but to satisfy curiosity and increase knowledge. Speeches of Catiline, erotic letters from Dellius to the Queen of Egypt and juvenilia by famous authors are all welcomed as 'revealing new and startling information'.[41] Christian ethics do not seem to have inhibited Christian writers from participation in this practice.[42] Orthodoxy encouraged literary dishonesty.[43] The promotion of special views and doctrines under the authority of a well-known name was one aspect of this practice, well exemplified by Jerome's quarrel with Rufinus over the publishing of forgeries under Jerome's name.[44] From another point of view, more of a good thing could in this way be supplied to a receptive audience. Thus it was 'love of the Apostle' which inspired the presbyter defrocked for composing the fictitious *Acts of St Paul and Thecla*, as Tertullian tells us.[45] Even blatant forgeries might be accepted by the faithful. Jerome seems to accept the correspondence between St Paul and Seneca,[46] while Eusebius and the pilgrim Egeria accept the correspondence between Christ and King Abgar of Edessa.[47] The insertion of forged passages into established texts was another practice indulged in all too easily in

---

[40] Mommsen (1895) 2.
[41] Syme (1968) 120.
[42] Rist (1972). Also Bardy (1936) Metzger (1972) and Gudeman (1894).
[43] Momigliano (1966) 144.
[44] Jerome, *Apologia aduersos libros Rufini*, 3. 25 = PL 23. 476.
[45] Tertullian, *De baptismo*, 17.
[46] Jerome, *De uiris illustribus*, 12 (cf. Augustine, *Ep.* 153. 14).
[47] Eusebius, *Hist. eccl.* 1. 13; *Itinerarium Egeriae*, 19.

the age of the copyists: it is against this form of pseudepigraphy that the author of *Revelation* writes of his prophecies:

If anyone adds to them, God will add to him the plagues described in this book, and if anyone takes away from the words of the book of the prophecy, God will take away his share in the tree of life and the holy city, which are described in this book.[48]

If set in rather drastic terms, this is typical of the *envois* found in many early manuscripts. And the copyist was not the only potential corrupter of a text: perhaps worth mention in this context is the latitude in the treatment of his original allowed himself by the fourth-century translator. Rufinus provides an obvious example here.[49]

Pseudepigraphy, of course, has a long and disreputable history, stretching back to the early centuries BC, but even this brief survey of the part it played in the later period reinforces a growing impression of a completely unworried attitude towards the factual and historical. An insatiable appetite for what has been termed 'historical romance',[50] combined well with the later tendency bred by school exercises towards rhetorical exaggeration and elaboration, and interest in the typical. The new literature growing up about the figure of the martyr-hero in the Christian sphere can soon be seen to be far from out of tune with more general contemporary historical and literary interests. There is no need to keep the reading public of Marius Maximus and the *Peristephanon* in separate compartments.

One at least, however, of the contemporary 'sectatores disciplinarum liberalium' claimed to rise above the standards he implicitly disdained in Marius Maximus—that is, Ammianus Marcellinus. He was the only historian of the time to attempt to break away from the biographical cast of contemporary historiography, and the only one to return to the example of Tacitus in order to write in Latin a serious history in the classical style. He seems to indulge in polemic directed obliquely against current historical interests and standards, when he dwells on the topic of the dignity proper to genuine history, which should for him 'dis-

---

[48] Rev. 22: 18–19.
[49] Neyrand (1978) and Oulton (1929).
[50] Syme (1968) 102.

currere per negotiorum celsitudines',[51] ignoring 'minutias igno-
biles',[52] and which is 'quae per squalidas transiere personas'.[53] He
is not interested in retailing trivia like an emperor's dinner-party
conversation, the stuff of Marius Maximus and the *Historia
Augusta*. Thus he praises brevity which cuts through 'moras
intempestiuas' in an historical work, but insists that he will give all
the information he discovers, 'nihil obtrectatores longi (ut putant)
operis formidantes'.[54] In other words, he wants to escape from
the inventive all-inclusiveness of the biographies, but also to avoid
the unsatisfactory brevity and omissions of the epitomes. He is
preoccupied with *ueritas* in the writing of history, careful to dis-
tinguish between information received from others and what he
has gained at first hand, the 'uisa uel lecta'.[55] So, in his description
of Thrace, he rejects the 'obscura uarietas' of earlier authors in
favour of 'quae uidisse meminimus expedire', 'what we ourselves
remember having seen'. He wants to describe in order the 'rerum
summitates', 'cum explicandae rerum memoriae oblique debeatur
integritas fida.'[56]

However, even the historian of these explicitly high standards
is betrayed by what must be his unconscious involvement in the
tastes and tendencies of the age. Thus, although he aspires in his
Res gestae to a more annalistic structure, this has been seen to clash
somewhat with the strong biographical elements clear in the por-
trayal of the emperors and Caesars necessarily central to the His-
tories. The reader is constantly aware of the emperor, even if only
in the background.[57] The description of key figures may be short,
anecdotes told in connection with the emperors may be brief and
in accord with the historian's moral purpose, yet the vividness of
the language and imagery in which they are expressed is far from
giving the impression of even the classical historian's degree of
objectivity. An exaggerated realism enters the high style of his-
tory, every scene is painted in dramatic terms, details of gesture

---

[51] Ammianus Marcellinus, *RG* 26. 1. 2.

[52] Ibid., 27. 2. 11.

[53] Ibid., 28. 1. 15, cf. 26. 1.

[54] Ibid., 15. 1. 1.

[55] Ibid., 22. 8; cf. 15. 1; 27. 4. 2; 29. 1. 24. For the importance of *ueritas*: *RG* 22. 8. 1;
31. 16. 9; 16. 1; 14. 6. 2; 26. 1. 1; 27. 9. 4; 29. 1. 15; 31. 2. 12; 16. 9. Interest in the reality
behind the lies: 15. 2. 9; 16. 8. 6; 31. 5. 10.

[56] Ibid., 27. 4. 2 for description of Thrace; 'rerum summitates': *RG* 31. 5. 10.

[57] Ammianus' tendency towards the biographical: Blockley (1975) 33 ff.; also Seeck
(1894) 1848.

and colour are picked out for description, the theatricality of which is explicitly pointed by constant comparisons with the presentation of scenes on the stage. The frequent use of animal imagery is striking: crowds and persecutors rage and grind their teeth like wild beasts, and even lengthy epic similes appear. Thus Ursicinus is compared to a 'lion of huge size and terrible fierceness which did not dare to go to save from danger his whelps that were caught in a net, because he had been robbed of claws and teeth'.[58] Small-scale descriptive digressions of this sort find extended form in digressions from the main narrative which, for instance, describe the Huns, the Gauls, or the Saracens. Geographical digressions might be excused within the genre of history, but as Ammianus pauses, in a dramatic description of the siege of Amida, to discuss the origins and different types of disease of the kind which attacked the besieged, the feeling arises that the historian is happy to display his erudition in this discursive passage.

Other digressions, too, draw in displays of erudition on subjects only marginally relevant to the narrative in progress. Ammianus is keen to illuminate his readers on the subject of obelisks, hieroglyphics, eclipses, rainbows, comets, and the sexual mores of palmtrees.[59] He is torn, he tells us, between the urge to recount all the theories about the phenomena with which he deals and the need to hurry on with his narrative.[60] One cannot help but feel, however, that Ammianus succeeds—perhaps even unconsciously—in getting the best of both worlds. He, too, shares the predilection for curiosities of his audience and feels no real scruple in giving us both the 'uisa' and the 'lecta' indiscriminately on occasion. Thus, much of the information which he supplies is from literary sources: either the earlier classical historians or poets, or perhaps the sorts of manuals represented by Solinus[61] Even in cases where Ammianus' personal experience forms a sound basis of 'uisa' for his digressions, he cannot resist resorting to the second-hand:

[58] Ammianus Marcellinus, *RG* 19. 3. 1–3. This vivid realism in Ammianus is discussed and illustrated by Auerbach (1953) 50 ff.
[59] Obelisks and hieroglyphics: *RG* 17. 4. 6; eclipses: 20. 3. 1–2; earthquakes: 17. 7. 9–14; rainbows: 20. 11. 26–30; comets: 25. 10. 2–3; palm trees: 24. 3. 12–13. See Dautremer (1899) 183–94.
[60] Ammianus Marcellinus, *RG* 25. 10. 3.
[61] Dautremer (1899) 186, and Mommsen's edition of Solinus, 21. On the pearl, compare Ammianus Marcellinus, *RG* 23. 6. 85–8 and Solinus 53. 23–8. Perhaps a common source was used by both authors?

hence his treatment of the pearl, which closes his description of Persia. Thus even the most self-consciously serious historian of the late fourth century, who tries to set himself outside and above the general run of reading interests and the historical standards of his less exacting contemporaries, also exemplifies the tendencies to be seen at work in the age of *curiositas*.

The demands of rhetoric partially explain the stylistic aspects of Ammianus' vivid and dramatic history, but it would be wrong, as some have done, to undervalue or dismiss Ammianus' credulity in the *Res gestae*: once again, anachronistic interpretations cannot accept belief by a fourth-century intellectual in supernatural phenomena now recognized as incredible or scientifically explicable. Thus Ammianus is chastised for his confusion of scientific data with mythology and for retailing the incredible as though he believed it. The point is, rather, that Ammianus is here simply reflecting one aspect of the general level of credulity of the age. That is, the belief in what were seen as miraculous occurrences. These could happily be accepted on hearsay, since there was little opportunity for gathering first-hand information and not much interest in research in general. Such miracles could also easily be accepted at first hand, through a lack of a scientific knowledge thorough enough to reduce them to natural laws and rational explanation. In a world of largely unexplained, or, at best, only partially-understood natural phenomena, events regarded as miraculous were far from uncommon and never regarded as incredible unless transmitted by an obviously untrustworthy authority. Scepticism, of course existed, but on uncertain grounds. Thus, the same person might reject one story or fact as incredible, but be ready to accept another on no better grounds.

Ammianus cannot be blamed for his belief in, for instance, a baby born with two heads, two sets of teeth, a beard, four eyes, and two very small ears, as a prophecy of the degeneration of the state. To this portent he can even add the complaint that, although such portents are numerous, they pass by unheard-of and unknown because not expiated by public rites as in earlier times. In Book 21, he speaks in favour of augury and prophetic dreams: the gods are behind such phenomena, and it is not the dreams that are to be doubted but the mistakes of their interpreters. In the same passage he compares the art of divination with those of grammar, medicine and music. They are all techniques in which mistakes may be made. He quotes with satisfaction the 'fine saying' of Cicero in his *De natura deorum* to support his remarks.[62] Ammianus does not say what he thinks of the sort of ouija-board activities which Hilarius tells about in his evidence at the Antioch treason-trials,[63] but he says nothing to suggest that he considered the whole thing incredible, or simply untrue.

There was no reason why he should. Such belief had a long history and was by no means excluded by the highest intellectual or even philosophical interests of the day: one need only think of the growth of later Neoplatonist interest in theurgy, in spite of Plotinus' own lack of interest in magic, for instance.[64] The various *Lives* of prominent philosophers and the so-called aretalogies provide evidence for the belief of members of the same school in the miraculous powers of these philosophers. Lucian's *Life of Alexander of Abonuteichus*, the Pseudomantis, parodies such *Lives*, and those whom Lucian suggests were taken in by similar charlatans. But the credulity which they illustrate and assume even among those of more specifically intellectual, philosophical interests was typical of Late Antiquity as a whole. What was accepted with no difficulty by the man in the street was at least likely to be admitted to be a strong possibility by those of the highest contemporary education. It is this general and marked credulity which Lucian satirizes in a more general way as early as the second century in his *Philopseudes*, or *Lover of Lies*.

Belief in magic, divination, and astrology was a living and powerful force in the pagan outlook of the time, and it is therefore far from surprising or paradoxical to find Ammianus in this matter writing under the influence of his cultural environment. He does not represent an awkward example of *naïveté* at odds with intellectual outlook, but rather a case exemplifying the general rule for the period. Augustine here provides at once a parallel case and a useful transition back to the Christian sphere: he can truly be said to represent the highest degree of contemporary culture over the widest range of subjects and interests, while also giving an insight into the outlook of an intellectual converted to

---

[62] Ammianus Marcellinus, *RG* 19. 12. 19–20; 21. 1. 14. Cicero, *De natura deorum*, 2. 4. 12; cf. *De diu.* 1. 52. 118. For a more particularly political interpretation of the miraculous in Ammianus, see Cracco Ruggini (1977) 114–116 and Meslin (1974).

[63] Ammianus Marcellinus, *RG* 29. 1. 25–32.

[64] Dodds (1947); cf. Blockley (1975) 104 ff. Also MacMullen (1967) 121–7, 322–5; and Barb (1963).

Christianity. It is difficult to disentangle in Augustine a more neu-
tral attitude towards the miraculous in the widest sense from his
more narrowly religious approach to the inexplicable;[65] to separ-
ate, in other words, an attitude representative of general secular
attitudes from that shaped by Christian *fides*. However, several
significant qualifications of Augustine's attitude towards the
miraculous in a Christian context might be suggestive of a more
basic intellectual attitude. It is worth reconsidering the often
noted evolution of Augustine's attitude towards miracles within
the Church.

He moves from a position of reserve and disbelief in contem-
porary miracles in the closing years of the fourth century to the
total acceptance which made the institution of the *libelli miracu-
lorum* a task high on his list of priorities at Hippo, as he records in
the *City of God*.[66] His original reserve is not, however, the result
of a completely rationalistic outlook: he is ready enough to admit
the miracles of the Apostolic Age. It is rather the product of
Augustine's own high spiritual standards and the emphasis in his
religious outlook on the spiritual rather than on the earthly and
tangible. Miracles may have been needed as signs in the earliest
years of the Church, but now the faith is strong enough not to
need to look for miracles. The Church is not supported by the
proof of miracles, but the miracles are to be accepted only because
of their place within the Church. Spiritual miracles within the
soul are the sort to be looked for today.[67] On the other hand, bib-
lical miracles are accepted by Augustine as real and are explained
in terms of the operation of the whole of Nature by and through
the will of God.[68] Miracles are due to the *semina seminum*
implanted in the world by God at Creation.[69] He calls these seeds
elsewhere *causales rationes*, or *seminales rationes*.[70] They represent a
second level of potential natural order above that of the better
known order of the normal natural laws which we are able to see
in operation every day. Thus the only difference between a
miracle and something which is not a miracle is that the miracle is

[65] On Augustine and miracles: Courcelle (1950) 139 ff; de Vooght (1939a) Brown
(1967) 414 ff; Van der Meer (1961) 527–57; Dodds (1985) 156–210; Momigliano (1977).
[66] Delehaye (1910). Augustine, *De ciu. dei*, 22. 8 for AD 426.
[67] *Sermo* 90. 5.
[68] *Ep.* 137. 11–16, cf. *De ciu. dei*, 21. 7.
[69] *De trinitate*, 3. 8. Grant (1952) 218–19.
[70] *De Genesi ad litteram*, 6. 14, 9. 17.

to be attributed to a different mode of causation from that of ordinary events. Both classes of events are, strictly speaking, 'natural', since they both have their origin in God. Augustine can, therefore, conclude that nothing really happens contrary to nature, but only to what we know of nature in our limited and ignorant way.[71] A miracle cannot be measured by anything so feeble as current understanding.[72]

Even in Augustine's earlier period of reserve towards contemporary miracles, however, he had—as he tells us later—either witnessed, or at least learnt of and accepted, the cure of the blind man which had taken place at the *inventio* of the Milanese saints Gervasius and Protasius.[73] His enthusiastic acceptance and promotion of contemporary miracles in the 420s was apparently, not 'a sudden and unprepared surrender to popular credulity',[74] and in any case had a firm basis in his earlier analysis of the acceptability of the miraculous in a Biblical context. Evidence of God's direct action in the Church could be used to make an important polemic point in the troubled years of the early fifth century, but it would be wrong to see Augustine's change of position on the question of miracles as a cynical exploitation of their practical value for the survival and prestige of the Church in these circumstances. His belief and acceptance seem to have been sincere and all the more interesting for not being a product of crude superstition. He is at pains to bring a sceptical and even experimental attitude to bear on the miraculous. He does not expect his readers to accept rashly all the marvels of which he tells in the *City of God*:[75] he himself only believes implicitly those which have come either under his own observation, or those which 'anyone can readily verify'. Hence his enthusiasm for the first-hand information to be included in his 'casebooks' of miracles, the *libelli*, at Hippo. He is concerned to define the miracle thoroughly enough to avoid the over-inclusiveness of the popular style.

However, Augustine's very acceptance of the possibility of the miraculous fits in with his susceptibility to the more general attitude of the day towards the marvellous and inexplicable in a less

---

[71] *Ep.* 72. 2 to Jerome, for AD 398; cf. *De ciu. dei*, 21. 8.

[72] *De ciu. dei*, 3. 15.

[73] Augustine, *Conf.* 9. 7. 16.

[74] Brown (1967) 415.

[75] *De ciu. dei*, 21. 7.

narrowly religious sense. His theoretically high standards of veri-
fication and his cautious attitude are forgotten as he accepts and
relays to his readers *mirabilia* accepted on hearsay or from the
literary tradition. Thus he tells us of the apples of Sodom which
are filled with dust and smoke, of the miraculous fountain at
Epirus, and the salamander which lives in the midst of flames, to
name but a few examples. In spite of efforts to give his informa-
tion convincing credentials, it is Augustine the *curiosus*, typical of
his age, who is speaking here. If, in spite of attempts to rationalize
and explain strictly Christian miracles in human terms, a man of
more than average education and intellectual independence can be
shown to betray symptoms of less exacting credulity, then it is not
difficult to understand the prevalence of a much higher degree of
credulity among those with less capacity or time for hard thought
on the same subject.

Augustine the intellectual may be said to balance Augustine the
man of Christian *fides* in this evolution of attitude towards
Church miracles, but both aspects of the man are based on a
common receptiveness to the marvellous. Having reached the
Christian end of the argument through Augustine, it is instructive
here to consider Christian attitudes towards specifically pagan
dealings with the supernatural.

Far from dismissing this as baseless fantasy, Christians showed
the extent to which their world was at one with that of the pagans
by attributing what they accepted as real manifestations of super-
natural powers to the demons.[76] Divination and magic were
attributed by Tertullian to the activities of fallen angels.[77] In fact,
hardly a human being is not attended by a demon.[78] Demons
sometimes masquerade as angels, the better to deceive pagans
who vaunt their success with magic. The deceit involved in magic
for Augustine is that the magicians think it is *they* who are work-
ing the marvels really performed by demons.[79] Why, Augustine
argues, if pagans accept such wonders, can they remain incredu-
lous with regard to analogous phenomena mentioned in the
Bible?[80] His only consolation in considering the miracles of the

[76] Ibid., 2. 24–5.
[77] Tertullian, *De anima*, 57.
[78] Augustine *De ciu. dei*, 10. 9.
[79] *Conf.* 10. 42.
[80] Keenan (1940); Thorndike (1923), 462–79 and 504–22.

gods of the Gentiles in the past is that they 'are in no way compar-
able in power and grandeur with those performed among the
people of God' (*de ciu. dei*, 10. 16).

Acceptance of Christian miracles and religion did not exclude
an awareness of the powers of magic and the supernatural outside
it—hence the continuation of imperial legislation on magic even
after Christianity was officially recognized for the Empire. Con-
stantine upholds the traditional ban on 'magic arts' used either to
hurt people or to seduce to love, but can still add that there is
nothing wrong in medicinal magic or spells to prevent bad
weather.[81] The condemnation only of black magic and the
acceptance of the white version even under the Christian
emperors provides significant proof of the similarity of mentality
and outlook on these matters among both Christians and pagans.
Their different religious outlooks were found largely on the same
basic set of assumptions about the supernatural. Accepting the
possibility of the inexplicable and miraculous, they shaped their
attitude towards them according to their different religious
beliefs.[82]

At this point I would like to return to the sphere of strictly
Christian literature, to the new genre of martyr-literature repre-
sented in poetry by Prudentius' *Peristephanon*. As I hope I have
gone some way towards showing, in a rather rapid survey, a lack
of concern for historical verification centred on the narration of
key *Lives*, and the inclusion of the miraculous, are far from being
ingredients which it would have been difficult for the educated
Christian to accept without an artificially imposed mentality
based on Christian *fides*. A general loosening of historical stand-
ards, a growing interest in a form of biography unbothered by the
need for factual accuracy, and an insatible enthusiasm for the
exotic, the weird, and the wonderful can be traced among the
reading tastes of the educated classes as a whole for the period.
With this background in mind, there is naturally no need to re-
strict judgements of other Christian writings to purely religious
explanations. Thus it is no surprise on one side to find interest in
the *Apocrypha* spreading over the whole social scale, or, on the
other, to see the *Ecclesiastical History* of Eusebius recording con-
temporary miracles with no trace of scepticism, although this is a

---

[81] *CTh* 9. 16. 13 and 9. 16. 3. See MacMullen (1967) 121–7, 322–5.
[82] Thorndike (1923) 523–47.

work which has been particularly praised for its untypical concern for documentation.[83] A history like this was intended for an audience of some culture and is the work of a scholar; and yet it, too, displays features which are to be viewed in the light of its complete cultural context. Mention might also be made on the Christian side of the *Lives* of the saints which were enjoying such popularity in the West. The *Life of Anthony* started a trend which was continued by Jerome with his *Lives* of Paul, Malchus, and Hilarion, and by Sulpicius Severus in his *Life of St Martin*. It is into this pattern of interests that the *Peristephanon* should be fitted. The Christian and the secular interests of the period converge to provide a full explanation for the combination of its particular content with a presentation in a literary form which situates it in the realm of private leisure-reading for men of culture.

The poems of the *Peristephanon*, however, are representative of a fourth-century phenomenon even more far-reaching than the continuity of taste among educated Christians and pagans. The poems must also be viewed in the light of the *naïveté commune* of the period which I mentioned earlier. This *naïveté* is, of course, encapsulated in the '*curiositas* and credulity' of the title of this chapter, but if I have succeeded in demonstrating the prevalence of the outlook this implies among the educated classes at the end of the fourth century, it remains to note how far this tendency was typical of *all* levels of society. It comes as no surprise for this period, as for any other, to discover that this *naïveté* was a feature of lower-class culture. But the late period is remarkable for the extent to which both upper and lower classes are drawn together in a unified cultural outlook represented by a shift in taste affecting the whole of society. This shift can be expressed, at least partially, in terms of a popularization of culture; a growing receptiveness, that is, to the products of uneducated, unclassical, and un-Roman tastes.[84] This can be clearly seen at a mundane level, for instance, in the influence of the East and barbarian tastes in general in matters of dress: hence the marked increase in this period of the use of bright colours and the adoption of the *bracae*,

---

[83] Momigliano (1960) 145.

[84] MacMullen (1964a). This democratization in late antique culture is discussed by Momigliano (1977: 155): '... there is no way of defining a clear separation between an upper-class culture and a lower-class culture in the second half of the fourth century and in the first half of the fifth century.' He sees this process initiated by the Christians and assumed by the pagans.

which became so common in the fourth century that a law was passed to make sure that Romans continued to wear the toga (*CTh* 14. 10. 2, AD 399). The extreme popularity of the theatre and animal-shows with all classes of society is perhaps one of the most striking examples of the wide influence of more popular forms of entertainment, which was reflected in contemporary art. Ammianus' use of animal and theatrical imagery in his *Res gestae* has already been noted above: this can be paralleled in other works of the period. It was accompanied by a new note of realism contained in the preoccupation with lengthy and lurid descriptions of violence and death. Auerbach, in discussing this aspect of the literature of the fourth century in connection with Ammianus Marcellinus and his unconscious stylistic tendencies, speaks of the 'invasion of glaringly pictorial realism into the elevated style' as a feature typical of the age, and of the breakdown under this popular pressure of the classical rhetorical requirements of the high style.[85] Thus the literature of the Late Empire, together with the other arts, reveals 'a partial turning away from stale imitations, laboriously mastered, to a richer source of images in popular culture'.[86] The poems of the *Peristephanon* can obviously be fitted into this pattern.

The change and unifying of taste in the late period should be seen as another aspect of the 'social mobility' often discussed for the period;[87] in other words, the possibility of movement upwards in society for those of lower-class and perhaps provincial origins. The imperial administration, both civil and military, provided opportunities for this sort of advancement: in this way men of different non-Roman cultures came to move and mix freely about the Empire and within imperial society. The classical Roman culture which had once been the possession of a ruling minority was now sufficiently widely diffused throughout the Empire in the form of the contemporary school curriculum to provide an increasing number of provincials with at least the minimum degree of literacy necessary for admission to the civil administration: counterbalancing this 'Romanization' of the culture of the Empire, provincials naturally retained, or brought to bear on their assimilation of Roman culture, their own cultural backgrounds. It was not surprising that all this should gradually result

[85] Auerbach (1953) 50 ff.   [86] MacMullen (1964*a*) 455.
[87] See Hopkins (1961) and MacMullen (1964*b*).

in a new culture belonging peculiarly to the new circumstances of
the Late Empire, a culture with a fresh homogeneity and fresh cri-
teria of taste. It accompanied the social movements of those who
were unconsciously helping to form it. Even an emperor's literary
tastes might betray his origins: Valentinian's rather more salacious
poetic interests fortunately found an accomplice in his fellow-
provincial Ausonius.[88]

A share in the contemporary version of classical culture led to a
large amount of this sort of social movement, most clearly within
the imperial civil service. Here the possession of literary culture
was, according to the Emperor Constantius, 'the greatest of all
virtues' (*CTh* 14. 1. 1, AD 357/60), and a sure route to success, if
not always as spectacular as that of someone like Ausonius. Those
with a minimal education might rise too far: contemporaries
complain about the illiteracy of judges, for instance. A two-way
cultural movement is, in fact, well reflected within the civil ad-
ministration by the development of what has been called a form
of 'bureaucratese': men moving up through the ranks took some-
thing of their original and perhaps low level of culture with them,
while down through the administration filtered a rhetorical
bureaucratese perfected by the bureau-chiefs and ministers of state
chosen originally for their high level of literary culture.[89]

The effects of social mobility were thus more far-reaching for
fourth-century culture than the immediate results of material
advantage or geographical movement. It is in the context of the
attendant change of taste affecting the whole of a more fluid
society that the *Peristephanon* can most fully be appreciated.

These observations on the late fourth century help to set Pru-
dentius' *Peristephanon* poems firmly enough in their cultural
milieu to dispel any idea of a tension between their form and con-
tent, or of any strict isolation of these poems from the culture of
the period as a whole. Apart from the Christian bias necessarily
involved in a treatment of the martyrs, they conform to the
general taste of their period, and must have been well received on
all counts by the cultured Christian audience for which they were
written.

---

[88] Ausonius, *Cento nuptialis*, 19 (Teubner edn., p. 159).

[89] MacMullen (1962). See p. 366 for illiterate judges with references to Lactantius' *De
mortibus persecutorum*, 22 and *CTh*. 14. 1. 1. (AD 357/60). The pomp and theatricality of the
court also had their effect on the lower levels of society.

3

The Form and Purpose of the
Peristephanon

MY aim in this chapter is twofold, to reopen the question of whether or not these hymns were written originally for liturgical use;[1] and, by close analysis of their form, to establish a clearer picture of the public for which Prudentius was writing. The need to relate these poems to a living context has long been recognized.[2] I hope that the study presented here goes some way towards answering this need, since the form and contents of the poems are inevitably the products of a particular religious and cultural background. In the case of the *Peristephanon*, they are the only clues available in the search for the original purpose of the poems, and must therefore be analysed with special care. Awareness of a complex background must be maintained: on one side lies the increased enthusiasm for the cult of the martyrs and the parallel development of martyr-literature; on the other, a literary heritage formed by the still vital tradition of classical poetry (see Chapter Four) and also by the embryonic tradition of Christian Latin poetry.[3]

Linking all these elements is the central figure of Ambrose. His importance for the *Peristephanon* lies both in his active promotion of martyr-cult in the West at the end of the fourth century,[4] and in his composition of an influential corpus of Latin hymns, which improved on and replaced the earlier hymns of Hilary. The fusion of poetic traditions achieved in turn by Hilary and Ambrose[5] undoubtedly provided Prudentius with an important starting-point for the composition of his own lyric poetry. It is therefore

---

[1] The later evidence of Sidonius Apollinaris, *Ep.* 2. 9, and the role of Prudentius' poems in the *Mozarabic Hymnal* will be discussed below, pp. 67 ff. and p. 91 ff.

[2] The importance of this has been noted by Cunningham (1976). He cites a comment to this effect made by Fontaine (1974b) esp. 255–61, with n. 34.

[3] Raby (1953), early chapters.

[4] See chap. 1, p. 130 with n. 105.

[5] See Fontaine (1974a) esp. 330.

useful to begin with a brief sketch of early Latin hymnody, with
the aim of supplying significant points of comparison for a full
study of the form and purpose of the *Peristephanon*.

Hymnody in the West: Hilary and Ambrose

Metrical hymnody developed in the first place in the Eastern
Church.[6] It was influenced by its Jewish ancestry, in particular by
the Psalms which were so constantly in use, and also by the pagan
tradition of metrical hymns which had been preserved in the Hel-
lenistic world. Some awareness of this dual background emerges
from the Vulgate translation of the Greek ψαλμός by the Latin
word *hymnus*.[7] As prayer and praise and a didactic instrument for
both orthodox and heretical propaganda, the hymn held an im-
portant place within and outside the liturgy. It was popular in the
sense of reaching and being enthusiastically received by the wide
range of social classes included in the Christian congregation of
the fourth century.

Greek was the language of the Western liturgy as late as the
fourth century,[8] and a Latin hymnody appeared correspondingly
late. Its first surviving metrical examples were provided by the
bishops Hilary of Poitiers (?AD 315–67) and Ambrose of Milan
(*c*. AD 337–97). The overwhelming influence of these two writers
of hymns was recognized in the Council of Toledo in the seventh
century. Their hymns provided the pattern for the composition
of other non-Scriptural hymns 'like those which the blessed
Hilary and Ambrose composed'.[9]

Isidore of Seville says of Hilary 'hymnorum carmine floruit

---

[6] For full accounts and discussions, see: Leclercq (1925*b*); *ODCC* 681–4; Szövérffy
(1966 and 1964); Wellesz (1947, 1961, and 1969); also Anglès (1969); Darre (1968); Mearns
(1914) 1–6; Norberg (1967); Wagner (1907); Reese (1940); Baumstark (1914); Avenary
(1953); Altaner (1960) 90 ff., 402, 405, 427, 431, 449 ff., 458 ff., 638 ff.; Quasten (1950 and
1960); Charlet (1982) esp. 11–18; Thompson (1973).

[7] The Vulgate calls the Psalms of David *hymni*: for example, Ps. 136: 3; 64: 1; cf. Matt.
26: 30; 14: 36.

[8] Mohrmann (1957) 16: 'Greek remained for a long time the language of liturgical
prayer, at least of the Eucharistic Liturgy'. Textual evidence is provided by Marius Victori-
nus in *Adu. Arianos*, 2. 8 (a *Greek* quotation from the Roman canon of the Eucharistic
Liturgy), and the author of the *Quaestiones Veteris et Noui Testamenti*, AD 374–82: the Latin
text from the same liturgy is quoted by Mohrmann (1957) 50. See also Charlet (1982) 19.

[9] Mansi 10. 622. Did Hilary and Ambrose both write hymns in honour of the martyrs?
The Council mentions hymns 'to the praise of God and the Apostles, and on the victories
of the martyrs'. But no hymns of Hilary for the martyrs survive under his name.

primus',[10] and Jerome records that he was the author of a 'liber hymnorum'.[11] Unfortunately, only a fragmentary and representative sample of these hymns have survived in the authentic hymns of the Arezzo MS.[12] Important background to Hilary's compositions can be found in his contact with Eastern practices in the liturgical use of hymns during his period of exile in the East.[13] His originality and his significance for later Latin hymnology lay in his approach to the problem of emulating the Eastern metrical hymns by means of the Latin poetic idiom. This meant attempting to present to Western congregations compositions which combined the elements of prayer and praise inherited from the Psalms[14] with the didactic element noted above. The latter was particularly important for Hilary in his struggle against the Arians.[15] These elements were expressed through poetry which drew on the rich classical tradition of lyric and epic for language and form. The success of the later hymns of Ambrose was really the fruit of Hilary's primary inspiration and the synthesis of traditions which can be seen in its early stages in Hilary's poetry.[16]

It may be assumed that the hymns of Hilary were written to be sung in a liturgical context, since they are not distinguished from the Ambrosian hymns when mentioned with them.[17] The practical use of the latter is well attested in connection with their first famous appearance.[18] The fact that Hilary's complete *liber hym-*

---

[10] Isidore of Seville, *De ecclesiasticis officiis*, 1. 6.

[11] Jerome, *De uiris illustribus*, C. 100.

[12] I follow here Pellegrino (1947) 204 ff.; cf. Raby (1953) 41 and 42, no. 2 and Fontaine (1974a) 318 ff. See also Mason (1904); Walpole (1905 and 1922, 1–2). The text of the fragments can be found in *CSEL* 65 (1916) 208–16, with *Hymnum dicat turba fratrum* at 217–23.

[13] 'His defence of orthodoxy led to his condemnation at the Synod of Biterrae (AD 356) and to a four-year exile to Phrygia by the Emperor Constantius', *ODCC* 649.

[14] Mohrmann (1957), 160 and (1961) 108–9. See the great number of early Latin translations, *ODCC* 1140.

[15] Hilary in particular would have had personal experience of the polemic role of Ephraem's hymns during his exile in the East. See *DACL* 6, 2902 and Beare (1957) 224.

[16] Fontaine (1974a), and Mohrmann (1955) esp. 234 ff.

[17] For example, the 4th Council of Toledo, Mansi 10. 622: it is hymns 'like those of Hilary and Ambrose' which are permitted, with no distinction made between them.

[18] Augustine, *Confessions* 9. 7. Were the hymns written before this occasion or not? Walpole (1966: 16) thinks that they were: 'Ambrose had already written some hymns for the liturgy of the Milanese Church, though we do not know when.'; ibid., n. 1, 'Some scholars . . . maintain that amid the storm and stress of the siege of the Basilica, Ambrose found time and leisure to write his hymns, no improvisations, but carefully worked out poems. That he should have done so may not be absolutely impossible, but it is improbable.'; cf. Van der Meer's views (1961: 329): these were 'hymns which were probably

norum did not survive, while the hymns of Ambrose did, suggests
that the Hilarian hymns were found to be less suitable for con-
gregational use. Their unsuitability was presumably bound up
with their form, and this is worth consideration in analysis of the
form and purpose of the *Pe.* for a possible liturgical function. Pru-
dentius probably knew Hilary's hymns if they were well known
to Jerome in the 390s.[19] Examination of the characteristic features
of the surviving hymns reveals their possible influence on Pruden-
tius' lyric compositions.

In two of the surviving hymn fragments, Hilary adopted the
abecedaria form, in which successive verses began with successive
letters of the alphabet. This was intended to act as an *aide-mémoire*
for the congregation, and in this way contributed to the didactic
function of the poems. The same form was later used by Augus-
tine to help the less able among his congregation in his *Psalm
against the Donatists.*[20] Hilary was careful to surround the complex
didactic material of his hymns with the more commonplace
hymnic elements of prayer and praise.

It was probably the metrical aspect of Hilary's hymns which
finally ensured their reduced popularity in the face of their
Ambrosian successors, especially at a time when quantitative
metres were giving way to accentual rhythms.[21] From the few
hymns left, it seems that Hilary was interested in metrical vari-
ation and experimentation. Three different and complex metres

already known to a small circle of ascetics and other personal intimates.' The innovation of
the occasion for Walpole is not the hymns themselves, but the method of singing them
antiphonally, with the whole congregation participating. Walpole's views seem sensible,
but Van der Meer's idea of limited circulation for Ambrose's hymns explains their impact
in the midst of the crisis in AD 386.

[19] Kelly (1975: 174–8), points out that Jerome's honesty over his actual reading matter
is not unimpeachable: 'Unfortunately, as the analyses of modern investigators have made
plain, its pretentious façade is largely a sham' (p. 176). This need not, however, call into
question the actual existence of the *Liber hymnorum* mentioned by Jerome.

By talking of the failure of Hilary's hymns, I do not intend to suggest that these hymns
were never in general use although, as Norberg points out (1974: 136), Hilary's hymns
were never absorbed into the liturgy, but remained a separate corpus in their *Liber* (unlike
those of Ambrose). They were simply generally acknowledged to be less well suited for
congregational singing once Ambrose's hymns were available. The 4th Council of Toledo
in the 7th century mentions Hilary's hymns as well as those of Ambrose (see n. 17 above),
so they were still known, used, and even imitated as late as this.

[20] Vroom (1933).

[21] Mohrmann (1957) 166. This period 'avait vu la ruine du système rythmique fondé
sur la quantité syllabique'; cf. Norberg (1952) and Beare (1957) 206 ff.

are used in the four surviving hymns. Even if the prosody is not
absolutely classical in its attention to quantity, it is still basically
metrical and closely attached to the combinations of classical
poetry.[22] Hilary also paid some attention to the classical doctrine
of decorum in his choice of metre. Thus in the hymn which tells
of Christ's victory over Satan, *Adae carnis gloriosa*, the metre is one
well-known from marching songs and *carmina triumphalia*, the
trochaic tetrameter catalectic (the metrical scheme for this is
$-\cup-\underset{\smile}{-}-\cup-\overset{\cup}{\underset{\smile}{}}:-\cup-\underset{\smile}{-}-\cup-$).[23]

A metre familiar from use in the theatre was chosen by Hilary
for the hymn which celebrates the mystery of the Passion and
Resurrection *fefellit saevum*, the iambic *senarius* ($\bar{\cup}\overset{\cup\cup}{-}\cup-\bar{\cup}:\overset{\cup\cup}{-}$
$\cup:-\bar{\cup}\overset{\cup\cup}{-}\cup\underset{\smile}{-}$). In *Ante saecula qui manes*, Hilary uses a purely
literary lyric metre, which consists of a glyconic line followed by
the shorter Asclepiad line ($\overset{\cup}{\underset{\smile}{}}\bar{\cup}-\cup\cup-\cup-/---\cup\cup--$
$\cup\cup-\cup-$) arranged in two pairs of lines to form a four-line
stanza. Horace draws on this form no less than eleven times in his
Odes.[24] Although in all three metres Hilary aims at a regularity of
line presumably designed to suit a recurring fixed melody, the
very length of the lines (and the variation of length within *Ante
saecula qui manes*) was a disadvantage for easy memorization, par-
ticularly in the face of the simpler alternative of Ambrose, so
admirably suited to congregational use.

The style and contents of Hilary's hymns were also perhaps too
far above the heads of the average congregation. His mixture of
the classical and Christian was sometimes too crude. In dealing
with abstract theological ideas or more concrete Biblical images
(there is a preponderance of the former), his language tended to
become obscure and abstract. This tendency was the result of his
regard for the classical canons of style: lyric form demanded a
sublime style and in Hilary's hymns, this resulted in what has been
termed a 'désordre pindarique'.[25] There are echoes of classical

---

[22] As Cunningham notes (1955: 509–14); cf. Cunningham (1976) 60.

[23] Raven (1965) *ad loc.* Also useful for hymn metres in particular is Connelly (1954)
xviii–xxi. In the following discussion, each metre mentioned will be followed by a brief
representation of its scheme, with possible resolutions of feet represented by the long and
short signs raised above the basic scheme.

[24] Horace, *Odes*, 1. 3, 13, 19, 36: 3. 9, 15, 19, 24, 25; 4. 1 and 3. See Nisbet and Hubbard
(1970) xxxviii ff. This metre is there termed the Fourth Asclepiad.

[25] Fontaine (1974*a*) 334.

authors in the hymns, but these are mingled with the specifically Christian terminology which Hilary does not hesitate to introduce.[26]

Like the soul in Hilary's second hymn, Christian poetry was 'renata nouis legibus' with his lyric compositions. His pioneer work on Latin hymnody was taken over and perfected by Ambrose.[27] The testimony of Augustine leaves no room for doubt concerning the practical function of the ambrosian hymns:

> At this time was it here first instituted after the manner of the Eastern churches, that hymns and psalms should be sung, lest the people should wax faint through the tediousness of sorrow; which custom being retained from that day to this, is still imitated by divers, yea, almost by all thy congregations throughout other parts of the world.[28] (Loeb translation, from William Watts, 1631.)

Just as hymns had already been used as an important weapon of religious propaganda by heretical sects, so the hymns of Ambrose first appeared in the midst of the struggle against the Arians in Milan. The bishop himself, in a letter to the Emperor Valentinian, unashamedly makes their value clear as orthodox propaganda by which the *populus* is 'deceptus': 'Facti sunt omnes magistri, qui vix poterant esse discipuli'.[29] However, the hymns appealed to a wider audience than just the ignorant *populus*. Augustine provides moving proof of their impact on one of deeper understanding and a higher level of culture. The hymns of Ambrose were thus truly 'popular'.[30]

The striking circumstances under which the hymns were introduced must have contributed to their immediate success, but this was surely also the result of the author's 'sentiment du style

---

[26] For example, the reference to 'angeli' in the second hymn. See Mohrmann (1947) 294.

[27] On Ambrose, see Fontaine (1974*a*); Cunningham (1955); Walpole (1966); Mohrmann (1947); Norberg (1974); Blume and Dreves (1909); also Raby (1953) 32–6. The hymns of the Ambrosian corpus can also be found at *PL* 17. 1171–222.

[28] Augustine, *Conf.* 9. 7. 15; cf. Paulinus of Milan's *Life of St Ambrose* 13: 'hoc in tempore primum antiphonae hymni ac uigiliae in ecclesia Mediolanensi celebrari coeperunt.'

[29] Ambrose, *Ep.* 21. 34.

[30] In considering the Ambrosian hymns, I shall not discuss problems of authenticity, but shall restrict my comments to the limited number of hymns generally agreed to be genuine. The question of authenticity is discussed by Norberg (1974) 138–9. The 14 hymns generally agreed to be genuine are given by Dreves and Blume (1909).

délicat'.[31] Ambrose was able to learn from Hilary's *liber hymnorum*. Thus he retained the unit of the stanza for use in antiphonal performance after the Eastern style, with perhaps greater emphasis than ever before on the participation of the whole congregation rather than choirs and precentors.[32] This participation must have been most important for dispelling the 'maeroris taedium' of the Milanese Christians during their vigil in the basilica. The hymns are not of the well-known Eastern type which required simply a repetition of a refrain by the congregation. Instead, the whole verse of a hymn was sung by one side, and then the second verse was sung by the other side, and so on through the hymn.[33] The end-stopped stanzas and the even number of stanzas in each hymn are designed for this sort of presentation. In the brevity of his hymns (thirty-two lines), Ambrose recognized the limitations of the simpler members of the congregation: 'A hymn of just so many verses would not on the one hand be so long as to weary the singers, nor on the other would it be so short as to preclude the teaching for which it was specially written.'[34]

[31] Mohrmann (1947) 295 speaks of 'un sentiment du style délicat de saint Ambroise . . . qui a trouvé l'équilibre entre les éléments essentiels d'une poésie chrétienne et les éléments traditionnels de l'héritage littéraire romaine'.

[32] Vroom (1933) speaks of two choirs of people with a refrain sung by the whole congregation. Avenary makes it clear that the whole Jewish congregation was involved in responsorial performance. Mearns (1914: 1) cites the 4th-century Council of Laodicea for a prohibition of all but 'the canonical singers who sing from the book' from singing in church, but other texts suggest the participation of the whole congregation, for example, Sozomen, *Hist. eccl.* 3. 6; Ambrose *In ps.* 1 = *PL* 14. 968; *Hexaemeron*, 3. 5 = *PL* 14. 178. In a hymn like the Ambrosian, however, it needs to be asked whether a limited choir was involved, or whether the whole congregation was divided for the singing. Either interpretation would fit the basilica scene of Augustine's *Confessions* (9. 7), although the innovation felt in the use of hymns on this occasion, and the extent to which the singing of them relieved the whole congregation might suggest complete audience participation. Pope Celestinus in the 5th century in the fragment of a sermon (*PL* 50. 457) seems to point to the participation of all: 'Recordor beatae memoriae Ambrosium in die Natali Domini nostri Jesu Christi *omnem populum* fecisse una uoce canere: Veni Redemptor . . .' Norberg (1974: 139–40) points out in addition that the simplicity, clarity and brevity of the hymns were all features designed for their use by the whole congregation. The *Life of St. Ambrose* by Paulinus of Milan also speaks of the incident. He interestingly adds the detail that the soldiers set to guard the basilica joined with the congregation in lifting up their voices on behalf of the Catholic faith. This also suggests the participation of all.

[33] Walpole (1966) 16. Very little is known about the earliest Ambrosian chant: 'It is impossible to say at the moment whether the extant melodies of the hymns which are the genuine productions of St Ambrose are the same as those already sung at Milan in the Fourth Century'. Anglès (1969), 68; Reese (1940) 104.

[34] Walpole (1966) 23.

Where metre was concerned, Ambrose—like Hilary—was not
prepared to relinquish the elevation of a classical quantitative
metre, but also realized that an over-complicated metrical system
would represent too much of an anachronism in a period which
was losing the taste for such metres (see n. 21). His solution to the
problem was inspired: he chose for his hymns the iambic di-
meter acatalectic ($\bar{\cup} - \cup - \bar{\cup} - \cup -$). This metre had been popu-
lar since the time of Hadrian.[35] Ambrose is far from neglecting
classical prosody with this metre, but the ictus and accent on
words in the line often coincide, resulting in a compromise
between the classical tradition and the contemporary tendency to-
wards accentual rhythms.[36] Those members of the congregation
who were less thoroughly acquainted with classical authors and
who were accustomed to the increasingly accentual rhythms in
general use, would have taken readily to this isosyllabic metre.
For Ambrose avoids resolution of the iambic feet in the line and in
this way maintains an even eight syllables (the short syllables of
the first and third iambs may be replaced by a long one). This had
obvious advantages from the musical point of view over its more
classical version.[37] Ambrose was also wise to use only a single,
well-adapted metre, rather than the variety of Hilary. This was
bound to make his hymns more easily memorized by the con-
gregation as a whole, which could cope with a simple melody.[38]

The fixed form and length of Ambrose's hymns were unclassi-
cal features deliberately chosen by the author to suit the circum-
stances of performance.[39] The form itself imposed a certain
economy and simplicity on the actual contents of the hymns. This
does not mean that the hymns were popular in the sense of cater-
ing for the lowest taste and intellectual capacity of the congrega-
tion.[40] On the contrary, it has been well demonstrated how far

[35] Mohrmann (1947) 165.
[36] See Norberg (1952).
[37] Hughes, quoted in Brittain (1951) 8: 'The use of classical metre must have created a
natural demand for this change, for in most of the classical metres the number of syllables
may vary: amphibrach may replace trochee, dactyl may become spondee and so on. To
sing a number of stanzas, the corresponding lines of which might contain a varying
number of syllables in different verses, to a fixed recurring melody is impossible without
continual adaptation and "footnotes".'
[38] Norberg (1967) 116.
[39] Cunningham (1955) n. 22, where he points out that this is not a classical feature.
[40] This idea, posited by Simonetti (1952), is refuted by Fontaine (1974a) 331 and by
Marrou (1953).

Ambrose represents in his hymns a balance between the tradi-
tional poetic elements of the literary Roman heritage and the new
Christian contribution to poetry. It is a rich synthesis which 'con-
verts' the features of classical hymnody and the language and
spirit of Latin lyric to Christian purposes, combining them with
the lyric element necessarily involved in the individualistic self-
expression of Christian prayer. The Christians of the period had as
their supreme example in this the model of their beloved
Psalms.[41] This synthesis will be discussed further below, but it
must be noted here that it hardly represented the language, style
or thoughts only of the common Christian of the period.[42] In-
deed, it was not intended to do this. It should be viewed rather in
the light of the liturgical language of the early Church.[43] The
Ambrosian hymns, however, do contrast with those of Hilary in
the clarity of their images and the expression of the thought
through such images. Word order within the iambic line is never
contorted or strained. Ideas develop in a series of readily grasped
concrete images—the *gallus* of 'Aeterne rerum conditor', for in-
stance, or the day/night antithesis of 'Aurora' in 'Splendor pater-
nae gloriae'. A clear image is presented in a single line, with wide
use of parallel phraseology, and antithesis within this, for
example:

> Egressus eius a patre,
> Regressus eius ad patrem,
> Excursus usque ad inferos,
> Recursus ad sedem Dei.

or in the hymn for St Agnes:

> Matura martyrio fuit,
> Matura nondum nuptiis.

[41] So the hymns of Ambrose are sung in conjunction with the Psalms: 'tunc hymni et
psalmi ut canerentur ... institutum est' (Augustine, *Conf.* 9. 7). Wagner (1907: 9) talks of
the emphasis laid on knowing the Psalms by heart.

[42] Puech (1888) 83: 'à vrai dire, ces hymnes n'ont pas grand caractère littéraire ...
quelque chose y reste du Nouveau Testament; c'est bien là le language populaire qu'il faut
parler aux âmes naïves'. This is surely too dismissive.

[43] Mohrmann (1957) chap. 1, 'Sacred and Hieratic Language'. Liturgical language was
from its origins intended to represent a language set apart, not necessarily equally compre-
hensible to all in the congregation. So the Latin West used a Greek service as late as the 4th
century. The less educated would accept and use a suitably 'elevated' style and language.

[44] *Intende qui regis Israel*, 25–6, Blume and Dreves (1909) 10. For parallels, cf. the hymn
in honour of Agnes, 5–6; and of course, the Psalms, *passim*.

The lyric side of Hilary's prayers in the hymns had involved use of the first person plural.[45] This reappears in Ambrose's compositions:

> Te *nostra uox* primum sonet;
> Et ora *soluimus* tibi.
>
> (*Deus, Creator omnium*, 30–2)

and 'Christum rogemus et patrem' (ibid., 29). This reflects the same usage in prayers. It is less in evidence in the hymns in honour of the martyrs, where the lyric side of the hymn gives way to the narrative requirements, and to a more directly didactic tone. In the hymn in honour of Victor, Nabor and Felix, for example, Ambrose makes a statement about the armour of true faith:

> Munitus armis ambulat
> Veram fidem qui possidet.
>
> (23–4)

Invocation of Christ or God the Father is replaced by a statement about the martyr's feast day (for example, in the hymns for Agnes and for Peter and Paul), or his connection with Milan (as in the case of Victor, Nabor, and Felix), or Rome (with Lawrence). A narrowly personal element enters the hymn in honour of Gervasius and Protasius, where Ambrose records that he is 'novi repertor'. He must have judged that his role as 'inventor' of the martyrs' remains entitled him to a direct reference to this event within the hymn. This personal note, however, is suppressed in the more general first person plural of the third stanza:

> Nequimus esse martyres,
> Sed repperimus martyres.
>
> (11–12)

Ambrose manages to compress the narrative side of the martyr-hymns into the scope of thirty-two lines. This involves a certain amount of abbreviation and simplification in order to fit the stanza unit. The result is a series of tableaux which highlight the key scenes of the martyrdom. Thus the hymn in honour of St Lawrence, for example, ends at the climax of the martyr's famous exchange with his torturer while still on the grill. Direct speech is

---

[45] Cf. Hilary's hymns for the use of the first person plural, for example, in *Hymnum dicat turba fratrum*, 2, 4, and 65 ff.

kept to a minimum but is all the more effective for its brevity. Agnes' defiant speech, for instance, is only five and a half lines long, but loses none of its force.

The *Peristephanon*

The influence of Ambrose must have been particularly strong for Prudentius when he came to write poems in honour of the martyrs,[46] but this does not necessarily mean that the poet's compositions were also written for practical use in the life of the Church. Most critics have in fact accepted that these poems were not intended for liturgical use, but have not reached this conclusion through a thorough study of their form in relation to the known liturgical hymns.[47] Room for controversy has been admitted,[48] but where discussion of the problem has drawn on some analysis of the poems, the conclusion has been reached that they were indeed written expressly for sung performance.[49] This view is, in my opinion, mistaken, and I would like to reopen the question here with a full analysis of the poems. The ground will then be clear for a reconsideration of the purpose of the poems *outside* the liturgy.

One aspect of the *Peristephanon* which has been mentioned before in passing,[50] but never fully analysed or interpreted, is their part in the Mozarabic liturgy,[51] where their use as sung hymns and their influence on the hymnic celebration of saints, both Spanish and foreign (not necessarily those of the *Peristephanon* itself) has been observed to have been formative.[52] It would be wrong, however, to conclude from their use in the Mozarabic liturgy that the poems were originally written to be sung. For

---

[46] Another influence on Prudentius' martyr poems was provided by Damasus' epigrams, composed to adorn the martyrs' shrines in Rome. This influence is discussed in chapter 8, pp. 240 ff.

[47] See e.g. Puech (1888) 83; Raby (1953) 50; Darre (1968) 25 ff. and 34; Walpole (1966) 28; Faguet (1883).

[48] Sanford (1936).

[49] Cunningham (1963) and (1976), repeated in the *New Catholic Encyclopedia* 9 (1967) 928.

[50] By Fontaine, (1974a); also (1975b); by Leclercq (1925b) 2909; by Marrou (1953); by Raby (1953) 50; and by Walpole (1966) 115 ff.

[51] On the Mozarabic liturgy, see Cabrol (1935); King (1930); Messenger (1944) and (1946); Blume and Dreves (1897) 35 ff.; and Szövérffy (1970).

[52] See n. 51 esp. Messenger (1946); also Szövérffy (1970) 195; and de Bruyne (1913).

although 'le rite Mozarabe est plus ancien que les textes liturgiques qui le représentent' and the texts have a history going back to pre-Visigothic Spain and perhaps even to a period earlier than the third century, it is impossible to date the entry into the liturgy of any particular text.[53] With reference to Prudentius' poetry, it is worth noting again the reluctance of Spain in particular to admit non-Scriptural hymns into the liturgy.[54] It was only in the seventh century that this ban was lifted by the Fourth Council of Toledo (AD 653) to allow the use of hymns by Ambrose and Hilary.[55] Thus, it seems most unlikely that Prudentius' poems were officially accepted into the liturgy before this period, let alone written specially for it in the fourth–fifth centuries. It might, of course, be argued that the recurrence of the prohibition in Church legislation points to a general practice which could not be suppressed. Even if this were so, there is nothing to suggest that the *Peristephanon* was written for this popular use: indeed, the internal evidence of the poems themselves makes this unlikely.

The certain later use of the poems in the Mozarabic liturgy, however, cannot be ignored. But it provides in fact evidence for the extent to which they were recognized to be *non*-liturgical in both form and content at an early stage, at the time when they were included in the hymnal. For, as I shall demonstrate below, the poems underwent certain modifications which were evidently seen as necessary for adapting them for congregational use.[56] Such changes reflect those features which were *not* suited to their practical use as sung hymns, and thus the role of the *Pe.* in the Mozarabic liturgy forms a useful part of the discussion to follow.

To argue that the poems of the *Pe.* were not liturgical in purpose is not to suggest that they were written without any reference to their liturgical counterparts, which were very clearly part of their inspiration. They could not fail to be influenced by them,

---

[53] See Férotin (1904) I.

[54] 2nd Council of Braga, AD 563, can. 12: 'Nihil extra psalmos ... nihil poetice compositum in ecclesia psallatur'. Mansi 9. 778, and Vives *et al.* (1963), 73. 4th Council of Toledo, AD 633, Mansi 10. 622–3, Vives *et al.* (1963) 197. The 13th canon upholds the validity and appropriateness of hymns by Christian authors against those who would restrict the hymnody of the Church to the Psalms of the Old Testament. 8th Council of Toledo, AD 653. Mansi 10. 1218, can. 8, Vives *et al.* (1963) 260 ff. This forbids the ordination of candidates to the priesthood who were ignorant of psalms, canticles, and hymns.

[55] 4th Council of Toledo, can. 13, Mansi 10. 622–3. See King (1930) 276 and Messenger (1944) 103–12.

[56] For a list of Prudentian centos in the Mozarabic Hymnal, see Szövérffy (1964) 82.

granting the instantaneous success of the latter. Prudentius did not need to visit Rome to get the idea of writing hymns for martyrs, as it has been suggested with reference to *Pe.* 12. 60, where the native Roman's reply to the pilgrim/poet includes the injunction, 'et his et illis perfruamur hymnis'.[57] It should be noted here that Rome, in any case, was even slower than Spain to admit non-Scriptural hymns into the liturgy (if that is what is in question at *Pe.* 12. 60).[58]

Prudentius in fact shows himself in several places to be well aware of the general role of non-Scriptural hymns in the life of the Church. In the Praefatio, the poet refers to the *Cathemerinon* with the words 'hymnis continuet dies' (37), and at *Cathemerinon* 4. 75 he says, 'grates reddimus et sacramus hymnos.'[59] In particular, the poet is aware of the use of hymns in martyr-cult. Cunningham might also have mentioned, for instance, *Pe.* 2. 515–16, especially in the context of Roman celebration of saints:

> Christi frequentans atria
> *hymnis* resultat martyrem

or the poet's encouragement at *Pe.* 1. 118:

> State, nunc, hymnite matres.

(This will be discussed further below); or *Pe.* 6. 151:

> Laudans Augurium resultet *hymnus*.

Even more significantly, Prudentius may also show an awareness of the antiphonal performance of contemporary hymns. This could explain his address to the 'matres' of *Pe.* I, where he implies the sort of male/female division of the congregation (or some part of it) attested by Eusebius at least for the beginning of the fourth century (though see n. 105 below). The exhortation in *Pe.* 3 of the 'uirgo puerque' (207) could also be explained in this way, although the reference is made in a context of classical reminiscence, complicated further by the classically inspired image of the garlands (discussed below). The reference to 'psalmis' at *Pe.* 4. 148

[57] Cunningham (1976) 57–8.
[58] The hymns could be sung simply in the course of the procession across Rome from St Paul's-without-the-Walls to St Peter's. For Roman reluctance about hymns, see Leclercq (1925*b*) col. 2911–12.
[59] cf. *Cath.* 5. 121 ff: Felices animae prata per herbida/*concentu pariles*, suaue sonantibus/ *hymnorum* modulis, dulce canunt melos/calcant et pedibus lilia candidis.

might be used with particular meaning for the performance of such a hymn.[60] The chorus suggested at *Pe.* 6, 145–50 seems to be more realistic than that of *Pe.* 3, and includes a mixture of the whole congregation, which probably reflects the recent Ambrosian innovation. Thus there is no reason why Prudentius should not have been able to write hymns suitable for the sort of contemporary performance of which he was evidently aware, if he had been interested in this sort of composition.

The Form of the *Peristephanon* Poems

Even a cursory glance at the 'hymns' of Prudentius reveals their differences from their Ambrosian counterparts. Far from restricting himself to the thirty-two line limit of the authentic hymns of Ambrose (or even the fifty-two line maximum admitted in the Ambrosian corpus as a whole),[61] Prudentius writes poems ranging widely in length from the eighteen lines of *Pe.* 8, to the 1140 lines of *Pe.* 10. Even if these two hymns are to be distinguished from the rest of the poems[62] only *Pe.* 12 is less than 100 lines long (66 lines) while *Pe.* 2 and 5 are 584 and 576 lines long respectively—ironically the two poems which are the most 'Ambrosian' through their use of the iambic dimeter in four-line stanzas. This is surely far too long for congregational singing, even granting the suitability of content, and the clues provided by the *inscriptiones* discussed below. Even a well-trained choir (assuming the possible use of such a body within the congregation), would find the inclusion of such a long composition in their repertoire a severe strain on the memory, if such a feat was possible or desirable within the liturgy. It is surely significant that where these poems are later drawn on for the Mozarabic hymnal,[63] *Pe.* 2 is reduced to a selection of only twenty lines,[64] with the addition of a five-line doxology; while *Pe.* 5 is halved to give lines 1–289, which represents the maximum length of any

---

[60] *Pe.* 4. 147–8: perge conscriptum tibimet senatum/pangere psalmis! For antiphonal performance of the Psalms, see Wagner (1907) 15–19; Wellesz (1947) 54; Avenary (1953); and Vroom (1933).

[61] See the collection of Ambrosian hymns in *PL* 17. 1171–222.

[62] Cunningham (1963) sees *Pe.* 8 as an inscription and *Pe.* 10 as a separate book, but all the other poems as hymns.

[63] *PL* 86. 885–940, ed. Lorenzana; and Blume and Dreves (1897).

[64] *PL* 86. 1179, using lines 15, 17, 397–8, 20–32, 549, 550, 565.

hymn used in the hymnal. And this in a liturgy remarkable for the manifestation of its religious enthusiasm by its endurance of lengthy services.[65] Excesses might particularly be expected in the celebration of saints' days, in its enthusiasm for which it again surpassed other contemporary liturgies.[66] It is true that the first of the authentic hymns of Hilary must have been at least 104 lines long when its *abecedaria* form was completed,[67] but it should be remembered that this form in itself was intended to help the least intellectually able of the congregation in a hymn which Hilary himself recognized to be somewhat lengthy. In any case, Hilary's hymns evidently did overtax his congregations, since they were discarded as more suitable ones appeared.

One attempt has been made to show that Prudentius' poems were not too long for liturgical performance. It is based on the length of Augustine's *Psalm against the Donatists*, which is nearly 300 lines long.[68] The Augustinian text *Retractationes*, I. 19–20 is used to show that Augustine intended this long rhythmical statement of orthodox doctrine to be sung in its entirety by the whole congregation. The simplicity of the rhythm supposedly balances out the difficulty for the performers of following continuous doctrinal exposition: how much easier to sing are the simple narratives of Prudentius, albeit in such a wide variety of lyric metres.

Metrical considerations apart,[69] no account is taken in this argument of the probable form of performance of this *Psalm of Augustine*. It consists of a series of verses, usually twelve lines long,[70] preceded by a *hypopsalma* which recurs as a refrain between each verse of the *abecedaria*-plan composition. As has been convincingly shown, this structure is clearly suited to the *cantus responsorius* (see n. 60). Augustine himself refers to the Psalm in the following way:

Volens etiam causam Donatistarum ad ipsius humillimi uulgi et omnino imperitorum atque idiotarum notitiam peruenire et eorum, quantum fieri per nos posset, in-haerere memoriae, *psalmum qui eis cantaretur*, per latinas litteras feci, sed usque ad V litteram ... Hypopsalma etiam *quod*

[65] Blume and Dreves (1897) and Messenger (1946).
[66] Blume and Dreves (1897) 35: '... die Mozarabischen vor einem langen Hymnus nicht leicht zurückschreckten, namentlich wenn er das Lob eines Heiligen besang'.
[67] Augustine stops at the letter 'V'.
[68] Sanford (1936). The *Psalmus* is 288 lines long.
[69] Vroom (1933) 16.
[70] There is irregularity in the stanzas for C (11 lines), and for Q (10 lines).

respondetur, et prooemium causae, quod uoluimus ut cantaretur, non
sunt in ordine litterarum; earum quippe ordo incipit post prooemium.[71]

One person (or perhaps a small group) is intended to sing the
verses to the congregation, who, while they may be expected to
follow the thought of the verses, in fact only have to memorize
and repeat a *single* line, not all 288. Augustine, like Ambrose, was
perfectly aware of the intellectual limitations of the congrega-
tion.[72]

This is not to deny the endurance expected of a congregation
with regard to the liturgy. The length of the *lectiones* might make
the congregations' passive role a quasi-martyrdom.[73] The
Spanish pilgrim Egeria does not register surprise at the huge de-
mands made on the people following the Easter liturgy in Jerusa-
lem.[74] However, the active vocal participation of churchgoers in
general was accepted and expected to be as small as Augustine's
Psalm suggests. The often repeated thirty-two lines of an Ambro-
sian hymn, particularly when used antiphonally, and in combina-
tion with the stylistic features discussed above, may have
represented the maximum capacity of the congregation as a
whole.

Ambrose catered for his congregation's needs and capacities
and so succeeded with his hymns, while Hilary tried for too great
a length and variation of metre, and perhaps in this found the
reason for calling his Gallic flock 'indociles'.[75] It seems unlikely
that if Prudentius *did* intend his hymns for singing, he would have
ignored the lead of Ambrose, whose success in hymn-writing he
had certainly experienced at first-hand in Milan. The size of the
Ambrosian corpus of hymns is witness to the lack of embarrass-

---

[71] Augustine, *Retractationes*, 1. 19. The text of the *Psalmus contra partem Donati* is also
given in Vroom (1933) 7–15.

[72] Augustine, *Retractationes*, 1. 19–20; cf. *De ciu. dei* 22. 8 for the congregation's short
memory. See chap. 2, p. 33, with n. 5.

[73] For the quasi-martyrdom of listening to lengthy readings and sermons on the
martyrs, see Augustine, *Sermo* 274: Longam lectionem audiuimus, breuis est dies, longo
sermone etiam nos tenere uestram patientiam non debemus. Nouimus quia patienter audis-
tis, et diu stando et audiendo tamquam martyres compassi estis. Qui audit uos, amet uos et
coronet uos. (*PL* 38. 1253.)

[74] Egeria tells about the Jerusalem liturgy for Holy Week at 27. 1–40. Her travel diary
is translated by Wilkinson (1982). The passage on the Jerusalem liturgy is discussed at
54–88, and the translation appears at 128–40.

[75] Jerome, *Praef.* to *Comm. in Galat.* 2, 'cum et Hilarius Latinae eloquentiae Rhodanus,
Gallus ipse et Pictauis genitus, in hymnorum carmine Gallos indociles uocet' (*PL* 26. 355).

ment felt by Ambrose's other hymn-writing successors in adopting his form.

Pe. 2 and 5 do indeed use the Ambrosian stanza, but Prudentius does not restrict himself to this form: 'sunt enim ex Prudentianis hymnis ad exemplar Horatianorum, Catullianorum operum dispositi, sunt qui Ambrosianos hymnos imitentur sunt quorum dispositio a Prudentio inuenta est'.[76] It is true that, as far as we can guess, Hilary seems to have used a wide range of metres, including the Horatian combination of the Asclepiad minor with a glyconic line, and may have inspired Prudentius in the use of a variety of metres modelled on, if not always in exact imitation of, classical metres.[77] However, the musical disadvantages of these metres have been mentioned above in connection with Hilary's comparative failure, and an interesting insight into Prudentius' purpose can be gained by a comparison of the poet's iambic dimeters with those of Ambrose in the light of such difficulties. It can be shown that whereas in the Ambrosian hymns, no feet besides spondees and iambs are allowed, presumably the better to fit a fixed melody, the Prudentian version of the metre allows both anapaests and tribrachs in the first and third feet of quite a considerable number of lines.[78] These are irregularly placed, so that one could not argue for any sort of regular psalm-like *initium* or *flexa*, which in any case does not seem likely to have been a feature of the antiphonally-used fixed melody suggested by the Ambrosian stanza. The *cantus directaneus* was probably not yet in use.[79] Thus, even in a metre established as the hymn metre *par excellence* and currently widely in use, Prudentius shows how little concerned he was with a sung performance of his poems, by his frequent departure from the features of this metre most suited to its practical function.

Great weight has also been placed on Prudentius' use of the stanza form, which had already been taken up by Hilary and

[76] Faguet (1883) 126.

[77] So, for instance, Prudentius begins the *Pe.* with a poem in the trochaic tetrameter of Hilary's 'Adae carnis gloriosa'. The trochaic tetrameter's connection with marching songs and *carmina triumphalia* makes it particularly suitable for the celebration of two soldier-martyrs. Prudentius also uses the iambic trimeter in *Pe.* 10.

[78] Faguet (1883) 126 ff.

[79] In this, the whole people sang together a series of verses without refrain. But this style of singing is not mentioned before the *Regula S. Benedicti* in the 6th century, and is presumed not to have been in use before this date. Wagner (1907) 24; Vroom (1933) 24. Cunningham (1976) 60.

Ambrose as 'appropriate for and acceptable to ordinary people, the people for whom they were composing'. This statement in itself implies a slight misconception of the sense in which liturgical hymnody aimed at being 'popular' (see n. 40) but also seems to ignore two important points. In the first place the use of the stanza in classical lyric poetry must not be forgotten, particularly in the context of literary hymnology.[80] This use is clear in the *Pe.* in the use of the Sapphic stanza in *Pe.* 4, for instance. Secondly, some explanation must be found for those poems which do *not* make use of the stanza, that is, *Pe.* 9, 11,[81] 12, 13, and 14. *Pe.* 9 uses the Horatian combination of dactylic hexameter and iambic trimeter found in *Epode* 16 $(-\,\overline{\cup\cup}\,-\,\overline{\cup\cup}\,-\,\overline{\cup\cup}\,-\,\overline{\cup\cup}\,-\,\overline{\cup\cup}\,-\,\overset{\cup}{\_}\,/$ $\overline{\cup}\,-\,\cup\,-\,\overline{\cup}\,-\,\cup\,-\,\overline{\cup}\,-\,\cup\,\overset{\cup}{\_})$, while *Pe.* 12 is in couplets made up of an Archilochian line in combination with an iambic trimeter acatalectic $(-\,\overline{\cup\cup}\,-\,\overline{\cup\cup}\,-\,\overline{\cup\cup}\,-\,\cup\cup:-\,\cup\,-\,\cup\,-\,-\,/\,\overline{\cup}\,-\,\cup\,-$ $\overline{\cup}\,-\,\cup\,-\,\overline{\cup}\,-\,\cup\,\overset{\cup}{\_})$. This is also a Horatian combination. *Pe.* 13 uses the Great Archilochian line κατὰ στίχον, and *Pe.* 14 the Alcaic hendecasyllable in the same way $(\overset{\cup}{\_}\,-\,\cup\,-\,-:-\,\cup\cup\,-\,\cup\,\overset{\cup}{\_})$. None of these metrical arrangements seems to fit either of the current styles of sung performance. Reference to the Mozarabic liturgy is illuminating here: the Prudentian form of *Pe.* 11, 12, and 13 is implicitly judged to be unsuitable for singing, and is rejected in all three cases. The hymn in honour of St Cyprian, for example, who is one of Spain's earliest and most popular 'imported' saints, is presented in Ambrosian stanzas, albeit studded with reminiscences of Prudentius' poem.[82]

Among those poems which *do* favour the stanza form, *Pe.* 3 has an odd number of stanzas, obviously less suited to antiphonal performance. In the other poems, no particular care is taken to end-stop the stanzas, which is another feature of the sung hymn. The proportion of end-stopped stanzas seems directly related to the proportion of direct speech in each poem. Thus, *Pe.* 4, which contains no direct speech has the greatest number of end-stopped stanzas, while *Pe.* 2 and 5 combine the highest proportion of stanzas which are not end-stopped with the highest proportion of

---

[80] Cunningham acknowledges the importance of this aspect of the hymns, which is also emphasized by Fontaine (1975*b*).

[81] Cunningham (1963) calls *Pe.* 11 a letter, but then decides that it was also intended to be a hymn; cf. his later article (1976).

[82] On Cyprian, see Blume and Dreves (1897) 152–3.

direct speech. Unbroken series of grammatically linked and con-
tinuous stanzas tend to occur particularly within the speeches. As
we have seen, the Ambrosian hymns have consistently end-
stopped stanzas designed for antiphonal use, and also avoid ex-
tensive use of direct speech within their brief scope. Thus, even in
the Ambrosian-style poems *Pe.* 2 and 5, Prudentius' use of the
stanzas is far from suitable for any liturgical use according to
accepted practice.

The Contents of the *Peristephanon* poems

Procrustean attempts to prove the homogeneity of the *Peristepha-
non* 'in character, intent and function' as liturgical compositions[83]
fail ultimately when it comes to a consideration of the contents of
the poems and the variety with which the poet treats his chosen
theme of martyrdom. The *inscriptiones* of the poems here provide
a good starting place for discussion.

First, it is worth pointing out that the *inscriptiones* need not
necessarily be attributed to the author himself. From Prudentius'
own period comes a discussion by Jerome about the authenticity
of such titles. Jerome is aware of their value: they give an indica-
tion of the author's name and the subject-matter to be treated. He
mentions their usefulness in the case of manuscripts made up of a
number of short poems—the Psalms for instance. However, he is
also well aware that copyists can make mistakes in transferring
this vital information. Some ignorant emendators have omitted
the titles from his own works, he notes. He also significantly talks
of works without any title, and says that occasionally titles may be
added without authority, as in the case of certain psalms, whose
titles were missing in the Hebrew text, but added to the trans-
lations.[84] In the light of this discussion, the authenticity of the
inscriptiones of Prudentius' poems should be viewed with a certain
scepticism.

Five of the poems (1, 3, 4, 6, and 7) bear the *inscriptio* 'hymnus'
in the manuscripts, while the rest (2, 5, 9, 10, 11–14) are labelled
'passio'. *Pe.* 8, which is written in the form of a brief inscription
for a baptistery, bears the title: 'De loco in quo martyrs passi sunt,

---

[83] Cunningham (1963) 44.
[84] For all the relevant texts, with discussion, see Hulley (1944).

nunc baptisterium est Calagurri'. The relation of the *inscriptio* to particular poems is not always clear. So, for instance, *Pe.* 2 in the oldest manuscripts bears the title 'hymnus', while in more recent manuscripts it is called a 'passio'. *Pe.* 11, too, provides an exception. Its title is 'ad Valerianum de passione Hippolyti'. Thus the *passio* proper is only a section within a poem, which takes the form of a letter to the bishop. Consideration of the title of this poem can lead to more fruitful conjecture about the origins of the *inscriptiones* and the way in which they reflect the actual contents and form of the poems.

The title of *Pe.* 11; 'Ad Valerianum episcopum de passione Hippolyti beatissimi martyris', clearly refers to its letter form, which is introduced by the poet in the first line of the poem by the direct address 'O Christi Valeriane sacer'. Although an important part of the martyrdom of Hippolytus (125 ff.) is set in the form of a description of a painting, *Pe.* 11 is in fact no less a *passio* in over-all contents than, for instance *Pe.* 9 and 12, in spite of its letter form. In *Pe.* 9 and 12, the passions are set within a dramatic frame-work which is distinct from that of the martyrdom itself. In *Pe.* 9, the *aedituus* at Imola describes the passion of Cassian to the pilgrim/poet, whom he sees before the painting of the martyr-dom. In *Pe.* 12, a native Roman explains the feast day celebrations of 29 June to a visitor by briefly outlining the passions of the apostles Peter and Paul. Yet *Pe.* 9 and 12 bear the title of *passio*, while *Pe.* 11 is given the title of a letter *de passione*. Thus, the dis-tinction in the title bears a fairly superficial relation to the form of the poems, and does not seem to take into account a careful con-sideration of their contents. *Pe.* 11 is called 'Ad Valerianum ... de passione Hippolyti' because the very first line of the poem shows its letter form, but no mention of their dramatic form is made in the titles of *Pe.* 9 and 12. These are allowed to remain plain *passiones* in spite of their complex forms. These observations seem to bear a warning against taking the poems' titles as a certain indi-cation of their practical purpose, provided by the poet himself. He would surely have provided equally accurate descriptions of all his poems in their *inscriptiones* if he had composed these himself.

It seems more likely that these titles arose from later, inept dis-tinctions made by copyists/editors of the text, simply on the basis of a superficial appraisal of the nature of the contents. Prudentius himself in the *Praefatio* refers to the whole corpus of whatever poems he thinks of at this stage as constituting this section of his poetry, in the line '*carmen* martyribus deuoueat, laudet apostolos' (42). The use of 'carmen' here may admittedly represent nothing more than variation of terminology, 'hymnus' having been used immediately before, but it certainly discourages the notion that the poet is himself taking care to distinguish between the *hymni* and *passiones* of the *inscriptiones* among *Pe.* 1–7, 9, 11–14. 'Carmen' may even be a calculatedly all-inclusive term for a collection of poems which he himself sees as heterogeneous in every sense. It is interesting here to note that in the *Praefatio* the poet himself also draws a distinction between the martyrs in general and the 'apostles', Peter and Paul, the subject of *Pe.* 12. The poet may only be making the same distinction which is found elsewhere in the literature of the period,[85] but his attitude may be another indication that the *inscriptiones* should not be given too much weight in seeking for a homogeneous function for the poems.

Comparison of the *inscriptiones* with the contents of *Pe.* 1–7 also undermines the titles' authenticity. The internal evidence of *Pe.* 1 and *Pe.* 3–6 has been used to prove that these poems were intended for singing, in conjunction with the use of the word 'hymnus' in their titles.[86] This argument ignores the fact that *Pe.* 5 is termed 'passio' in its title, and that *Pe.* 2 is sometimes labelled 'hymnus'. The internal evidence needs to be analysed more strictly within its immediate context within the poems. Then inconsistencies appear which give a further warning against taking the *inscriptiones* too literally.

In all but one of the poems entitled *hymni* (the exception is *Pe.* 7, out of 1, 3, 4, 6, and 7), the poet directly addresses the reader/congregation, and exhorts them, or some section of them, to venerate the martyr concerned or to join with him in doing so. Thus at the end of *Pe.* 1, Prudentius addresses the *matres*:

> State, nunc, hymnite, matres, pro receptis paruulis!
> coniugum salute laeta uox maritarum strepat!
> sit dies haec festa nobis, sit sacratum gaudium!

---

[85] e.g. Jerome, *In Ezech.* 12. 40. 5.
[86] Cunningham (1963).

At the end of *Pe.* 3, the poet addresses 'uirgo puerque':

> ista comantibus e foliis
> munera, uirgo puerque, date!
> ast ego serta choro in medio
> texta feram pede dactylico,
> uilia, marcida, festa tamen.

> (206–10)

In *Pe.* 4 the poet suggests:

> Publium pangat chorus, et revolvat
> quale Frontonis fuerit tropaeum . . .

> (153–4)

and finishes with:

> sterne te totam generosa sanctis
> ciuitas mecum tumulis; deinde
> mox resurgentes animas et artus
>   tota sequeris.

> (197–200)

Pe. 5 ends with a prayer to Vincent (545–76):

> si rite sollemnem diem
> ueneramur ore et pectore,
> si sub tuorum gaudio
> uestigiorum sternimur,
>
> paulisper huc inlabere . . .

> (561–5)

At the end of *Pe.* 6, the poet encourages his choir:

> circumstet chorus ex utroque sexu:
> heros, uirgo, puer, senex, anulla,
> uestrum psallite rite Fructuosum!

> (148–50)

In the same poem, he says for Augurius, 'Laudans Augurium resultet hymnus' (151). In all of these cases, the poet seems to suggest the circumstances of an actual performance by setting himself up by implication as a form of chorus or choir leader. This role must be examined with reference both to the secular Latin poetic tradition, and to the more recently formed conventions of Latin hymnology.

The Latin hymns of the fourth century provide no example of the hymn composer referring to or addressing the members of the congregation in a comparably detached way. The lyric, psalm-like element of the hymns as group-prayer[87] is expressed by means of a first person plural which makes no distinction between author and congregation,[88] and which does not refer to the technicalities of composition or performance. So Hilary says 'Bis *nobis* genite',[89] or Ambrose 'votis *vocemus* et patrem', and

> Christus *noster* sit cibus
> ... Laeti *bibamus* sobriam
> ebrietatem spiritus.[90]

This is the first person of the *Pater Noster*, or the *Gloria*: 'We praise you, we bless you, we adore you, we glorify you ...', or that contained in the injunction 'let us pray', included within many prayers in which priest and congregation speak together. In authentic hymns, therefore, the author does not figure as distinct from the congregation,[91] and no distinctions are made between the members of the latter. This is in sharp contrast to the 'uirgo puerque', the 'matres' or the 'chorus ex utroque sexu' in terms of which Prudentius exhorts his congregation within the *Peristephanon*.

In the Prudentian poems called *hymni*, the poet in effect assumes a speaking role within the poem: it is the poet as author of the poems concerned who organizes the performance and issues instructions, and it is significant that in two of these *hymni*, the poet's orders are given in close conjunction with references to his own role as 'maker'. So in *Pe.* 3 he is the one producing the dactyls: 'Ast *ego* serta .../texta feram pede dactylico' (208–9), while in *Pe.* 6 he appears 'dulces hendecasyllabos reuoluens' (161–2). In *Pe.* 1, speaking *in propria persona* as poet, he asks, 'Quid *loquar* purgata longis alba morbis corpora?' (112–14). Comparison might be made here with the end of *Pe.* 2, where the poet speaks of himself, again in the first person singular, as the 'poetam rusti-cum' (573), in a poem which has at least ambivalent status in the

---

[87] Fontaine (1975a).

[88] Cf. the use of the first person plural in the biblical Psalms, for instance, in Ps. 46 and 47: 'God is our refuge and our strength'.

[89] *CSEL* 65, 209.

[90] The third stanza of 'Splendor paternae gloriae', Blume and Dreves (1909) 8.

[91] Though see the Ambrosian exception mentioned above, p. 66.

inscriptiones of the later MSS, a point not insignificant in the present argument. In those poems indisputably labelled *hymni*, however, this internal role of the poet together with use of the first person singular is not only unparalleled in the Christian hymn tradition, but is also obviously artificial and unacceptable in a conjectured liturgical performance of the poem by the whole congregation. It introduces matter too far from the subject and aim of the hymn—the praise and glorification of the martyr.

Reference to earlier Roman lyric soon makes it clear that Prudentius has here picked up a purely literary technique, which has its origins in the techniques developed in Hellenistic poetry as this became divorced from the circumstances of actual performance. The development of the literary hymn was one result of the general tendency to produce lyric poetry bearing an indirect relation to life.[92] Prudentius here felt the influence of the Augustan poets and their successors (see Chapter 4). In the *Pe.* he is particularly influenced by the lyric poetry of Horace. This poet was popular even among the Latin Fathers of the fourth century, both for the moral content of his poetry and for the virtuosity of his use of diverse metrical forms. Familiarity with the latter was encouraged by the exemplary function which they had acquired among Latin *grammatici*.[93] I shall be concerned in the next chapter with the extent and form of Horace's influence on the *Peristephanon* in general, but the classical poet's evident influence on Prudentius' pseudo-hymnic technique must be discussed here.

The tradition of the stanza in early Latin hymnology has already been mentioned, and its practical use in classical times is confirmed by Horace's *Carmen saeculare*.[94] The use of choirs of boys and girls for the performance of these hymns is confirmed for the classical Greek and Hellenistic periods, as well as for the early Roman Republic and the Augustan era.[95] This actual usage finds its way into Horace's literary lyric via Callimachus and other Hellenistic poets in just the form in which Prudentius uses it here: the poet apparently becomes involved in the direction of the performance of the hymn. In connection with Horace, *Odes*, 1.

---

[92] Williams (1968) discusses this transition in his first chapter.
[93] Hagendahl (1967) 464, on Horace and Ovid; cf. Hagendahl (1958) 281 ff. on Jerome's interest in Horace.
[94] Fraenkel (1957) 364–82; cf. Horace, *Odes*, 4. 6 and *Ep.* 2. 2.
[95] Fraenkel (1957) 379–80, esp. 380 n. 3.

21, 'Dianam tenerae' (which was also influenced by Catullus' earlier poem, *C.* 34), Nisbet and Hubbard in their commentary usefully note that:

> though Horace's poem draws on the technique of hymns, it could not conceivably have been sung. This is shown not simply by the artificial style and metre [which is Asclepiadic: $- - - \cup\cup - \vdots - \cup\cup - \cup \overset{\cup}{-}$ ×
> 2 followed by $- - - \cup\cup - \overset{\cup}{-} / - - - \cup\cup - \cup \overset{\cup}{-}$] but by the mode of addressing the boys and girls. Horace's 'dicite' is of course intended to recall the way in which genuine cult-songs open, but it can only be spoken by the poet, not the chorus ... the poem is no more a real hymn than those of Callimachus, in which we find similar addresses (οἱ δὲ νέοι μολπήν τε καὶ ἐς χορόν ἐντύνασθε, 2. 8).[96]

Horace's use of the hymn form is 'rhetorical and allusive';[97] the hymns[98] are 'a fusion of the old and the new, of ritual formulas and literary references, with a modern setting to give them relevance'.[99] Thus the use of the first person singular and the instructions of poet to choir within the poem are features of the literary hymn as it was developed in Latin by Horace.[100] Both are features obviously unsuited to actual sung performance of a Christian hymn.

It is true that a first person singular appears in Horace's *Carmen saeculare*, but here it is the chorus itself which speaks in the final stanza, not the poet:

> haec Iovem sentire deosque cunctos
> spem bonam certamque domum *reporto*
> doctus et Phoebi chorus et Dianae
> dicere laudes.

$$(73–6).$$

However, although the actual performance of the *Carmen* is well

---

[96] Cf. *Pe.* 5. 137 ff., 6. 1 ff. and 118 ff.; Nisbet and Hubbard (1970), p. 254; cf. p. 255.

[97] Nisbet and Hubbard (1970) xvii, on *Odes*, 1. 10.

[98] As qualified by Nisbet & Hubbard (1970) 254; cf. Williams (1972) 26, also on *Odes*, 1. 21: 'a complex poem because it is not a hymn, but the poet purporting to be instructing a choir in a hymn'. See also Williams (1968) 154 ff.

[99] For example, Horace *Odes*, 1. 19, 21, 30, 35; 3. 18, 19, 22. See Cairns (1971) esp. 440–7 on 1. 21 and 1. 30 and also Cairns (1979) 121–7.

[100] Horace can also give these features a non-hymnic setting, for example in *Odes*, 3. 1. Prudentius' reference to his own role as poet (for example *Pe.* 6. 160–3) make it clear that it is the poet instructing the imaginary chorus, not the chorus or chorus leader addressing itself.

attested,[101] the circumstances of the performance and the brief
which Horace was given for its composition put it outside the
realm of traditional hymns. It is more literary in orientation than
the normal cult song. The hymn was an artistic ending to the rites
of the *ludi saeculares*.[102]

It is, therefore, as an aspect of purely literary technique that
Prudentius' injunctions to various forms of choir should be
understood. When he exhorts the 'matres': 'hymnite', or the
'chorus ex utroque sexu': 'uestrum psallite rite Fructuosum!', he is
referring not to the actual circumstances of performance, but
simply to the poem before the reader. So Horace '*appears* to ask
for a song of praise', but 'the song of praise is nothing other than
the Ode itself'.[103] The Ambrosian hymns never use such a device.
The only explicit reference to the mode of performance uses the
first person plural, occurs near the beginning of the hymn con-
cerned, and clearly refers to the actual circumstances of perform-
ance.[104] The literary quality of Prudentius' usage is emphasized in
Pe. 3 with its 'uirgo puerque': this sort of choir represents classical
practice not generally accepted among Christian communities at
the end of the fourth century.[105] It is set, too, in the context of a
highly poetic image: this reference to the boy and girl forms a
bridge between the offerings of real flowers and the poet's own
gift of metrical garlands, his poems, 'Serta texta pede dacty-
lico'.[106] Flowers are a suitable gift for a virgin martyr, and gar-

---

[101] See Fraenkel (1957) 367–8 for the epigraphic evidence. He sees the Carmen as a
'compromise between a Horatian Ode and a traditional sacred song'.

[102] Williams (1972) 42.

[103] Nisbet and Hubbard (1970) 254 on *Odes*, 1. 21; cf. ibid., 302 on 1. 26 and 359 on
1. 32.

[104] Lines 4–5 in the hymn *Aeterni Christi munera*, Blume and Dreves (1909) 1. 14: Laetis
canamus mentibus/Ecclesiarum principes.

[105] Reflected in Catullus, *C.* 34 and 61, and in Horace, *Odes*, 3. 1, the *Carmen saeculare*,
and *Odes*, 4. 6. On reservations about the singing of women in church, see Quasten (1941).

[106] For the word 'serta' used of poetry, cf. Martial, *Ep.* 8. 82. 4, 'scimus et haec etiam
serta placere tibi', where it is used in the closing dedication of the book of poems to Domi-
tian. The idea of the poet 'weaving' his songs may look back to Virgil's picture of himself
at the end of the *Eclogues* as the shepherd who '... sedet et gracili fiscellam texit hibisco'
(*Ecl.* 10. 71). The basket might be taken to symbolize the pastoral poetry of the *Eclogues*:
Servius (writing in the 4th century) sees a metaphorical reference to the *gracilitas* of pastoral
poetry in 'gracili ... hibisco'. It is worth comparing Prudentius here with himself at *Cath.*
3. 26–30: sperne, Camena, leues hederas,/cingere tempora quis solita es,/sertaque mystica
dactylico/texere docta liga strophio/laude dei redimita comas. For the word 'dactylico', see

lands are particularly apt for the martyr who has earned not only earthly but heavenly garlands. Other poems mention the singing of hymns to celebrate the martyrs' feast days, but obliquely. At *Pe.* 2. 516, 6. 151 and 12. 60, the references are detached even from the 'reality' of the poem, and are set within its narrative progress.

Explicit reference to the poet's involvement in his literary creation is another product of an awareness of the techniques evolved by Horace in his very self-conscious and personalized form of literary lyric.[107] Reference can be made here to *Odes*, 1. 1, 2. 1, 3. 3, 30, 4. 2, 3, and 6, where the poet's allusion to his task often comes at the *end* of the ode—a point perhaps not without relevance for the cases cited in Prudentius,[108] both of which occur at the end of poems and which might therefore reflect the poet's impression of Horace's technique in this matter. *Odes*, 4. 6 provides an important Horatian example: it combines the literary address to 'uirgines' and 'pueri' discussed above with a reference to the poet's own production, including an oblique mention of the actual metre being used, 'Lesbium ... pedem' (35: cf. *Pe.* 6. 209). Thus Prudentius picks out this combination of literary topics to achieve a similar personalized hymn form. He shows an awareness of the actual performance of Christian hymns,[109] is at pains—like Horace—to create the impression of a real situation, but simultaneously (also like Horace) undercuts this by his own obviously artificial and literary role within the framework he suggests. This sort of artifice is not the stuff of genuine hymns, as the Ambrosian 'control' proves.

However, use of this sophisticated technique could well have led to the contents of the *inscriptiones*, which are the result either of a rather superficial perusal of the poems, or of a purely literary judgement based on classical criteria exemplified by Horace. Even if the poet himself, rather than an editor or copyist, was indeed behind these titles he could have intended them as literary labels,

---

TLL 5. 1, 2–3. The only poet to use this technical term in poetry is Ausonius (18 *Epistularum Liber*, 6 'Inuitatio ad Paulum', line 37), who is certainly master of the metrical craft, and whose poetry undoubtedly presented a polished technical model for Prudentius.

[107] Although, of course, it is a Christian poet in question here: for him, the literary creation and the poet's pride in it are seen in the perspective of Christian *humilitas* and the renunciation of earthly fame. These are subordinated to the importance of the subject-matter.

[108] That is, *Pe* 3 and 6. Cf. *Pe.* 2 where the 'poeta rusticus' is mentioned at 574.

[109] See p. 69 above.

not as an indication of any practical function within the liturgy.[110]

It is significant that where Prudentius abandons this literary technique, the poems are termed *passiones*, except the interesting border-line case of *Pe.* 2, which refers to the 'poeta rusticus', but not to the supposed circumstances of performance. An exception here in the case of the undisputed *hymni* is *Pe.* 7, which, on the one hand, records the martyrdom of Quirinus in the completely *impersonal* way familiar from the Ambrosian hymns in honour of Lawrence and Agnes, but on the other, seems to deserve the title *hymnus* (in terms of the *inscriptiones* and their suggested origins) less than the *passio* of Agnes, *Pe.* 14, which ends with the lyric prayer of the poet (*qua* Christian of course) and the otherwise odd juxtaposition of first person singular and plural:

> purgabor oris propitiabilis
> fulgore, nostrum si iecur impleas.

> (132–3)

Without resorting to a theory of complete arbitrariness (a certain—albeit misguided—method is likely to have led to the *inscriptiones*), a less desperate answer may be found in the metre of *Pe.* 7, glyconics written κατὰ στίχον ($\overset{\smile}{-}\,\overline{\cup}\,|-\cup\cup-|\cup-$). This metre was associated with the hymn as early as Anacreon, and reappears in Latin poetry in the literary hymns of Catullus, *C.* 34 and 61, where it is used in mixed stanzas.[111]

While the title '*hymnus*' does not bear any real relation to the function of the poems it is supposed to describe, the heading '*passio*' in the manuscripts for *Pe.* 5, 9, 12, and 13 is hardly adequate for these poems either. Apart from their length and metrical form, they seem in their contents to wander too far from the simple treatment of subject-matter suitable for the practical

---

[110] No help is given in this matter by the MSS of the poems. In the earliest MSS of the 6th century, the titles are written in the same script as the text. See Lowe (1950) 16 on Bibl. Nat. Lat. 8084, with photograph.

[111] Fordyce (1973) reproduces fr. 1 (D) of Anacreon at p. 171, in his introduction to *C.* 34. For analysis of glyconics, see Raven (1965) 137; for aeolic verse, ibid., 140; cf. Seneca, who is found writing whole series of glyconics with an invariably spondaic base: $--|-\cup\cup-|\cup-$, e.g. *Hercules Furens*, 875–94. Faguet (1883) comments on Prudentius' glyconics in chap xvi, 'De Glyconico': 'Glyconicum semper sic scandit Prudentius $---\cup\cup$, quod non sine taedio est'. Once again, Prudentius follows the later, standardized version of a lyric metre (cf. Phalaecian hendecasyllables used in *Pe.*; see below chap. 7, n. 20).

function of liturgical readings, let alone hymns. Thus *Pe.* 9, 11, and 12 are set in the dramatic frameworks described above (p. 76). An account of the relevant martyrdom is included in each case, but also much else besides. These are compositions which represent to an important extent Prudentius' own poetic flights of imagination, and his skill as a latter-day *poeta doctus* who plays with novel *variatio* in the presentation of his chosen and well-known theme of Christian martyrdom. This may also refer to audience tastes, but it is surely far from the sort of material suitable for annual use or memorization, even by a limited section of the congregation. Concentration on the figure of the martyr with, at most, an element of lyric in keeping with collective prayer, would be more suited to this.

Confirmation for this is supplied by the Mozarabic hymnal, which, while it is a constant witness to the success and popularity of Prudentius' poems, is also a constant measure of their unsuitability as hymns. Thus, *Pe.* 9, 11, and 12 do not appear in any form in the hymnal: a new stanza form composition appears for Hippolytus' feast, which, however, obviously bears some relation to the traditional elements in Prudentius' version.[112] Cassian, on the other hand, does not figure at all in the hymnal (too foreign a saint for the Spaniards, perhaps in any case), while Peter and Paul are significantly celebrated by the *Ambrosian* hymn in their honour. This is a true measure of the unsuitability of *Pe.* 12 for liturgical use, since the Ambrosian hymn to Agnes gives place to a cento of *Pe.* 14. This cento significantly omits the more personalized lines, 130–1.[113] Cyprian's *passio* also appears in the hymnal in 'Ambrosianized' form: a negative judgement, here, on the highly literary metre in which Prudentius sets his version of this martyrdom.[114]

Mozarabic treatment of the *hymni* among the *Pe.* gives some indication of the unsuitability of their contents for congregational

[112] Blume and Dreves (1897) 183–4. For the Ambrosian hymn for Peter and Paul, see *PL* 86. 144.

[113] *PL* 86. 1050. This hymn uses lines 1–4, 7–9, 67–9, 83–8, 125–8. That is, 20 lines only from 133 lines in Prudentius' hymn. It has, in addition, a 4-line prayer to the Trinity; cf. the full version of Prudentius' poem given in *PL* 86. 1052–4, where, however, the personalized ending of Prudentius' prayer is adapted to more general use: Purga iam corda propitiabili / Fulgore, nostrum si iecur impleas.

[114] Blume and Dreves (1897) 152–3. The hymn uses the Greater Archilochean metre κατὰ στίχον. See above, p. 74.

purposes. Difficult for my theory here is the inclusion of the full versions of the *hymni* to Eulalia and Fructuosus, including the more personal references to the poet's art and role at the end of each. The local popularity of these native saints may provide an explanation here, though it should be noted that in the case of both these poems (as in that of the others incorporated in some form into the liturgy), a doxology is added to close the hymn. The addition of this more prayerful ending shows the need to modify for congregational use what is in itself not quite suitable. However, there are brief centos of *Pe.* 3 and 6 in the hymnal, as well as the full-length versions. Comparison with the very impersonal and stark endings of the Ambrosian hymns to Agnes and Lawrence is instructive here.

The same tendency is at work in the reduction of the other *hymni* to manageable form. Speeches and lengthy anti-pagan harangues are omitted. *Pe.* 2 provides a striking example here, only surpassed by that of the massive *passio Pe.* 10, which is reduced to only twelve lines, plus eight lines of prayer and doxology at the end.[115] The more literary features of the poems are also jettisoned: thus, for instance, in the centos of *Pe.* 4 created for the saints Engratia and Zoilus,[116] the decorative but over-baroque pageant of cities (16–53) is omitted in both cases, together with Prudentius' self-conscious play with ideas from his Christian poetic ('cura de sanctis' takes precedence over 'carminis leges' (164–76)). The greatest reduction in length corresponds to a recognition of the greatest unsuitability for congregational use. Thus *Pe.* 10, 'contra gentiles dicta', is reduced by 99 per cent in full recognition of its difference from the other poems included more regularly in the *Peristephanon* manuscripts.

The Purpose of the *Peristephanon*

The next task is to replace Cunningham's over-simplified view of the purpose of the *Pe.* with a convincing alternative. To do this, it is necessary to approach the poems as individual compositions, and without any preconceived idea of a unified collection com-

---

[115] The Mozarabic cento (*PL* 86. 1249) extracts lines 1–10, 928, 930, and adds a prayer of 8 lines.

[116] The hymn for Engratia (96 lines + doxology), appears at *PL* 86. 901–3; the 25-line hymn for Zoilus at *PL* 86. 1140–1.

posed as such. This view is promoted by the manuscript tradition of the final collection. Bergman pointed out in 1908 that the earliest manuscripts of Prudentius' works (*Parisinus lat.* 8084, saec. VI 'Puteanus', and *Cantabrigiensis Corp. Chr.* 223, saec. IX) do not, in fact, record the Greek title *Peristephanon* for the collection. Gennadius, writing in the fifth century, gives their Greek titles to the three didactic poems (*Apotheosis, Hamartigenia,* and *Psychomachia*), but only describes the *Cathemerinon* and *Peristephanon* poems without mentioning these titles (see Chapter 1 n. 40). This suggests that the Greek titles of the lyric poems in the corpus were late additions, made by analogy with the existing Greek titles, after Gennadius' own time.[117] In other words, the collection may not at first have been seen as a united whole by the poet himself, but was a later creation compiled from a number of poems written earlier on different occasions and circulated separately. This theory is perhaps confirmed by the variable order of the *Pe.* in the manuscripts,[118] and by the frequent appearance of *Pe.* 10 as a separate book preceding or following the other *Pe.* poems.[119] It was certainly accepted practice in the period in question to circulate individual poems (see Chapter 1 n. 37), at a time when papyri were still in use as well as the new parchment *codex*, which would have suited the omnibus edition of AD 405 so well. *Pe.* 10 would certainly have filled a separate papyrus, its length thus giving it the status of a book in its own right in the eyes of later compilers and editors of the collection. Although Prudentius probably did not write his martyr-poems originally with any collection with its

[117] Bergman (1908) 35. Brožek (1970: 31–6) makes a convincing case for the first collection of Prudentius' poems having been made in Gaul in the 6th century. He uses the evidence of Gennadius' entry and Sidonius Apollinaris' probable knowledge of at least the *Pe.* (p. 32). Gennadius' list is ordered according to works based on the Bible, polemical poems, and lyric. He supposes (p. 34) that the *Praefatio* and *Epilogus* both came together at the end of the collection, as they would have done in the complete form of the codex *Puteanus* (8084). It was a later scribe who thought that the terms of the *Praefatio* fitted it better for its position at the beginning of the collection. In any case, Prudentius' poems on this argument would have been circulating separating until the 6th century.

[118] Bergman (1908) 14 ff., 17, and 35; cf. Bergman (1926) xix–liv, discussed by Ludwig (1976) 321 ff., who argues, however, for an early (? 5th-century) archetype for the *Pe*: 1, 2, 3, 4, or 5, 5 or 4, 6, 7, 8, 9, 11, 12, 13, 14. This conclusion is not incompatible with the theory of the collection gradually forming as such during and after the poet's lifetime, until the martyr-poems were collected and circulated together by the time of Gennadius at the *end* of the 5th century. It does not mean, either, that the order of the poems does not reflect something of the poet's own wishes during the earliest stages of the collection's history.

[119] Winstedt (1904) and Bergman (1908) 8.

own title in view, his reference in the *Praefatio* of AD 405 to his poems to martyrs and apostles 'carmen martyribus deuoueat, laudet apostolos' (42) implies that by then at least he regarded this section of his work as a collection with a uniting theme. His very distinction between martyrs and apostles suggests his awareness of the collection's heterogeneity.

The poems of the *Pe.* have indeed the linking central theme of the commemoration of martyrdoms, as the poet points out at *Praefatio* 42, but in general, in each poem, the poet answers his particular brief for the occasion by a variety of formulae created for dealing with his subject. He is not limited in the same way as Ambrose by the form and scope of lyrics intended for congregational singing. He can experiment with different ways of treating the basic theme. His only limiting factors are to be found in the nature of his source-material for each martyrdom (see Chapter 8), and perhaps in the tastes and expectations of the particular readers he has in mind in each case. Thus the collection probably evolved in the end from a series of poems written at different points in the poet's career for different audiences. It is the result of the poet's gradual realization of the potential of the theme of martyrdom. This view makes better sense of the variety of the collection than any strained attempt to give such disparate poems the same practical function by a Procrustean effort to make them all hymns. Once it is admitted that the form and contents of the poems preclude their composition in the first place for sung performance, the way is clear for a more realistic interpretation of their varied forms. There is then no need to be so troubled by the inclusion of *Pe.* 10 or *Pe.* 8 in the final collection, or by their exclusion or omission,[120] since all these variations are the result of the judgement of editors and copyists after Prudentius' own time.

It has been thought possible to explain the variety of the *Pe.* in terms of a chronology based on analysis of apparent stylistic developments surrounding treatment of the subject matter.[121] *Pe.* 7, 13, and 14 are then seen as poems written early in the evolution of the collection, at a time when the poet was content with flat and simple versified accounts of the martyrdom in each case. His

---

[120] *Pe.* 10 does not appear in the (admittedly incomplete) MS Par. Bibl. Nat Lat. 8084, and *Pe.* 8 is missing from Ambrosianus D. 36 Sup., saec. VII.

[121] Cunningham (1976). On this argument, *Pe.* 2 is early because written before a visit to Rome.

treatment of the material becomes more sophisticated, more consciously literary in the (therefore) later poems *Pe.* 1–6. The complex forms and descriptive detail of *Pe.* 9, 11, and 12 point to their composition having taken place later than the other poems, and this fits in with the association of *Pe.* 9, 11, and 12 with a visit to Rome which took place late in the poet's lifetime. As I have pointed out in my first chapter, it is unwise to push this biographical association too hard. But in any case, such an overall chronological scheme for Prudentius' poetry must be approached with caution, since other factors may also affect the stylistic variation of the poems, as suggested in the previous discussion of the manuscript variations. Closer examination of the poems themselves discredits too rigid a timetable of composition. So *Pe.* 14 ends on a lyric note and may have been written *after* a visit to Rome (see below p. 252): *Pe.* 13 too has a more lyric ending (100 ff.). The narrative part of *Pe.* 2 might be considered to be 'early', in that it is fairly simple, yet it, too, displays lyric features which suggest a later date of composition.

A more fruitful approach to consideration of the poems' heterogeneity lies in an evaluation of the poems' purpose set in terms of the reading public for which they were written. The fact that they were not composed to be sung by mixed Christian congregations provides an important limiting factor here. The choice of particular saints for celebration and the use of particular sources for their histories is also likely to affect the form of the poet's treatment.

At the end of *Pe.* 1, 2, 3, and 9, Prudentius explicitly alludes to his personal religious motivation in writing in honour of a martyr. His statements here recall those made in the *Praefatio*, where he talks of his vocation as a Christian poet and his hope of salvation as the result of this new role. However, the reader's appreciation of the poet's task should not be limited too narrowly by these personal religious preoccupations, sincere as they no doubt are at another level. They constitute a literary device, a sort of *captatio beneuolentiae* as well as a religious statement. They provide the means of justifying the poetic setting of the subject for a Christian audience by emphasizing the wholeheartedly Christian standpoint of the poet and his message. In inverted Lucretian terms, it is the *contents* of Prudentius' poetry which is the 'honey' for his Christian readers, while the attractions of the poetry itself

are paradoxically the 'wormwood', if a stern Christian rejection
of the blandishments of poetry is upheld.[122] Prudentius rehabili-
tates poetry for Christians in writing poetry which convinces
Christian readers of the conversion of the Muses to Christianity.
But he still feels a certain anxiety to clarify his own combined role
of practising poet *and* Christian. In the *Praefatio* he issues an invi-
tation to the Christian reader to relax and enjoy all aspects of a
poetry safely dedicated to Christian ends.

   This is all part of writing for a particular audience. The nature
of the poems themselves gives the only clue in the search for the
specific identity of this audience. Fontaine neatly describes these
poems as 'paraliturgical':[123] their contents, and to a limited
extent, their form, have obvious reference to their liturgical
counterparts, but for the reasons put forward above, they are
clearly written to be read and not to be sung. They thus belong to
the category of devotional literature. Such a categorization at
once restricts the poems' audience within the Christian congrega-
tion, and requires full emphasis to be laid on both its main ele-
ments, the Christian and the literary: one helps to limit and define
the other.

   The poet assumes the pose of the 'poeta rusticus' (*Pe.* 2 *ad/fin.*),
producing poetry which he claims is 'vilia, marcida, festa tamen'
(210). Yet, objectively speaking, he is producing poetry of a high
literary standard, which draws not only on recent Christian
attempts to channel the Latin poetic tradition into Christianity via
hymnology, but which also looks back directly to classical
models. The poet's pose of humility may well reflect genuine re-
ligious feeling, a true awareness of the subordination of his art to
its message of salvation, but should also be seen in the light of new
Christian tenets of style developed against the background of the
sermo humilis of the Bible[124] as judged by Late Antiquity, which
saw a new form of sublimity in its lowly didactic style, and tran-
ferred the spirit of this at least to its embryonic Christian litera-
ture. Prudentius is aware of the desirability from the Christian
point of view of this spirit of *sermo humilis*, which had found

---

[122] Jerome, *Ep.* 22. 30. See, for instance, the neurosis behind Jerome's famous dream;
cf. chap. 1, n. 41.

[123] (1975*a*) 773.

[124] For discussion of the Christian change of perspective on the classical genres, see
Auerbach (1965), esp. chap. 1.

natural expression in the new genre of martyr literature. A kind of simplicity and realism associated with the Bible and the concept of *sermo humilis* are prevalent even in the later excesses of this genre. Yet Prudentius is also very aware in his treatment of this genre in poetry that he is presenting the reader with a composition which is highly wrought at the more worldly level of art. His humility as a Christian conceals the artist's pride in the success of his new combination.

This is interesting, however, not so much from the point of view of Prudentius' psychology, as for the sake of narrowing the limits of his audience for the *Pe*. His literary awareness here is directed towards appreciative private readers, not the Christian congregation at large.

It is thus the literary form which sets Prudentius' poems apart from the hymns of Ambrose, and which leads to the assumption that he is writing for an audience of higher than average literary culture, which has the leisure time to satisfy religious preoccupations by the reading of devotional poetry. Prudentius' own background and career at the Western court in combination with these assumptions based on the nature of the poems themselves, suggest as his reading public some section of the Christianized circle of the Western aristocracy. The *Pe*. were not the educated man's substitute for Ambrosian hymns, but provided a supplement to the church diet, a means of supplying the Christian's leisure hours and devout imagination with acceptably pious and improving images. Worth mention here is the sort of sitting-room context suggested by a passage in a letter of Sidonius Apollinaris, where the poems are mentioned among the books in a Gallic aristocrat's private library:

... in another part were books in any number ready to hand; you might have imagined yourself looking at the shelves of a professional scholar or at the tiers in the Athenaeum or at the towering presses of the booksellers. The arrangement was such that the manuscripts near the ladies' seats were of a devotional type, while those among the gentlemen's benches were works distinguished by the grandeur of Latin eloquence; the latter, however, included certain writings of particular authors which preserve a similarity of style though their doctrines are different; for it was a frequent practice to read writers whose artistry was of a similar kind—here Augustine, there Varro, here Horace, there Prudentius ... (*Ep.* 2. 9. 4; Loeb translation.)

A suitable setting here for the de luxe edition represented by the earliest manuscript of Prudentius' work, the revised edition in fine rustic capitals which belonged to the consul of AD 527, Vettius Agorius Basilius Mavortius.[125]

In the *Pe.* readers enjoyed the advantages of good literature as well as religious edification. Meditation on the lives of the saints was generally accepted as a true sign of piety and as an aid to self-improvement. This explains the compilation of later *legendaria*.[126] An interesting note on this is provided by the prologue to the *Life of St Willibrod*, sent to the Abbot Beornrad in the eighth century.[127] The author explains that he is sending the abbot two books, 'unum prosaico sermone gradientem, qui publice fratribus in ecclesia ... legi potuisset; alterum *Piereo pede* currentem, qui in secreto cubili inter scolasticos tuos tantummodo ruminari debuisset ...' The author thus provides a prose version for reading in Church and another in verse for the monks to meditate upon in their cells, and to serve as models for the basis of meditation in their schools. The poetic treatment is a supplement to the prose version, and is intended as devotional reading. This passage is suggestive in consideration of the purpose of the *Pe.* which, by the end of the fifth century at least, was already popular among the monasteries of Southern Gaul, if the witness of Gennadius, writing in this context, is given full weight. The original audience may not have been so narrowly monastic. Even so, the same function held true for the poems. In church could be heard the prose readings and the Ambrosian hymns; but the import of both these could be recalled at will by private reading of the poems, which evoked both reading and hymn in their mixing of narrative and lyric.

The breadth and variation which Prudentius felt necessary for the treatment of this basic theme, and the acceptability within the collection of such diversity, can be explained in terms of the high level of literary culture of Prudentius' readers. The works mentioned alongside those of Prudentius in the letter quoted above give some indication of this. The poetry itself also confirms the same conclusion, with its rich evocation of classical authors. The

---

125 See Lowe (1950), chap. 1, p. 18 above with n. 38 and chap. 4, p. 104 with n. 26.
126 See García Rodríguez (1966) 73. Also de Gaiffier (1954a)
127 de Gaiffier (1967) 475.

sophistication of its metrical variety and its often allusive style are surely aimed at readers qualified to appreciate them.

The informative and prayerful elements are not the only ingredients of the poems. Polemic against the pagans is another important strand, most noticeably in *Pe.* 10, but also in *Pe.* 2, 3, and 5. This provides another clue to the possible nature of the poet's audience. Prudentius has been seen as playing the role of missionary to the Western aristocracy: 'Let us not forget that the Church at the close of the fourth century still had to wage a concerted campaign to win the upper classes'.[128] The pagan revival of the 390s had bitter results,[129] and in this context it is significant that the earliest manuscript of the poems[130] also features a fierce invective against the very Flavianus who helped to lead the pagan forces at the Frigidus, and who lost his life in this battle.[131] The so-called *Carmen ad senatorem ex Christiana religione ad idolorum seruitutem conversum* 'may reflect the general success of the pagan party in winning Christians to apostatize'.[132] It is possible that the strong polemic note of the *Pe.*, which certainly jars with its ostensible purpose of hymning the martyrs, may bear some relation to the general anxiety generated among Christians by this situation. The repetition of apologetic commonplaces might, however, also be taken as an expression of solidarity on the part of convinced and practising Christians, and not only as a practical warning or strengthener in a campaign against apostasy. The poems assume a degree of religious conviction compatible with the acceptance of martyr-cult, and as such are perhaps hard to see in the role of outright Christian propaganda.

The poems, however, also make a more general and implicit polemical point. They should be viewed in the light of Jerome's anxiety in his *De uiris illustribus*[133] to show that Christians did not

---

[128] Smith (1976) 103.

[129] Piganiol (1972) 288–95 and Matthews (1975) 223–52.

[130] Lowe (1950) 16.

[131] Matthews (1970) 464–79. Matthews re-argues the traditional view that the poem is written against Flavianus. Cracco Ruggini (1979) has more recently tried to argue a case for Praetextatus. Her case does not seem stronger than the accepted one for Flavianus.

[132] Smith (1976) 94. The *Carmen ad senatorem* is edited by Peiper, *CSEL* 23 (1881).

[133] *Prologus*, 14 ff: Discant igitur Celsus, Porphyrius, Iulianus, rabidi aduersum Christum canes, discant sectatores eorum qui putant ecclesiam nullos philosophes et eloquentes, nullos habuisse doctores, quanti et quales uiri eam fundauerunt, struxerunt, adornauerunt, et desinant fidem nostram rusticae tantum simplicitatis arguere, suamque potius imperitiam recognoscant.

lack their own varied culture. Although Prudentius' poetry must have become generally known too late to figure in Jerome's Christian answer to Varro,[134] it filled the gap which was evidently felt. The evidence of Sidonius Apollinaris is again revealing—Prudentius on the religious book-shelf balances Horace on the profane side, the delights of which are restricted to the more discerning male minds of the household.

Jerome's anxiety, it must be noticed, finds expression in answer to the preoccupations and perhaps the suggestion of a Spaniard. Two things are to be noted: first, the high general level of piety among upper-class Spaniards, which found political expression in the court activities under the Spanish and highly orthodox emperor, Theodosius. These members of a predominantly Spanish court would have provided the sort of audience demanding devotional reading-matter of a high literary quality to grace their libraries in place of, or at least in addition to the classics. Secondly, the Spanish nationality of Prudentius himself, his preoccupation in particular with Spanish saints in the *Pe.* and his likely involvement along with many compatriots in the Spanish court circles at Milan is to be taken into account. The extent of the audience may in this way once more be plausibly narrowed down. There is further justification for this in the Spanish enthusiasm for its native poet as witnessed in the frequent appearance of his compositions in the Mozarabic hymnal. This might also indicate the Spanish nationality of most of the original recipients of the individual poems. The Spaniards of the period seem to have been keen to ensure a final resting-place in Spain for their worldly goods and also their mortal remains.[135] They were equally keen to demonstrate clearly their claim to a national Christian poet.

A Spanish reading-public helps to explain not only the treatment of Spanish martyrs in the *Pe.*, but other aspects of the collection as well. The descriptive side of *Pe.* 11 and 12 provides an example. Here the reader is given a clear insight into the activities in Rome on major feast-days in the year of the Church. This information would be valuable as a pilgrimage-substitute for those Spaniards unable to visit the shrines concerned, either through living in far-away Spain (see *Pe.* 2), or through being kept in

---

[134] Kelly (1975) 174–7; cf. chap. 4, n. 16.

[135] The *missorium* of Theodosius and the remains of Cynegius found their way back from Constantinople to Spain. Matthews (1967) cf. Matthews (1975) 112.

Milan by official duties in the emperor's court. Such poems might also provide Spaniards returning to their families in Spain with a souvenir of Roman martyr-cult and the catacombs, whether or not these had in fact been directly experienced by the recipients of the poems. Prudentius may thus have been sharing his experience of foreign martyrs with those who remained in Spain, providing a sort of 'arm chair pilgrimage' as a substitute for the strenuous reality.[136] The epistolary form of *Pe.* 11 is suggestive in this context: here, Prudentius allows the actual purpose of his poem to find explicit expression in its form. Poems may even have been commissioned by Spanish patrons or connections, and this could explain the emphasis of *Pe.* 9, 11, 12, as well as the end of *Pe.* 2, where Prudentius angles his treatment of the martyrs and their cult to suit those who are not intimately acquainted with the cult-places in each case. At the end of *Pe.* 2, he is at pains to stress the universal influence of the martyr and the effectiveness of prayer in any part of the world (537 ff.) for the sake of those unable to visit Lawrence's tomb.[137] *Pe.* 2 may also demonstrate the indirect influence of the Spanish pope Damasus on the poet, who was probably aware of this pope's interest in the Roman martyrs. To Damasus' reign belongs the new church in Rome dedicated to St Lawrence.[138]

A patriotic pride in native Spanish saints is evident in *Pe.* 1, 3, 4, 5, and 6: it seems reasonable to suppose then that these poems were written for Spaniards of the governing classes known to Prudentius either from his earlier career in Spain, or from his later connection with the Milanese court. The poet is careful in each poem to involve the population of each city in his celebration of the martyr, in a way which suggests his awareness of a definite audience with a particular expectation of inclusion in the poem. Perhaps each poem represents the saint local to the recipient of the

[136] See the passage from Sidonius Apollinaris quoted above, p. 91, where a Gallic aristocrat's private library is in question. Prudentius' work is considered testing enough only to be appreciated by the male members of the household.

[137] The idea had the approval of Ambrose and came to notice with the *inuentio* of Gervasius and Protasius in Milan. See Matthews (1975) 190.

[138] Matthews (1975) 363–5, with reference to *Pe.* 2. 541 ff.; cf. Ferrua (1942), 58. Matthews draws out the significance of the scene depicted by Prudentius: '. . . in supporting the functions of the Catholic Church, the converted senators enjoyed the opportunities so essential to them, to be seen by whole crowds, active in the public pursuit of their religion.'

particular poem, or each recipient's favourite patron saint—hence
again, pride in particular martyrs for their nationality, mingled
with due emphasis on the saint's role 'patronus mundi', for
example, *Pe.* 1. 13. Comfort here, perhaps for Spaniards in tem-
porary exile for reasons of official duties, cut off from the focal
point of the cult, the saint's actual tomb. The 'Spanish' poems in
this sense might even be thought of as 'home thoughts from
abroad', an assurance of the maintenance of religious ties unaffec-
ted by earthly geographical limitations: Fructuosus in *Pe.* 6 under-
takes quite emphatically to pray 'cunctis pro populis' (84).

However, the note of patriotic fervour which mingles so well
with the expression of religious feeling in the context of martyr-
cult[139] is conspicuous by its absence in some poems: in *Pe.* 7, 13,
and 14. Interestingly, foreign saints are in question in these poems,
and it could be that they are also written for foreign patrons. *Pe.*
13 seems to give a clue to what is going on. Cyprian was one of
the first foreign saints to be adopted by the Spanish Church,
which was generally devoted to martyr-cult and which had from
early times had close links with the Church in Africa. Yet no
special mention is made in the poem of Spanish devotion to
Cyprian, or to the possibility of this, in contrast, for example, to
the treatment of Lawrence in *Pe.* 2. When Prudentius talks of
Cyprian as 'decus orbis et magistrum' (*Pe.* 13. 2) and adds 'Est
proprius patriae martyr, sed amore et ore *noster*', 'noster' is used in
a neutral sense, 'of us Christians everywhere', and this meaning is
balanced and clarified by some significant lines at the end of the
poem. At 103–5, Cyprian's influence is mentioned in connection
with Libya, Gaul, and even Britain. Spain and the Iberian penin-
sula are indeed mentioned at the end of the list, but without any
special emphasis of the sort to be found in the poems concentrat-
ing on Spanish saints:

> Nec Libyae populos tantum regit, exit usque in ortum
> Solis et usque obitum, Gallos fouet, imbuit Britannos,
> praesidet Hesperiae, Christum serit *ultimis Hiberis*;
> denique doctor humi est, idem quoque martyr in supernis;
> instruit hic homines, illinc pia dona dat patronus.

> (13. 102–6)

---

[139] Matthews (1975) 147–8. See Ambrose, *Ep.* 22 (*PL* 16. 1019–26) and Paulinus' *Life of
St Ambrose*, C. 14, for his view of the saints as the allies, protectors, and patrons of Catholic
Milan. See below chap. 7, nn. 37 and 38.

The flat tone and lack of emphasis here on Spain as the poet's or reader's native land seem to indicate that the poet is writing *ad hominem/homines* in a case where the recipient is *not* a fellow Spaniard. The same conclusion might be applied to *Pe*. 14, which was perhaps written for a non-Spaniard who has not visited Rome. This would explain the scene-setting of the opening lines. *Pe*. 7 remains something of a puzzle, but the difference of stylistic level may also reflect the inspiration Prudentius found in a prose source as well as lack of personal experience of Quirinus' cult. It may also reflect the nature of Prudentius' involvement in his brief, which would naturally have been shaped and controlled by the poet's knowledge of the recipient's tastes and expectations. Thus the heterogeneity of the *Peristephanon* is best to be understood in the light of a variety of treatment and approach shaped by the variable factor of each recipient's tastes, in combination with the poet's own artistic inspiration and his knowledge of the sources for each martyr's story.

The particular audience which I am suggesting for the *Peristephanon* not only fits the evidence supplied by the poems themselves, but also supplies the poems with a clearer social context and function. Through the poems, further insight can be gained into the extent to which the religious interests of the Spanish Christian court in the West pervaded every aspect of its life. Even leisure literature must undergo conversion, to become devotional reading matter. To suggest vaguely that 'Prudentius' patron is the Church at large',[140] is, for the *Peristephanon* at least, to throw away the evidence of the poems themselves. I hope that the discussion of the purpose of these poems in this chapter has contributed towards giving further definition to Prudentius' particular audience, and indirectly, towards a wider perspective on the activities and life-style of the 'coterie religieuse espagnole'[141] both at home and abroad.

---

[140] Smith (1976) 72.
[141] Piganiol (1972) 238.

4

Prudentian *Imitatio* and Christian 'Augustanism'

PRUDENTIUS' role as the 'Christianorum Maro et Flaccus'[1] was recognized at an early date in scattered comments which reveal an appreciation of his poetry as the Christian equivalent of and, indeed, substitute for the heritage of secular Latin poetry. Isidore of Seville (d. AD 636) sees him as a rival of the great classics and recommends him to the Christian reader:

> Si Maro, si Flaccus, si Naso et Persius horret,
>   Lucanus si te Papiniusque taedet,
> Par erat eximio dulcis Prudentius ore,
>   carminibus uariis nobilis ille satis.

> (*C.* 9 = *PL* 83. 1110)

Bishop Sidonius Apollinaris a century earlier notes that Prudentius provides the Christian counterpart of Horace in a friend's library (*Ep.* 2. 9, *c.* AD 472, quoted above p. 91). Although the poet makes no explicit statement about his attitude towards the

---

[1] Bentley, *Horatius Flaccus* (1711) on 2. 2. 15. Much work has been done from an early date on Prudentius' debt to previous Latin poets, in particular to Virgil, whose influence on Prudentius was noted by Arevalo in his 1788 edition (*PL* 59), by Obbarius (1845: xvi–xvii), and Dressel (1860: xix–xx). Puech (1888) alluded briefly to the influence on Prudentius of Virgil, Horace, Ovid, Lucretius, Lucian, Seneca, and Juvenal, noting that Virgil was 'le principal modèle' (261–2). Bergman (1926: 455–69) has an *index imitationum* for secular authors. Lavarenne notes parallels with non-Christian authors throughout his edition of the poems, together with Guillén and Rodríguez (1950). Parallels are also listed by Cunningham (1966). Exhaustive lists of parallels with Virgil have been compiled by Dexel (1907), Schwen (1937), and Mahoney (1934). There is brief discussion in all three works, but no full analysis of the implications of particular references to their context. More detailed work on this has been done by Richard (1969). For Horace and Prudentius, see the (over-inclusive) list of parallels without analysis in the dissertation of Breidt (1887); also Martija (1935); Strzelecki (1955); Opelt (1970); Salvatore (1956) and (1958) 59 ff. For the influence of other authors on Prudentius, see below, chap. 6, with notes. The subject is covered by Lavarenne (1933) 568–96, and also in Hanley (1959). Both these studies leave the parallels drawn without sufficient discussion.

models of earlier Latin poetry,[2] his poetry speaks for itself in its clear reference to these secular works, both in its range of forms and in the details of its language. The accumulation of classical features is just as conscious an adoption as the fully Christian inspiration expressed in the *Praefatio*. The poet's intentions, therefore, should be examined: for what sort of audience was he writing, and how exactly did he view his own Christianity in relation to classical culture?

As a result of the traditional opposition of Christianity to classical culture, the development of Christian Latin poetry had been slow until the fourth century. Poetry as the vehicle of pagan falsehood has to be rejected: *eloquentia* and *veritas* could not go together,[3] and only the simplicity of the Gospel texts could express the truths of the Church established by simple fishermen.[4] This early attitude was well summed up in the famous antitheses of Tertullian: 'What is there in common between Athens and Jerusalem, the Academy and the Church?'[5] However, while the Church was not of this world, it could not help being increasingly involved in it, and naturally found it difficult to maintain complete isolation from contemporary culture.[6] Christian attempts to find a solution to this situation and to assimilate aspects of Greek culture bore significant fruit in the East at the end of the second century with the work of the Alexandrian school under Clement and Origen,[7] but it was not until official recognition of the Church under Constantine at the beginning of the fourth century that the problem demanded a more general solution, especially at a time when more educated converts were flooding into the Church.

These people brought the fruits of their secular education with them into the Church. This was bound to continue since the pagan school curriculum, based completely on pagan authors, had

---

[2] The nearest that Prudentius comes to a statement on the subject seems to be at *Cathemerinon*, 3. 26 ff.: sperne, camena, leues hederas,/cingere tempora quis solita es,/sertaque mystica dactylico/texere docta liga strophio,/laude Dei redimita comas. Cf. Paulinus of Nola, *Carmen* 15. 30–1: 'non ego Castalidas, uatum phantasmata Musas/nec surdum Aonia Phoebum de rupe ciebo . . .'.

[3] Hagendahl (1967) 455.

[4] Sulpicius Severus, *The Life of Saint Martin*, Preface, 3 ff.

[5] Tertullian, *De praescriptione haereticorum*, 7; cf. Jerome, *Ep.* 22, Ad Eustochium. See chap. 1, n. 41, with bibliography.

[6] Hagendahl (1958) 310–11 on Jerome's attitude.

[7] Chadwick (1967) 94–113; Cochrane (1944) 226 ff; and Bartelink (1986) 1–44.

not been replaced by a Christian alternative.[8] Educated Christians
might resolve in theory to abandon their non-Christian cultural
heritage, but in practice they continued to show the influence of
the familiar pagan authors in their own writings. This explains the
discrepancy between theory and practice in the use of pagan
authors in Church writers like Jerome and Augustine. At one
extreme lie the genuinely neurotic dreams of Jerome and vows to
reject all pagan literature,[9] at the other, an increasing willingness
to appropriate aspects of secular literature for Church use. Augus-
tine and Jerome express this new openness by means of Biblical
analogies: the beautiful captive woman of Deuteronomy made
suitable for marriage with the Jew, and the Egyptian treasure
which, although bad in itself, the Jews can appropriate for their
own uses when they leave Egypt.[10] This second analogy appears
in Book 4 of Augustine's *De doctrina christiana*, where he even ad-
mits that eloquence should also be enlisted on the side of truth. He
outlines his scheme for an ecclesiastical rhetoric in terms which
strongly recall the rhetorical treatises of Cicero.[11] Augustine
maintains some distance from pagan rhetoric by emphasizing that
its study should be restricted to youth (*De doct. Christ.* 4. 3), and
that intelligent reading and listening can themselves have the same
results. He points out that he can in any case exemplify all the
formal features of eloquence from the Bible and from Church
writers—but it is noticeable that it is still in terms of the system of
pagan rhetoric that he analyses these writers' merits. Augustine
here exemplifies both the new willingness to assimilate at least the
formal aspects of pagan culture and the more traditional position
of suspicion and detachment.

The same tension lies behind attempts in the fourth century to
supply Christians with an alternative literature. In order to satisfy
an audience feeling the need for a substitute for the profane litera-
ture in which it was steeped, Christian authors presented the new
subject-matter as far as possible in recognizable classical forms.
Just as Augustine had viewed Biblical style in terms of the classical

---

[8] Marrou (1965) 451–84.

[9] Hagendahl (1958) 310–11.

[10] The captive woman: Jerome, *Ep.* 21. 13. 4, with reference to Deut. 21: 10–13. The
Egyptian treasure: Augustine, *De doctrina christiana*, 2. 40, with reference to Ex. 3: 22; 11: 2;
12: 35.

[11] Hagendahl (1967) 565; cf. Clarke (1953) 151 ff.; Deferrari (1927) 105; Baldwin
(1925).

genera dicendi, so the Gospels were seen in the perspective of classi-
cal forms, in particular the epic. In the preface to his epic version
of the Gospel story, the Spanish poet Juvencus explicitly refers to
the 'dulcedo Maronis' and his undying glory, in spite of his equal
awareness of the 'mendacia' of ancient epic.[12] The result of this
dual outlook is a Gospel narrative in Virgilian hexameters and
Virgilian language, a mosaic of Virgilian reminiscences now con-
verted to a new Christian context. This form of Christian Latin
poetry reaches its climax in the cento poems, perhaps the best
known example of which is that of Proba:[13] 'Vergilium cecinisse
loquar pia munera Christi'. Proba's narrative consists entirely of
lines and half-lines taken straight from the poems of Virgil.

The inability of Christians to look outside the forms of classical
literature was put to the test by the rescript of the Emperor Julian
which banned Christians from teaching in pagan schools.[14] This
prohibition helped to define and throw into relief the deficiencies
of existing Christian literature. However, when it came to
supplying an alternative to the pagan authors for use in a new
Christian curriculum, attempts were made simply to mould Bib-
lical material into classical forms. So the Old Testament was used
as the basis for epic and tragedy and the Gospels were turned into
Platonic dialogues.[15] These efforts did not stand the test of time
and at the end of the century it was still possible to assert that
Christians did not possess a literature exclusively their own. It was
in reply to this assumption on the part of the Spaniard Dexter that
Jerome embarked on his *De uiris illustribus* in the early 390s.[16]

It is against this background and in the perspective of the
limited development of a Christian Latin poetry that Prudentius'
achievement must be evaluated and understood. He marks a new
and more complex stage in the development of a Christian litera-
ture. His poetry embodies an implicit involvement in classical cul-
ture; the poet has absorbed and assimilated the substance and

---

[12] Juvencus, *Praef.* 10 ff. (*Evangeliorum Libri IV*). See McClure (1981) on Bible Epic.
[13] *CSEL* 16, 511 ff.; see Raby (1953), 16 ff.; Ermini (1909); Fontaine (1981) 95 ff.
[14] *CTh* 13. 3. 5 (AD 362); Julian, *Ep.* 36.
[15] Socrates, *Hist. Eccl.* 3. 16. = *PG* 67. 418–19. The two Apollinarii (father and son)
worked together to rewrite the Bible in classical forms (*ODCC*, 72).
[16] For the date of Jerome's *De uiris illustribus* see chap. 1, n. 66. Prudentius is not men-
tioned in this work, presumably because his poetry was not widely known at this date, or
perhaps was hardly begun. He does, however, figure in Gennadius' later continuation of
Jerome's work.

techniques of classical poetry, but has managed to produce a Christian poetry which is fresh and individual. Earlier attempts had, in general, relied in too narrow a way on the 'Egyptian treasure' of secular literature: the technique of assimilation was superficial and crude in the centos and in the various Christian attempts to see Virgil, for instance, as a 'Christian without Christ'.[17] Only Ambrose had so far achieved a more balanced and original synthesis of classical and Christian elements (see above, pp. 62 ff.). I hope to show here that Prudentius imitates and assimilates classical models in such a way as to give a Christian significance, not only to the formal aspects of secular poetry, but also to many of the major values which it expresses. In doing this, I shall try to analyse Prudentian *imitatio* in terms of creative imitation of his models in a way which reflects more recent and more sympathetic attempts to do this for the rest of Prudentius' corpus.

In fact, the poet's realization of his models is the mark of an originality which even appears in the range of forms adopted. The traditional poetic genres are covered in the use of epic and didactic hexameters and lyric metres, but in every case the apparent genre is widened with novel results. The *Peristephanon*, for instance, contain features traditionally associated with lyric, but also features associated with epic and satiric poetry. Prudentius uses lyric metres with obvious reference to the classical poetic tradition (see, for instance, the Horatian Sapphic stanzas used for the panegyric of *Pe.* 4), but demonstrates his metrical virtuosity by some novel lyric combinations (see, for instance, the metres of *Praefatio* and *Epilogue*). In tune with the lyric tone set by the metres, the poet enters his poems to speak at times *in propria persona* as he intercedes with the martyrs in the prayers which end some poems (*Pe.* 1–6, 14). Yet a strong narrative thread runs through the poems, conforming to the pattern set by Prudentius' Christian sources: the arrest of the martyr, his trial and interrogation, the tortures and final execution for the faith. The narrative impetus established by this well-known and often-repeated pattern is broken, however, by the speeches of the protagonists. Ample space is devoted to anti-pagan polemic in the mouths of the martyrs (Romanus speaks out in *Pe.* 10, for instance, and Lawrence in *Pe.* 2), and here a satiric–didactic note creeps in. The poems are

---

[17] Hagendahl (1967) 437–42; Comparetti (1966), 99–100; Courcelle (1957).

thus an unusual combination of elements which might otherwise be kept separate in the traditionally more distinct genres of poetry. They are an even richer and more complex mixture than Raby's comparison of them with ballads allows.[18]

Verbal reminiscence of earlier authors is an important aspect of Prudentius' technique in evoking classical models. Here, too, the poet is more subtle than his predecessors in his *imitatio*, more varied in technique and aims. His art assumes an audience equally familiar with his secular models, since often an appreciation of the original context is required in order to achieve the fullest understanding of the new Christian context. Prudentius is very much the *poeta doctus* who writes for an audience of like-minded *litterati* with the background of the same form of secular education.

This audience was in the best possible position to appreciate Prudentius' poetry. Detailed study and memorization in youth of the set school authors[19] led to a thorough knowledge of the texts. Virgil in particular was revered as the national poet: 'poeta sublimis, non Homerus alter . . . sed primus Homerus apud Latinos',[20] the fund of all knowledge, 'nullius disciplinae expers'.[21] He was studied in all the word-by-word detail exemplified by the treatment he receives in Macrobius' *Saturnalia* and Servius' commentary. His poetry became so imprinted on the schoolboy's memory that even in later years he could recite the text with little prompting.[22] It was this degree of awareness of a text which made the cento form a possibility, and such a success in the non-Christian sphere, too, as Ausonius proved with his *Cento nuptialis*. Such an awareness justifies the careful analysis of Late Antique poetry in terms of its debt at various levels to earlier secular poetry.

Virgil of course provided a major influence in the composition of late Latin poetry, but other authors were also popular. The fourth century seems, in fact, to have been a period of renewed interest in the authors of the Empire. Livy and Juvenal, for instance, are taken up again in this period.[23] Among the poets,

[18] This is discussed by Fontaine (1975a).

[19] Marrou (1965) Part 2, chap. 5; cf. Brown (1967) 36–7.

[20] Jerome, *In Mich.* 7. 5–7 = *PL* 25. 1220; in general, for Virgil's standing, see Hagendahl (1967) 384 ff. Also Comparetti (1966) and Hudson-Williams (1966).

[21] Macrobius, *In Somnium Scipionis*, 1. 6. 44.

[22] For instance, Augustine's friend who could produce the penultimate line of every poem of Virgil, and the line preceding it: *De anima*, 4. 7. 9.

[23] This is discussed by Cameron (1964a).

Horace was the object of attention among Christian as well as non-Christian authors. He was the source and example of a wide range of metrical forms, as the grammarians appreciated,[24] and also to be admired for the moral-philosophical content of his verse, in particular his hexameters.[25] It is interesting to note that the consul of AD 527 whose name appears on the earliest manuscript of Prudentius (Bibl. Nat. Lat. Puteanus 8084), was also responsible for an edition of Horace.[26] Of Republican poets, Terence was used in the school syllabus, while Lucretius certainly, and Catullus probably, were still being read.[27] Propertius was naturally shunned by Christian readers for his frivolity as a love poet, but seems to have been generally available in the Late Period.[28] The works of Ovid were well known, and were even cited by the Church Fathers.[29] His poetry was popular enough to form the basis for Ovidian *centones*.[30] The *Fasti* and *Metamorphoses* seem to have been more popular than the *Amores*. Of later poets, Lucan, Statius, Persius, Juvenal, and Martial were all still read and cited. Jerome mentions commentaries available on Sallust, Cicero, Terence, Lucretius, Horace, Persius, and Lucan (*in Rufinum* 1. 16 = *PL* 23. 409–10). These commentaries are unfortunately not known from other references, but even this single mention indicates the width of reading expected of an educated man of the fourth century.

Before embarking upon detailed analysis of the text of the *Peristephanon*, it is necessary to decide how reminiscences from earlier authors are to be recognized and categorized in order to achieve

---

[24] Froebel (1911); Strzelecki (1935).

[25] Hagendahl (1958) 269 ff.; and (1967) 690 ff.

[26] That is, Vettius Agorius Basilius Mavortius. See Winstedt (1903); also *PLRE* 2, 736–7 and *CSEL* 61, 'Prolegomena', xxv n. 2.

[27] Lucretius: Hagendahl (1967) 383 and (1958) 20. Also Jerome, *In Rufinum*, 1. 16 5 = *PL* 23. 410; Catullus, *C.* 4 appears in Augustine's *De musica*, 4. 5, although it must be noted that the same example is used for the iambic trimeter in Terentianus Maurus, from whom Augustine draws many examples of metre.

[28] Enk (1962) 54–77: 'Tabula poetarum qui Propertium aut imitati sunt aut saltem legerunt'. Hosius (1932); Helm (1957), *RE*, 792–3. On the absence of Propertius 792–3. On the absence of Propertius from Augustine, see Hagendahl (1967) 468.

[29] Augustine knows at least the *Metamorphoses* (Hagendahl (1967) 468); Jerome in *Ep.* 123. 4. 3 quotes *Amores*, 3. 2. 83, and refers to two passages from *Metamorphoses*. For Ausonius and Ovid, especially the *Fasti*, see Green (1977) 441. Also Manitius (1899) 727, on Prudentius (with no reference to the *Peristephanon*).

[30] For Ovidian *cento* poems, see Ermini (1909) 40. The poetry of Lucilius, Lucan, Silius Italicus, and Statius also seems to have been used for *cento* poems.

the fairest evaluation of their contribution to the later composition. To be avoided here is the mechanical paralleling of texts which tended to be the hallmark of early attempts to approach an analysis of Prudentius' *imitatio*.[31] They form part of a line of criticism which discussed Prudentius' poetry in terms of the merely imitative and derivative. Such lists leave unexplained the compiler's exact criteria for admission of particular parallels which, in the end, cover too wide a range of similarity. Examples of verbal parallel may exist only in the mind of a compiler keen to include as many points of imitation as possible. A single word, in a different case and metrical position, can be used to support reliance of the later author on the earlier. This in itself need not supply insufficient grounds for claiming reminiscences or dependence, but in this sort of case in particular, a full discussion of the context of both texts is also required. The structure of the later passage, the thought behind it, the thought expressed in the original passage, together with *its* structure and context, all have to be explored in order to see how the original passage is used in its new setting and how far an understanding of this explains why Prudentius bothers at all with such reminiscences.

The answer to this question may admittedly not always be very positive. At the lowest end of the scale of imitation, the poet is simply concerned to draw on the traditional diction of earlier Latin poetry in order to lend his own poem the literary polish expected by an audience steeped in its classical heritage. Such diction is the common property of the later poets and not to be pinned down too closely to particular passages in any one earlier author. To satisfy his audience, Prudentius needs to supply the stylistic equivalent of the much-read poets of the past. These more trivial and basic reminiscences consist of isolated phrases or adaptations of phrases which seem coined for no obvious reason in the context, apart from the stylistic. See for example a formulaic phrase like 'nec mora' discussed below (p. 169, with n. 46). Mahoney (1934: n. 1) lists such phrases under the headings 'probable' and 'possible' imitations. The meaning of the phrase in its original context lends nothing to the new setting, or may even be changed completely to fit the new context. Virgilian reminiscence is most open to this use. This rather superficial concern with, in this case,

[31] For example, Dexel (1907); Sixt (1892); Breidt (1887).

epic diction should not, however, be dismissed as completely
without significance: although apparently trivial phrase for
phrase, and much filtered through the medium of intervening
epic poetry, it is itself significant for the epic terms in which the
poet views his Christian heroes and their world. Among these
sorts of reminiscences can be counted the purely formulaic (for
example, the introduction and ending of speeches) and the simply
ornamental or descriptive, used in the setting of scenes. Such
reminiscences have been termed 'unconscious'. This description
seems to go too far in reducing the poet's conscious role in com-
position and seems meaningless for the immediate purpose of pin-
pointing and evaluating reminiscences in the work in general.
The poet's role in composition *may* at times be reduced to one of
unconscious imitation on smaller points of diction, but it is more
useful to place all reminiscences on a scale ranging from the *trivial*,
that is, with no immediately apparent special meaning or function
in its context, to the obviously *significant*, that is, having far-
reaching implications for the new context.[32] 'Trivial' may, in this
way, be taken to cover possible unconscious 'echoes'.[33] Whatever
the level of consciousness in the use of such reminiscences, they
cannot be ignored, since they at least contribute to the quality of
style of the new context.

'Significant' reminiscences provide more matter for discussion.
It is a question here of deliberate imitation of perhaps a whole pas-
sage in the earlier poet. Both its structure and its thought are
recalled by means of verbal reminiscence, either by direct and
clear imitation or by calculated variation of the original. Pruden-
tius is far removed from the crude technique of the centonist.
Close verbal parallel in Prudentian usage need not be extended,
but can be a matter of restricted but recognizable reminiscences at
key points. These act as vital indications which help the reader to
recognize the whole.[34] The reader is asked for a sophisticated
appreciation of the poet's technique: he must recognize the

---

[32] On techniques and expectations of imitation, see Du Quesnay (1979) esp. 38–9.
Cameron (1970) 279 ff. discusses different categories of borrowings, rightly stressing the
complexity of imitation which has to be divided into a range of categories.
[33] Green (1977) 441. Green distinguishes between borrowing, reminiscence or imita-
tion, as implying some degree of deliberate purpose, and an 'echo' which represents an
unintentional reminiscence with no particular reason behind the choice.
[34] This technique is explored for Claudian by Clarke (1950–1) and for Prudentius by
Alexander (1936).

reminiscence in the poetry under his eyes, remember the passage referred to in the earlier poet, and consider both its context and meaning there. This knowledge must then be set against the new context in order to reach the fullest conclusions about the meaning of the later poet. By a process of *contaminatio*, the later poet may combine reminiscences of more than one model in a single passage.[35] Such reminiscences derive their significance from their involvement with the underlying thought of both old and new contexts. They are more than superficial literary echoes of poetic diction (which do *not* make such heavy demands on the reader). They have more far-reaching implications,[36] particularly in a setting where secular poetry is being recalled in a Christian context. Appreciation is constantly required of how far the Christian poet accepts or rejects, or at least feels the need to adapt the content of his pagan author. This can lead to an understanding of the later poet's attitude towards inherited secular culture.

This form of reminiscence has rightly been termed 'dynamic'[37] and entails more than simply 'Christian matter in pagan form'. It involves the two-way movement of ideas and epitomizes on the literary level the wider synthesis of Christian and pagan taking place in a society no longer interested in or capable of the artificial isolation of two earthly cities.[38] It is with this level of reminiscence that I shall be dealing in the final section of this chapter.

The *Peristephanon Liber*

The difficulty of giving these poems a single generic label has been outlined above (p. 102). It would be wrong, however, to try to dissect the poems too mechanically into their classical components without being conscious of the richness of the Christian background into which these threads are woven. This aspect of the poems partially explains their originality and should be kept firmly in mind when attempting any analysis or appreciation.

[35] The expectation of this sort of appreciation of a text drawing on an earlier one is perhaps confirmed by some early criticism of Virgil for his use of Homer. Some interesting examples of early critics, comparing Virgilian passages with the original, are cited by Russell (1979) 7–9. On *contaminatio* see ch. 5, n. 37 below.

[36] This point is emphasized by Cameron (1970) 279 ff.

[37] Rapisarda (1950) 48 n. 11. Also discussed by Salvatore (1958) 11–34, esp. 12.

[38] This is the main point of Fontaine (1972: 571–95), in which he explores the continuity of the 'withdrawal' motif among pagans and Christians.

That is why these chapters on Prudentian *imitatio* are framed by chapters dealing with the relation of the *Pe.* to the recent developments in Latin hymnology and to a wide variety of martyr-literature.

The fourteen poems of the *Peristephanon* are very varied, and some effort must be made to explain their unevenness of stylistic level. *Peristephanon Liber* seems to be an 'umbrella-title' for poems only loosely linked by unity of basic subject-matter. The poems represent a wide range of forms, from the brief elegiac 'inscription' for a baptistery, with its subtle symbolism and elliptical treatment of the martyrs concerned (*Pe.* 8), to the unadorned versified version of known *Acta* in *Pe.* 6, or the baldness of *Pe.* 7 which outlines only the essentials of Quirinus' history in a completely impersonal narrative. These poems stand in strong contrast to the more complicated dramatic frameworks used as the setting for the martyr-narratives of *Pe.* 9, 11, and 12, or the lively lyric treatment of 1, 3, and 4. This range of forms within a single collection reflects the width of literary background behind the conception of poetic treatment of martyrdom. The quality of the Christian sources is influential: a well-known and 'canonical' written version of a story dominates the poet's treatment of it, for example, *Pe.* 6 (see below, chapter 7), whereas a story drawn from the oral tradition may be familiar in outline, but have many variants which leave the poet more freedom. This helps to explain the differences between *Pe.* 6, and 5, or 7 and 11.

Variety of treatment may, of course, also reflect both the evolving literary interests and preoccupations of the poet himself and his perception of the level of literary appreciation or expectations of his audience in any poem. It seems likely that the collection developed gradually as the result of individual commissions from a variety of probably Spanish patrons.[39] The tastes of a different patron may be reflected in each poem. Such an evolution may be confirmed by the manuscript tradition of the collection: the order of the poems is variable, while *Pe.* 10 was probably not originally included in a collection of noticeably shorter poems.[40]

Thus it is difficult to treat all fourteen poems in the same way as representing a totally unified collection with consistent stylistic

[39] See above, chap. 3, pp. 91 ff.
[40] Lavarenne (1963*b*) 117–19 (introduction to *Pe.* 10).
[41] Fabre (1948); Charlet (1975); Fontaine (1972); Walsh (1970) 568.

features. The number fourteen is itself probably accidental, par-
ticularly if *Pe.* 10 can be discounted. The fourteen poems of Pauli-
nus of Nola might be cited as a significant precedent, but these
poems were spread over the years AD 395–409,[41] and would prob-
ably not have been known to Prudentius as a finished series (unless
the *Pe.* collection was incomplete for the 'omnibus edition' of
AD 405).[42] In any case, the last *Natalicia* poem (*C.* 29 in *CSEL* 30)
is only fragmentary and is spoken of in one manuscript as the
fifteenth poem of the series.[43]

It can be assumed, however, that in the final stages at least, the
poet himself decided to gather at least a number of these poems
together into a collection. This seems to be the implication of
Praefatio, 42. It is therefore worth considering the whole collec-
tion in terms of possible secular precedents. A starting-point is
provided by the purely Christian scope of the poems. It is notice-
able that the *Peristephanon* poems conform to the vital cultic
points of reference, the so-called 'hagiographic co-ordinates',[44]
through their interest in the actual feast-day of the martyr, that is,
the 'natalis dies' of his death,[45] and his place of burial. So, for in-
stance, *Pe.* 1 is framed by reference to 'hic locus', line 5, and 'dies
haec', line 120. Possession of a martyr's remains is considered a
great prize for a town: pride in this provides a new Christian focus
for patriotism. This is expressed in the opening stanzas of *Pe.* 1:
'Pollet hoc felix per orbem terra Hibera stemate,/hic locus dignus
tenendis ossibus visus Deo ...' (4–5). The idea is repeated in *Pe.* 3.
6–10:

> Proximus occiduo locus est
> qui tulit hoc decus egregium,
> urbe potens, populis locuples,
> sed mage sanguine martyrii
> uirgineoque potens titulo.

In *Pe.* 11 and 12 this patriotic interest is concentrated on Rome

---

[42] Lavarenne (1955) xxiv–xxv discusses the contents of the MS Bibl. Nat. Lat. Puteanus 8084.

[43] Fabre (1948) 114, on *C.* 19 of Paulinus; cf. Lienhard (1977) 154 ff. on 'The Chrono-
logy of Paulinus' Works', with a table of conclusions, 189–90.

[44] Delehaye (1934) 8 ff.

[45] Delehaye (1933*b*) 24 ff.; cf. Paulinus of Nola, 14. 1 ff. Thus, *Pe.* 1 begins with a refer-
ence to the place ('hic locus', 5), and ends with a reference to the feast-day ('dies haec', 120).
Rand (1920) 74. Salvatore (1958) 35. Also Salvatore (1959) vol. 2, 257–72; Alexander
(1936).

itself, the 'Romula urbs' (*Pe.* 11. 1) in an exciting way which will be discussed in detail below (pp. 116 ff.). The Roman focus of these poems in combination with various features of their presentation recalls two earlier collections of secular poetry, the interests of which were both aetiological and patriotic, with emphasis on the celebration of the monuments and religious festivals of Rome in the light of their origins: Book 4 of Propertius' *Elegies* and Ovid's *Fasti*. The strongly religious focus of the latter is particularly relevant in a consideration of the *Peristephanon*.[46] The works of both authors were certainly being read in the fourth century, when the *Fasti* were particularly popular. It can be argued that Prudentius felt the influence of Propertius only through the medium of Ovid's poems which had been influenced by the Propertian precedent.[47]

Features of the works of both poets caught Prudentius' attention as suitable for adaptation to a new Christian setting, but his debt to Propertius is slight in terms of clear and direct reference to the text of the *Elegies*.[48] Some observations can be made however about structural similarities. Thus, the 'periegesis'[49] form of Propertius 4.1 may have played its part in giving Prudentius an idea for the form of *Pe.* 9 and 12 (though see below for more obvious Ovidian parallels), while the inclusion of an elegiac letter in Propertius' book may have encouraged Prudentius to choose the letter form of *Pe.* 11. The variety of poems included by Propertius in his book and the probable evolution of the book from the two commissioned poems 4. 6 and 9[50] may be suggestive for the shape of the *Peristephanon*, which could also have developed out of individually commissioned poems.

Central to many of the *Peristephanon* poems, in particular to *Pe.* 9, 11, and 12, is the poet's role as Christian pilgrim. Prudentius can most suitably take part in these poems through participation

---

[46] Rand (1920) 74; Salvatore (1958) 35 and (1959) 2, 257–72; Alexander (1936).

[47] On the background to the *Fasti*, see Kraus (1942) 1950 ff., esp. col. 1953. Also, Wilkinson (1955) 241–84, and Bömer (1957–8) vol. 1, introduction.

[48] *Pe.* 9. 3 'maxima Roma' may echo Propertius 4. 1 'maxima Roma', though cf. *Aen.* 8. 602–3 where 'maxima rerum Roma' seems more probably the model behind 'rerum maxima Roma', *Pe.* 9. 3. Also, cf. *Pe.* 9. 20, where the framing of the line by the words 'ueram fidem' may recall the identical framing at Propertius 4. 1. 98: 'fatales pueri, duo funera matris auarae!/*uera*, sed inuito, contigit ista *fides.*'

[49] See Kraus (1942) and Bömer (1957–8) 1, 25. Also Macleod (1976); Hubbard (1974) 116; Camps (1965).

[50] Hubbard (1974) 117.

in the cult for which he is helping to promote interest. The poet
becomes an example and encouragement to the reader. His role as
peregrinus to Imola and Rome represents in personalized form
(whether or not strictly autobiographical) recognition of the
value of pilgrimage to cult-centres. This finds implicit recogni-
tion elsewhere in the *Peristephanon*.[51] The involvement of the
poet-pilgrim figure also fulfils the promise of the *Praefatio*, where
the writing of Christian poetry was seen to represent a form of
Christian vocation by which the poet's 'peccatrix anima' is
encouraged: 'carmen martyribus deuoueat, laudet apostolos'. Just
as in writing anti-heretic polemic, his soul would actually be
fighting against these forces (*Praef.* 39–40: 'pugnat contra
hereses'), so praise and commemoration of the martyrs is ex-
pressed through the poet's participation in the cult within the
dramatic framework of the poems. His role as pilgrim is a humble
one, befitting the *humilitas* with which he treats himself every-
where in his poetry. It is the natural Christian extension of the tra-
ditional classical commonplace of the author's humility.[52] This is
a more natural role for the Christian poet as Spaniard abroad; it
expresses too the humble hopes of every Christian pilgrim who
prays for help at the martyrs' tombs. The poet-pilgrim's role as
the *hospes* or guest is perhaps more valuably discussed in the light
of Ovid's *Fasti*, to which Prudentius owes a more direct debt than
to Propertius.

The *Peristephanon* and Ovid's *Fasti*

The *Fasti* displays a wide variety of ways of involving the poet in
the acquisition and retailing of information about the rites and
feasts which are the subject of the poem. Ovid's involvement in a
developed dramatic role within his poem is more marked than
that of Propertius and was probably more influential in shaping
Prudentius' role as a poet-pilgrim within his poems. Prudentius is
thus indirectly more of a Callimachean than the 'Roman Callima-
chus' himself, since Ovid's practice probably represents more
fully the role of the poet in Callimachus' *Aitia*.[53] Ovid's chrono-

---

[51] For the importance of pilgrimage in the 4th century, see Hunt (1982), and Bardy
(1949).

[52] Junod-Ammerbauer (1975). See chap. 1, p. 9.

[53] Kraus (1942), 1958.

logical framework for his aetiological interests is another feature
of the *Fasti* which makes them an obvious model for Prudentius,
since the celebration of the *dies natalis* for each martyr is a vital
part of his cult. The *Pe.* might be said to aspire to play the role of a
poetic version of the Christian calendar being formulated in the
fourth century (see below, pp. 255 ff.).

There was another aspect of the Ovidian adaptation of his
Callimachean model which would have naturally answered Pru-
dentius' stylistic expectations and needs, particularly for a writer
of the fourth century, whose view of 'classical' literature was em-
bodied in the poets of the Augustan age and the early empire.
Ovid's poetry shows his attraction to that aspect of Alexandrian
baroque which encouraged the breaking-down and mixing of the
traditional genres, particularly in the field of lyric. Both the *Meta-
morphoses* and the *Fasti* cover a wide range of genres within a
single poem, and defy generic categorization.[54] With these
models and those of the Silver Age before them, writers of the
fourth century arrived at their own form of baroque. The most
classicizing authors among them strained to reproduce the classi-
cal ideal as they saw it in the earlier poets, but in doing so repro-
duced their models' perspective of the unclassical in Hellenistic
literature. This explains the Hellenistic-style lack of generic
rigidity in authors like Claudian,[55] in whose court-poetry for in-
stance, the barriers between narrative and panegyric are lowered,
or Ausonius in his poetic *jeux d'esprit*, both large and small.[56]
Ovid's freedom in the selection of material for his large-scale
poems might have provided the Christian poet with a 'classical'
confirmation for the freedom to combine a variety of elements to
form a new Christian form of lyrical ballad. By writing indi-
vidual poems about different martyrs, Prudentius may have
implicitly recognized the essential lack of unity in his model.
Ovid's clever transitions, after all, hardly transforms his long
poems into a continuous whole.[57] Prudentius' modification is
clearest in the individual dramatic episodes of *Pe.* 11 and 12, each
of which in fact represents the dramatic structure of separate epi-
sodes in the *Fasti*.

[54] Fontaine (1975a) 760 ff. and Rossi (1971); also Kroll (1924) 202 ff.
[55] Cameron (1970) 253 ff.
[56] Fontaine (1975a) 766-8.
[57] Barsby (1978) 28, 30 n. 17.

The most consistent unifying factor in the *Fasti* is the poet himself in his role within the poem and the resulting subjectivity of the narrative style. Ovid is not a detached narrator: he identifies himself with his prayers (for example *Fasti* 5. 377), offers comment to the reader (for example 2. 419) and apostrophizes the participants in his stories (for example 2. 811). Ovid here follows the precedents of Callimachus' *Aitia* and, to a lesser extent, Propertius in Book 4, although he develops it further than either. In the *Peristephanon*, this subjectivity finds a new setting in poems which look both to the tradition of classical lyric and the Christian hymn. The religious focus of the *Fasti* lives on in the *Peristephanon* in intensified form, since without doubt Prudentius is a more committed Christian than Ovid was ever a seriously committed follower of Roman religion (although his poem does have a patriotic purpose in a more general way). It is not insignificant that most of the Ovidian influence can be felt in *Pe.* 9, 11, and 12, in poems in which the greatest effort is made to combine traditional Roman patriotism with the new Christian outlook.

The acquisition of aetiological information in the *Fasti* depends on the poet's questioning of a variety of potential informants: the Muses or a god, for instance (cf. Callimachus, *Aitia*, Books 1 and 2 at least, and *Propertius* 4. 2, where the god Vertumnus explains himself), or simply a human bystander or host. Ovid goes back directly to Callimachus in his use of this question-and-answer technique.[58] Each question/answer situation, together with the resulting narrative is an individual episode within the poem as a whole. The possible influence of this structure on the Prudentian 'Fasti' poems is clear. Each poem involves the exchange of information: in *Pe.* 9, the *aedituus* of St Cassian's shrine points out the painting and explains its significance to the poet-pilgrim; in *Pe.* 11, the poet, as experienced pilgrim, describes in a letter to the Spanish bishop Valerianus the origins of the feast-day of St Hippolytus, that is, his martyrdom. He also describes the contemporary celebration of his feast, the site of the catacombs and the latest architectural additions to the cult-site; in *Pe.* 12, a native of Rome explains the feast-day of SS Peter and Paul to an unidentified pilgrim, who may be the poet-pilgrim of 11 and 9.

There are striking parallels for all these situations in the *Fasti*.

---

[58] Kraus (1942); on the nature of Callimachus' *Aitia*, see Herter (1931) 408 ff.

The interlude with the shrine attendant in *Pe.* 9 can be compared
with two passages in the *Fasti*: 4. 685 ff. and 4. 905. The proximity
of these two passages may be a significant factor in Prudentius'
conflation of them to produce the situation of *Pe.* 9. In the first
Ovidian passage, the poet visits a friend who explains to him the
origins of the custom of burning a fox at the festival of Ceres. The
episode begins:

> frigida Carseolis nec oliuis apta ferendis
>   terra, sed ad segetes ingeniosus ager;
> *hac* ego Pelignos, natalia rura, *petebam*,
>   parua, sed assiduis uuida semper aquis.

> (4. 683–6)

Pe. 9 begins with an aetiological explanation of the name of the
town, which was named after its founder, Cornelius Sulla, and
then goes on,

> *Hic* mihi cum *peterem* te, rerum maxima Roma,
>   spes est oborta prosperum Christum fore.

> (*Pe.* 9. 3–4)

The slight verbal similarity built into the also similar general out-
line of events (journey, halt on way to destination, information
given), suggests that Prudentius had the Ovidian passage in mind.
The poet, however, may not be thinking only of a single passage
here. Further on in Book 4 of the *Fasti*, the poet again pauses in
the course of another journey with words echoed by *Pe.* 9. 3
(quoted above): 'Nomento Romam cum luce redirem' (905). He
comes upon a 'candida turba' in the middle of the road, a crowd
under the supervision of a *flamen*, which is going off to celebrate
the feast of Robigo. The poet addresses the Flamen and asks what
is the meaning of the crowd. The Flamen, in reply, explains the
rites in which they are engaged. The Flamen, as religious leader
and adviser, provides the pagan counterpart to the Christian
aedituus: both are officially involved in a day-to-day capacity in
their respective rites, and both are uniquely qualified to provide
the poet with information. There are admittedly no extended
close verbal reminiscences in the Prudentian passage, but the
structure and *personae* of the scenes are strikingly similar. The
aedituus in *Pe.* 9 is *consultus*—a key verb in the *Fasti*, where the
exchange of information is the substance of the poem. So at *Fasti*

6. 425, for example, 'consulitur Smintheus ...'[59] The *aedituus* is a
suitable Christian substitute for the pagan priest or god, and in the
setting of a cult-shrine carries the attraction of a dramatically
credible member of the shrine personnel. Prudentius improves on
the Ovidian original in a striking way, since his own apparent
personal involvement in the cult in *Pe.* 9 gives the poem more
dramatic point and cohesion than either of the passages from the
Fasti.

Pe. 9 contains one feature with a background wider than that of
the *Fasti*. The description of the painting at the shrine, which is
used to embody the passion-narrative, represents a device which
has its roots in the Hellenistic tradition of the description of works
of art, particularly as an inset within another poem. This device
had found its way strikingly into Roman poetry through the
work of Catullus and Virgil.[60] Ovid had also seen its potential as a
means of giving variation to his narrative in the *Metamorphoses*,
for instance.[61] In *Pe.* 9 this literary device is given dramatic form,
with the description of the painting in the mouth of the *aedituus*.
The poet may also have in mind the Christian practice of adding
inscriptions to paintings, which he at least evokes with his own
Dittochaeon.[62] There is something of the flavour, too, of the
sepulchral epigram with its salutation of the passer-by and its bio-
graphical content.[63] The latter is particularly relevant to a
martyrdom-narrative, in the light of Pope Damasus' recently
composed elegiac inscriptions, which Prudentius had no doubt
seen in Rome.[64] All these elements combined to produce the de-
scription given by the *aedituus*, which certainly introduces a wel-

[59] Deferrari, Barry, and McGuire (1968), 355, gives other examples. Another key-
word in the *Fasti* is *celebrare* (ibid. 278–9). The *Peristephanon* makes frequent use of this
verb: *Pe.* 2. 34, 532; 3. 182; 4. 105; 11. 198.

[60] Fordyce (1961) 273–4, introduction to *C.* 64; and Gransden (1976) 161, on *Aen.* 8.
626–738 and the shield of Aeneas.

[61] See e.g. the tapestries of Arachne and Minerva in *Metamorphoses*, 6. 70–128.

[62] For instance, Paulinus of Nola tells of the verses inscribed on different parts of the
basilica at Nola in *Ep.* 32. Goldschmidt (1940: 97–8) notes that these verse-inscriptions and
those of Prudentius' *Dittochaeon* 'inaugurate a genre of inscriptions which had a great
vogue, especially in the 9th and 10th centuries'. The subject is treated by Steinmann (1892),
and also by Engemann (1974). See below, pp. 273 ff.

[63] Fordyce (1961: 273–4) cites Cicero, *Tusc.* 1. 101 (translating Simonides), Varro, *Sat.*
12. 8,, Propertius, 4. 1, and Seneca, *Ep.* 21. 10; cf. Horace, *Odes*, 1. 28, with notes in Nisbet
and Hubbard (1970) 317–20. See, too, Lattimore (1942) 266 ff.

[64] Damasus inscriptions: edited by Ferrua (1942) and Ihm (1895); cf. *Pe.* 11. 7–8: 'Plur-
ima litterulis signata sepulcra loquuntur/martyris aut nomen aut epigramma aliquod ...'

come variation in Prudentius' narrative technique in these poems. The device is thought good enough to repeat in a different setting in *Pe.* 11 where the martyrdom of Hippolytus is described in horrific detail through the medium of the description of a painting (*Pe.* 11. 123 ff.: 'exemplar sceleris paries habet inlitus ...', which recalls the spirit, if not the actual form and words, of Ovid's version of the pagan Hippolytus' death (*Metamorph.* 15. 492 ff.). Prudentius' literary sophistication in using the description of a painting device has an Ovidian feel to it. Whether or not the paintings described in fact existed is another question, which is discussed below (pp. 273 ff.).

Before returning to consideration of the relation of the *Peristephanon* to the *Fasti*, it is worth noting one more general Ovidian parallel, in connection this time with *Pe.* 11. The epistolary form and metre of this poem can be viewed partially in terms of a concern for variation of form (cf. Propertius Book 4). It can also be seen in the perspective of Ovidian elegiac letters. This emerges from the contrast felt between the described experiences of the poet abroad and the more limited experiences of the recipient. For Prudentius, however, there is a reversal of the situation: exile is transformed into the more positive experience of Christian pilgrimage. The poet's undefined troubles are now set at *home* (*Pe.* 9. 8, 104–5; *Pe.* 2. 575). The *Peristephanon* poem gives a glowingly positive account of the voluntary exile of pilgrimage.

Pe. 11's link with the *Fasti* is, however, clearer, and is emphatically established in the first line, where the phrase 'Romula in urbe' recalls Ovid's phrase:

> ... 'habeto
> tu quoque Romulea' dixit 'in urbe locum'
> (Mars speaks to Flora, *Fasti* 5. 259–60)

Pe. 11 is also striking for the poet's insistence on his personal observation and experience of what he describes to the bishop. Autopsy is repeatedly stressed: 'uidimus' (2), 'haec dum lustro oculis ... inuenio Hippolytum' (18–20), 'Rorantes saxorum apices uidi' (127). Nisbet and Hubbard in their note on Horace, *Odes*, 1. 2. 13 and the use of *uidimus* there, associate the usage with 'the appeal to experience' as a 'familiar rhetorical device', where *uidere* is often used of unpleasant experiences. Parallel passages are produced.⁶⁵ Perhaps there is something of this rhetorical device at work here, particularly in connection with the study of all the macabre and colourful detail of the painting of Hippolytus' death (127 ff.). Worth comparison is the passage at *Pe.* 4. 137 ff.: '*Vidimus* partem iecoris reuulsam/iugulis longe iacuisse pressis ...', where 'uidimus' can hardly represent an accurate historical statement, but is used rather to impress the scene vividly on the reader's imagination. As a literary device, this certainly recalls the *Fasti*, since it is impossible to know how far Ovid's apparently autobiographical statements are true concerning his presence at a wide variety of festivals. But it is much more likely that Prudentius *is* in some sense reporting the result of an actual experience of pilgrimage to Rome in his letter to the Spanish bishop.⁶⁶ Prudentius' own visits to Rome are surely relayed to the reader through *Pe.* 9, 11, and 12. Of all three poems, *Pe.* 11 can most justifiably be taken at face-value, where the poet addresses the bishop in *propria persona.*

Pe. 11 is written after the poet's return from his trip to Rome:

> Quod laetor reditu, quod te uenerande sacerdos,
>   complecti licitum est, scribo quod haec eadem,
> Hippolyto scio me debere ...

(179–81)

The poet, therefore, also resorts to references to the power of memory, which he brings to bear on the task of recalling the circumstances of his visit, and the date of St Hippolytus' feast-day:

> Sexaginta illic defossas mole sub una
>   reliquias memini me didicisse hominum ...

(13–14)

> Si bene commemini, colit hunc pulcherrima Roma ...

(231)

In the context of what must be at root an historical visit to Rome, these words carry some force, since Prudentius indeed composed this poem after the visit. They find their counterpart in Ovid's insistence on his personal memory of rites and their dates in the *Fasti*: for example, 2. 4, 'exiguum, *memini*, nuper eratis opus', and

---

⁶⁵ Nisbet and Hubbard (1970) 24.
⁶⁶ See chap. 1, p. 29, with n. 98.

3. 792, 'hac si *commemini*, praeteritaque die', where the use of an open condition reinforces the personal involvement of the potentially fallible narrator (cf. *Pe.* 11. 231). Ovid adopts this role in order to inject life and immediacy into what might become a dry catalogue. Other passages in the *Fasti* where this device is used are 4. 377, 5. 646 and 6. 237. Behind Ovid's usage is the problematical Virgilian precedent at *Georgics*, 4. 125, in connection with what Virgil claims are his memories of the old gardener of Tarentum: 'namque sub Oebaliae *memini* me turribus arcis .../Corycium uidisse senem ...'. This is strikingly the only occasion on which Virgil explicitly refers to his own experience, but doubts have been raised about the authenticity of the memory in view of the literary precedent for the passage in the two retired bee-keeping soldiers of Varro (*Res rusticae*, 3. 16. 10).[67] Whatever doubts surround the Virgilian passage, they can be doubled for the repeated use of this device in Ovid, but perhaps dismissed for Prudentius. The Christian poet's restriction of the device to a single poem suggests its reference to actual personal experience.

In *Pe.* 12, apart from the entrance of the narrator into the poem as witness of what is described, Prudentius concentrates on a completely impersonal exchange between Roman and visitor, which is introduced with an abruptness reminiscent of Propertian rather than Ovidian technique (for example Propertius 4. 1). However, although verbal parallels with the text of the *Fasti* do not abound in *Pe.* 12, the similarity of situation here and in several episodes of Ovid's poem is striking.

Pe. 12 opens with an unintroduced speaker, presumably a stranger to Rome and her feast-days, asking another unexplained character, presumably a native of the city, the meaning of the exceptional crowds on what turns out to be the double feast-day of SS Peter and Paul:

> Festus apostolici nobis redit his diec triumphi
> Pauli atque Petri nobilis cruore ...
>
>   (3–4)

---

[67] *Georgics*, 4. 125. See Bömer (1957–8), vol. 2, 80: this line is 'als Zeichen für die Erinnerung an ein kirchliches Erlebnis gewertet'. Willeumier (1930) esp. 332: 'pourquoi Virgile prendrait-il soin de nous conduire en erreur par son "memini" exceptionnel dans son œvre, que rien ne permet de suspecter et que confirment d'autres témoignages?' For example, Propertius, 2. 34. 67–8, Horace, Sat. 1. 5, and Servius on *Georgics*, 4. 125. See also Williams (1979) on *Georgics*, 4. 125, and Wilkinson (1969) 178.

The dramatic device of question and answer recalls its recurrence in Ovid, although here the abruptness of the poem's opening lends it an impersonality which the Ovidian versions do not achieve. The poet is clearly present throughout the episodes of the *Fasti* as observer and questioner. Prudentius, however, chooses barely to suggest a dramatic framework in *Pe.* 12. The questioner might be identified with the poet in the role of the pilgrim, who appears more clearly in *Pe.* 9 and 11, but this identification is not important for the poem; more important is the presentation of a setting designed specifically to provide the opportunity to tell of the double martyrdom and feast-day of the Apostles. Prudentius' technique here is reminiscent, too, of Propertius 4. 1, where the figure of the *hospes* loses importance in the poem once his dramatic usefulness has been exploited.

The question-answer structure has numerous parallels in the *Fasti*. At 4. 769, the host-native points to the surrounding countryside (the native is on home ground, as in *Pe.* 12), and tells Ovid the story of the burning fox and its significance for the festival of Ceres. At 4. 377, an old man sitting next to Ovid at the games explains how he earned his seat through service under Caesar. At 6. 395 ff., an old woman whom Ovid meets on his way home during the festival of Vesta explains the history of the site of the Fora. Each of these exchanges of information forms a separate episode which corresponds to the individual poems of the *Peristephanon*. The feast-day setting in the last two passages from the *Fasti* is recalled in *Pe.* 12 and also in *Pe.* 11. There are also passages in the *Fasti* which give detailed and lively descriptions of feast-day scenes, for example, 3. 525–42, the description of revelry at the feast of Anna Perenna, and 1. 78 ff., where the description of a festival celebration going on under the speaker's eyes provides an interesting parallel for the immediacy of the feast-day described at the end of *Pe.* 12.[68]

In conclusion, I would like to point out two more general Ovidian touches in the *Peristephanon*. Firstly, the recurrence of *fama* in both authors' works is noticeable. This is partly, of course, the result of the nature of the subject-matter in both cases, where tradition has often to be relied on. One case, however, seems to

---

[68] Bömer (1957–8) vol. 2, 15 on *Fasti* 1. 75 ff. as an ἔκφρασις on a Roman feast-day.

offer a clearer case of Prudentian borrowing. In telling of the Fabii at *Fasti* 2. 203–4, Ovid says:

> illa *fama refert* Fabios exisse trecentos;
>   porta uacat culpa, sed tamen omen habet.

In *Pe.* 13. 76 Prudentius says, in connection with the 'massa candida':

> *fama refert* foueam campi in medio patere iussam

The similarity of phrasing is striking,[69] and reinforced by the context: Ovid speaks of the three hundred who went out to their death and Prudentius numbers the Christians who made up the 'massa candida' at three hundred (83), in spite of the actual uncertainty surrounding the number in other sources.[70] Again, the personified 'Fama' of *Pe.* 1. 11 seems Ovidian in spirit, if not identifiable by definite reminiscence:

> Fama nam terras in omnes percucurrit proditrix
>   hic patronos esse mundi.[71]

Perhaps another Ovidian touch may be discerned in Prudentius' naming of himself as poet at the end of *Pe.* 2:

> Audi benignus supplicem
> Christi reum Prudentium,
> et seruientem corpori
> absolue uinclis saeculi!

>   (581–4)

---

[69] The phrase does not occur in this form in any other earlier authors whom Prudentius read; that is: Horace, Virgil, Lucan, Statius, Propertius, Lucretius, Ausonius. It is, however, a favourite phrase of Ovid: it occurs not only at *Fasti*, 2. 203, but also at *Tristia*, 5. 12. 12; *Pont.* 3. 2. 51 and 4. 3. 28. Other examples of *fama* in the *Peristephanon* are to be found at *Pe.* 1. 11, 74; 2. 541; 10. 189, 225. *Fama* appears in the *Fasti* at 2. 237; 3. 168; 3. 662; 4. 145, 311; 5. 84, 625; 6. 104, 557.

[70] In speaking about the Massa Candida, Augustine puts their number at 'more than one hundred and fifty-three' (*PL* 36. 571: 'Solo in proximo quae dicitur Massa Candida plus habet quam centum quinquaginta tres martyres'), cf. *Sermo* 306: 'In natali martyrum Massae Candidae', *PL* 38. 1400–5; *Sermo* 311, *PL* 38. 1417; and *Enarr. in psalm.* 49. 9. = *PL* 36. 571. See Lavarenne (1963b) 184–5.

[71] Cf. Ovid, *Metam.* 9. 137; 12. 43 ff. A personified *Fama* of course, also has a Virgilian precedent, for example, *Aen.* 4. 173, 666; 7. 104.

This *sphragis* is set in the form of a prayer and could recall a similar prayer of Ovid at *Fasti* 5. 377–9:

> floreat ut toto carmen Nasonis in aeuo,
> sparge, precor, donis pectora nostra tuis.

The poet here addresses the goddess Flora. The prayers of the two poets are, however, very different. Ovid looks for the immortality of his verse, Prudentius for his own eternal salvation as Christian. In the *Praefatio* he sees his role as Christian poet as part of his claim to salvation (*Praef.* 43–5), but never hopes that the products of his poetic vocation should also win immortality. The pagan poet can only hope to win immortality through his poetry: the Christian wins salvation which takes him beyond the importance of such worldly and ephemeral trivia.[72]

Prudentius the Christian Augustan

In the previous section I have tried to show that there is some evidence to suggest that Prudentius was aware of the forms and techniques of presentation of material in the aetiological poems of Propertius Book 4 and Ovid's *Fasti*. This is particularly clear in those poems of the *Peristephanon* which have a clear Roman focus and the most sophisticated dramatic form (*Pe.* 9, 11, and 12). These poems form the kernel of a collection which seems to reflect and extend the calendar-interests of the *Fasti* in Christian form. The topographical and religious preoccupations of Propertius and Ovid both lend themselves to the importance of the physical presence of martyrial remains emphasized in each poem, and particularly in the 'Roman' poems. In the next section, an attempt will be made to show that Prudentius' interest in the Propertian and Ovidian originals is not superficial or simply literary at the formal level. As *Pe.* 9–12 suggest, it is the patriotic preoccupations of the Augustan poets which have caught Prudentius' attention. They provide him with the basis for his own expression of a renewed Christian consciousness of an empire still centred emotionally and historically on Rome. By focusing on this aspect of Prudentius' poems below, I shall attempt to show the ways in

---

[72] On the *sphragis*, see Bömer (1957–8) 2. 313 at 5. 377. He cites Callimachus fr. 7, 13 (Pfeiffer) and the ends of Books 1 and 2 of the *Ars Amatoria*. See also Kießling (1929) and Kranz (1961).

which the Christian poet adapts and assimilates not only the expressions, but also the values of this earlier Latin poetry.

Rome, for Prudentius, can now be seen as the head of an empire, founded providentially by Christ for the promotion of universal conversion.[73] Rome's traditional greatness has been re-established and set on a new and more secure footing by her overwhelming richness in the remains of the new heroes of the empire, the martyrs, and the new monuments in their memory which now decorate Christian Rome (*Pe.* 11. 215 ff. and 12. 31 ff.). This new empire-wide patriotism could, to some extent, be countered by the individual and local pride of Spanish towns over their martyrs. This is apparent in Saragossa's anxiety to keep her claims on St Vincent, although he did not suffer martyrdom in his native city:

> *Noster est*, quamuis procul hinc in urbe
> passus ignota dederit sepulcri
> gloriam uictor prope litus altae
>   forte Sagynti.
>
> (*Pe.* 4. 97–100)

In general, however, Prudentius encourages a wider awareness of the martyrs as belonging to and uniting Christians everywhere. In *Pe.* 1, this point is stressed in connection with SS Emeterius and Chelidonius:

> Exteri nec non et orbis huc colonus aduenit,
> fama nam terras in omnes percucurrit proditrix
> hic patronos esse mundi, quos precantes ambiant.
>
> (*Pe.* 1. 10–14)

So, too, Prudentius comforts those Spaniards who are distant from the remains of St Lawrence in Rome:

> Sed qui caremus his bonis
> nec sanguinis uestigia
> uidere coram possumus,
> caelum intuemur eminus.
>
> (*Pe.* 2. 545–9)

Fructuosus in *Pe.* 6 says he will pray to Christ '*cunctis* pro populis'

---

[73] Cf. *Contra Symmachum*, 1. 580 ff. Also *Pe.* 2. 423–36; and Paschoud (1967).

(84).[74] But it is Rome with her exceptional richness in martyrs which cannot help but provide an earthly focus for a Christian patriotism which represents both an assimilation and an extension of the traditional view. At the literary level, it is most appropriate for the new enthusiasm of this Christian patriotism to be expressed through the forms and language of Augustan poetry. Both periods inspired their poets as the beginning of a new Golden Age of peace, security and unity, based on right regard for divine power in conjunction with overall moral regeneration. In this situation, Prudentius naturally realizes the relevance to his own poetic brief of the two Augustan poets who were most sincerely concerned to voice the new ideals, that is, Virgil and Horace.

In considering the importance of these poets to Prudentius, I would like to concentrate on examination of the more dynamic, conceptual end of the scale. In the *Peristephanon*, this revolves around one major theme: the new Christian form of patriotism, with its corresponding focus on Christian Rome. In close connection with this can be taken the new perspective on the Christian heroes which contributes to the legitimacy of the new patriotism. The traditional patriotic emotions centred on Rome were still very much alive in the second half of the fourth century. This finds expression in the importance attached to visits to Rome by the emperor,[75] and in the strong attachment to the old capital felt by the Roman aristocracy. This focus could now be maintained in a consciousness of Rome's richness in martyrs and her preeminence as a place of pilgrimage. The promotion in this period of the feast day of SS Peter and Paul deliberately encouraged a Christian perspective on Roman patriotism.[76]

These interlocking themes of heroism and patriotism, based on the key concept of *pietas*, with all this implies, are central to the Augustan epic of Virgil. It is therefore not surprising to discover that it is Virgil's *Aeneid* which is most often imitated in the *Peristephanon*. The patriotism of the *Georgics* finds a smaller but no less

[74] This prayer does, however, reproduce an identical prayer in the authentic prose *Acta* (in Musurillo (1972: 181): 'Passio Sanctorum Martyrum Fructuosi Episcopi, Auguri et Eulogii Diaconorum' 3. 6). See below, chap. 7, p. 218.

[75] Paschoud (1967) 11: 'La plupart des empereurs visitèrent en grande pompe ce qui demeurait le centre idéal de l'empire. See, for example, Ammianus Marcellinus, *RG* 16. 10.

[76] Paschoud (1967) 9–21; Piétri (1961); Klingner (1961) 645.

important place. In both poems, it is noticeably on passages of the
highest patriotic interest and intensity that Prudentius concen-
trates his attention in channelling the Virgilian enthusiasm for the
Augustan régime into the new enthusiasm for the Christian rule
of Theodosius.[77] The epic side of the celebration of Christian
heroes is balanced to some extent by its lyric presentation: Pru-
dentius' debt to Horace is also clear and does not exist only at a
purely formal level.[78] Horace's 'Augustanism', too, becomes part
of Prudentius' vision of a rejuvenated Rome (Contra Symmachum,
1. 504 ff.).

Prudentius seems most concerned to recall his Augustan fore-
bears in those poems which have the most clearly Roman focus,
that is, Pe. 2, 9, 11, and 12.[79] The secular history of Rome had
found its fullest expression in the Aeneid as far as the Romans of
the Late Empire were concerned. When the poets of this period
called on the words of the Aeneid in their own poetry, it was not
simply because of an incapacity to express themselves with any
originality and without the use of Virgilian clichés, but rather
because all the important political events of their own period
were necessarily seen in the perspective of episodes in the national
epic. In recognizing the Christian Empire in his poetry in Virgil-
ian terms, Prudentius makes it clear that Roman power is not a
gift from Jupiter, but a spiritual strength acquired by the Chris-
tian Emperor. Although the poet contests the power of Jupiter, he
accepts the Virgilian promise of eternity for the Empire, insofar as
it protects the Christian Rome.[80] All this is expressed through the
evocation and adaptation of key Virgilian passages. It emerges
strikingly outside the Peristephanon, in a passage in Contra Symma-
chum, 1. 541 ff., where the poet enumerates for a converted Rome
the benefits bestowed on her by her Christian Emperor, 'quantum
praecipuus nostro sub tempore princeps/prospexit tribuitque
boni' (528–9). At 541–4 he ends the passage:

---

[77] Thus there is a higher concentration of reminiscences from Aen. 1, 6, 7, and 8, and
they key patriotic passages within these books.

[78] This is well brought out by Salvatore (1958) 59 ff.

[79] Dexel (1907) does not include Pe. 12 in his list of poems which show particularly
high concentration of Virgilian reminiscences, but he does not seem to take the relative
length of the poems he deals with into account. Pe. 12 is one of the shortest poems of the
collection (60 lines only). He does mention Pe. 3 in this list: the number of Virgilian remin-
iscences here is high through a concern to portray the martyr-heroine in epic colours.

[80] Courcelle (1976).

> denique nec metas statuit nec tempora ponit:
> imperium sine fine docet, ne Romula uirtus
> iam sit anus, norit ne gloria parta senectam.

Prudentius here refers to the climactic passage of Jupiter's prophecy in *Aeneid*, 1, in particular 279–80, which is now given a new tone and import in the context of a Rome aware of the 'tumulorum milia circum', the constant witness to the new glory won by 'sanguine iustorum' (*Contra Symmachum*, 1. 513–16).[81]

Outside the 'Roman' poems of the *Peristephanon*, less effort is made to evoke the larger patriotic ideals of the Augustan poets by 'significant' verbal reminiscence. The strong local patriotic element (in *Pe.* 4, for instance) does not rouse the poet to such constant emulation of the Augustans. This may, of course, be the result of the influence of the poet's purely Christian source for any martyr (see, for instance, the relation of *Pe.* 6 to the historical *Acta*, analysed below in Chapter 7), and may also reflect the literary interest and tastes of the patron for any poem. In many of the non-Roman poems, however, Virgilian reminiscences are used to establish the epic stature of the martyr and his struggle.

Peristephanon 2

Although the narrative interest centres on the arrest and martyrdom of Lawrence, several passages which stand outside the simple account point to a preoccupation of the poet with the wider questions raised by the existence of a Christianized Empire. The fact that Lawrence is a Roman martyr gives Prudentius the chance to consider this new role of the imperial city with all its implications for the evolution of a new Christian patriotism centred on Rome. The traditional patriotism had had a religious dimension: Rome's greatness had been god-given. Prudentius here tries to show how this is still true, but in a *Christian* sense, and chooses to make Lawrence's martyrdom mark a turning-point in the conversion of Rome to Christianity:

> Refrixit ex illo die
> cultus deorum turpium:
> plebs in sacellis rarior,
> Christi ad tribunal curritur.

> (*Pe.* 2. 497 ff.)

---

[81] Cf. *Contra Symmachum*, 1. 587, and *Aen.* 6. 794 ff., 806 and 890.

The martyr in his final speech and prayer voices Prudentius' own view of an empire founded providentially for the promotion of Christianity. He invoked Christ as 'auctor horum moenium',

> qui sceptra Romae in uertice
> rerum locasti . . .
> Hoc destinatum, quo magis
> ius Christiani nominis,
> quodcumque terrarum iacet,
> uno inligaret uinculo.
>
> (*Pe*. 2. 417 ff.)

He prays 'sit christiana ut ciuitas' and, secure in the knowledge that 'hic nempe iam regnant duo apostolorum principes' (that is, SS Peter and Paul), he prophesies a 'futurum principem' (473), who can only be Theodosius. In other words, in this poem Prudentius is interested in expressing more than simply St Lawrence's martyrdom: he wants to make an optimistic statement about the conversion of Rome which has been officially completed in his own day and about his Christian view of this as the climax of Rome's imperial history.

This interest is concentrated in the five-stanza introduction to the martyrdom narrative (21 ff.), and in Lawrence's final prayer (431 ff.) with its prophecy of Rome's future conversion in the reign of Theodosius. The poem's opening stanzas throw into relief Lawrence's achievements through martyrdom by contrasting them, in juxtaposition, with Rome's apparent achievements of the past. Each four-line stanza contains a contrast betwen past forms of glory and the present truer glory of the martyrs. In the first stanza Rome is addressed with high patriotic emotion by means of a personification: '*Antiqua* fanorum parens'. She is Christian now, however: '*iam* Roma Christo dedita'. Here the past/present, pagan/Christian opposition is clear. Rome is now 'Laurentio uictrix duce', but her 'triumph' ('triumphas') is over the 'ritum . . . barbarum', an unexpected form of triumph from the point of view of ordinary worldly imperial history. The next stanza opens (5–6) with a more traditional view of Rome's success in the past:

> Reges supervos uiceras
> populosque frenis presseras.

But again, the stanza ends with a strong contrast, which is intro-
duced by the emphatic 'nunc':

> *nunc* monstruosis idolis
> imponis imperii iugum.
>
> (7–8)

The next stanza starts again with the traditional terminology of
success, 'gloria', but now the poet refers to the only glory *lacking*
'urbis togatae insignibus', that is, the glory which resides in
defeating paganism. The poet returns for the third time to a
theme introduced in each stanza so far. The fourth stanza tells
how the triumph over paganism is to be achieved:

> *non* turbulentis uiribus
> Cossi, Camilli aut Caesaris,
> *sed* martyris Laurentii
> non incruento proelio.

A contrast appears here again between the past ideas of heroic tri-
umph and the different demands of the new situation.

In this passage, Prudentius is trying to show how far the spir-
itual triumph represented by the victory of martyrdom is an
extension of traditional Roman values of courage, glory and
achievement. Prudentius stretches the traditional vocabulary in
order to do this: so Rome will be 'uictrix', but on the spiritual
plane; Lawrence is to be the *dux* to help her to achieve her *triumph*
(now a spiritual one), over barbarian gods. In the context of
'uictrix' and 'triumphas', there may be some play on Lawrence's
name, and its possible associations with the victor's 'laurea': so
Lawrence will become part of Rome's triumphal garland of mar-
tyrs, an image which Prudentius also uses for a city at *Pe.* 4. 22 ff.:

> Tu *tribus gemmis diadema pulchrum*
> *offeres Christo*, genetrix piorum
> Tarraco, intexit cui Fructuosus
> sutile uinclum.

He continues this image at *Pe.* 4. 53 ff.:[82]

---

[82] The crown of victory was, of course, the martyr's traditional prize. See St Paul, Eph.
6. 10–19; Rom. 13. 12; 1 Cor. 9. 5, and cf. Cyprian, *Ep.* 10. The image finds its place in the
title given to this collection of poems, and recurs throughout the poems in descriptions of
the triumphant martyrs. For example, *Pe.* 2. 276; 4. 73; 5. 4, 526; 6. 25; 4. 20; 10. 71 and 14.
119. The subject is treated by Brożek (1954), 137–8, with bibliography.

Tu decem sanctos reuehes et octo,
Caesaraugusta studiosa Christo,
uerticem flauis oleis reuincta
        pacis honore . . .

The passage in *Pe*. 2 is, however, particularly interesting for the
way in which it draws on one of the most famous passages in the
Aeneid, the patriotic fervour of which provides the basis for Pru-
dentius' promotion of his Christian patriotic ideal. *Aeneid* 6.
756 ff. is the passage in question, where Anchises explains the
'pageant of heroes' to his son Aeneas in the underworld.[83] Aeneas
here is fired with love for the Rome he is to found by a vision of
her future kings and heroes. Throughout the passage, emphasis is
laid on the coming *imperium*: the repetition of this word at regular
intervals almost becomes a refrain (782, 795, 812), with its climax
in the famous injunction of 851. In describing the succession of
figures, Anchises gives a roughly chronological survey of Roman
history from the earliest kings: Silvius Aeneas is introduced (765)
as 'regem regumque parentem'. An anachronistic centre-piece in-
troduces Augustus as a key point, significantly introduced by way
of the founder-hero, Romulus. Anchises then returns to a series of
kings until 'Tarquinios reges animamque superbam/ultoris Bruti'
(817–18). This is followed by a brief review of some of the names
associated with the establishment of empire: 'Decios, Drusosque
procul saeuumque securi ... Torquatum et referentem signa
Camillum'. Pompey and Caesar introduce a more pessimistic
note. Though unnamed, they arouse unhappy thoughts of the
turmoil of civil war. The passage draws to a close with a brief
catalogue of the achievements of Memmius, Cato, Cossus, the
Gracchi, the Scipios, Fabricius, and Fabius Maximus, inserted in a
series of apostrophes which sets the right heightened emotional
tone for the famous climax of the pageant, ending with the in-
junction:

> tu regere *imperio populos*, Romane, memento
> (hae tibi erunt artes), pacique *imponere* morem,
> parcere subiectis et debellare *superbos*.
>
> (*Aeneid*, 6. 851–4)

---

[83] This reference to Virgil was not discussed by Thraede (1973). Some aspects are dealt
with by Buchheit (1966).

It has seemed worth-while recalling this well-known passage in some detail in order the better to be able to demonstrate how Prudentius recalls it in the first twenty lines of *Pe.* 2.

Prudentius' technique here is not one of continuous, exact verbal parallel. Instead, he uses key words from a restricted passage in the original in order to promote his own ideas, thereby gaining both the support of the original context and an inevitable contrast with the new. So, in line 5 in the second stanza, Prudentius conflates the rather unexpectedly separated 'reges' and 'superbia' of *Aeneid,* 6. 817–18, in order to arrive at his own 'reges superbos'. The 'superbos' may also owe something to *Aeneid,* 6. 854, quoted above, since *Pe.* 2. 6–8 seems to evoke the vocabulary used in the lines central to the Virgilian imperial vision (851–4). Hence, Prudentius' use of 'populos' in the context of Roman conquest, and the idea of 'imponere imperii iugum'. The context of *Pe.* 2 requires a readjustment of this vision from *Aeneid* 6. In Virgil, the reality of empire is set in potential terms—this was what the Augustan age was still in the process of achieving. After centuries of empire, Prudentius can put this achievement firmly in the past: 'reges superbos *uiceras*/populosque frenis *presseras . . .'.* In doing this, he certainly does not try to devalue imperial rule. But, as Lawrence himself remarks later in this same poem, Christ is now to be considered as the 'auctor horum moenium' (*Pe.* 2. 416), who founded the empire to make a world-wide and united Christendom possible (*Pe.* 2. 417–32). In *Aeneid* 6, Augustus replaces Romulus as the second founder of a renewed Rome; in *Pe.* 2 and for Prudentius in general, Christ now replaces Augustus as the true founder of the Christian empire and can be described in the same terms.

In the passage from *Pe.* 2, Prudentius is at pains to point out the contrast between past worldly victories and the present need to achieve *imperium* over 'monstruosis idolis' (*Pe.* 2. 7). This phrase itself ironically recalls another 'imperial' passage from the *Aeneid*: the scenes from the divine shield of Aeneas which is delivered and described at the end of Book 8. Here, the battle of Actium is commemorated. Augustus' victory is seen not only in terms of his battle against Cleopatra, but also in terms of a 'theomachy', in which the Roman gods join battle with the outlandish and bestial Egyptian gods. These are described collectively (699) as 'omnigenumque deum *monstra*'. The Roman gods, by contrast, represent a noble anthropomorphic picture. Prudentius evokes this passage subtly with his adjective 'monstruosus' for the pagan gods. But he turns the picture from *Aeneid* 8 on its head, since now all the traditional Roman gods must be regarded as 'monstra' in comparison with the one true God. And it is these traditional gods who are now defeated in turn by Rome's conversion to Christianity. A further indication that Prudentius had this Virgilian passage in mind might be found later in *Pe.* 2 when the martyr alludes to the traditional gods as 'tot monstra deum' (451).

Thus, *imperium* now acquires a completely spiritual value. In the opening stanza, Rome was to celebrate a triumph—but one in the religious sphere, one over 'ritum ... barbarum'. The passage from *Aeneid* 6 sinks from view in the third stanza (9–12), although another context of patriotic prophecy is drawn upon in the phrase 'urbis togatae' (10). This should be read in the light of *Aeneid*, 1. 282, where Jupiter prophesies to Venus the glorious future of her son's descendants and refers to the Romans as 'rerum dominos gentemque togatam'. Prudentius was certainly sufficiently aware of this phrase (he also uses it at *Contra Symmachum*, 1. 35), to vary it consciously to produce its form in *Pe.* 2, used again at *Pe.* 12. 56. The verb 'domare' at *Pe.* 2. 12 reflects the use of 'dominabitur' at *Aeneid*, 1. 285. It must be noted that Prudentius has an important point to make in drawing on patriotic Virgilian passages of prophecy at the opening of *Pe.* 2. He is setting the achievement of Christianity in terms of what was still, for the Roman reader, the definitive expression of Roman patriotism. By building his own statement of the Christian patriotic ideal for Rome around the Virgilian frame, Prudentius assimilates the well-known and well-worn values in a way which makes clear their continued worth in modified Christian form. The setting of prophecy is made explicitly relevant towards the end of the poem in Lawrence's prophetic prayer (413 ff.).

Before leaving the third stanza, it is worth looking at line 11 more closely:

> haec sola derat gloria
> urbis togatae insignibus,
> *feritate capta gentium*
> domaret ut spurcum Iouem.
>
> (9–12)

Here there seems to be an attempt to recall a famous Horatian pas-
sage (*Ep.* 2. 1. 156–7), where he alludes to the civilizing influence
which Rome's conquest of Greece had on her cultural life:

> Graecia capta ferum uictorem cepit et artis
> intulit agresti Latio . . .

The words 'feritas' and 'capta' in such close proximity in the Pru-
dentian passage recall the Horatian context, but are used to make
a very different point. It is now no longer cultural matters but re-
ligious which are in question. Rome may no longer be 'fera' in the
worldly sense, but the 'feritas' of her gods must be subdued
('feritas' here recalls the adjective 'monstruosus' used of the gods
in line 7). Christianity here is portrayed obliquely as the new
civilizing force by this subtle evocation of the Horatian lines.

With the fourth stanza, Prudentius is undoubtedly once more
involved in the passage from *Aeneid* 6. The poet explains how the
new spiritual form of victory is to be gained. To do this he begins
the stanza with a negative statement which recalls by name the
heroes usually associated with Rome's imperial greatness:

> non turbulentis uiribus
> Cossi, Camilli aut Caesaris,
> sed martyris Laurentii
> non incruento proelio.
>
> (13–16)

This effectively alliterative combination of Roman names must
surely have its roots in the citing of these figures as part of Rome's
hopes for an imperial future within a similarly limited scope in
Aeneid 6. So here Camillus is named at 825, Cossus is addressed at
841, and Caesar is addressed without being named at 834, in the
context of civil war:

> ne, pueri, ne tanta animis adsuescite bella
> neu patriae ualidas in uiscera uertite uiris . . .
>
> (832–3)

This troubled context is perhaps recalled in Prudentius' passage
with the words '*turbulentis* uiribus' ('uiribus' points back to 'uiris'
in the Virgilian passage). 'Turbulentis' is an adjective commonly
used of civil disturbance[84] and might seem a rather strange choice

---

[84] Lewis and Short's *Latin Dictionary* gives some examples of this usage under: 'turbu-
lentus, II'.

of adjective to use of Cossus and Camillus in view of Prudentius' general approval and acceptance of past imperial successes. The disapproving tone of the adjective here is likely to stem from the introduction of Caesar and memóries of 'vires' put to bad use as they are recalled in the Virgilian passage. The harsh alliteration of 'c' in the Romans' names, together with the judgement implicit in the choice of adjective for their achievements points to the poet's new perspective on Rome's apparent past glories. There seems no need to identify Caesar with Augustus, or to connect this reminiscence of Virgil with *Aeneid*, 6. 789–92, where the name 'Caesar' probably does refer to Augustus.[85] Such a connection neglects the disapproving tone of 'turbulentis uiribus', which is surely better-suited to Julius Caesar and the reference to civil wars at *Aeneid*, 6. 826 ff., particularly as this falls between the mention of Camillus and Cossus in the Virgilian passage. Proximity there facilitated transposition to a new context.

A parallel has been seen between Lawrence and Augustus as the inaugurators of a new age. More useful is comparison of the 'catalogue of heroes' with the Horatian version or with the custom of citing the *exempla maiorum* in the *laudatio funebris*.[86] The importance of this background to 13–16 lies in the general point which Prudentius seems to be making: the final and true glory for Rome to win by rejecting the old gods necessitates a new form of Christian hero, the martyr. He fights for very different ends and he is, in one sense, involved in a 'caelestis militia' which is the antithesis of the worldly 'turbulentis uiribus' of *Pe.* 2. 14. There is a clear contrast between Augustus' rule, won by war and bloodshed, and Christ's 'Kingdom of Peace'.[87] Yet, Prudentius is dealing with more here than a clear opposition of ideals. Lawrence may replace Augustus as the climax of a 'catalogue of heroes', but he fits the progress of the catalogue just as well as Augustus, in the sense that his victory is won 'non incruento proelio', as Prudentius puts it, with ironic understatement. Lawrence betters the pagan heroes even on their own terms, as the next stanza drives home, with its emphasis on the bloody struggles of a now abstract 'armata ... fides' (17). The Christian martyr is not simply a poor substitute

---

[85] This identification is discussed by Austin (1977) 243.

[86] Buchheit (1966) 129. Horace: see *Odes*, 1. 12 and Nisbet and Hubbard (1970) 144–5, with notes on the traditional *exempla maiorum*.

[87] Buchheit (1966) 129.

for the traditional heroes, but a full replacement qualified to match the virtues of ancient heroism. To a large extent they fight on the same terms for much the same stakes, life or death. But death for the martyr is only the start of a new and glorious heavenly existence. Christian writers apart from Prudentius also recognized the heroic traits of their own martyrs and compared them favourably with well-known Roman heroes like Regulus and Mucius Scaevola.[88]

Thus Prudentius provokes reminiscence of the Virgilian passage only to suggest that now is the time for a change of view on the old concepts of *imperium* and *gloria*: the old values are not to be completely invalidated or devalued, but are given a new spiritual force. Earthly *imperium* is still important, but only insofar as it facilitates spiritual *imperium* over the forces of evil. Prudentius' reluctance to relinquish or devalue earthly *imperium* appears strikingly at the end of *Pe.* 2, where he gives a picture of St Lawrence enjoying his heavenly reward:

> Illic inenarrabili
> allectus urbi municeps
> aeternae in arce curiae
> gestas *coronam ciuicam.*
>
> Videor uidere inlustribus
> gemmis coruscantem uirum,
> quem *Roma caelestis* sibi
> legit *perennem consulem.*

> (553–60)

A vivid picture is painted, drawing on some of the traditional terminology of Roman rule: Lawrence is described as 'consul' in the heavenly Rome, he wears the 'corona civica'. Prudentius converts these Roman honours to their Christian setting in a completely new way, establishing a novel set of associations. Prudentius is the first to coin the phrase 'Roma caelestis', the first to see the martyr as the heavenly consul and the first to equate his martyr's crown with its earthly counterpart, the 'corona civica'.[89] In this accumu-

---

[88] Regulus is cited by Augustine, *De ciu. dei*, 1. 15, and Octavius by Minucius Felix at *Octavius*, 37, where Mucius Scaevola also appears.

[89] Buchheit (1966) 143 discusses the *corona civica*, but does not bring out the suitability of this decoration for the martyr, who in any case, expects a *corona caelestis* as the reward for martyrdom. *Corona* is used in this context at Augustine, *De ciu. dei*, 8. 27 and Damasus, *Epigram* 47 (Ihm (1895) 50). On Prudentius' novel idea of the heavenly consul, see

lation of traditional language may lie an attempt to hint at
Lawrence's role as a Christian Augustus: the consulship and the
'corona civica' had special meaning for Augustus.[90] But perhaps
more significant is the complete picture of the 'Roma caelestis'
which far outshines its earthly counterpart, yet which also con-
tributes a new spiritual dimension to the centre of the Christian
world. The earthly system of rule with its hierarchy and honours
(cf. *Pe.* 2. 517–28) finds some justification in Prudentius' picture of
its heavenly version. Implicit in this picture is the added weight
given to the position of the emperor on earth. He is now the
counterpart of God in Heaven: 'te minor laetum reget aequus
orbem', in the words of Horace's prayer at the end of *Odes*, 1. 12,
where 'te' refers to Jupiter. Such an idea of a 'Roma caelestis' can
only exist because of the poet's certainty of the Christian status of
its worldly reflection.

In the next stanza, Lawrence's gruesome struggle, only hinted
at in line 16, is set against the wider context of a battle waged by
the whole of Christianity: 'Armata pugnauit Fides ...'. This per-
sonified abstraction may come indirectly from *Aeneid*, 1. 292,
where 'cana Fides et Vesta, Remo cum fratre Quirinus/iura
dabunt'. Prudentius uses the expression 'cana Fides' at *Hamarti-
genia*, 853, but here uses the developed picture of a 'pugnatura
Fides' which he uses in the *Psychomachia* at line 22. The word *Fides*
in *Pe.* 2 may also have a Christian precedent in the Damasan in-
scription for Lawrence which records:

> uerbera, carnifices, flamina, tormenta, catenas,
> *uincere* Laurentii *sola fides* potuit.
>
> (Ihm, no. 32, pp. 37–8)

Prudentius prepares for the simpler martyr-narrative by closing
these introductory stanzas with two alliterative and riddlingly
expressed lines (2. 19–20), one of which refers to St Paul's Letter
to the Hebrews (2. 14). This passage sums up the basic Christian
paradox of Christ's victory over the power of death, won by his

---

Cameron (1968*b*). Dr Adrian Hollis has suggested as a possible parallel here Horace, *Odes*,
4. 9. 39–40 where Lollius is addressed as 'consulque *non unius anni*,/sed quotiens bonus
atque fidus/index honestum praetulit utili ...'

[90] Austin (1977) 273, gives the background for the *corona civica* as a military decoration.
Augustus mentions it in his *Res gestae*: 'corona civica super ianuam meam fixa est' Brunt
and Moore (1975) 34.

own death. The martyr's achievement is in this way viewed in its truest and widest perspective as Prudentius moves away from the rather controversial content of his introduction to the simplicity of the martyrdom narrative itself.

He returns to the more general question of Rome's new role as a Christian power in Lawrence's prophetic prayer (413 ff.), in which the martyr prays for the conversion of Rome and predicts the coming of a *princeps* (that is, Theodosius), who will finalize the Christianization of the empire by closing the pagan temples (473 ff.). This passage has been thoroughly analysed in comparison with the structure, and some of the content, of Jupiter's prophecies from *Aeneid* 1 and 12.[91] Verbal reminiscence at key points underlies the parallels. The address to Christ as world-ruler at *Pe.* 2. 413 ff. can be compared with the address to Jupiter at *Aeneid* 1. 229, '... o qui res hominumque deumque/aeternis regis imperiis ...'. Reference can also here be made to some Virgilian uses of the word 'auctor'. At *Aeneid*, 5, 17, Jupiter himself is termed 'auctor' for instance. There is clearly some parallel of thought at *Pe.* 2. 417–28 and *Aeneid*, 1. 264 and 12. 834. Jupiter's prophecy of unity of speech and culture for the Romans finds it true fulfilment in the Christian empire, the founding of which it was designed to facilitate. The emphasis on the peacefulness of the Christian empire at *Pe.* 2. 437 ff., reflects *Aeneid*, 1. 291 ff.: 'aspera tum positis *mitescent* saecula bellis ...'. The verb *mitescent* finds its counterpart in the repetition of 'mansuescere' in the Prudentian passage. That Peter and Paul should replace Romulus and Remus in Prudentius' vision of Christian Rome fits in with contemporary propaganda.

One significant verbal reminiscence should not escape notice in an examination of Lawrence's speech. It ends with the phrase: 'Hic finis orandi fuit ...'. This is admittedly, to some extent, a formulaic ending for a speech (and, in this sense, a 'trivial' reminiscence lending a general epic flavour), but is also a reminder of *Aeneid*, 10. 116, where the phrase 'hic finis fandi' closes the speech of Jupiter at the 'Council of the Gods'. This reminiscence thus supports the view that Lawrence's speech has the same weight in its Prudentian context as the prophecies of Jupiter.

On the other 'Roman' poems, *Pe.* 9 offers little of interest in the present discussion apart from line 3, where Rome is described as

[91] Buchheit (1966), 138–41, with a detailed analysis on 140.

'rerum maxima' in a phrase recalling *Aeneid*, 7. 602. In the *Aeneid*, this description of Rome is used in an aetiological passage programmatic by its position for the increasing presence of Rome in the background of the poem as Aeneas moves through Italy towards the actual site of Rome. In the *Peristephanon* poem, there is unfortunately no hint given about the purpose of the poet's visit to Rome. If it is completely a matter of pilgrimage, then Rome as 'rerum maxima' in Christian terms could be seen as an extension of the Virgilian patriotic description. But nothing tells us exactly what the poet means when he rejoices that 'dextris successibus utor' in Rome. He may be engaged on either public or private business—he is not interested in filling-in a complete personal picture. The real interest of the poem is the story of St Cassian.

Pe. 11 is a different matter. Here we are more or less on the site of Rome with the poet as he describes his pilgrimage experiences to Bishop Valerianus. Line for line, this poem has the highest concentration of reminiscences at every level from both *Aeneid* and *Georgics*. This may reflect the level of Valerianus' literary culture, but since Virgil was such common property, it is tempting to see at work here Prudentius' own patriotic intensity, aroused by dealing with the site of Rome itself, particularly in a context of personal reminiscence.

The poem opens with a line which strikes a clear Roman note by an echo of a phrase from Ovid's *Fasti* (5. 260; see above p. 116): 'Romula in urbe'. The beginning of the line, however, strikes the balance for this poem and its projected promotion of the Christian form of patriotism: Rome is memorable for 'innumeros cineres sanctorum', the new heroes who are to replace the Romulus mentioned immediately afterwards. There may be some irony in play here. The reference to 'furor impius' at line 5 inevitably recalls the picture of a chained *Furor* at *Aeneid* 1. 294, in a passage prophesying the greatness, peace and stability of the future Rome. The Christian poet implies that 'furor impius' was still at work against persecuted Christians under the pagan empire, but that now it is chained, as in the Virgilian picture, under the Christian Augustus, Theodosius. The phrase 'Troia Roma' at line 6 is evocative. It should be compared with the use of 'error Troicus' which confounds the Roman senate before its conversion to Christianity in *Pe.* 2. 445. The 'Trojan error' for Augustan poets had been a way of referring to Rome's perjury and wickedness in the past and a way of expressing the present burden of guilt earned by her involvement in civil war (see for example, Horace *Odes* 3. 3 and Virgil, *Georgics*, 1 ad fin.). The 'error Troicus' for Prudentius is something different: it is Rome's past devotion to the wrong gods. In *Odes*, 3. 3, Juno warns the Romans against re-claiming Troy's site and greatness: they will only suffer the same fate as Troy, the 'Troiae ... fortuna' (61–2). So, too, for Pruden-tius, if Rome persists in the Trojan error of its pagan religion, then it will suffer destruction in a far more final sense by losing its chance of salvation.[92]

An echo of the *Aeneid* occurs at *Pe.* 11. 43–4:

> non contentus humum *celsae intra moenia Romae*
> tinguere iustorum caedibus assiduis.

The echo of *Aeneid*, 1. 7, 'altae moenia Romae' carries almost ironic weight: persecution is the sort of low slaughter to which a lofty imperial power has sunk. And yet it is the very presence of these 'caedes' on Roman soil which will indeed make Rome truly 'celsa' in the Christian future.

The new monuments built to celebrate the martyrs are part of Rome's Christian wealth. They not only equal, but outshine the pagan monuments of Rome. The splendour of Hippolytus' new basilica is set in terms at least partially reminiscent of a Virgilian description of a temple, that of Juno at Carthage:

> hic templum Iunoni ingens Sidonia Dido
> condebat, *donis opulentum* et *numine diuae*
> aerea cui gradibus surgebant limina *nexaeque*
> *aere trabes*, foribus cardo stridebat aenis.

> (*Aeneid*, 1. 446 ff.)[93]

Pe. 11. 215 ff. picks up the passage with the structure of the line: 'superba/maiestate potens muneribusque opulens', and with the phrase 'auratis ... trabibus'. Ideas and scenes from the Virgilian passage are picked up by these words, although there are admit-tedly no exact extended examples of verbal reminiscences. The passage offers an example of *contaminatio*, that is, the conflation of points from more than one original model. Two other obvious

---

[92] This complex of ideas is explored by Pari (1975) and by Galinsky (1969), 194–9 and 222.

[93] This is the suggestion of Dexel (1907).

and exact reminiscences occur here from two other passages in the
Aeneid. So 'laquearia tecti' at *Pe*. 11. 219, reproduces the same
phrase in exactly the same metrical position at *Aeneid* 8. 25. The
Virgilian context has no real relevance to the new passage beyond
the descriptive (the phrase occurs in a simile in the Virgil). Also,
'fronte sub adversa' at the beginning of *Pe*. 11. 225 exactly repro-
duces the same phrase, again at the beginning of a line at *Aeneid*, 1.
166, where, however, the description is in itself of little value for
the description of a Christian basilica. These are both examples of
'trivial' reminiscences, metrically useful and adaptable to different
descriptive contexts. The picture of the basilica is thus lent a com-
posite epic grandeur by the combination of three Virgilian
passages.

Perhaps there is more patriotic weight in 231 ff., where Pruden-
tius returns to the feelings and implications behind the opening
lines of the poem:

> si bene commemini, colit hunc pulcherrima Roma
> Idibus Augusti mensis . . .
>
> (231–2)

The poet here conflates two Virgilian passages of high patriotic
emotions. The first is *Georgics*, 2. 534, where at the end of a de-
scription of the life of the ancient Sabines, Virgil exclaims:

> hanc olim ueteres uitam coluere Sabini,
> hanc Remus et frater, sic fortis Etruria creuit
> scilicet et rerum facta est *pulcherrima Roma.*
>
> (532–4)

The identical phrase describing Rome as 'pulcherrima' holds an
emphatic position at the end of the line in both passages. Virgil's
phrase comes as the climax to an exposition of the ancient founda-
tions of Rome's present supremacy. Prudentius leaves this part of
the Virgilian precedent unspoken. But perhaps in the context of
martyrdom, the single Virgilian phrase is enough to suggest that
Rome has earned her status as *pulcherrima* in a new and truer sense
through the sufferings of martyrs like Hippolytus. Another Vir-
gilian passage may be recalled here:

> Mos erat Hesperio in Latio, quem protinus urbes
> Albanae coluere sacrum, nunc maxima rerum
> Roma colit . . .
>
> (*Aeneid*, 7. 601 ff.)

The 'mos' in question here is the opening of the *Belli Portae* at the start of war. It is true that the Prudentian lines do not reproduce exactly the words of Virgil (in fact it is at *Pe.* 9. 3 that Rome is described as 'rerum maxima'). But there seems to be some similarity of sound and sense: the word 'colit' appears in both contexts (though admittedly not in the same position in the line), the word 'nunc' is echoed by 'hunc', while Rome in both cases is described in superlative terms in contexts which are patriotic. Both record current practice after a narrative dealing with past events. The military side of the Virgilian passage might even lend some colouring to Prudentius' lines: the 'wars' of the martyrs against their pagan persecutors now replace in importance for Rome the worldly wars proclaimed by the opening of the *Belli Portae*. This might be pushing a slight verbal reminiscence too far. But Prudentius certainly draws to some extent on the Virgilian contexts for ways of expressing a new Christian pride in Rome.

Pe. 12 has, surprisingly, less to say in a direct way about the new patriotic interest in Rome, which in fact it was thought possible and desirable to promote at the end of the fourth century through the celebration of the feast of SS Peter and Paul (see above, n. 76). The dramatic framework perhaps made the sustained comments of *Pe.* 2, for example, difficult to insert. Details of the two balanced martyrdoms dominate the poem, though when the *urbs* does appear, in its role as the recipient of 'duas ... dotes' (55), it is described as 'togata', with all the associations which that adjective has with the prophecy passage in *Aeneid* 1. The plebs who celebrate the feast-day before the visitor's eyes are described emphatically as 'Romula': again, an adjective used in passages of pointed patriotic feeling. Horace, for instance, at *Odes*, 4. 5. 1 talks of the 'Romula gens' in a highly emotional address to Augusta as the guardian of his people and uses the same expression in the *Carmen saeculare* at line 47 in an obviously patriotic context. Although these touches in *Pe.* 12 are slight, they are important as indications of the width of perspective in which the achievements of Rome's Apostles can be viewed.

5

'Egregiae Animae'

THE old Rome had required for its foundation the efforts of men of superhuman strength and endurance, men supported by *Fatum* and divine aid, 'cum coleret patrios *Troia Roma* deos' (*Pe.* 9. 6). In the *Aeneid*, Virgil recorded the exploits of those first heroes, and of one in particular who was 'insignem pietate' (*Aeneid*, 1. 10). Aeneas sets out from the ruins of fallen Troy on a mission to found Rome, taking the Trojan gods with him. The defeat and destruction of the eastern city are the necessary conditions for the founding of the new city. This point is explored in *Aeneid* 12 in the interchange between Jupiter and Juno, and in Juno's speech in Horace, *Odes*, 3. 3. 18 ff. The Trojan background provides some of the negative notes sounded in Augustan literature, when the subject of Rome's origins and moral state are in question. The *Aeneid* is partly a rejection of Troy and the 'Laomedonteae . . . periuria Troiae' (*Georgics*, 1. 501).[1] Prudentius, however, sees his 'rerum maxima Roma' (*Pe.* 9. 3) in a new, clear light as representing the true climax of Rome's history. Associations with a defeated Troy cease when she ceases to worship 'patrios . . . deos', the defeated gods of the East. Rome is renewed and refounded in her total conversion to Christianity. The temporal and spiritual are united in the empire's providential rule. Patriotism becomes a necessary constituent of full Christian belief.

The new Christian Rome also required 'founding heroes'. It was not established without a struggle. The martyrs who suffered and died in witness of the faith naturally assume the role of heroes in a reinforced sense. They display the same qualities as the epic heroes of the *Aeneid*: remarkable courage and endurance, a fearless willingness to lay down their lives for a cause, the earthly fulfilment of which they will not live to see. They, too, benefit on occasion from divine assistance, though now from the one true God.

---

[1] Cf. Horace, *Odes*, 3. 3; 1. 18; *Ep.*, 16. 9; Propertius, *Elegies* 4. 1. 87; Ovid, *Fasti*, 1. 523.

Prudentius was not the first Christian writer to see the martyrs in an epic perspective. Without reference to epic literature, Eusebius at the beginning of the fourth century speaks of the martyrs as the champions of the Church describing the 'unshakeable determination of the champions of true religion, their *courage* and *endurance*, their *triumphs* over demons and victories over invisible opponents, and the crowns which all this won for them at the last.' (*Historia Ecclesiastica*, 5, *Praef.* 1. 4.)[2] The church historian restricts the martyrs' victories to the spiritual sphere, but their triumphs are won by the traditional human traits of heroism which Eusebius enumerates at length.

Augustine, a century later, explicitly puts the martyrs in an epic context when he uses a quotation from the *Aeneid* itself to extend his description of the martyrs' heroism at *De ciu. dei* 2. 29. At *Aeneid* 11. 24–5 Aeneas pays homage to the fallen heroes, those 'egregiae animae' (24):

> quae sanguine nobis
> hanc patriam peperere suo . . .

Augustine applies these words to the Christian martyrs:

de quorum *uirtute perfecta* et *pro fide uera* etiam passionibus gloriamur, qui usquequaque aduersus potestates inimicissimas confligentes easque fortiter moriendo uincentes 'sanguine nobis hanc patriam peperere suo'. Ad quam patriam te inuitamus et exhortamur, ut eius adiciaris numero ciuium.

Augustine's *patria* is of course the 'caelestis patria'. Yet, by quoting from the poem which, in the later period, epitomized in its main character the traditional Roman *uirtus* and *pietas* in action in an epic setting, Augustine makes a significant comparison of heroic actions in the non-Christian and Christian spheres. He appropriates and reapplies Roman *uirtus* and *fides* to the situation of the Christian hero, the martyr. Not only does he substitute a Christian for a Roman heroism, but he implies that the Christian version is the true one: 'uirtute *perfecta* et pro fide *uera* . . .'[3] The Christian hero requires some of the same qualities implicit in the traditional interpretation of *uirtus*:

---

[2] Translation by G. A. Williamson, *Eusebius, The History of the Church* (Penguin, 1965).
[3] This passage is discussed by Hagendahl (1967) 440. The same point is discussed by Buchheit (1966: 129–30), where other references to Christian authors are given.

labor inpiger, aspera uirtus,
uis animi excellens, ardor uiolentia.

(*Contra Symmachum*, 2. 24–5)

But he does not fight alone:

sua dextera cuique est,
et Deus omnipotens ...

(ibid., 35–6)

His reward is a spiritual *corona*.

Prudentius goes even further than Augustine. Once the
worldly *patria* is justified in terms of God's providential plan for
the Christianization of the world, there is no need so severely to
separate and exclude the earthly kingdom from the heavenly. The
Christian empire is an extension of its spiritual counterpart: the
martyrs as champions achieved the triumph of the Church on
earth, before experiencing their own triumph in heaven. Thus
there is every reason to hymn the martyrs as 'founding heroes',
parallel to the old in terms of qualities and aspirations, but going
beyond them in the greatness of their achievement and the eternal
heavenly glory of their reward.

The martyrs shed their blood for the Church in 'peaceful wars'
(εἰρηνικωτάτους πολέμους, Eusebius, 5, *Praef.* 1. 4) by passive
resistance rather than armed warfare. Their activity can, however,
be described in military terms as the *militia Christi*, which for
dedicated Christians must, in the end, replace *militia Caesaris*. The
alternative *militia Christi* is a recurrent theme in martyr-literature
and takes several forms. Martyrs from all walks of life, including
women and children, become 'soldiers for Christ' by their heroic
end. Yet another Christian paradox may be set up in this way. On
the other hand, these soldiers for Christ may, in fact, also be
soldiers by profession in the world. In this case, their martyrdom
is the result of their rejection of the *militia Caesaris* when it in-
volves an acknowledgement of pagan divinities.[4] Soldier-martyrs
of this type constitute a large category in themselves. While civil-
ian *milites Christi* provide examples of untypical extremes of hero-
ism (the traditional physical manifestations of *uirtus* appear in

---

[4] For *militia Christi*, see Harnack (1905); Auer (1980); Fontaine (1965). Fontaine gives a
bibliographical survey of recent literature on the subject. He also gives a useful brief discus-
sion in his edition of the *Vita Martini* by Sulpicius Severus (*SC* 133–5, 1967–9), especially
in vol. 1, 143–8. See also M.-D. Valentin (1977) 111 n. 5.

unexpected quarters), soldier-martyrs demonstrate the re-channelling of the *uirtus* which is professionally expected of them. Thus they provide the opportunity for examining the Christianized ideal of *uirtus* against the background and standard of the traditional form.

Prudentius, in fact, begins his collection of poems about martyrdom with an account of the end of two Spanish soldier-martyrs, Emeterius and Chelidonius. They are the only soldiers in the collection, in which the martyrs portrayed include young *uirgines* (Eulalia, *Pe.* 3, and Agnes, 14),[5] children (*Pe.* 10), clerics (*Pe.* 2, 5, 6, 7, 11, and 13), a school-master (*Pe.* 9), and apostles (*Pe.* 12). The soldier-martyrs are placed prominently at the opening of the collection, a position which probably reflects the author's intentions, since it appears in all the manuscripts, in spite of the variable order of the other poems.[6] Various explanations for this have been suggested: *Pe.* 1 may reflect Prudentius' Spanish patriotism or even his personal association with the martyrs' region of Spain;[7] or it may represent the poet's interest in martyrs who put the *militia Christi* before the *militia Caesaris*, as he himself did in giving up the *militia Caesaris* at court, in which he had been so successful, for the vocation of Christian poet.[8]

However, the poem can be explained as a suitable introductory poem in several other ways. It is programmatic for the whole collection by its introduction of recurrent themes and by its means of expressing them. The opening and closing sections of the poem which frame the martyrdom narrative itself (1–30, 94 ff.) describe the continuing effect and meaning of the martyrdom. These considerations are not directly relevant to the central narrative. Thus the opening lines express patriotic pride felt in the possession of the martyrs' earthly remains:

> Pollet hoc felix per orbem terra Hibera stemmate,
> hic locus dignus tenendis ossibus uisus Deo . . .
>
> (4–5)

---

[5] These *uirgines* form a rather similar pair; many of the details of Eulalia's story seem to reproduce the circumstances of Agnes' martyrdom according to Damasus' inscription (see below p. 240). The martyrs appear side-by-side in the mosaics of S. Apollinare Nuovo in Ravenna. For Prudentius' interest in the girl-martyrs in the *Peristephanon*, see Fontaine (1970).

[6] Lavarenne (1955 edn) xxiv–xxx; Bergman (1926) xxv–xlviii; Cunningham (1966a) xi–xix.

[7] Arevalo, Prolegomena, *PL* 59. 390; Bergman (1921) 31 ff.

[8] This idea is suggested by Fontaine in a discussion of *Pe.* 1 (1980: 141–71).

An element of local pride is present, but the poet also carefully emphasizes the martyrs' powers as 'patroni ... mundi' (13), available to 'exteri ... orbis ... colonus' also (10). This theme reappears at *Pe.* 2. 545 and *Pe.* 6. 84. The fulfilment of petitions made to the martyrs at their tomb is emphasized both in the opening stanzas (13–18) and at the close of the poem, where the power of healing invested in the martyrs is vividly illustrated by the description of an exorcism (97 ff.). Successful supplication at a martyr's tomb occurs also at the end of *Pe.* 9 and 11. In other poems, the poet only goes as far as the prayer for help and protection (*Pe.* 2, 3, 4, 6, 10, 14).

In *Pe.* 1, 'spurcum latronem martyrum uirtus quatit' (106). This statement forms the climax of an exploration of the meaning of *uirtus* for Christian martyrdom, which has important implications for the presentation of the martyr-hero throughout the collection. In *Pe.* 1 *uirtus* is redefined for the reader in the light of a new struggle fought for new ends, in a way which is particularly striking because the martyrs have been soldiers in the world. Prudentius' exploration of *uirtus* is given an extra dimension through the language used: by a mosaic of references, the poet evokes a famous Augustan treatment of the same theme. In Horace's second 'Roman' Ode (*Odes*, 3. 2), *uirtus* is redefined for his period in the context of the traditional ideals of military achievement. In drawing on his Augustan predecessor at this point, Prudentius does not rely on extended verbal parallels, but a scattering of key words and phrases which not only evoke the stylistic quality of the original in a superficial way, but which also refer significantly to the ideas and values expressed there. In this way, the Horatian passage contributes to an adjustment of the ideal of *uirtus* in what is now a Christian context.

This pattern of ideas is mainly developed at *Pe.* 1. 25–73, where the poet turns from a detailed picture of the *beneficia* bestowed by the 'patroni mundi' to a consideration of martyrdom in a general sense: 'hoc genus mortis decorum, hoc probis dignum viris' (25). The poet then moves on (31 ff.) to the particular circumstances of the death of Emeterius and Chelidonius. This movement from the general to the particular may in itself be seen as a piece of Horatian technique, learnt from the large-scale lyric of Pindar,[9]

---

[9] For Pindaric generalizations and their function, see Bowra (1964), 346–8. For Horace and Pindar, see Fraenkel (1957) 283 ff., 293, 426 ff.; also Nisbet and Hubbard (1970) xiii. For Prudentius and Pindar, see Brožek (1954) and (1957–8a).

and demonstrated, for instance, in *Odes*, 3. 4. In *Pe.* 1, the two stanzas of generalized comment on martyrdom provide a transition from the stanzas which tell of supplication to the martyrs and its rewards, to the story of the soldiers' actual martyrdom. At 31–9, the future martyrs' profession as soldiers is discussed, and then the poet turns to the persecution itself, which is first described in general terms (40–52) as a great *pestis* (43), and then with special reference to the two soldiers (52 ff.). The actual torture and persecution fills only a single stanza (70–3), and the real climax of this section is the speech of the martyrs (58–69), where they justify their course of action.

The Horatian references in *Pe.* 1 revolve around the ideals and values woven into the second ode of Book 3. This poem begins with a suggestion for the hardy training suitable for young soldiers who will be involved in Augustus' military efforts (the reference 'Parthos feroces' in line 3 ties the opening general statement to the realities of Roman foreign policy). The brief reference to the *Parthi* is then allowed to recede in favour of a picture with a very epic flavour: the warlike exploits of the lion-like young soldier are viewed from the standpoint of the betrothed of the enemy prince whom he fights (6–12). This picture of military *uirtus* in action gives way to a general statement about the noblest application of this *uirtus* to patriotic ends: 'dulce et decorum est pro patria mori'. The next two stanzas (17–24) broaden Horace's concept of *uirtus*. The very word becomes a refrain introducing each stanza. In 17–20, *uirtus* is related to political life and the courage of convictions which is unaffected by popular whim. Lines 21 ff. animate the figure of *uirtus*, which rises above the common herd 'recludens immeritis mori/caelum' (21–2).[10]

For Prudentius, military *uirtus* finds its truest development and extension in 'martyrum uirtus' (*Pe.* 1. 106), which, moreover, gives them special powers both before and after death. The martyrs, too, endure death for a cause and win eternal glory by their courage. But it is for the sake of Christ that they die, and their 'caelum' is the Christian heaven. The Christian application of *uirtus* in fact requires the rejection of the earthly army which had been the usual sphere for its operation.

---

[10] Williams (1969: 37) analyses the movement of the poem. Horace's ideas 'move from honest poverty to soldierly qualities, to bravery, to *uirtus* that faces opposition, to the trusty silence that acquiesces in what is right, but not popular'.

However, Prudentius leaves no doubt that Emeterius and Chelidonius achieved the highest standards of ordinary military *uirtus*. Horace's opening exhortation from *Odes*, 3. 2 is translated into the statement of *Pe*. 1. 31–3:

> *Nec rudem crudi laboris* ante uitam duxerant
> milites ...
> *Sueta uirtus bello et armis* militat sacrariis.

The position of Prudentius' stanza is in itself significant. The earthly military ideal takes second place to a set of more general statements about the glory of the martyr's choice of death, but in such a way as to imply that Christian *uirtus* is by no means completely divorced from its secular counterpart, which could indeed be seen as part of the martyr's necessary training. The moral and physical requirements of full military *uirtus* (alluded to by Prudentius at 31–3), are also valuable to the martyr in his endurance in the face of martyrdom. Just as the soldier needs training in the martial arts (this point is emphasized by Horace again in lighter mood at *Odes*, 1. 8), the *miles Christi* finds an ideal training in secular military life,[11] which is converted to Christian ends. Prudentius draws attention particularly to the soldiers' *sodalitas* (53), the comradeship of fellow soldiers in the camp and in battle. Just as the *sodalitas* of Emeterius and Chelidonius had kept them shoulder-to-shoulder in battle, so now they stand together ready to face whatever trial awaits them as Christians. The statement in line 54 could just as well be applied to their stubborn resistance in battle, as well as to their courageous patience in awaiting martyrdom:

> stant parati ferre quidquid sors tulisset ultima.

This aspect of the martyrs might recall the close friendship of Nisus and Euryalus from Book 9 of the *Aeneid*, although there seem to be no verbal reminiscences. In any case, the martyrs' *sodalitas* is about to take them through very different trials—the tortures of 55–7, which provide the explanation of 'quidquid' in line 54. Thus a quality associated with military *uirtus* can be reapplied in the Christian sphere of *militia Christi*. In coining the phrase 'fida sodalitas', Prudentius may also be aware of the religious connotation of the word *sodalitas*.[12] This is obviously very

---

[11] Fontaine (1980) 161–2.
[12] For *sodalitas* in a military setting, see Livy, 2. 3 and Horace, *Odes*, 2. 7. 5. For its use in religious contexts, see the *Oxford Latin Dictionary* (1982) 1780.

suitable for describing the companionship in death of two members of the Christian brotherhood.

The stanza at 55–8 balances and reflects, in the context of martyrdom, an earlier stanza (37–9). Here, a statement of the soldiers' earlier participation in military life and their decision to reject 'Caesaris uexilla' (34) is followed by a devaluation of the details of military life: now,

> *Vile censent* expeditis ferre dextris spicula . . .
> *inpias manus* cruentis inquinare stragibus.
>
> (37–8)

The word 'inpias' used of the martyrs' activities in war implicitly expresses a condemnation of warlike activities which are traditionally included in any definition of *pietas*, and obliquely sets forth a redefinition of the latter in a Christian context. This leads to something of a paradox: the poet hymns the rejection of violence and military activities in an age which gloried in the triumph of the Christian Empire on the battlefield. The apparent opposition at work here may be reconciled in the figure of the *miles Christi* embodied in the secular soldier. In *Pe.* 1, Prudentius refers to the Gospel text of Matt. 22: 21, when the soldiers claim:

> Sit satis, quod capta primo uita sub chirographo
> *debitum persoluit omne functa rebus Caesaris,*
> *tempus est Deo rependi quidquid est proprium Dei.*
>
> (61–3)

Prudentius may even consider his own career in the same light: he served the Christian emperor, and then devoted his time more completely to service of God.[13]

Prudentius' extension or renewal of the old values reflects Horace's broader definition of *uirtus* in *Odes*, 3. 2. Here Horace refers partially, perhaps, to his own views on true *amicitia*, and partially to the particular difficulties and needs of Augustus in stabilizing his new régime. He recalls a fragment of Simonides, and several Pindaric statements along the same lines, with his idea:

> est et fideli tuta silentio
> merces.[14]

[13] For discussion of traditional *pietas* at work in the Aeneid, see Grimal (1959) and Williams (1973). On Prudentius' view of his own role, see Fontaine (1980).

[14] On Simonides, fr. 66 and *Odes*, 3. 2, see Pasquali (1920) 680–1; cf. *Ol.* 2. 91, *Nem.* 5. 16, and Pindar, fr. 180, (ed. H. Maehler (post B. Snell), Teubner (1975), Part 2, p. 128).

True *uirtus* in the political sphere (*Odes*, 3. 2. 17–20) is not moved by 'ambitio popularis aurae'. In Prudentius poem, 'uox fidelis plectitur' (48) at a moment of crisis for the Church in the midst of persecution. There seems to be an echo of the Horatian passage here, but with a reversal of sense revolving around the key word, *fidelis*: *fides* requires positive assertion by the *uox* of the Christians, not silent acceptance. Their reward is not the pagan hope of hero-ization and glory, but 'lux . . . longior' (24).

Prudentius' confirmation of Emeterius' and Chelidonius' soldierly worth in secular terms follows three stanzas in which the value and honour of a martyr's death are laid out in general terms which recall the universal statements of the Horatian poem at 13 ff., when he moves out and away from the epic-style τειχοσκοπία scene of the second and third stanzas. At the begin-ning of his poems, Horace encouraged the 'robustus acri militia puer' to 'angustam amice pauperiem pati'. Poverty suggests moral qualities, hard work and absence of selfish ambition which, for the soldier, should be played out amidst the rigours of military life (stanzas one and three). The finest manifestation of military excellence gained in this way is patriotic endeavour, the willing-ness to lay down one's life for one's country (13). While Pruden-tius does not concern himself with the ideal of *paupertas* for the soldier, he does (22–5) translate martyrdom into terms of profit and loss, though now the 'poverty' to be endured is the loss of one's life. The martyr stands witness to the one true God 'sangui-nis dispendio/sanguinis'. There is no question of death as the end in the battle of this *militia*; but, as in Horace, 'uirtus . . . intaminatis fulget honoribus' (17–18), so Prudentius balances the expenditure of one's life against the compensation after death: 'sed tale *damnum* lux rependit longior'.

This connection of thought may be considered tenuous, unsup-ported as it is by any touch of verbal echo. But it is supported by the clearer surrounding references to the relevant Horatian con-text. So the beginning of Prudentius' next stanza recalls the devel-opment of thought and also the language of Horace 3. 2. 14 ff. Horace turns to the patriotic ideal of death in battle with the famous line 'dulce et decorum est pro patria mori'. Prudentius at 25 has '*Hoc genus mortis decorum*, hoc probis *dignum* uiris . . .' and at 28, '*Pulchra res* ictum sub ense persecutoris pati'. The association of 'decorum' with a form of 'mors' strongly recalls the Horatian passage, especially in conjunction with the thought and grammatical structure of 28: 'pulchra res' replaces 'dulce et decorum', while 'sub ense ... pati' recalls the construction of 'pro patria mori' (preposition plus noun, with dependent infinitive). 'Pati' itself might echo out of context the 'pati' of *Odes*, 3. 2. 1. The substitution of 'pulchra res' for 'dulce et decorum' might also recall *Aeneid* 2. 317, 'pulchrumque mori sucurrit in armis'. If Horace's 'dulce' is dropped here, it is picked up later by Prudentius (51), where in the context of a general picture of Christian *uirtus*, which is 'ense caesa' in the persecution, he remarks 'dulce tunc iustis cremari, dulce ferrum perpeti', a use of the neuter adjective with the infinitive which recalls Horace in the context of laying down one's life for a greater good. For Horace, it is the tangible 'patria', for Prudentius the heavenly, which is opposed to the 'aula mundialis' of the persecutors.

To return to *Pe.* 1. 25 ff.: Prudentius, having echoed Horace 3. 2. 15, at 25 follows the thought of the Horatian stanza right through. Horace follows his famous dictum with a far less often quoted alternative to the patriotic ideal: 'mors et fugacem persequitur uirum'. In other words, even if you do not die heroically for your country, cowardice only ends in death too, but an inglorious one. The coward not only loses his life, but the chance of eternal glory as well. 'A man's life is forfeit anyway, and then it is for him to exploit that fact positively.'[15] Prudentius provides the same logic to support his encouragement to the 'genus mortis decorum'. So the material body which will be lost by martyrdom is, in any case, a prey to earthly ills which will culminate in death:

> membra morbis exedenda, texta uena languidis,
>
> (26)

Instead of awaiting the inevitable end, why not rather 'morte mortem vincere' and voluntarily 'hostico donare ferro'.[16] Not to

---

[15] Williams (1969) 35.

[16] Most MSS have 'morte et mortem' at line 27, but two MSS have '(h)ostem', which Bergman adopts. However, if 'hostem' was the original reading, 'mortem' must be explained as an attempt to reproduce the Pauline echo at *Pe.* 2. 19. On this hypothesis, the suppression of 'et' might have been expected both for metrical reasons and because of the parallel text on which this 'emendation' was supposedly modelled. Prudentius' use of the phrase at *Pe.* 2. 19 is, however, a strong argument for its restoration here; and this is supported by the following textual analysis: at an early stage, 'et' was inadvertently interpolated after 'morte' and so copied faithfully by most scribes; but for at least one scribe the

make this sacrifice when the opportunity arises is to be a deserter from Christ, one of the 'Christi defugas' (42). Prudentius' use of military language here extends the theme of *militia Christi* and is particularly appropriate in the case of two soldier-martyrs. Prudentius employs the same play on military language when he describes the martyrs as 'quos *ad perenne cingulum* Christus uocat'. It is the word 'perenne' which points the difference between secular and Christian *militia*.[17] The phrase 'Christi defugas' might recall the 'fugacem uirum' of Horace at Odes, 3. 2. 14, whom *'mors* persequitur'. The implication in Prudentius' poem is that eternal *mors*, that is, damnation, awaits the deserter from the true *militia* of Christ and from the death of the body. It is the martyr who, paradoxically, wins 'lux longior' (that is, in Heaven) by his death.

Not only is it 'decorum', 'dulce', and 'pulchra res' to die in martyrdom (*Pe.* 1. 25, 51, and 28), but 'nobilis per uulnus amplum porta iustis panditur' (29). A Horatian passage, again from Odes, 3. 2, may once more lie behind Prudentius' line. At 21 ff. Horace speaks of the power of *uirtus* to separate its possessors from the crowd:

> Virtus, recludens immeritis mori
> caelum, negata temptat ire uia,
> coetusque uulgaris et udam
> spernit humum fugiente penna.

A path to glory and eternal fame is open to those 'immeritis mori', who show their excellence in a *uirtus* pictured here as a winged deity forging an upward path. At *Pe.* 1. 29, Prudentius uses a rather macabre image to imply the idea of transition from the earthly to the heavenly sphere by exceptional *uirtus*: the gaping wound of the martyr is a 'nobilis ... porta' open wide, presumably for the martyr to pass through to Paradise. The image of the 'uiam ... caeli' occurs more explicitly, however, later in the poem (84), in the context of the miracles of the 'anulus' and 'orarium'. These seals and symbols 'subuehuntur usque in astra'.

metrical difficulty made emendation imperative. He chose to write 'ostem' for 'mortem'. But this upsets the balance of the line, which begins with 'hostico'. My emendation is both simpler and more consonant with Prudentius' style.

[17] Christian commitment in baptism in a less militant context could be treated as *militia*: some Christian sarcophagi show scenes of the enrolment of the 'soldiers of Christ', with Christ himself presiding in the place of the emperor. See Piétri (1962); cf. St Lawrence in *Pe.* 2, the 'perennis consul' (2. 560).

The terminology used of their ascent is reminiscent of the traditional terms used to represent the reward of *uirtus*, but is transferred from the martyrs themselves to the mechanics of the miracle. This is witnessed by the executioner:

> Vidit hoc conuentus adstans, *ipse uidit carnifex*,
> et manum repressit haerens ac stupore obpalluit;
> Sed tamen peregit ictum, ne periret gloria.
>
> (91–3)

The 'gloria' here is surely that of the martyrs, not that of the executioner.[18]

The torturers' activities in the persecutions are described in terms which refer back to Horace, to another passage in the Roman odes. At line 47, Prudentius says:

> barbaras forum per omne tortor exercet manus.

At *Odes*, 3. 5. 49, Regulus

> sciebat quae sibi barbarus
> tortor pararet . . .

Prudentius intensifies the horror of his picture of the torturer by focusing on his hands, to which the adjective 'barbaras' is transferred. It is the hands of the torturer which inflict pain. However, the reference to the Horatian passage is still clear. Prudentius uses the same Horatian line again at *Pe*. 4. 121, where the reminiscence is more exact:

> Barbarus tortor latus omne carpsit.

Odes, 3. 5 in fact provides a rich complementary background for *Pe*. 1. It not only deals with the question of 'uera uirtus' (29), in a military context, with both contemporary relevance and historical point, but it also represents an interesting example of a pre-Christian martyr-soldier, Regulus, who chooses death rather than dishonour, and who calmly explains himself in a speech which is central to the poem's development of ideas and structure.

The 'barbaras . . . manus' of Prudentius' torturer may recall the 'inpias manus' of the unfavourable description of soldierly activities at line 39. If this is a consciously inserted similarity, perhaps the poet intends soldiers to be regarded in the same light as tor-

[18] Lavarenne (1963*b*) 26.

turers. In any case, the presence of the torturer early in Pruden-
tius' poem points forward to the scene of exorcism at the end
where:

> Audias, *nec tortor adstat*, eiulatus flebiles.
>
> (103)

In other words, true torture is possession by evil spiritual forces. A
true *uirtus* based on spiritual strength and *fides* can beat such
forces: so the 'martyrum uirtus' exorcises the evil demons.[19]

Pe. 1 uses a mosaic of references to well-known Horatian ex-
plorations of *uirtus* in order to underpin and throw into relief the
nature and operation of the Christian development of this quality.
In this way, the poem is programmatic for the rest of the collec-
tion in its presentation of the form of Christian heroism which it
suggests has assimilated and replaced the old. This forms the
kernel of the poem and figures in the description of the martyrs'
arrest, speech and execution. The frame for the narrative also con-
tains preoccupations programmatic for the whole *Peristephanon*,
for example, the poet's evident involvement in contemporary
martyr-cult, which later appears so clearly in *Pe.* 9, 11, and 12.

Pe. 1 also illustrates the poet's policy towards the selection and
treatment of his material. At 73–8 he bemoans the cruelty of the
'blasphemus . . . satelles',[20] who caused the records of this martyr-
dom to be destroyed, and thus implicitly recognizes the possibil-
ity of genuine *acta*. More important, the way is left clear for the
poet to rely on oral tradition, which in fact seems to have been in-
complete for Emeterius and Chelidonius. No details about their
imprisonment are known:

> Hoc tamen solum uetusta subtrahunt silentia . . .
>
> (79)

although the poet is keen to emphasize how much *is* remembered,

---

[19] For another poetic treatment of possession and exorcism, compare Paulinus of Nola
C. 19. 266 ff. See too, Fontaine (1964a).
[20] Prudentius must here be referring to the results of the edict of Diocletian AD 303,
which required the handing-over of sacred books for burning (Frend (1965) 491 ff.). In
Pe. 1, it is unclear exactly who the 'blasphemus . . . satelles' is. Prudentius uses the word
'satelles' to cover all the pagan opponents of the martyrs, from the governor himself
(*Pe.* 5. 13) to the executioner (*Pe.* 3. 171), and down to any servant in the governor's house
(*Pe.* 6. 121).

in spite of the efforts of the 'blasphemus ... satelles'. He is able to
tell of the miracle of the ring and the napkin:

> illa laus occulta non est nec senescit tempore
>
> (82)

Pe. 1 is, in fact, the first written account of this martyrdom,[21] and
the poet can thus treat his subject matter more freely than if a
well-known written version of the martyrdom already existed.
This is clear in *Pe.* 1 in the framing of the narrative, for instance,
by matter with a more general and contemporary reference. It
makes it possible for Prudentius to include in his martyrdom
account an exploration of Christian *uirtus* which he can express by
free imitation of his favourite non-Christian writers. Not only
can he produce a more literary version of his chosen popular
theme from the stylistic point of view, but he can also introduce
the very ideas which form the basis of the poet's exploration of his
theme. Where a known version of a martyrdom exists, the poet
has none of this liberty. The poems most influenced by a strong
Christian tradition contain the fewest classical reminiscences. *Pe.* 6
analysed below in Chapter 7, provides the most striking example
of this. At the other end of the scale are the 'Roman poems', *Pe.* 9,
11 and 12, which draw on the classical tradition in form and direct
verbal reminiscence in order to promote a new Christian patriotic
ideal. Between *Pe.* 6 and these poems come *Pe.* 2, 3, 4, 5, and 14,
which use classical reminiscences mainly to qualify the actions of
the martyrs who are viewed in this way as the heroic proponents
of the new *uirtus* posited as a Christian ideal in *Pe.* 1.

Thus, the martyrs exemplify superhuman endurance and cour-
age in the face of overwhelming odds, and naturally lend them-
selves to poetic portrayal in epic terms which inevitably draw on
the most famous expression of epic heroism, the *Aeneid*. In *Pe.* 1,
the poet taps Horace's more abstract terms of analysis in order to
compile a set of programmatic general statements. In *Pe.* 2–5 he
sets out to show the new *uirtus* in action, by setting the martyr in
an heroic framework. This is established by use of a pattern of
Virgilian reminiscences which evoke for the poem's audience the
heroic actions and qualities of Aeneas, his followers and their
opponents. The new application of the old heroic ideal to the

---

[21] See below, pp. 237–9 for the sources for *Pe.* 1.

martyrs highlights the superiority of the new Christian heroism. The audience is expected to set the original context of the Virgilian reminiscence against the new, in order to form a judgement. The martyrs win a 'path to heaven', in a new sense, and an eternal reward greater than heroization.

The best way to demonstrate Prudentius' reworking of epic values is to analyse fully a single poem. I propose here to look in detail at Pe. 3. The intervening poem about St Lawrence (second in the ordering of the earliest MSS) provides a certain number of points at which the martyr's heroic stature is reinforced by verbal reminiscence from the Aeneid,[22] but the effect of these references is diluted by their wide distribution over a long poem which is evidently strongly influenced by popular tradition and recent treatments of the martyrdom (see below, p. 243 ff.). The main points of interest for classical imitation are contained in the 'Roman' sections discussed above (pp. 125 ff.), and in the Juvenalian diatribe against paganism.[23] In other words, Pe. 2 also has other preoccupations outside the simple narration of the martyr's heroism.

By contrast, Pe. 3 is a more straightforward and economical martyr-narrative. Only two stanzas at the beginning of the poem (1–10) and six at the end (186–215) are used to emphasize Emerita's luck in possessing Eulalia's remains, and to allude to the current architectural developments of the cult-site together with the pilgrims' practices at the shrine. The actual events of the narrative are developed within a far smaller scope than in Pe. 2, and the result is a more coherent dramatic treatment. Lawrence's lengthy diatribes in Pe. 2 are reduced in Pe. 3 to a single short speech against the pagan gods (66–95), which is balanced by a reply from the praetor of almost equal length (97–125).

The story of Eulalia is also one which Prudentius records for the first time in a written version, and he thus feels freer to describe the martyr in terms recalling those used of the Virgilian epic hero. A poem about a martyr who is also a young girl presents an extreme and intriguing form of heroism.[24] The con-

[22] So, for instance, Lawrence at Pe. 2. 529 echoes the words of Aeneas from Aeneid, 1. 94. A full list of Virgilian reminiscences is given by Mahoney (1934).

[23] So Pe. 2. 514 recalls Juvenal, Sat. 6. 343–4. On the influence of Juvenal on Prudentius, see below pp. 180 ff.

[24] See Fontaine (1970) 58, 65. Fontaine sees a certain contradiction and tension between a negative picture of women drawing on a Christian tradition with its roots in pre-Christian Roman literature and an heroic picture of virginity.

tradiction implicit in her case is pointed by the explicit antithesis
of line 35, where '*femina* prouocat arma uirum', or by the paradox
of 39–40 where Eulalia is 'fera ... puella'. Prudentius was inter-
ested enough in the militant figure of the virgin martyr to depict
her twice more in his *Peristephanon*: Encratis in *Pe.* 4. 109–40 is a
'uiolenta uirgo' (111) reminiscent of Eulalia, the 'uirgo animosa',
and her martyrdom figures at comparative length in the catalogue
of martyrs briefly treated in *Pe.* 4; Agnes is featured in *Pe.* 14
where she gives vent to her 'furor' (63) against her persecutors. In
the case of Eulalia, the most striking of the three examples in Pru-
dentius' treatment,[25] the contrast between the martyr's youth and
sex and her masculine courage is deepened and explored by de-
liberate frequent reference to Virgil's poetry. The effect is far
from merely ornamental and is enriched by an admixture of
Ovidian references.[26]

In the introductory passage (1–10), Eulalia already figures as
'decus egregium', a phrase with a long history in epic after the
Virgilian coinage at *Aeneid*, 7. 473, where the words are used with
reference to the young Latin prince Turnus. It is true that repeated
use of the phrase in later epic may devalue its fullness of reference
in the Prudentian context, but the surrounding context in the Vir-
gilian passage is so suggestive for Eulalia that it is tempting to sup-
pose that Prudentius intended to evoke this occurrence of the
phrase in particular.[27]

It stands in a passage in the central section of *Aeneid* 7, where
the Fury Allecto, roused by Juno, goads Amata, then Turnus, and
finally all the Italians, to war against the Trojans. The words in
question occur in two lines which explain Turnus' power to
excite his followers to war:

> hunc decus egregium formae mouet atque iuuentae
> hunc ataui reges, hunc claris dextera factis.

This description of the young hero contains points also suitable
for a characterization of Eulalia. She too has 'forma' and 'iuuenta',

[25] A brief comparison of the three virgin martyrs and their treatment in Prudentius
may be found in Riposati (1979).

[26] The concentration of Virgilian reminiscences in *Pe.* 3 is noted by Mahoney (1934)
181 ff. For the Ovidian reminiscences, see Hanley (1959) 208–13. At 271–2, she notes the
primary importance of the *Metamorphoses* and *Fasti* for Prudentius' poetry.

[27] This Virgilian reference is recognized by Lavarenne (1963*b*: 55), Bergman (1926 edn:
466), Dexel (1907: 25). Paronetto (1957 edn: 61), and by Mahoney (1934: 158). The phrase
is frequently borrowed by later poets. See Schumann (1980; *MGH* 4. 2) 19–20.

though the 'forma' of a young girl and extreme 'iuuenta' (11–12: 'curriculis tribus atque nouem/tris hiemes quater adtigerat ...'). This makes the recognition of her as the 'decus egregium' of Emerita all the more striking. Eulalia outstrips her Virgilian predecessor in those very 'claris ... factis' for which he is famed. Her *uirtus* is clear:[28] she too demonstrates it in her 'facta' in true heroic manner. Just as Turnus has a family background of 'ataui reges', so Eulalia is not only 'germine nobilis' (1) but also 'mortis et indole nobilior' (2). She represents a new and higher form of Christian *nobilitas*, which disregards the old class distinctions of the world, and which takes its seat by right in the heavenly senatus after death.[29] In the Virgilian passage, Turnus' 'decus egregium' moves and excites his followers. So, too, Eulalia as a 'decus egregium' in the Christian sphere inspires the response of the pilgrim which is depicted at the end of the poem and supplies the poet with a moving example with which to edify his Christian audience.

The next Virgilian reminiscence occurs in 16–17:

> Iam dederat prius indicium
> tendere se *Patris ad solium.*

The italic phrase looks back to the Virgilian phrase 'Iouis ad solium' at *Aeneid*, 12. 847, where it is used of the appearance of the Dirae.[30] The replacement of the word 'Iouis' by the word 'Patris' with all its Christian connotations represents a case where Prudentius deliberately converts a reference to the pagan gods to a Christian reference.[31] There may be a polemical point being made implicitly by this,[32] but the chief function of the phrase in this context is to emphasize the extent of Eulalia's heroic aspirations

---

[28] 'Clara facta' form the basis for the manifestation of true *uirtus*. So at *Aeneid*, 6. 806, 'et dubitamus adhuc uirtutem extendere factis?', and *Aeneid*, 10. 467: 'stat sua cuique dies, breue et inreparabile tempus/omnibus est uitae; *sed famam extendere factis hoc/uirtutis opus.*'

[29] So Lawrence in *Pe*. 2 is 'perennis consul' after death, elected by 'Roma caelestis', where he had taken his place 'aeternae in arce curiae' (*Pe*. 2. 551–60). See Cameron (1968*b*). In *Pe*. 4, the martyrs are described *en masse* as 'chorus ... niueus togatae nobilitatis'.

[30] Cf. *Pe*. 7. 55 'aeterni ad solium patris', and *Pe*. 10. 639, 'uexit ad solium patris'. The phrase also occurs in Horace, *Ep*. 1. 17. 34.

[31] Hagendahl (1958) 382 ff.

[32] This point is made about all Virgilian references in the *Psychomachia* by Smith (1976), who sees Prudentius' use of Virgil in this poem as ironic throughout. The *Psychomachia* is thus an *anti*-Virgilian epic. This thesis seems too extreme, and does not fit Prudentius' attitude towards Virgil's poetry as demonstrated elsewhere in his own corpus.

by drawing on the grandeur of Virgilian epic language. It might be pressing the point too far to see the awesome and infernal figures of the Dirae behind Eulalia, even if she is characterized as 'ferox' and 'fera' elsewhere.

The unfeminine and unchildlike qualities of Eulalia are emphasized early in the poem. Her rejection of girlish toys and fripperies (19–22) recalls the warrior-maiden Camilla from *Aeneid*, 7. 803 ff. and 12. 532 ff.:

> bellatrix, *non illa colo calathisue Mineruae*
> *femineas adsueta manus*, sed proelia uirgo
> dura pati ...
>
> (*Aeneid*, 7. 805–7)

This heroine also rejects the traditional occupations of a woman. The reminiscence here, however, seems to be one only of a general picture, not reinforced by particular verbal similarity (and the emphasis in *Pe.* 3 is as much on Eulalia's unchildishness as on her unfemininity). Prudentius points the paradox represented by Eulalia by coining the diminutive 'pusiola', which is used to express the girl's soft fragility (see n. 52 below). The girl evokes the use of a diminutive again later in the poem (103) where the Praetor addresses her as 'torua puellula'. The diminutive here once again emphasizes Eulalia's paradoxical role in an oxymoronic phase.

The picture of the girl 'canitiem meditata senum' (25) refers to a τόπος with a long history. Curtius calls it 'the *puer senilis* topic' and traces its roots back to non-Christian literature. It became a favourite paradox in the Late Antique period, particularly with the Church Fathers. It had Biblical precedents as well as classical. At *Pe.* 3. 25, 'canities' refers figuratively to the wisdom associated with old age. This figure was a popular one (Curtius lists some Christian occurrences) recalling a passage in the *Wisdom of Solomon*, 4, 8 ff.: 'cani sunt sensus hominis' (Vulgate version). Prudentius draws on this topic in order to depict Eulalia in as remarkable a light as possible. Spiritual precocity forms a suitable introduction to her courage later in the poem.[33]

At lines 31–5, Eulalia's 'sacer ... spiritus' is described in terms which recall the Sibyl's frenzy, described at *Aeneid*, 6. 45–102.

---

[33] Curtius (1979) 98–101; cf. Gnilka (1972).

Protracted verbal imitation is not so much in question here as a complete parallel picture supported by suggestive, if isolated, instances of similar vocabulary. Virgil describes the Sibyl:

> ... cui talia fanti
> ante fores subito non uultus, non color unus,
> non comptae mansere comae; sed *pectus anhelum*
> et rabie *fera corda* tument, *maiorque* uideri
> nec mortale sonans, adflata est numine quando
> iam propiore dei.
>
> (46–51)

And again,

> ... ea frena *furenti*
> concutit et stimulos sub pectore uertit Apollo.
> ut primum cessit furor et rabida ora quierunt ...
>
> (100–2)

Compare this with *Pe.* 3. 31–5:

> infremuit sacer Eulaliae
> spiritus ingeniique ferox
> turbida frangere bella parat,
> et rude *pectus anhela* Deo
> femina prouocat arma uirum.

In both cases, emphasis is laid on extreme spiritual reactions and the effect of these on breathing. Both women become 'maior': the Sibyl grows in physical stature, while Eulalia becomes courageous beyond the usual capacity of her sex. Both women become capable of more than their conventional female role allows, and both in a religious context of spiritual inspiration. The important difference is, however, that the Sibyl is frenzied by the mumbo-jumbo of pagan religious rites and a bogus god, while Eulalia is more profoundly (for Prudentius) inspired by the one true God to sacrifice herself for His sake in martyrdom.

A similarity has been noticed between *Pe.* 3. 31–2 and *Aeneid*, 10. 711, where Virgil uses a simile to convey Mezentius' extreme and savage bravery when under attack. He is compared to an old boar at bay, which nobody dares to approach. In the simile, the boar

> substitit *infremuitque ferox* et inhorruit armos ...

The two italic words are both used in the description of Eulalia
quoted above, and thus it is possible that the boar simile is behind
Prudentius' characterization of Eulalia, who is also 'at bay' in the
face of her persecutor. She, too, struggles alone and with great
bravery in the face of overwhelming odds. A reminiscence of this
simile is suitable for the portrayal of the *fera* puella', and it also
grotesquely underlines anew her unfeminine qualities.

Although Eulalia presents the paradox of a 'uirgo animosa'
(Prudentius here draws on an Ovidian phrase, used of the goddess
Diana at *Heroides*, 19. 115), a 'fera puella', she is protected at first
by her parents (the genitive is here surely subjective rather than
objective):

> Sed *pia cura parentis* agit
> uirgo animosa domi ut lateat . . .
>
> (36–7)

The phrase 'pia cura parentis' recalls a reference to Aeneas'
fatherly affection towards his only son Ascanius: 'omnis in
Ascanio cari stat *cura parentis*' (*Aeneid*, 1. 646). In this way, Pru-
dentius invites comparison of the young girl-martyr with
Ascanius, boy-hero of the *Aeneid*. Points of similarity as well as
differences emerge which mould the reader's perception of the
martyr. Thus, alignment with Ascanius in the context of parental
affection helps to emphasize the pathos of Eulalia's extreme youth
and her normal ties of affection with her parents, which are to be
broken by her enthusiasm for martyrdom. These are played on
more explicitly and even more pathetically in the speech of the
Praetor later in the poem. Family ties are suggested in order to
show that greater responsibilities exist. So Christ rejects the claims
of his 'mother and brothers': 'Whoever does the Will of God is
my brother, my sister and my mother' (Luke 8: 19–21). Eulalia's
compulsion to stand witness to her faith causes her to dispense
with the natural response to the closeness of the family.

In the *Aeneid*, Iulus represents Aeneas' hopes for the future
greatness of the kingdom which he is founding. This is empha-
sized at several points in the poem. In the great prophecy in Book
1, the advent of Augustus is foretold, with reference to his ances-
tor 'a magno demissum nomen Iulo' (288). In Book 4, Mercury
urges Aeneas to remember 'Ascanium surgentem et spes heredis
Iuli/. . . cui regnum Italiae Romanaque tellus/debetur' (274–6).

This line of thought recurs in the *Lusus Troiae* demonstration of Book 5. 545–603, with its sudden insight into the Roman future, its families and customs. The same point is made by Apollo at Book 9. 641–2:

> macte noua uirtute, puer, sic itur ad astra,
> dis genite et geniture deos . . .

The optimism for Rome's future which is associated with Ascanius is transferred to Eulalia by the poet in his evocation of Virgilian references to the boy hero. But her heroism is acted out in spite of her youth and her sex in a way not allowed for Ascanius. It is part of the foundation laid by the martyrs for the future greatness of the Christian empire, the true climax of the history of the Roman empire.

Then Eulalia sets out on her lonely night-journey from her parents' home to the town (40–5). In conception, this can be paralleled by the night-exploits of Euryalus and Nisus in *Aeneid* 9. Here, the expedition is undertaken at Nisus' suggestion (184 ff.) because:

> aut pugnam aut aliquid iamdudum inuadere magnum
> mens agitat mihi, *nec placida contenta quiete est.*

This can be compared with the thought expressed at *Pe.* 3. 41–2:

> illa, *perosa quietis opem*
> degeneri tolerare mora.

There may be no exact verbal imitations, but the similarity of circumstance and motivation is striking. Also, Euryalus' participation in the night-raid represents the courage of the young, acted out in spite of parental opposition and in secret. Euryalus' deception of his mother by a 'sin of omission' in not telling her of his intended absence results in her tragic lament for his loss. Eulalia, too, sets off in secret by night for her journey to the town and martyrdom.

At *Pe.* 3. 47, the poet returns to *Aeneid* 6 with a clear reference to Aeneas' journey through the underworld as it is described by the hero himself to the silent ghost of Dido:

> sed me iussa deum, quae nunc has ire per umbras,
> *per loca senta situ* cogunt noctemque profundam,
> imperiis egere suis.

> *(Aeneid,* 6. 462–4)

Aeneas' words convey his fear and horror at having to undertake this journey to reach his father in the underworld. By transferring the descriptive phrase 'per loca senta situ' to Eulalia's situation in *Pe.* 3, Prudentius emphasizes the roughness and danger of the girl's journey and puts it on the same level of heroism as that of Aeneas. Eulalia's journey is also one of 'death', but of real physical death through martyrdom. Paradoxically, this death leads to the life and vision of the true Christian 'Elysium': Heaven. In Christian terms, Eulalia's journey and its end are more truly heroic than those of Aeneas. His guide in *Aeneid* 6 is the Sibyl. She is replaced for Eulalia by the 'angelico ... choro' (48) in a phrase which recalls Ovid, *Metamorphoses*, 2. 441, where the goddess Diana is pictured 'suo comitata choro'. Eulalia is thus once more compared implicitly to the 'uirgo animosa' (see above p. 159 on line 37). Angels, however, replace the nymphs of this classical version, and Eulalia's virginity must be viewed as part of her *Christian* dedication. Her heavenly guides bring a saving light to relieve the gloom of her journey, and this picture suggests the Old Testament parallel which is then drawn from Ex. 14: 20. Here, a column of light leads the 'generosa patrum/turba' out of Egypt. However, while the Jews are fleeing from Pharaoh, slavery, and death, Eulalia is in a sense pursuing death in martyrdom. It is interesting to observe the way in which the classical scenes evoked by Virgilian and Ovidian references merge into specifically Christian scenes, which are introduced in a manner similar to that used for an epic simile ('sic ... non aliter', 51 and 56). The Biblical parallel plays the part of a Christian simile.

It is as the '*pia* uirgo' that Eulalia 'uiam nocte secuta [est]' and thus 'diem meruit' with heavenly assistance. So it is by *pietas* that 'pius Aeneas' (see n. 13 above) wins through to Elysium, as Anchises notes at their meeting:

> ... tuaque exspectata parenti
> uicit iter durum pietas.

Thus the obligations and code of behaviour contained in the term *pietas* find a Christian meaning and application, with new commitments and priorities. Eulalia's *Pietas* as a Christian causes her to leave her natural parents in order to do the will of her heavenly Father. This paradoxical situation is emphasized by the contrast set up with the earlier reference in the poem to '*pia* cura parentis'

(36), with all its normal feelings and duties. In *Aeneid* 6, of course, Aeneas' *pietas* helps him to *go to* his own father. Once again, the demands made on the Christian hero are shown to be greater still.

However, the martyr's end can still be described in terms reminiscent of the non-Christian literary expression of the hero's reward. At line 60, Eulalia

> ... super astra pararet iter.

This recalls phrases like 'sic itur ad astra' (*Aeneid*, 9. 641, where the phrase is used significantly by Apollo of Ascanius; see above p. 160) or 'aliquem infere astris' (Ovid, *Metamorphoses*, 9. 272).[34] An exact parallel occurs at the end of the *Metamorphoses* (15. 875–6) where Ovid claims immortality:

> parte tamen meliore mei *super alta* perennis
> *astra ferar*, nomenque erit indelebile nostrum ...

The Prudentian echo of this thought contains a certain irony: the non-Christian poet can only hope for immortality through the enduring qualities of his verse. Eulalia as a Christian martyr can be certain of true spiritual immortality as her eternal reward. There may also be some contamination of sources here, as the phrase 'super astra' also occurs in the Vulgate Old Testament at Isa. 14: 13 'super astra dei exaltabo solium meum'. If Prudentius has this passage also at the back of his mind, the reminiscence is purely superficial, since the phrase occurs in Israel's taunt against the King of Babylon, where it forms part of the King's proud statement of ambition. This hardly seems to fit the context of *Pe.* 3. It must, therefore, be the Ovidian passage which is the true forerunner of Prudentius' lines.

Almost superhuman speed and strength bring Eulalia to the city in a single night. Two swift and alliterative lines with an epic flavour (e.g. 'Eoa polum'), convey this:

> Illa, gradu cita peruigili,
> milia multa prius peragit
> quam plaga pandat Eoa polum;
>
> (61–3).

---

[34] Cf. Virgil, *Eclogue* 5. 52: 'Daphnimque tuum tollemus ad astra'; and Horace, *Odes*, 4. 2. 23: 'educere in astra'. The idea of moving 'ad astra' after death is also common on Christian grave inscriptions. See *TLL* 2 col. 973–4: *Carm. epigr.* 669 (AD 382), 2, 'fecit ad astra viam' and 787. 42, 'decedis martyr ad astra'. The theme is treated by Lattimore (1942) 311–12: the theme of 'the soul among the stars' represents 'a real strand of pagan thought worked into the Christian doctrine'.

In the morning, when she reaches the tribunal, she is described as 'superba'. The epithet is heroic, suitably so at a point when Eulalia's courage, already tested by her night-journey, is to face the greatest test of all. The true hero remains proud in the face of death, may even earn his death by this and by the resolve to support his cause to the end. Eulalia's pride is all the more impressive for her youth and apparent feminine frailty. This was emphasized in the opening stanzas of the poem. With Eulalia's arrival at the tribunal, Prudentius begins his portrayal of the young martyr as 'uirgo animosa'. She courts death and provokes the Praetor in a way which invites a highly dramatic treatment from the poet.

This emerges in Eulalia's fierce and scathing denunciation of the pagan gods at 66 ff., and her confession of faith at 75. Virgilian reminiscences enrich this outburst. She begins (66–70) with a single rhetorical question, which is immediately followed by a second and shorter question in which she addresses the pagan gathering with the words, 'o miseranda manus' (71). This phrase recalls a passage in *Aeneid* 11 where Venulus reports to the Rutulians Diomedes' reply to their envoys (252 ff.). Diomedes speaks of the sufferings of the wandering Greeks after their taking of Troy and refers to them in their pitiable state as 'Priamo miseranda manus' (259). By using this form of address to the non-Christians at her trial, Eulalia suggests that they too are to be pitied: they will one day pay the penalty for their lack of faith. The phrase 'miseranda manus' takes on a prophetic force in its new context. It also puts the Christians in the position of the Trojans, the race of Priam, which in the end wins through to the founding of a new empire in spite of defeat at Troy. So the Christians endure persecution to enjoy not only a heavenly kingdom, but also a Christian Rome, which has in fact reached its completion in Prudentius' own time. Just as Troy had had to fall for the new city of Rome to rise,[35] so the Trojan gods brought down from the defeated city gave way in turn to the Christian god.

Eulalia's use of the phrase marks her own superiority over the unenlightened pagans. She then turns to her own situation with the exclamation 'en ego sum ...' (72). Her words recall several passages from the *Aeneid*. At 5. 672, Ascanius cries out 'en ego uester Ascanius!' to the Trojan women who are frenziedly setting

---

[35] Cf. n. 1 above. Juno makes this point clear at *Odes* 3. 3. Dexel (1907: 23) points out that the phrase 'miseranda manus' occurs in the same position in the verse in both contexts.

fire to the Trojan ships while the men are engaged in the funeral
games held in Sicily in honour of Anchises. Ascanius tries to rouse
the women from their divinely-induced frenzy by announcing his
identity. Eulalia, the young heroine, is once again matched with
the boy-hero by the Prudentian evocation of a Virgilian passage.
Both children face the fury of a crowd: Ascanius that of the
Trojan women, Eulalia that of the pagans led by the Praetor. But
for Eulalia, the hostility of those she faces will lead to her death at
their hands. Her exclamation is thus invested with even greater
heroic defiance.

Two other Virgilian passages may also be important for
Eulalia's exclamation. At *Aeneid*, 7. 452, the Fury Allecto uses the
words 'en ego …' as she sheds her disguise as an old priestess and
reveals her true identity to Turnus. This may provide a fitting
background for Eulalia's behaviour at her trial. She is externally a
uirgo but a *uir* in spirit. Allecto comes 'dirarum ab sede sororum'
and is another example of an unnatural female force, reminiscent
of the association of Eulalia with the Dirae which may be implied
by the reference to *Aeneid*, 12. 849 at *Pe.* 3. 17. Eulalia in this way
is shown to be stepping beyond her normal feminine nature in her
behaviour at the trial.[36]

At *Aeneid*, 9. 427, Nisus cries out to draw attention to himself
in the shadows when he sees Volcens advancing to attack his com-
panion Euryalus:

> me, me, adsum qui feci, in me conuertite ferrum,
> O Rutuli!

Nisus here announces himself in order to invite attack and pos-
sible death. This is very much the spirit of Eulalia's announcement
in *Pe.* 3, made in answer to her own opening rhetorical question.
It does not seem unlikely that Prudentius should evoke all three
Virgilian passages in Eulalia's exclamation. Such contamination of
models only increases the resonance of the new phrase in its con-
text.[37]

The martyr's speech continues with a denunciation of pagan

[36] Mahogany (1934: 160), notes this reminiscence. See too Richard (1969). The Chris-
tian paradox of the 'mulier uirilis' is discussed by Giannarelli (1980), and also by Fontaine
(1970).

[37] For *contaminatio*, the combined imitation of two models (without pejorative over-
tones), see West and Woodman (1979) 212 n. 86, and 229 n. 4, with reference to Kroll
(1924) 171–4.

gods, culminating in an exposition of the emperor's stupidity in worshipping such man-made, inanimate deities. Prudentius here steps outside the epic world of the *Aeneid* to insert a sarcastic cut at the pagan emperor by means of a reference to Horace, *Odes*, 4. 5. 5, where Horace wholeheartedly eulogizes Augustus and asks 'lucem redde tuae, *dux bone*, patriae . . .'[38] It is with heavy irony that Eulalia refers to the Emperor as 'dux bonus' at line 86.

This last point is noted in an interesting article on the figure of the persecutor in the *Peristephanon*.[39] The poems are considered in terms of the central *agon* between Roman magistrate and martyr. Attention is drawn to Prudentius' frequent characterization of magistrate as 'tyrannus', and to how he is influenced by the literary treatment of this type. The confrontations of martyrs and magistrates can be compared with the treatment of this theme in the tragedies of Seneca the Younger. The exchange between Ulysses and Andromache in the *Troades* (578 ff.) is particularly relevant to the exchange between the Praetor and Eulalia in *Pe.* 3.[40] However, actual close verbal similarity is lacking, and Opelt draws attention rather to the common background to the tragedy and the *Peristephanon* in the declamation exercises practised in the rhetorical training experienced by both poets. Examples are drawn from the *Controuersiae* of the Elder Seneca, in particular from 2. 5: 'Torta a tyranno pro marito'. This example is particularly apt in a consideration of *Pe.* 3, with which it has many features in common, not least the sex of the victim. There is the same emphasis on the number and cruelty of the tortures (*Controuersiae*, 2. 5. 6–7), the same bullying threats from the tyrant and the same defiance from the woman. The silent resistance of the woman (2. 5. 6 and 8) is reminiscent of *Pe.* 3. 126–8, although Prudentius adds an act of wild defiance to Eulalia's silence:

> Martyr ad ista nihil, sed enim
> infremit inque tyranni oculos
> *sputa iacet* . . .

---

[38] This parallel is noted by Bergman, Lavarenne, and Guillén, ad loc. In 87 'sanguine pascitur' may recall *Amores*, 8. 10 'sanguine pascitur eques', also used in the context of disdain for the rich and powerful.

[39] Opelt (1967).

[40] Opelt (1967) 254. It should also be noted in connection with this exchange that attempts at dissuasion by the Roman officer in charge do occur in historical martyr-acts. Musurillo (1972. xiv) notes that in the case of Polycarp, 'Herod and his father Nicetes, with the proconsul, all attempt to break down [Polycarp's] resistance in a kindly way. It would appear that they are still acting on the directives of Pliny's rescript (*Ep.* 10. 97).'

This rhetorical influence on Prudentius' treatment of his heroine is
rather far removed from the influence of Virgilian epic on the
Christian poet's characterization of Eulalia, but it must be men-
tioned in passing to give the fullest picture of Prudentius' tech-
nique in this poem. The influence of Senecan tragedy on the
Peristephanon is discussed below, pp. 188 ff.

The Praetor reminds Eulalia of the joys of marriage which she
will forego by her premature death and the impact of her death
on her family (104–13). The death of a virgin before marriage was
a pathetic theme with a long history in both Greek and Latin liter-
ature. Homer speaks of 'tender virgins' among those souls which
are called forth from Erebus

> παρθενικαί τ᾽ ἀταλαί νεοπενθέα θυμὸν ἔχουσαι
>
> tender maidens with hearts yet new to sorrow
>
> (*Od.* 11. 39)

This is taken up by Virgil in his picture of the underworld in
Aeneid 6 when he speaks of 'pueri innuptaeque puellae' (307). The
theme receives tragic treatment from the Greek dramatists, where
Sophocles' *Antigone* provides the most striking example. The
heroine is an interesting prototype for Eulalia: she too dies for her
religious convictions at the hands of a 'tyrannus'. In her last
exchange with the chorus, Antigone laments her own death in
terms of the marriage she will never know:

> οὔθ᾽ ὑμεναίων
> ἔγκληρον, οὔτ᾽ ἐπί νυμ-
> φείοις πω μέ τις ὕμνος ὔ-
> μνησεν, ἀλλ᾽ Ἀχέροντι νυμφεύσω
>
> (813–16)

I who have had no portion in the chant that brings the bride, nor hath
any song been mine for the crowning of bridals; whom the lord of the
Dark Lake shall wed.

These ideas recur at 869, 878, and 917–18 in the tragedy. As Latti-
more has pointed out, they also constitute a theme common to
Greek and Roman epitaphs.[41]

---

[41] Lattimore (1942) 192 ff.

Eulalia's family will lament:

> flore quod occidis in tenero,
> proxima dotibus et thalamis.
>
> (109–10)

Bergman[42] at this point keeps the reading 'sole' for 'flore' on the basis of the occurrence of 'sole' in the MS Bibl. Nat. Lat. 8084 (Puteanus) and in the margin of the MS Cantabr. Corp. Chr. 223. He supports his reading by reference to *Psychomachia*, 845:

> *seu pueros sol primus agat*, seu feruor ephebos
> incendat nimius . . .

where the italic phrase is used figuratively to express the idea of childhood. The sixth-century date of the Puteanus MS is obviously persuasive in the case for the reading 'sole', but the reading 'flore' seems preferable for two reasons.[43] Firstly, every other MS has 'flore'. The marginal note on the variant 'sole' seems to argue against rather than for this reading, especially in a MS which in other ways seems to be derived indirectly from Puteanus' model. Secondly, the word 'flore' is simply much better in the context in all respects. The 'parallel' from the *Psychomachia* may easily be dismissed, since the metaphorical phrase in which 'sol' is used of childhood is set in a series of phrases which cover the whole of a man's life in terms of the progression of the sun, its heat and light from dawn to noon:

> seu pueros sol primus agat, seu feruor ephebos
> incendat nimius, seu consummabilis aeri
> perficiat lux plena uiros . . .
>
> (845–7)

The adjective 'tener' at *Pe.* 3. 109 seems an unsuitable one to use of the sun in any context, and it does not appear in this connection elsewhere in Latin poetry. On the other hand, the word 'flore' at this point is richly suggestive and evocative. It recalls the metaphorical use of the word 'flos' in just the same context in epitaphs: 'et uirtute potens et pulcher flore iuuentae'; 'flos aetatis hic iacet intus condita saxo'.[44] It also has a literary background. Perhaps

---

[42] Guillén (1950 edn.: 530) is alone in following him.
[43] It is adopted by Lavarenne, Cunningham, and Thomson.
[44] Lattimore (1942) 192 ff.

there was the echo of an epitaph in Virgil's mind when he composed the simile which is used to mark the pathos of the young hero Euryalus' death in *Aeneid*, 9. 435 ff.:

> purpureus ueluti cum *flos* succisus aratro
> languescit *moriens*, lassoue papauera collo
> demisere caput pluuia cum forte grauantur.

The image emphasizes Euryalus' youth and beauty and the cruelty of his early death.[45] The Prudentian lines have the same pathetic force which might be associated with the similarity between Eulalia's secret night-journey and Euryalus' night-exploits.

However, flower imagery used of young girls belongs in particular to the wedding hymn, an obvious connection to make here in view of the Praetor's references to Eulalia's marriage. Comparisons can be made with the recurrent flower images of the Catullan wedding hymns *C*. 61 and 62. At *C*. 61. 34, the bride is compared to clinging ivy. At line 57 the poet refers to her as 'florida puellula', using a diminutive which the Praetor significantly uses of Eulalia at line 103 in his appeal. At *C*. 61. 89, the bride is compared to a hyacinth, at line 187 to a white daisy or yellow poppy. At *C*. 62. 139–44, the unmarried girl is compared to a flower in a garden, 'nullo conuulsus aratro'. Catullus expresses the bride's youth and virginity by these comparisons, and perhaps also in the last example, her fragility. Prudentius' line uses the metaphor of 'flos ... tener' to combine suggestions of the martyr's youth, her virginity and the imminence of death. Ironically, the Praetor here chooses an image which has its own positive associations in the context of martyrdom. Thus, by her death, Eulalia will become a bride of Christ and one more 'flower' in the Church's garland of martyrs. At *Pe*. 2. 544, Rome 'sacris sepulcris *floreat*'. At *Cathemerinon*, 12. 125 ff., the martyred Holy Innocents are hailed as 'flores martyrum', cut down by Herod 'ceu turbo

---

[45] Virgil's simile may itself be partly influenced by Catullus 11. 21 ff.: 'nec meum respectet, ut ante, amorem,/qui illius culpa cecidit uelut prati/ultimi flos, praetereunte postquam/tactus aratrost.' It has also, of course, a beautiful epic precedent in the simile at *Iliad*, 8. 306–8, used to describe the death of Gorgythion: μήκων δ' ὡς ἑτέρωσε κάρη βάλεν, ἥ τ' ἐνὶ κήπῳ,/ καρπῷ βριθομένη νοτίῃσί τε εἰαρινῇσιν,/ ὡς ἑτέρωσ' ἤμυσε κάρη πήληκι βαρυνθέν. 'And he bowed his head to one side like a poppy that in a garden is laden with its fruit and the rains of spring; so bowed he to one side his head, laden with his helmet.' (Loeb translation.)

nascentes rosas'. Here the same connection is made between death of the very young and the fragility of flowers.

The epic flavour of Prudentius' account of Eulalia's martyrdom is maintained by one or two touches over the next thirty lines. The 'nec mora' with which line 131 begins recalls several Virgilian uses of the phrase in the same position, and many other occurrences of the same phrase in later epic.[46] A piece of Horatian phraseology has been noticed in 'inuolitans umeris' (152), where reference is made to *Odes*, 4. 10. 3, 'umeris inuolitant'.[47] The Prudentian context is far from erotic, as it is in Horace: Eulalia's hair covers her and supports her modesty. Lines 151–2 do, however, build up a rather sensually pleasing picture of the young girl, whose soft prettiness is evoked at this point in order to intensify the pathos of the scene as she stands alone on the pyre. The 'crinis *odorus*' which introduces this stanza is part of this picture, whether or not this phrase is meant to evoke the description of Venus from *Aeneid*, 1. 403 ff.:

> ambrosiaeque *comae diuinum* uertice *oderem*
> spirauere . . .

At lines 156–60, Prudentius more obviously tries once more to relate Eulalia's experience to the heroic world of the *Aeneid*. He describes the final burning of Eulalia:

> *flamma crepans* uolat in faciem,
> *perque comas* uegetata caput
> occupat exsuperatque apicem;
> uirgo citum cupiens obitum
> adpetit et *bibit ore* rogum.

Two scenes from the *Aeneid* are here recalled. In *Aeneid* 7, an ominous flame appears on the head of Latinus' daughter Lavinia, who is destined to marry Aeneas:[48]

> praeterea, castis adolet dum altaria taedis,
> et iuxta genitorem astat Lauinia *uirgo*,
> uisa (nefas) *longis comprendere crinibus ignem*
> atque omnem ornatum *flamma crepitante* cremari

---

[46] See Schumann (1981) 3, 499–500.

[47] This parallel is noted by Bergman, Lavarenne, and Guillén.

[48] Mahoney (1934; 159), puts this passage among his 'probable' Virgilian reminiscences. It is not noted by Bergman, Lavarenne, or Guillén.

regalisque accensa comas, accensa coronam
insignem gemmis; tum fumida lumine fuluo
inuolui ac totis Volcanum spargere tectis.

(*Aeneid*, 7. 72–80).

The scene of sacrifice, the picture of 'Lauinia uirgo', the noise of
the 'flamma' (*crepitante* in the Virgilian passage is recalled by
crepans in Prudentius), and the detailed description of the flame's
possession of the girl's head and hair, all provide a series of strik-
ing similarities between the two passages, although no extended
verbal imitation is involved. Prudentius evokes the Virgilian pas-
sage by building up a similar scene, marked as such by the selec-
tion of telling details. Key words and phrases taken from the
original passage support the picture and lend it a deeper perspect-
ive. Thus, here Eulalia's positive reaction to the pyre ('adpetit et
bibit ore rogum') appears all the stronger in contrast to the passive
role of Lavinia in *Aeneid* 7.

In this passage, Prudentius may also be evoking another pro-
phetic flame from the *Aeneid*, the fire which appears over Iulus'
head at a crucial moment towards the end of *Aeneid* 2:[49]

ecce leuis summo de uertice uisus Iuli
fundere lumen apex, tactuque innoxia mollis
lambere flamma comas et circum tempora pasci.

(682–4)

The word 'apex' here might be behind Prudentius' rather unusual
use of 'apicem' at *Pe.* 3. 158. He may even have misunderstood his
Virgil here. In his picture of the martyr, Prudentius shows the
flame leaping into Eulalia's face, over her hair and head. Finally as
the climax 'exsuperatque apicem', where 'apex' evidently means
the top of Eulalia's head. This is an unparalleled use of the word.[50]
The Virgilian use of the word with regard to Iulus has been much
disputed,[51] but seems to refer to the actual point or tongue of fire
(a usage which can be paralleled), rather than to any sort of sacer-
dotal hat as in Servius, *Ad Aen.* 2. 683. The presence of this par-
ticular problematical word in an unparalleled sense in Prudentius'

---

[49] Also noted by Mahoney (1934: 159).
[50] See *TLL* 2, 'apex', col. 226–8.
[51] See Austin's discussion of *Aeneid*, 2. 683 (1964: 254–5).

description of a similar scene might suggest that he was alluding to the Virgilian picture.

By the double allusion at *Pe.* 3. 156 ff., a very full picture of the martyr is given: the youth and virginity of Lavinia are evoked, and the youth of Iulus, who stands in fact for the Trojans' hopes for the future. The flames of both Lavinia and Iulus are prophetic in a positive sense for the most part. By recalling these flames for his description of the funeral pyre, Prudentius confers on Eulalia's death not only an epic heroism enhanced by her youth and sex, but also a message of hope for the whole 'Christicolum genus'. Although the flame of Eulalia's pyre consumes in a way that the Virgilian flames do not, this flame and the death which it brings constitute victory for Christianity in the future in a more real and lasting sense than that contained in the *Aeneid*'s prophecies for the future greatness of Rome. Eulalia herself recognizes this—hence her enthusiasm to 'drink down' her death: 'et bibit ore rogum', where 'bibit ore' recalls a heroic Horatian passage. At *Odes*, 3. 3. 11, Augustus is pictured in heaven drinking nectar among the heroes and gods: 'purpureo bibit ore nectar . . .'. The 'rogum' replaces the pagan 'nectar' for Eulalia. But she will, by this heroic draught, reach the true Christian heaven and a reward more real than the pagan idea of heroization represented by Horace.

The sudden release of Eulalia's 'anima' at *Pe.* 3. 161 recalls the release of the dove at the funeral games of Anchises, *Aeneid*, 5. 500 ff. This dove 'uitamque reliquit in astris/aetheriis', while it is '*plaudentem*'. So Eulalia's soul 'flatus in aethere plaudit orans' (169). Eulalia is as innocent as the dove. The miraculous nature of Prudentius' dove-*anima* might even recall the miraculous climax of the archery contest in *Aeneid* 5, which immediately follows the death of the dove at 520 ff. At 525, 'uolans liquidis in nubibus arsit harundo'. The snow-white dove symbolizes Eulalia's purity: it is 'niue candidior'. At the superficial level, this phrase recalls Virgil's description of the horses of Turnus: 'candore niues anteirent' (*Aeneid*, 12. 84), or Ovid's description of the horses of the Dioscuri as 'niue candidiores' (*Metamorphoses*, 8. 37). The extreme purity of Eulalia's spirit is emphasized again at the end of the stanza with the adjective 'lacteolus' (165), milk-white. A precedent for this diminutive form may be found at Catullus *C.* 55. 17, where, however, the word occurs in an erotic context. Prudentius here wants the adjective in the softness of its diminutive form to

convey Eulalia's youth and innocence, as it is represented by the
snow-white dove of her soul.[52]

White as a symbol of youth and purity is important for the
second miracle which accompanies Eulalia's death (176 ff.):

> Ecce niuem *glacialis hiems*
> ingerit et tegit omne forum,
> membra tegit simul Eulaliae
> axe iacentia sub gelido
> pallioli uice linteoli . . .

Eulalia's body is modestly covered by the snow, as though by a
small linen cloak (the diminutives 'palliolum' and 'linteolum'
surely have a pathetic force in this context and emphasize the
diminutive proportions of the child-martyr's corpse). So had her
hair covered her 'pudibunda pudicitia' in the midst of torture.[53]
Just as the snow-white dove/soul had led the eye of the reader
heaven-ward, so now the falling of actual snow (another realiza-
tion of the symbolic force of white in denoting purity and inno-
cence) leads the eye gently back down to earth and to Eulalia's
earthly remains. The line introducing the snow miracle recalls a
Virgilian scene, though this time from the wanderings of Aeneas,
Aeneid, 3. 284–5. The old context contributes to the miraculous
nature of the new by its emphasis on the regularity of the *natural*
rotation of the seasons:

> interea magnum sol circumuoluitur annum
> et *glacialis hiems* Aquilonibus asperat undas . . .

---

[52] The single occurrence of the word in Ausonius (*Ep.* 13. 46, does not seem relevant
here: the word is used to describe the flesh of a mussel. The adjective is used again at *Pe.* 11.
245, to describe the 'agni' in Bishop Valerianus' 'flock'. Cf. Ps. 702 'lacteolam . . . ovem';
and *Ditt.* 115 'lacteolo . . . sanguine', which recalls the curious picture evoked by Pruden-
tius at *Pe.* 10. 700 (see p. 183). Prudentius' expressive use of diminutives is discussed by Sal-
vatore (1958) 207–22.

[53] Agnes in Damasus' epigram is covered by her hair, (cf. Eulalia on the pyre, 151–3):
'Nudaque perfusos crines per membra dedisse/Ne Domini templum facies peritura
uideret.' See below, p. 240. Dr John Matthews has drawn a passage of Ammianus Marcelli-
nus to my attention (*RG* 28. 1. 28), in which an executioner is himself executed for allow-
ing a woman to go naked to her death. This is termed 'nefas . . . immane'. This
demonstrates an almost puritanical preoccupation with modesty, even in the pagan sphere
in the 4th century. Christian morality did not necessarily break continuity with the tradi-
tional views, in spite of the negative view of pagan mores presented by the Church Fathers.
Cf. the case of Lucretia (Livy, 1. 57–9, Ovid, *Fasti*, 2. 721–852).

Even nature admits Eulalia's heroism and rewards it:[54]

> ipsa elementa iubente Deo
> exequias tibi, uirgo ferunt.
>
> (184–5)

The final miraculous snowfall is followed by an exhortation not to mourn the martyr. (The opening phrase may superficially recall the identical phrase in Ovid's *Remedia amoris*, 752; the reminiscence is verbal only, since the Ovidian context is too inappropriate for the situation in *Pe.* 3.) Then follows a description of the contemporary cult-site:

> quam memorabilis amnis Ana
> praeterit . . .
>
> (188–9)

A description of the basilica erected over Eulalia's remains is given at 191–200. The church is resplendent with local and imported marble (191–3); its vaulted ceiling is glorious with gold (196–7):

> Tecta corusca super rutilant
> de laquearibus aureolis . . .

Prudentius then brings the reader's eye down to the floor, which is decorated with colourful mosaics reflecting the floral colours of nature:

> floribus ut rosulenta putes
> prata rubescere multimodis.

This riot of colour creates the effect of a glorious triumph for the martyr after the ethereal restraint of the snowy hues in the previous scene. This rich and varied scene evokes a Virgilian scene of splendour, the palace of Dido in *Aeneid* 1.[55] Prudentius' phrase 'laquearibus aureolis' recalls *Aeneid*, 1. 726, 'dependent lychni laquearibus aureis'. This line occurs in a description of a rich and festive scene, presided over by Dido, Queen of Carthage, who, like Eulalia, come to a tragic end on the pyre. The diminutive adjective in Prudentius' version is perhaps intended to express a deli-

---

[54] As Hanley notes (1959: 210), with Mahoney (1934: 160), Prudentius may also here be aware of Ovid's use of the same phrase at *Metamorphoses* 2. 30, where it is used of the personified figure of Winter.

[55] See Mahoney (1934) 159.

cacy of decoration which reflects Eulalia's youth and femininity. The background of Dido's history is perhaps less important here than the visual richness and splendour of the Virgilian scene. *Pe.* 3. 199–200 suggest the description of St Peter's Basilica given at *Pe.* 12. 54. The poet there describes the mosaics and compares them to spring flowers:

> sic prata uernis floribus renident.

The floral reference in *Pe.* 3 is fuller and better integrated, pointing back to the association of Eulalia with flowers at *Pe.* 3. 109 and linking the description of the basilica with the poet's closing exhortation:

> Carpite purpureas uiolas
> sanguineosque crocos metite!

Thus the poem ends with the colourful and festive variety of the flower-like decorations of the church, and the feast-day bouquets which the imaginary choir of boys and girls are encouraged to gather (*Pe.* 3. 207). The flowers are themselves significant: they are 'purpureas violas' (the adjective is a Virgilian flower-epithet used at *Georgics*, 4. 54) and 'sanguinei croci'. The adjectives are carefully chosen, not only for the rich visual effect suggested by their contrast in juxtaposition, but also for the symbolic value which they give the flowers. 'Purpureus' conveys the purple colour of the blooms and their vividness, but it could also suggest the idea of a triumph, since the colour was particularly associated with the celebration of triumphs.[56] Eulalia after death is a martyr triumphant in Heaven, and wears the martyr's crown of victory. The adjective 'sanguineus' (noticeably *not* the unsuggestive though vivid 'rubentem' used of the crocus at *Georgics*, 4. 182) speaks for itself in the context of martyrdom. It is an unusual word to use of a flower[57] and here really refers obliquely to the bloody end of Eulalia. Red eventually became the liturgical colour for the celebration of martyrs' feast-days, when it has the

---

[56] Lewis and Short, 1493: *Oxford Latin Dictionary*, 1523–4. The word is used of flowers by Horace (*Odes*, 3. 15. 25) and Propertius (1. 20. 38).

[57] Lewis and Short, 1626, *Oxford Latin Dictionary*, 1688. Used of flowers by Columella (10. 242), of berries by Virgil (*Eclogues*, 10. 27) and of bushes by Pliny (*Nat. Hist.* 16. 74; 19. 180). Cf. Ovid, *Metam.* 10. 735: 'flos de sanguine concolor ortus', and 13. 394: 'rubefactaque sanguine tellus / purpureum genuit florem'.

same symbolic force.[58] These flowers at the end of *Pe.* 3 are all
'sweets to the sweet', but do not allow the martyr's death to go
unforgotten. Eulalia may be as fragile and lovely as a flower, but
dies a hero's death by violence.[59] The poet calls for flowers in a
way which recalls Anchises' words at *Aeneid,* 6. 883–5. He finishes
his lament for the young Marcellus, carried off by a premature
death, with a similar call for flowers to scatter as a gift for his dead
descendant:

> ... manibus date *lilia* plenis,
> *purpureos* spargam flores animamque nepotis
> his saltem accumulem donis ...

The theme of the death of a young person and the association
with flowers links the two passages (the adjective 'purpureus' is
used too commonly of flowers to allow too much weight to be
put on its occurrence in this passage from *Aeneid* 6). Anchises
speaks out of extreme sorrow, but a more joyful note enters Pru-
dentius' cry for flowers: the death of the martyr is really her *dies
natalis* in Christian terms and is commemorated and celebrated
joyfully as such by her fellow-Christians.

Prudentius leaves the epic world for the pastoral setting of the
Georgics and *Eclogues* as he comes to the end of his poem. The
rather harsh picture of the martyr painted in the centre of the
poem (she is 'ferox', 'fera', 'uirgo animosa') is allowed to fade be-
hind the softer colours and lighter mood of the festive close. The
flowers recall and replace the wedding celebrations which Eulalia
foregoes by her martyrdom. She spurned flowers as playthings
and ornaments in life (20 ff.), was cut off in the 'flower of her
youth', but is now showered with blooms in her martyr's tri-
umph. Nature relaxes its laws to provide these gifts for her winter
feast-day (10 December):

> Non caret his *genialis hiems,*
> laxat et arua tepens glacies,
> floribus ut cumulet calathos.
>
> (203–5)

[58] But a liturgical colour-scheme for vestments was not in use as early as the 4th or 5th
centuries. See 'Vêtements', *DACL* 15 (2) (1951–3), col. 2989–3007; col. 3002–3, 'La
couleur des vêtements'.

[59] Hanley (1959) draws attention here to two passages in Ovid (*Metam.* 5. 392 ff. and
Fasti, 4, 435–42), where Proserpina is pictured collecting flowers just before she is carried
off to the Underworld. The general picture and atmosphere may be similar, especially in
the context of the shared youth and innocence of the girl-victims, Eulalia and Proserpina,
but this is not reinforced by close enough verbal similarities in the passages, even brief ones.

The phrase 'genialis hiems' echoes the identical phrase from *Georgics*, 1. 302, 'inuitat *genialis hiems* curasque resoluit'; 'laxat et arua tepens glacies' recalls *Georgics*, 2. 330 ff., 'Zephyrique trementibus auris/laxant arua sinus'. The language of pastoral and the rural scene promote a gentler mood for the end of the poem.

This tone continues in the last two stanzas. Floral gifts for Eulalia give way naturally to the appearance of the poet weaving 'garlands of song' in the midst of his choir:

> Ista comantibus e foliis
> munera, uirgo puerque, date!
> Ast ego serta choro in medio
> texta feram pede dactylico,
> uilia, marcida, festa tamen.
>
> (206–10)

Prudentius may have in mind here the Virgilian picture of the humble shepherd-poet who, at the close of *Eclogue* 10, 'gracili fiscellam texit hibisco'. Prudentius is more self-conscious about his own artistry: his garlands are explicitly those of verse, the metre of which is clearly stated.[60] The integration of this technical point into the course of the poem is a rather Ovidian touch,[61] but the lightness of tone here is then modified by the poet's humble attitude towards the products of his craftsmanship, which are 'uilia, marcida'. The poet's exuberance is qualified by his Christian outlook.

The movement from the epic to the pastoral world at the end of *Pe.* 3 is unusual (the *Aeneid* is the poet's main source of reference in the *Peristephanon*), but successful. The strident notes struck in the scenes of Eulalia's trial and death are softened. The opposition of the forces of light and darkness loses its harshness in the

[60] Cf. *Cathemerinon*, 3. 26 ff., quoted above p. 82, and *Pe.* 6. 163: the poet speaks of himself as 'dulces hedecasyllabos reuoluens'. At *Epil.* 7–8 he says: 'Nos citos iambicos/sacramus et rotatiles trochaeos . . .' The only other reference to poetry as garlands is at Martial, 8. 82. 4, cf. chap. 3 n. 106 above.

[61] Cf. Ovid, *Amores*, 1. 1. 30, for a playful reference to the metre of the poem: and *Remedia amoris*, 378, *Fasti*, 2. 126. Other references by poets to their metres may be found at Tibullus, 2. 5. 112, Horace, *Sat.* 1. 10. 1 and 2. 1. 28, *Ep.* 14. 12, *Ars poetica*, 80; Martial, 10. 9. 1, and Ausonius, *Invitatio ad Paulum*, 37–9. The dactylic metre of *Pe.* 3 may in itself have an oblique epic reference, though it is lighter than the hexameter. It also significantly evokes the metre of Ausonius' *Parentalia* 28, written in memory of the young relative Idalia. See Charlet (1982) 27 and (1980a) 96–7.

riot of festive colour at the poem's close. The girl-martyr recovers the feminine character which she lost in the midst of the narrative.

The epic scenes and personalities recalled by Prudentius through repeated reference to the text of the *Aeneid* add a depth of perspective to the figure of Eulalia which she might otherwise have lacked. An heroic framework is built up against which it is possible to measure and appreciate the girl-martyr's achievements. Not only are her courageous deeds *equal* to those of her Virgilian predecessors in number and quality, but at each point of comparison they surpass them. Eulalia is, after all, only a young girl. It is her spiritual strength which sustains her resolve and makes it possible for a girl to challenge men.[62] Prudentius makes no explicit negative judgement against the non-Christian heroism celebrated in the *Aeneid*.[63] He is more interested in showing how far Christianity exemplifies the same heroic qualities, and how far the new faith has assimilated them and extended their scope and value. The old values were admirable in themselves, but gain their true meaning through their Christian application.

Nowhere else in the *Peristephanon* does Prudentius create such a complete picture of a martyr's heroism by a comparably wide-ranging and complete set of epic references. Similar technique is indeed used in other poems, but more sparingly and more dilutedly. There are some Virgilian touches in *Pe.* 4, for example,[64] but no sustained epic references. The Sapphic metre of the poem and its celebration of the martyrs' victory recall, rather, Horatian panegyric in the same metre.[65] *Pe.* 5 uses quite a number of reminiscences from the *Aeneid* to build up an heroic picture of Vincent, but they are spread over a poem more than twice as long as *Pe.* 3. *Pe.* 6 is noticeably bare of reference to Virgil's heroes,[66] while 7 lacks significant Virgilian reminiscences after the striking

---

[62] See Fontaine (1980).

[63] See n. 32 above.

[64] Mahoney (1934) 161–2.

[65] For example, *Odes*, 1. 2 and 1. 12.

[66] Though see Mahoney's list (1934: 165–6). However, only the scene of Fructuosus' burning and its aftermath involves a large-scale reminiscence of a Virgilian scene, which is very lightly recalled by the repetition of one or two key words. Compare *Pe.* 6. 13 ff. with Misenus' funeral at *Aeneid*, 6. 227 ff. The binding of the martyr's hands recalls that of Sinon in *Aeneid*, 2. 57 (cf. *Pe.* 6. 103 ff), but the phrasing of this has taken on a formulaic character in Prudentius, who uses it again at *Pe.* 9. 43, and 10. 70. Apart from these reminiscences, the others may be regarded as trivial or superficial, contributing nothing to Prudentius' depiction of the figure of the martyr, except in a general way.

178   'Egregiae animae'

opening reference to Quirinus as 'insignem meriti uirum'. Aeneas
is 'insignem pietate uirum' at *Aeneid*, 1. 10.[67] After the patriotic
reference of the opening lines (see above pp. 135–6), *Pe.* 9 offers
no very striking examples of reference to Virgilian heroism:
Cassian's death at *Pe.* 9. 85 suggests that of Dido at *Aeneid*, 4. 693–
5, though in overall structure rather than by exact verbal reminis-
cence.[68] The patriotic function of the Virgilian reference in *Pe.* 11
has already been discussed. The martyr himself is not treated in
Virgilian terms,[69] but viewed rather in a tragic perspective, with
reference to Seneca's dramatic treatment of the martyr's mythical
namesake.[70] *Pe.* 12 and 13 lack significant Virgilian reminiscences
relevant to the presentation of their martyrs,[71] although Virgilian
language lends the poems in general an epic flavour. Mahoney[72]
has noted a number of Virgilian reminiscences in *Pe.* 14, which
have not been noticed by other commentators. The three most
significant for the figure of Agnes are accumulated towards the
end of the poem. Agnes after death:

> Miratur orbem sub pedibus situm . . .
>
> (94)

This recalls the deified Daphnis in Virgil's *Eclogue* 5 who:

> candidus insuetum miratur limen Olympi
> sub pedibusque uidet nubes et sidera . . .
>
> (56–7)

[67] Cf. *Pe.* 7. 49. Charlet brings out the significance of Prudentius' application of the tra-
ditional term for the hero, 'Vir' to the Christian martyrs (1980: 209). For other Virgilian
touches in *Pe.* 7, see Mahoney (1934) 166–7.

[68] In the *Aeneid*, as Dido suffers her death agony, Juno '. . . longum *miserata* dolorem/
difficilesque obitus Irim demisit Olympo/ quae *luctantem animam* nexosque resoluerat artus',
whereas in *Pe.* 9. 85–8 it is Christ who 'tandem luctantis miseratus ab aethere . . ./lubet
resolui pectoris ligamina;/difficilesque moras animae ac retinacula uitae/relaxat, artas et
latebras expedit.' See Schwen (1937) 63.

[69] Mahoney once again lists every possible Virgilian reminiscence in *Pe.* 11 (1934: 174–
8), but these seem mainly designed to create a general heroic background rather than to
make particular points about the heroic stature of Hippolytus. See Schwen (1937: 126) for
the same conclusion. Dr Adrian Hollis suggested here some similarities with the figure of
Mettus, whose death is briefly described at *Aeneid*, 8. 642–5. He too is dragged apart, by
chariots; the macabre results are painted with the line 'per siluam et sparsi rorabant san-
guine uepres'. Some of this vocabulary recurs at *Pe.* 11. 115–28, but there are no strikingly
exact similarities of expression. Perhaps the Virgilian scene was less consciously the model
for *Pe.* 11 here than the later poets.

[70] See below, pp. 188 ff., for the influence of Senecan tragedy on the *Peristephanon*.

[71] Mahoney (1934) 178–80.

[72] Mahoney (1934) 180–1.

At *Pe.* 14. 124 Prudentius directly addresses the martyr:

> o uirgo felix, o noua gloria.

Two points in the *Aeneid* are here recalled. Firstly, at *Aeneid*, 3. 321, Andromache refers to Polyxena as 'felix ... uirgo' because she died at Troy instead of living to know slavery, as she herself has done. The virgin Polyxena, sacrificed at Achilles' tomb, is a suitable counterpart to the girl-martyr Agnes, who, however, is more truly 'felix' in her heavenly state. It is Euander in *Aeneid* 12, secondly, who bewails the death of Pallas in battle and speaks bitterly of 'noua gloria in armis'. Agnes' 'noua gloria' in Heaven is also the result of her 'battle' on earth (in martyrdom), but her death in this battle is a matter for celebration, not for mourning. These Virgilian references give an heroic perspective to Agnes' death but highlight, by contrast, the more positive aspects of her Christian heroism. I leave discussion of the passage of Lucan relevant to *Pe.* 14. 94 ff. to the next section. No analysis of *Pe.* 10 is attempted here: the poem is long enough to merit separate treatment, and was indeed probably originally a work in its own right apart from the *Peristephanon* collection.[73] Virgilian language abounds throughout,[74] but the central figure of Romanus is not particularly coloured by significant allusion to heroic figures from the world of epic.

[73] See chap. 3, nn. 119 and 120, and Henke (1983).
[74] Mahoney (1934) 168–73.

6

Prudentius and the Imperial Poets

THE major Augustan authors still being read in the Late Antique
period provided the central inspiration for Prudentius' treatment
of his Christian themes, but other poets were also influential. Pru-
dentius' poetry reveals his participation in the whole range of
contemporary culture. He certainly knew the works of Juvenal,
Lucan, and Seneca. Statius' work was probably also in his library,
while he must have known the poetry of contemporaries: Auso-
nius, Claudian, and, of course, Ambrose (see above, Chapter 3).
In evaluating the influence of these poets on Prudentius, I shall re-
strict analysis to the poems of the *Peristephanon*, except in cases
where reference to the rest of his poetry helps to throw into relief
their individuality. Consideration of the influence of Ausonius has
been omitted here: it would constitute a major study in itself and
such a study already exists in the work of J.-L. Charlet.[1]

The collection is, in fact, untypical of the corpus as a whole.
This is partly the result of its large debt to martyr-literature and
the traditions surrounding the celebration of martyr-cult in Pru-
dentius' period. Both the content and the style of earlier martyr-
literature override the poet's more conventional poetic instincts at
many points, leading to a variety of stylistic levels which reflect
both the pressure of the Christian sources for particular poems
and the demands of the different audiences for which they were
written. (*Pe.* 6 provides a useful example to illustrate this point:
there is a full analysis in Chapter 7.)

The Influence of Juvenal

By the end of the fourth century,[2] the *Satires* of Juvenal had been

---

  [1] Charlet (1980*a*).

  [2] Syme (1968) 84–8; Cameron (1964*a*); Sanford (1931) 233 ff.; Highet (1954) 180–5;
Bartalucci (1973: 233–57) argues that the earliest commentator on Juvenal, Probus, belongs
to the early 4th century. This dating is not important here: widespread popularity by the
end of the 4th century is enough to supply Prudentius with a knowledge of the text of the
Satires.

rediscovered and had found widespread popularity, even among the lower ranks of the reading public.[3] There are clear indications in Prudentius' poetry that he too has read the *Satires* thoroughly, although reminiscence of Juvenalian thought and wording is mainly restricted to the hexameter poems. (There seem to be no reminiscences of any sort in the *Cathemerinon*.) The vividly expressed polemic of Juvenal's satire is most useful to Prudentius in his own polemic-didactic passages,[4] and it is in this context that it is recalled in the *Peristephanon*, at those points where the pagan gods and the materialistic values of the world are under attack from the martyrs. Thus, the clearest references to Juvenal occur in *Pe.* 2 and 10, poems in which the martyrs are given the opportunity to speak at unusual length.[5]

Both Juvenal and Prudentius attack the same extremes, the significant difference being that Prudentius does so from the Christian standpoint and with a new set of beliefs and values to promote. The verbal similarity of the texts in each case is clear and surely, therefore, deliberate: Prudentius does not hesitate to use Juvenal's unusual vocabulary and combinations of names. So, at *Pe.* 2. 514, the poet refers to:

> Quidquid Quiritum sueuerat
> orare *simpuuium Numae* . . .

The italic words recall Juvenal, *Sat.* 6. 343:

> et quis tunc hominum contemptor numinis? aut quis
> *simpuuium* ridere *Numae* nigrumque catinum . . .[6]

In recalling the words of the satirist, Prudentius satirizes his position in turn. Juvenal remembers with regret the old-fashioned reverence which is now lost: this reverence is symbolized for Juvenal by the articles used in the ancient rites. Prudentius hymns the Christianization of those Romans whose very neglect of the ancient rites and the ancient sacred objects is proof of the Chris-

---

[3] Ammianus Marcellinus, *RG* 28. 4. 14. See above, p. 38.

[4] See Bergman's list of *imitationes*; Highet (1954: 298) adds a few more.

[5] Delehaye (1966) 163–5 and 183 ff. Highet also parallels *Pe.* 14. 76 with Juvenal 14. 250 (but cf. Ovid, *Metam.* 8. 71). This is only a superficial verbal reminiscence and hardly even that; cf. Hanley (1962–3) 41–51.

[6] The word *simpuuium* is unusual. See Lewis and Short and the *Oxford Latin Dictionary*, ad loc.

tian victory confirmed by their conversion. The crowd that used
to participate in pagan religious activities now:

> Christi frequentat atria.

Those who were once 'luperci aut flamines' (*Pe.* 2. 518) now:

> apostolorum et martyrum
> exosculantur limina.
>
> (ibid. 519–20)

Prudentius' own polemical point here gains extra strength from
its reference to a passage in Juvenal.

At *Pe.* 10. 269–95, Prudentius makes a point against the pagans
by mentioning Myro, Polyclitus, Mentor, and Phidias: these men
are the 'fabri' of the ancient gods—so why not worship the sculp-
tors themselves as creators of the gods? The poet here echoes the
accumulation of these artists' names in Juvenal, *Sat.* 8. 102–4,
although with a very different end in view. Juvenal simply wants
to indicate with exaggerated expression, the great wealth avail-
able to the provincial governor.[7] Prudentius, on the other hand,
wants to call into question the divine status of the gods, who can
only be represented by statues made by men and their tools ('for-
ceps Myronis, malleus Polycliti'). Prudentius deflates the artists'
standing to that of human workmen ('forceps' and 'malleus' here
have bathetic as well as ironic force), while Juvenal uses their *high*
standing as artists to exaggerate the value of the governor's
plunder. Once again, Prudentius out-satirizes Juvenal's original
passage, while clearly drawing on the Juvenalian catalogue of
artists.

The satirical tone of both poets, however, is similar when it
comes to an attack on those who believe in a multiplicity of
gods—'genera deorum multa *nec pueri putant*' (*Pe.* 10. 675)—and
those who believe in the popular view of Hades:

> esse aliquos manes et subterranea regna
> et contum et Stygio ranas in gurgite nigras
> atque una transire uadum tot milia cumba
> nec pueri credunt . . .
>
> (*Sat.* 2. 149 ff.)

---

[7] Duff (1970) 306: 'their names are often mentioned together', for example Martial 8.
51. 1: 'Quis labor in phiala? docti Myos, anne Myronos?/Mentoris haec manus est, an,
Polyclite, tua?

The similarity of expression, and the way in which it is reserved in each case until the moment of denouncing obviously childish beliefs after these have been stated, seem to point to some reminiscence of Juvenal at this point.

At *Pe.* 10. 142–5, Prudentius picks up a theme common in philosophical writing—the transitory nature of worldly possessions and glories:

> ... nonne cursim transuent
> fasces, secures, sella, praetextae togae,
> lictor, tribunal et trecenta insignia,
> quibus tumetis moxque detumescitis?

At *Sat.* 10. 33 ff., Juvenal denounces wealth and its accompaniment, public office, and all its material trappings. These are not the things to ask from the gods in prayer. The message of Prudentius and Juvenal is the same, their expression similar. Both use the 'insignia' and props of office to emphasize the limited endurance of worldly advancement: these things are as finite as men's own bodies. Juvenal lingers over his caricature of men sweating and straining beneath the weight of their ceremonial clothing, while Prudentius concisely lists the offending objects. The brevity of his list treatment, however, is perhaps suggested by one asyndetic line which introduces Juvenal's indictment. In Rome, added cause for the philosopher's amusement is given by:

> praetextae trabeae, fasces, lectica, tribunal ...

Prudentius expands this list to two lines and adds other elements, but the original elements of Juvenal's list remain, and Prudentius recognizes the debunking force of this rapid and dismissive list. The speed with which he runs through the list reflects the speed with which such earthly glories pass: 'nonne cursim transeunt?'

At *Pe.* 10. 700, the vividness of the description in conjunction with similarity of wording seems to guarantee a Juvenalian influence on Prudentius' picture of the beating of the child:

> tenerumque duris ictibus tergum secent
> *plus unde lactis quam cruoris defluat.*

At *Sat.* 11. 68, Juvenal describes a kid, 'haedulus', as:

> necdum ausus uirgas humilis mordere salicti,
> qui *plus lactis habet* quam sanguinis ...

The 'haedulus' provides a fitting comparison for the youth and innocence of Prudentius' child, but the Christian poet pushes Juvenal's fanciful suggestion about the kid's constitution to its logical extreme in his grotesque picture of the child bleeding milk instead of blood. Prudentius thus tries to intensify the pathos of Juvenal's brief scene in his own scene of horror. The link between the two passages is confirmed and reinforced by their similar phrasing.

Bergman suggests nearly five times as many reminiscences from Juvenal in Prudentius' didactic hexameter poems. They cannot be discussed here.[8] From the evidence of the *Peristephanon* alone, it is possible to conclude that Prudentius knew his Juvenal and was ready to become a Juvenalian-style satirist in polemical passages. This involves reminiscence of Juvenalian language, but also careful treatment of the satirist's thought and arguments, which sometimes have to be adapted to their new Christian context. Sometimes, however, Prudentius can use Juvenalian language to the same satirical ends in attacking men's false values and common vices. Such awareness of Juvenal can occur only seldom in the *Peristephanon*.

The Influence of Lucan

Lucan's survival into the Late Antique and Mediaeval periods, his popularity and influence, have often been noted and discussed.[9] His poem was soon included in the school curriculum: Jerome's reference to a commentary available in the fourth century suggests that the poet was read in the schools.[10] The immediate popularity of Lucan's epic ensured its strong influence on later epic poets such as Statius,[11] and this indirectly widened its influence on later literature in general.[12]

Many of the characteristic stylistic features of Lucan's epic are derived from his involvement in contemporary rhetoric as taught

[8] There exists quite a full discussion in Hanley (1962).
[9] Schanz–Hosius–Krüger (1935), vol. 2, 492 ff. and 500 ff., with bibliography; Hosius' edn. of Lucan (Teubner, 1913); Manitius (1886) 81, 241 ff. and 401 ff.; Gotoff (1971); Fraenkel (1964) 243 ff.; Raby (1957) 34–6; Sanford (1931); Wessner (1929) 296–303, 328–35; Bonner (1966) 266–89; Thomson (1928); Vessey (1970).
[10] Jerome, *In Ruf.* 1. 16. For further discussion, see the authors cited in n. 9 above.
[11] Vessey (1970).
[12] Vessey (1973) chap. 1, with p. 11 n. 5 on *Silvae*, 2. 7, with bibliography.

and practised in the declamation schools.[13] This explains the number, length, and careful structure of the epic's speeches, and the amplified treatment of what are, in essence, set-piece descriptions. Scenes of battle, disease, and horror provide favourite subject matter, giving scope for the detailed treatment of the macabre and grotesque. Even a generalized characterization of Lucan's preoccupations points to the likelihood of his providing a strong influence for Prudentius' *Peristephanon*, which shares so many of its interests.

Lucan's influence on Prudentius has been closely studied.[14] Several descriptions of violence in the *Pharsalia* could have contributed at least in a general way to Prudentius' conception of scenes of martyrdom, for example, in the lengthy and detailed description of the sea-battle at Marseilles (*Phars.* 3. 572 ff., 657–8), or the deaths by different poisons described at 9. 767 ff.[15] There are passages of possible verbal imitation, for example *Phars.* 8. 708–10, where the fate of the body of Pompey is described:

> carpitur in scopulis hausto per uolnera fluctu
> ludibrium pelagi . . .

These lines may be echoed by Prudentius at *Pe.* 5. 437 and 441–3, where the praetor threatens to throw Vincent's body into the sea:

> mergam cadauer fluctibus . . .
>
> aut semper illic mobilis
> incerta per ludibria
> uagis feretur flatibus . . .

The use of the word *ludibrium* for the sea seems to be the strongest link between the two passages, which otherwise only have the general similarity of describing the fate of corpses in the sea.[16] Out of a list of other possible verbal parallels, only a very small proportion occur in the *Peristephanon*. When considering the influence of Lucan's violent scenes on Prudentius' poetry, it must be noted that similar accumulations of horrific detail might be found in other authors: Seneca, for instance. An explanation for this can

---

[13] Bonner (1966).

[14] Sixt (1892).

[15] Also 4. 541 ff.; 8. 671 ff. and 6. 540 ff.

[16] Lavarenne (1933) 585–6, para. 1728–33; cf. Virgil, *Aeneid*, 6. 75 'rapidis ludibria uentis'; and Horace, *Odes*, 1. 14. 15: 'tu nisi uentis/debes ludibrium, caue', and Nisbet and Hubbard (1970) *ad loc.*

be found in the popularity of themes of violence for expanded description in the rhetorical school exercises.[17] This formative common 'source' explains shared preoccupations without forcing the need for close verbal imitation, and in this way an over-inclusive list of cases of verbal imitation may be sensibly reduced.

There are some cases, however, which seem worth reconsideration,[18] where a similar scene might be evoked by minimum common vocabulary. Thus in the parallel between *Pe.* 5. 437–43 and *Phars.* 8. 709, there can be seen the striking use in both passages of 'ludibrium' in the description of the sea—a usage which seems to be original to Lucan. There are also convincing parallels in *Pe.* 10. A series of ideas here seems to be drawn from a single passage in Lucan's poem (2. 173–86), where the death of M. Marius Gratidianus is described in gruesome detail. In *Pe.* 10. 880, the praefect Asclepiades makes the wish:

> quot membra gestat, tot modis pereat uolo.

a line which gives a balanced and expanded version of *Phars.* 2. 177–8:

> Cum laceros artus *aequataque uolnera membris*
> uidimus ...

Admittedly, the wording is not identical, but the idea is strikingly similar. Soon afterwards in *Pe.* 10, the cutting out of Romanus' tongue occurs. This had been anticipated in the prologue to the narrative by the words:

> uox ueritatis testis, exstingui nequit,
> hic si recisis palpitet meatibus ...

> (9–10)

The picture of the cutting out of the tongue, and the poet's introduction to the idea may be linked to the picture of Marius' tongue after incision:

---

[17] Bonner (1966) 277. He quotes Seneca, *Controuersiae*, 2. 5 and 2. 5. 6 in particular: 'Describam nunc ego cruciatus et miram corporis patientiam inter tyrannica tormenta saeuientia ...' This seems a better explanation than the two poets' nationality as naturally passionate and violent Spaniards, used by Porebowicz (1921–2) 1–13. The interest in vivid descriptions of violent scenes seems rather a feature of later Roman culture.

[18] Lavarenne dismisses the Lucan parallels found for Prudentius' *Praefatio*, 2, *Cathemerinon*, 3. 8; 5. 53, 59; 9. 81; 12. 102 (Seneca's *Medea*, 1013 provides a good parallel here).

>   ... exsectaque lingua
>   palpitat et muto uacuum ferit aera motu.
>
>   (*Phars.* 2. 181–2)[19]

The picture of Romanus given at *Pe.* 10. 906:

>   immotus et patente rictu constitit
>   dum sanguis extra defluit scaturiens.

can be compared with *Phars.* (6. 224–5):

>   perdiderat uoltum rabies, stetit imbre cruento
>   informis facies ...

but there does seem little to link these passages apart from the
general idea of violence done to the face of the victim.

An exact verbal parallel occurs at *Pe.* 14. 89 where Agnes'
executioner 'uno sub ictu nam caput amputat'. The Lucan passage
(*Phars.* 6. 613) comments that 'uno sub ictu/stat genus
humanum', where, however, the poet is making a general state-
ment about the power of Fortuna. Prudentius' imitation here
seems to be a superficial echo which does not incorporate or refer
in any way to the underlying meaning of the original context.

The most striking instance of retreatment of a whole scene
from Lucan occurs at the end of *Pe.* 14. The ascent to heaven of
Agnes' soul and her detached review of worldly affairs and for-
tunes seem to recall the description of Pompey's soul after death
(*Phars.* 9. 1 ff.). The development of the two pictures is very simi-
lar: both souls leave behind earthly remains, both reach the
heavens and wonder with amusement at the earth now beneath
them. This similarity of structure is marked out by instances of
shared vocabulary used to describe the experience. Pompey's
'umbra' '*prosiluit* busto' (*Phars.* 9. 3): Agnes' 'spiritus' 'liberque in
auras *exilit*' (*Pe.* 14. 92). Pompey 'stellasque uagas *miratus* et astra/
fixa polis ...' (9. 12): Agnes '*miratur* orbem sub pedibus situm'
(14. 94). Pompey '*uidit quanta sub nocte iaceret/nostra dies, risitque
sui ludibria trunci*' (9. 13–14): Agnes '*spectat tenebras ardua subditas,
ridetque* solis quod rota circuit' (14. 95–6).[20] The main difference is
that Pompey's amusement is reserved for his own earthly fate,

[19] Lavarenne (1933: 586) doubts the parallel for *Pe.* 10 but passes no comment on the
parallel at *Pe.* 1. 880.
[20] 'Solis rota' also recalls Lucretius' terminology. For the influence of Lucretius on Pru-
dentius (minimal in the *Pe.*), see Brakman (1919–20) and Rapisarda (1950) and (1951) 3–33.

while Agnes laughs at all the ways of the world, which she now sees as meaningless and ephemeral in the light of eternity. Prudentius develops the opportunity provided by Lucan's picture[21] into a lengthy review of worldly vanities. He thus converts what is basically a Stoic picture[22] to a Christian interpretation, incorporating the Stoic philosophical outlook in a Christian worldview.[23] This development reflects only a hint of such an approach in the Lucan passage, but in any case, the structure of the two scenes seems close enough to argue Prudentius' awareness of Lucan's passage, particularly in conjunction with recurrent key words.

Lucan's poetry probably provided an important general influence for Prudentius in his descriptions of martyrdom (and for the treatment of the horrific and violent throughout his poetry).[24] This conclusion is confirmed in the *Peristephanon* by a few passages where the Christian poet shows a more detailed knowledge of Lucan's text, and an interest in evoking whole scenes, as well as particular expressions within them.

Influence of Seneca

The characteristic features of Senecan tragedy suggest its possible influence on Prudentius' often essentially dramatic presentation of martyrdoms in the *Peristephanon*. In the tragedies, the rhetorical element is strongly in evidence as the action advances through a series of debating scenes with set speeches which often explore the tension between harshly-contrasted attitudes. Emphasis is on the individual scene rather than the structure and balance of the whole. Characters are types rather than individuals, for instance the tyrant, and belong to the world of the declamatory exercise: 'By generalizing and exaggerating characteristics, Seneca could

---

[21] Pompey's words here contrast the permanent gloom of earthly day with the true light which he now sees above the world among the stars. There are touches of moral judgement of the world in Lucan's picture.

[22] Bougery and Ponchont (1926–9 edn.), 2. 129 n. 1. Also Housman (1926 edn.) 255.

[23] Cf. Seneca, *Consolatio ad Marciam*, 25–6: a father addresses his daughter about the 'commune fatum'; and *Consolatio ad Polybium*, 9. This inset *consolatio* at the end of *Pe.* 14 should be viewed perhaps as an abbreviated version of Christian *consolatio*, for which see Favez (1930) and (1937).

[24] Most of the other credible verbal parallels come from passages describing violent or warlike activities.

set up starker contrasts and intensify the clash of wills and arguments'.[25] Descriptions of scenes of horror and violence are also part of this 'declamatory drama'.[26] It is, of course, possible that Prudentius, like Seneca, might have absorbed his similar stylistic tendencies from the strong influence of the declamation schools.[27] Attempts have been made, however, to see more substantial parallels in the two authors based both on scene structure and verbal reminiscence. Weyman and Sixt, compiled the fullest and most thorough list of verbal parallels to date.[28] These lists do not present a very convincing case for seeing constant close references to Seneca in Prudentius. In the case of isolated verbal reminiscences (that is, those which are *not* built up into a mosaic of references which evoke a Senecan scene in the course of a whole passage in Prudentius), either the similarities are not striking enough to merit being listed as 'parallels', or in the few cases where there are definite similarities, these are so slight in themselves and so unrelated to the original context in meaning that they do not seem worth serious consideration.

Perhaps more striking are the larger-scale similarities of scene. Sixt (1892, 503) points to the confrontation of Ulysses and Andromache at *Troades*, 582 ff. as a possible model for the martyr-official scenes in *Pe*. 2, 3, 5, and 10. This parallel holds good in a general way, but there are no actual verbal points of contact between any of the texts. The opposition of women to tyrant is of course more particularly interesting for the case of the spirited Eulalia in *Pe*. 3, but without stronger textual evidence, it is justifiable to look as much at the general declamatory background as at Seneca's tragedy. The torturing of a woman by a tyrant can be found to be common stock for the basis of a *controuersia*.[29]

More solid evidence for comparison is provided by *Pe*. 11 and the death of Hippolytus, where Prudentius' unique description seems very near that of Seneca's mythological version, both in

---

[25] Costa (1974) 110–11.

[26] Costa (1974) 101.

[27] Due weight must also be given to Prudentius' Christian sources in the form of contemporary martyr-literature, which at the popular level displays many of the same tendencies as Seneca's literary drama.

[28] Weyman (1891) 283–7; 'Vermischte Bemerkungen zu lateinischen Dichtungen des christlichen Altertums und des Mittelalters, IV, Zu Prudentius, *Peristephanon* IX, XI and XII', *MM* 3 (1923) 176–81; Sixt (1892).

[29] See Seneca, *Controuersiae*, 2. 5 (cf. n. 17 above), 'Torta a tyranno pro marito.'

structure and language. The tearing apart by horses, the scattering of the martyr's/hero's remains over the countryside, then the collection of these by a faithful band of followers correspond in both narratives. Sixt inevitably produces a long list of verbal parallels.[30] These demonstrate a certain correspondence of vocabulary and thought, without any very striking or extended exact verbal imitation. Prudentius' knowledge of Seneca's play, however, is confirmed by his adaptation of the end of the mythological hero to the description of the end of his martyr. This is a Prudentian innovation, and one which is surely not founded on fact. Prudentius simply uses poetic licence to conflate the stories of two 'heroes' of the same name. The reason for this may even be found in Prudentius' appreciation of Seneca's play, to which his treatment of the death scene surely refers, albeit freely. The whole episode provides a literary variation on the rather repetitive theme of martyrdom, and the poet may be disclaiming responsibility for its factual accuracy by putting it in a painting, at one remove from reality.[31] Prudentius' adaptation of Seneca's version to a Christian context is most clear at *Pe.* 11. 133 ff., where Hippolytus' fellow Christians gather together his human remains. This passage is loosely based on a brief reference to Seneca's 'dolentum sedulus labor' (1114 ff.). Hippolytus' friends in Seneca's version are defeated in their task by the vastness of the area over which his remains are scattered—they cannot collect the whole body. Prudentius expands this brief reference to a passage of fifteen lines (131–

[30] The text to *Phaedra* is taken from the Teubner edition of Seneca's *Tragedies* by R. Peiper and G. Richter (1902).
  (i) *Phaedra*, 1068–9: 'inobsequentes protinus frenis equi/rapuere currum ...' *Pe.* 11. 89–90: 'uix haec ille, duo cogunt animalia freni/ignara insueto subdere colla iugo.'
  (ii) *Phaedra*, 1070: 'quacumque rabidos pauidus euexit furor.' *Pe.* 11. 112: 'qua sonus atque tremor, qua furor exagitant.'
  (iii) *Phaedra*, 1083–4: '... seque luctantur iugo./eripere ...' *Pe.* 11, 95: 'reluctantes bigas'.
  (iv) *Phaedra*, 1090: '(currus) non suum agnoscens onus.' *Pe.* 11. 114: 'nec cursus uolucer mobile sentit onus'.
  (v) *Phaedra*, 1092: 'deuio ... polo'. *Pe.* 11. 134: 'deuia ... semita'.
  (vi) *Phaedra*, 1093: 'late cruentat arua' *Pe.* 11. 122: 'madescit humus'.
  (vii) *Phaedra*, 1094–5: '... auferunt dumi comas,/et ora durus pulchra populatur lapis.' *Pe.* 11. 119–21: 'scissa ... frusta/carpit spinigeris stirpibus hirtus ager./pars summis pendet scopulis, pars sentibus haeret ...'
  (viii) *Phaedra*, 1109 ff.; description of 'dolentum sedulus ... labor'. *Pe.* 11. 133 ff.: description of collection of Hippolytus' body by 'maerore attonniti'.

[31] See Lavarenne (1963 b: 159–64) on the difficulties surrounding the figure of Hippolytus; and see below, chap. 8, pp. 248 ff. For a possible Virgilian model here, see chap. 5, n. 69.

46). One elegiac couplet describes the pieces of Hippolytus' body scattered over the countryside as they are painted on the wall (131: 'cernere erat ...'). Another couplet describes the search of the 'caros gressu lacrimisque sequentes'. Weeping, they pile their arms with 'uisceribus laceris'. This last macabre detail is not allowed to pass without further pathetic particularization: one follower picks up 'caput niueum ... ac reuerendam/canitiem molli confouet in gremio'. Another picks up

> ... umeros truncasque manus et bracchia et ulnas
> et genua et crurum fragmina nuda ...

(139–40)

The followers, too, soak up Hippolytus' blood with cloths and sponges. Prudentius here goes beyond the purely human anxiety to gather human remains for burial, in describing the anxiety of Christians to preserve as many relics as possible. The blood-soaked rags, in particular, are reminiscent of the world of relics.[32] And Prudentius' Christian followers of Hippolytus do better than their Senecan counterparts: they have complete success in their task. The burial of the body is the real Christian focus of interest once the martyrdom has taken place, and this provides a partial explanation for Prudentius' lingering over what had only been a brief suggestion in the Seneca. He finds here the necessary bridge back to his description of the monuments of contemporary Christian Rome, where Hippolytus' remains are buried, along with all the other remains which Prudentius had so proudly mentioned at the beginning of the poem. The burial place of Hippolytus is in the Roman catacombs, to which pilgrims come annually to celebrate his feast. And it is with the description of these that Prudentius ends his poem, in a world very far removed from that of the mythological hero Hippolytus. His form of death provided an exciting introduction to the more important part of the martyr's story and to his role within the Church. Prudentius saw its possibilities in reading Seneca, and freely modelled his new version of the martyrdom on the tragedy. There does seem, therefore, to be some basis for Sixt's comparison, without pushing the verbal similarities of the texts too hard.

Sixt records sixteen other cases of verbal imitation of Seneca in

---

[32] Delehaye (1933*b*) 120 ff.

the *Peristephanon*, of varying degrees of credibility. The death of
Astyanax at *Troades*, 1098 ff., for example provides a tempting
parallel for the death of the child in *Pe.* 10. (696 ff.). There is a cor-
responding feeling of horror behind the exclamation of Andro-
mache:

> Quis Colchus hoc, quis sedis incertae Scytha
> commisit, aut quae Caspium tangens mare
> gens iuris expers ausa?
>
> (1104–6)

and the comment of the poet at *Pe.* 10. 701–2:

> ... quae cautis illud perpeti spectaculum,
> quis ferre possit aeris aut ferri rigor?

There is some similarity of expression, although both passages
could also be drawing independently on the same stock theme.[33]
The Prudentian passage makes no other reference to the death of
Astyanax. The comparison of *Pe.* 10. 907 ff. ('sanguis extra defluit
scaturiens') with *Oedipus*, 999–1000 ('rigat ora foedus imber ...')
seems far-fetched, while *Pe.* 4. 9 ('deus dextram quatiens corus-
cam') can more convincingly be associated with passages in Virgil
and Horace.[34] Other brief expressions are very close to some used
by Seneca, but these are isolated and superficial echoes which may
be almost unconscious, rather than the result of deliberate imita-
tion.[35]

Prudentius was probably strongly influenced by Seneca's

---

[33] Cf. *Aeneid*, 4. 365 ff. (Dido's words to Aeneas); Catullus, 64. 154 ff.; Ovid, *Metam.* 7.
32–3. The τόπος goes back to Patroclus' speech to Achilles (*Iliad*, 16. 33 ff.). For full notes,
see Austin (1955) 114–15, and Pease (1935) ad loc.

[34] *Georgics*, 1. 328–9 and Horace, *Odes*, 1. 2. 1–3. See Nisbet and Hubbard (1970) 21.

[35] (i) *Hercules Furens*, 535: '*calcaluitque freti terga* rigentia ...' *Pe.* 5. 477: 'terga calcens
aequoris.'

  (ii) *Phaedra*, 255: 'mentis effrenae impetus'. *Pe.* 10. 966: 'mentis effrenae'.

  (iii) *Agamemnon*, 197: 'turbo rerum'. *Pe.* 14. 98: 'rerum quod atro turbine'.

  (iv) *Hercules Oetaeus*, 719: 'libet experiri'. *Pe.* 10. 881: 'libet experiri' (same position in
verse).

  (v) *Thyestes*, 896–7: 'discutiam tibi / tenebras ...' *Pe.* 13. 26: 'discutit et tenebras'.

  (vi) *Troades*, 771–2: 'Iliaca non tu sceptra regali potens / gestabis aula ...' *Agamemnon*,
10: 'superba sceptra gestantur manu'. *Pe.* 5. 22: 'qui sceptra gestat Romula'.

  (vii) *Hercules Furens*, 180: 'rota praecipitis uertitur anni'. *Pe.* 14. 96: 'solis rota'. (But cf.
n. 34 above.)

  (viii) *Octavia*, 455: 'calcat iacentem uulgus'. *Pe.* 14. 122: 'haec calcat Agnes'.

metrical practice in his tragedies. Seneca experiments with lyric metres, using them in ways unanticipated by Augustan practice, and which influenced later poets by encouraging them to experiment in turn. It may be Seneca's dramatic iambic trimeters which lie behind the choice of this metre for the lengthy 'tragedy' of Romanus in *Pe.* 10, although Prudentius' technique is not identical to that of Seneca, resembling rather that of Ausonius and Paulinus.[36] A more certain case can be made for seeing Seneca's influence at work in the glyconics used κατὰ στίχον in *Pe.* 7. Apart from Prudentius, only Seneca uses this metre, and also Septimius Serenus, whose four lines of fragments hardly provide enough evidence for comparison.[37] In two out of these four lines, Septimius Serenus uses a spondaic base for his line. An invariably spondaic base is the rule in Seneca, as in Horace, who uses a glyconic line in combination with other lyric metres. Prudentius models his glyconics on those of Seneca and Horace. This lyric metre is particularly suitable for a hymn, as Seneca suggests by his use of it for hymns in two out of the four examples.

It is safe to conclude that Prudentius read Seneca's tragedies and was influenced by them in his own poetry.[38] Their general influence can be felt to some extent in the dramatic form of some of the poems, the limited character portrayal, and the preoccupation with the violent and the macabre. *Pe.* 11 in particular supplies strong grounds for seeing awareness of a Senecan passage behind Prudentius' Christian reworking. Seneca's metrical practice influenced that of Prudentius.

The Influence of Statius

The poetry of Statius was certainly undergoing a revival of popu-

[36] Charlet (1972) 90.
[37] For glyconics, see Raven (1965) 140–1. Seneca, *Hercules Oetaeus*, 1030–1; *Medea*, 75–92, *Thyestes*, 336–403; *Hercules Furens*, 875–94. The metre is also used by Septimius Serenus (fr. 8 and 9 in Baehrens (1866) 385–6). Glyconics are also used by Prudentius in the preface to *Contra Symmachum*, 2.
[38] Philip (1968) esp. 175 n. 6. The earliest quotations from Seneca are found in the 5th and 6th centuries. Augustine quotes him, probably as early as AD 400. At *Contra Faustum*, 1. 20. 9 = *PL* 42. 374, and in a *Sermo* in Morin (1930: 231) he quotes *Phaedra*, 200–1 and *Troades*, 291 respectively, attributing the lines to 'quidam eorum tragicus' and 'quidam'. For Seneca's 'Fortleben', see Schanz–Hosius–Krüger (1935) 2. 469 and Weyman (1891) 281.

larity in the fourth century,[39] and it needs to be asked how far either the *Silvae* or the more popular epic, the *Thebaid*, influenced Prudentius' poetry. Although Statius' poetry probably did not form a regular part of the school curriculum in the fourth century, it may have attracted the interest of literati for the sake of what has been termed the 'mannerism' of the poetry. Dilke even talks of 'Statian baroque', using the words of L. P. Wilkinson to define the baroque spirit. It is

grandiose, arresting, theatrical. Full of restless and exuberant vitality, it seeks variety, strangeness and contrast. It is now fantastic, now playful, now picturesque. Indifferent to truth, it claims the right to exaggerate or deceive for artistic ends—anything to escape from a frigid classicism and to enforce attention.[40]

These features were particularly attractive to the writers of the fourth century with their taste for the melodramatic.[41] Statius' influence has been detected in the writing of Ausonius, Claudian, Sidonius Apollinaris, and Dracontius.[42]

   Where Prudentius is concerned, Statius' direct influence seems to be slight. The Christian poet may have been influenced at least indirectly by the metrical variation of the *Silvae* and in his use, for instance, of the phalaecian hendecasyllable.[43] His poetry could be said to reflect the pictorial aspect of Statius' poetry, in his descriptions of works of art and buildings, for instance, in *Pe.* 3, 9, 11, and 12, and his vivid visualization of individual scenes within his narrative.[44] However, as an overall tendency, this is one which can be related to the general characteristics of fourth-century tastes and aesthetic sensibilities. Something has been said above (Chapter 2, pp. 45 ff.) about the visual and dramatic quality of the history of Ammianus Marcellinus, which has been well discussed by Auerbach and Macmullen,[45] and which can be related to the

[39] Valmaggi (1893). I omit here mention of the poets Silius Italicus and Valerius Flaccus, who seem to have been little read in the 4th century. On Silius Italicus, see *RE* 3 A.1 (1927) 79–91; Schanz–Hosius–Krüger (1935) 2. 530. On Valerius Flaccus, see Summers (1894). Quintilian is the only writer of antiquity who mentions the poet (*Inst. Or.* 10. 1. 90).

[40] Dilke (1963) 502.

[41] Fontaine (1976a) 425–82.

[42] Schanz–Hosius–Krüger (1935) 2. 544; Valmaggi (1893) 481 ff.

[43] Phalaecian hendecasyllables are used for example in *Silvae*, 1. 6, 7; 2. 7; 4. 3, 9. See Newmyer (1979) 56–9, and below, chap. 7, n. 20.

[44] Duncan (1914) and Vessey (1973) 10–11.

[45] Auerbach (1953) 50 ff.; MacMullen (1964a).

whole quality and content of life in the period, with its love for show and ceremonial. Prudentius' poetry can more obviously be tied to this contemporary background in life and literature, than to particular points in Statius' poetry.

This is confirmed at the level of verbal imitation. Results are as disappointing as Bergman's brief list of parallels suggests.[46] A reading of both *Thebaid* and *Silvae* yields little fruit. Where exact parallels appear, they can almost invariably be explained away by their common occurrence as a poetic cliché, or by their more obvious reference to a Virgilian passage. I have found eighteen possible parallels, only six of which refer to the *Peristephanon*, and only two of which seem probably direct and uncontaminated by Virgilian or later models.[47] For the *Peristephanon*, I have found the following parallels, most of which are devalued by a possible Virgilian reminiscence. Thus the phrase 'pascere crinem' for growing hair occurs in slightly modified form at *Pe.* 1, 79–80:

> hoc tamen solum uetusta subtrahunt silentia,
> iugibus longum catenis an *capillum pauerint.*

At *Thebaid*, 8. 493, the poet tells of Polites as he is about to be slain in battle that

> ille genas Phoebo, crinem hic pascebat Iaccho.

The context of death is perhaps relevant to the Prudentian passage, but the phrase in question can be traced back to Virgil's *Aeneid*, where it is used in connection with Amata's madness when she is possessed by Allecto:

> te lustrare choro, sacrum tibi pascere crinem . . .
>
> (*Aeneid*, 7. 391)

At *Pe.* 4. 91, the poet address Vincent:

> nonne, Vincenti, peregri necandus
> martyr his terris tenui notasti
> *sanguinis rore* speciem futuri
> morte propinqua?
>
> (89–92)

---

[46] Lavarenne (1933) 590–1, dismisses even Bergman's modest list and reduces it by half.

[47] *Contra Symmachum*, 1. 566–7: 'sescentas numerare domos de sanguine prisco / nobilium licet . . .' *Thebaid*, 3. 598–600: 'Atqui hic ingenti Capaneus Mauortis amore / excitus et longam pridem indignantia pacem / corda tumens—huic ampla quidem de sanguine prisco / nobilitas . . .'

The 'dew of blood' could recall *Thebaid*, 5. 590:

> pallida *sanguineis* infectas *roribus* herbas.

But the phrase has a more obvious precedent at *Aeneid*, 3. 339, where it occurs as '*rores sanguineos*'. At *Pe*. 11. 220, the poet in describing Hippolytus' splendid basilica, speaks of '*ordo columnarum geminus*' which is '*auratus suppositus trabibus*'. At *Silvae*, 1. 3. 35, there is mention of '*auratas . . . trabes*' in a description of the villa of Manlius Vopiscus at Tibur. The phrase, however, first occurs in the *Aeneid*, where it is used of Priam's palace at 2. 448.[48] In describing the sacrificial bull used in pagan rites at *Pe*. 10. 1021, Prudentius talks of him as '*ingens fronte torua* et hispida'. Statius had used the same phrase of a tyrant at *Thebaid*, 1. 186 ('*torua sub fronte*'). Once again, however, Virgil provides a common source for the phrase. At *Aeneid*, 3. 636, Virgil describes the Cyclops, '*ingens* quod *torua* solum sub *fronte* latebat'. The use of '*ingens*' by Virgil brings his line nearer to that of Prudentius than Statius' use of the phrase.

More rewarding examples are found in *Pe*. 12. At *Pe*. 12. 10, Prudentius speaks of the double martyrdom of Peter and Paul in Rome:

> bis fluxit *imber sanguinis* per herbas . . .

The phrase 'imber sanguinis' occurs at *Thebaid*, 5. 598 in a description of the dead Achemorus:

> . . . tenuia ossa patent nexusque madentes
> sanguinis imbre noui . . .

This unusual image is, in fact, not found anywhere else in the same form,[49] so that it seems likely that its presence in Prudentius represents a direct piece of *imitatio*. The Christian poet likes the image so much that he uses it again at *Pe*. 10. 1032, 'inlapsus imber tabidum rorem pluit'. There seems, however, to be no significant reference to the Statian original in Prudentius' two passages. He simply uses Statius' words as a vivid image of violence.

---

[48] Cf. Propertius, *Elegies*, 3. 2. 10; Seneca, *Thyestes*, 646; Claudian, *Carmina minora*, 31. 42.

[49] *TLL* 'imber': some places are listed where 'imber' is used figuratively of blood, but never in the same way as in Statius; cf. Seneca, *Oedipus*, 349; Lucan, *Pharsalia*, 6. 224; Valerius Flaccus, *Argonautica*, 5. 176; 6. 186.

Another case where Prudentius does seem to be looking back to Statius directly is his description of the double feast-day of the apostles in Rome:

> Aspice, per bifidas plebs Romula funditur plateas,
> lux *in duobus feruet una festis.*

$$(57-8)$$

At *Silvae*, 1. 2. 230, Statius talks in similar terms of the double celebration of a marriage in the homes of the bride and groom:

> Vixdum emissa dies, et iam socialia praesto
> omina, *iam festa feruet domus* utraque pompa.

The words 'festus' and 'ferueo' in combination with the context of a double festival in both cases seem to give a strong indication of Prudentius' awareness of the Statian passage.

No more possible reminiscences from Statius can be found in the *Peristephanon*. Statius' influence was more important in a general way, insofar as he was influential for the variety of forms and the preoccupations of Late Antique poetry.

The Influence of Claudian

Prudentius was an older contemporary of Claudian, and since both worked for a large part of their career at the same imperial court,[50] it seems possible that the two poets met or at least knew each other's work.[51] Verbal parallels, together with other similarities[52] suggest mutual knowledge which has usually been assumed to argue for the influence of Claudian on Prudentius. Although Prudentius' poetry may not have been published in any form before AD 392 (the *terminus post quem* provided by the silence of Jerome in his *De uiris illustribus*[53]), nor in omnibus form before AD 404–5,[54] it is just possible that some of his poems may have been available to Claudian before his death in about AD 404.[55] On the whole, however, it seems safer to argue for larger-scale imita-

---

[50] See above, pp. 24 ff., for Prudentius' career. See too Clarke (1968).

[51] Cameron (1970) 469–70.

[52] Metrical similarities, for instance (cf. *Pe.* 14 and *Fesc.* 1 in Alcaic hendecasyllables κατὰ στίχον), or the use of personifications (Cameron (1970) 255).

[53] Kelly (1975) 174–8.

[54] Lana (1962) n. 2.

[55] Cameron (1970) Appendix B II, 469–73; cf. Vanderspoel (1986).

tion of the widely known court poet[56] by Prudentius, much of
whose poetry may have been written either in Spain or, at any
rate, for a narrowly Spanish audience, whether at home or in
Milan. This is obviously particularly true of the *Peristephanon*,
eight of whose fourteen poems seem primarily intended for the
poet's compatriots.[57] Furthermore, at least in the case of the
securely dateable *Contra Symmachum*, the Prudentian poem pro-
vides certain grounds for concluding that it is Prudentius who
imitates earlier poems of Claudian.[58] I shall, therefore, assume
that any verbal similarities in the *Peristephanon* are cases of Pru-
dentian reminiscence of Claudian.

Hoefer at the end of the last century discussed Claudian's in-
fluence on Prudentius.[59] He produced a lengthy list of verbal par-
allels, without further comments. Weyman, a little later,
criticized Hoefer's list for its over-inclusiveness: many of the
parallels were not similar enough to demonstrate dependence of
Prudentius on Claudian. Many could be dismissed on grounds of
similarity to a common earlier source, in particular Virgil.[60] So,
for instance, at *Pe.* 2. 529, the phrase 'ter quaterque' can obviously
be compared with the Virgilian passages *Aeneid*, 12. 155 and
Georgics, 2. 399,[61] without any recourse to the passage in Clau-
dian at *Carmina minora* 23. 18.[62] In any case, Prudentius does not
exactly echo any of the three passages, the point of his phrase
being to surpass the expression of his predecessors: the inhabitant
of Christian Rome is 'ter quaterque et *septies* beatus' in his prox-
imity to the buried martyrs. Hoefer makes none of these observa-
tions. He parallels *Pe.* 3. 6 'proximus occiduo locus est qui ...', the
introduction to Emerita as the burial place of Eulalia, with *In Ruf.*
1. 123, 'est locus extremum pandit qua ...', an ekphrasis-style in-
troduction to a description of Megaera's horrific abode. If Pru-
dentius were here calling on this passage, then he might be

[56] Claudian is, for example, known to Augustine in Africa; a statue was erected to his
memory in Rome after his death.

[57] See *Pe.* 1–6, 9, and 11. See chap. 3 above, pp. 94 ff.

[58] Cameron (1970) 469–73.

[59] Hoefer (1895).

[60] Weyman (1926) 64–71.

[61] Virgil, *Aeneid*, 12. 155 (Iuturna): 'terque quaterque manu pectus percussit honestum'.
Georgics, 2. 398–9: '... namque omne quotannis/terque quaterque solum scindendum
glaebaque uersis/aeternum fragenda bidentibus ...'

[62] Claudian: *Carmina minora* 23. 18: 'en pallidus omnia laudo/et clarum repeto terque
quaterque "sophos!"'

deliberately suggesting a sharp mood contrast between the glorious place of the Christian *martyrium*, and the gloomy haunts of the pagan Megaera. However, the ekphrasis introduction, 'est locus', is in itself too common[63] to allow a 'parallel' here, and the two passages following this stock phrase in fact hold nothing else in common. Attention to this passage of Claudian perhaps led Hoefer to attempt a parallel between *Pe.* 3. 24–5 and *In Ruf.* 1. 135. In *Pe.* 3, Eulalia's grave and measured step make her seem old beyond her twelve years:

> moribus et nimium teneris
> *canitiem meditata senum*

There seems little reason to associate this picture of the young girl with that of Megaera, who disguises herself (literally) as an old man:

> *longaeuum mentita senem* rugisque seueras
> persulcata genas et ficto languida passu . . .

The two passages seem at odds in theme and expression.[64] The same criticisms could be applied to many other parallels suggested by Hoefer, and Bergman in his edition sensibly reduces the list to twenty passages. Lavarenne in his *Études* reduces this list even further (pp. 594–6), and in his own edition of the *Peristephanon* lists no imitations of Claudian at all.

This is a move too far in the opposite direction: there *are* a number of verbal imitations in the *Peristephanon*. It is important, however, to judge how significant each imitation is, and to notice the distribution of imitations. If, as Bergman prefers, Hoefer's less likely parallels are dismissed, then very few parallels remain for the *Pe. Pe.* 1, 2, 3, 5, 6, 7, 8, and 14 do not even provide tenuous reminiscences from Claudian, while a possible reminiscence in *Pe.* 4 could be called into question by an earlier occurrence of the same combination of noun and verb.[65] The cases of imitation in *Pe.* 12 and 13 can be dismissed on grounds of the clichéd nature of the phrases in question. So 'egregium decus' (*Pe.* 13. 73) has a long poetic history going back to *Aeneid*, 7. 473, through Apuleius,

---

[63] Bonner (1966) 278, on *ekphraseis*.

[64] For this topic, see above p. 157 with n. 33.

[65] *Pe.* 4. 130: 'et diu uenis dolor haesit ardens'. *In Ruf.* 2. 280: 'sensu dolor haeret in alto/ abditus et tacitis uindictae praestruit iras'; cf. Cicero, *Phil.* 2. 26. 64: 'infixus animo haeret dolor'.

Silver Age epic, and Senecan tragedy. *Pe.* 12. 54 'sic prata *uernis floribus* renident' (cf. *Stil.* 1. 86 'cum *floribus* aequora *uernis/* Bosphorus indueret') presents a poetic cliché going back to Horace (*Odes*, 2. 11. 9 'non semper idem floribus est uernis'), Ovid (*Metamorphoses*, 4. 315; 5. 554), and Statius (*Thebaid*, 5. 580).

Pe. 9 and 11 provide some grounds for arguing Prudentian awareness of Claudian's poetry in the *Peristephanon*. This fits in with the conclusions reached above in the study of these poems with regard to *imitatio* of Augustan poets. *Pe.* 9 and 11 stand out from the collection as a whole because they seem more literary compositions, less trammelled by the usual expectations of martyr literature. Even in these poems, however, evocation of Claudian is not completely secure. At *Pe.* 9. 3, the expression 'maxima rerum' can be more valuably associated with *Aeneid*, 7. 602 than with Claudian's *Carm. min.* 30. 48. The other two possible parallels in *Pe.* 9[66] may be allowed to stand, although the reference to Claudian seems only superficial, and the Prudentian context gains nothing in particular from an awareness of Claudian's context in each case.

Of the nine imitations of Claudian by Prudentius in *Pe.* 11,[67]

---

[66] (i) *Pe.* 9. 11: 'plagas mille gerens, totos lacerata per artus'. *In Ruf.* 2. 431: 'laceros iuuat ire per artus/pressaque calcato uestigia sanguine tingi.'

   (ii) *Pe.* 9. 103: 'et post terga domum dubia sub sorte relictam'. *In Ruf.* 2. 245: 'si calcare Notum secretaque noscere Nili/nascentis nubeas, mundum post terga relinquam'.

[67] (i) *Pe.* 11. 17: 'Haec dum lustro oculis et sicubi forte latentes/uerum apices ueterum per monumenta sequor.' *In Ruf.* 2. 5: 'Iamque tuis, Stilicho, Romana potentia ciuis/et rerum commissus apex.'

  (ii) *Pe.* 11. 115: 'Incendit feritas, rapit impetus et fragor urget/nec cursus uolucer mobile sentit onus.' *Gild.* 472 ff.: 'Ilicet auguriis alacres per saxa citati/torrentesque ruunt; nec mons aut silua retardat.'

 (iii) *Pe.* 11. 151: 'metando eligitur tumulo locus; Ostia linquunt'. *Eutrop.* 2. 418: '... non commoda castris/eligitur regio.' (But cf. *Georgics*, 4. 296, 'eligitur locus'.)

 (iv) *Pe.* 11. 211: 'uix capiunt patuli populorum gaudia campi'. *De rapt. Pros.* 1. 221: 'fines inuade Sicanos/et Cereris prolem patulis inludere campis'.

  (v) *Pe.* 11. 212: 'haeret et in magnis densa cohors spatiis'. *4. Cons. Hon.* 87: 'qui modo tam densas nutu mouere cohortes'.

 (vi) *Pe.* 11. 216: 'tunc adeat cultu nobile regifico'. *Ruf.* 2. 340: 'desiluit stratis densaeque capacia turbae/atria regifico iussit splendere paratu.' (But cf. *Aeneid*, 6. 605, 'regifico luxu'.)

 (vii) *Pe.* 11. 219: 'ordo columnarum geminus laquearia tecti/sustinet auratis suppositus trabibus.' *Nupt. Hon.* 88: '... trabibus smaragdi/supposuit caesas hyacinthi rupe columnas.' (But cf. *Aeneid*, 8. 25, 'laquearia tecti'.)

(viii) *Pe.* 11. 225–6: 'Fronte sub aduersa gradibus sublime tribunal/tollitur'. *Ruf.* 2. 382: 'scandat sublime tribunal'. (But cf. *Aeneid*, 1. 166.)

 (ix) Prayer at *Pe.* 239–45: cf. *Carmina minora* 50. 3–14. On this, see Vanderspoel (1986).

only one seems to go beyond the superficial: *Pe.* 11. 115 seems to refer to *Gildo*, 472 ff. Cameron thinks the parallel striking enough here to suggest a definite terminus post quem for the *Peristephanon* poem (that is, after AD 399). The Prudentian passage describes the rushing of the horses dragging the martyr Hippolytus to his death:

> Per siluas, per saxa ruunt, non ripa retardat
> fluminis, aut torrens oppositus cohibet.
> prosternunt saepes et cuncta obstacula rumpunt
> prona, fragosa petunt, ardua transiliunt.
>
> (115–18)

The corresponding passage in Claudian describes the enthusiastic rushing of soldiers to war after a favourable omen. The whole picture and the terms in which it is described in both passages are very close. 'per saxa ... ruunt' is common to both passages. The 'torrens' of Prudentius' negative statement corresponds to the 'torrentes' of Claudian's opening statement:

> ilicet auguriis alacres per saxa citati
> torrentesque ruunt; nec mons aut silua retardat ...

Prudentius replaces the 'torrentes' by the 'silvae' which appear in Claudian's negative closing statement, 'nec mons aut *silua* retardat'. 'Retardat' also appears at the end of the hexameter line for Prudentius. The balance of positive and negative statement in Prudentius corresponds to the same structure in the Claudian passage. *Pe.* 11. 115 ff. provides an example of Prudentian *contaminatio*: the general structure at least evokes the death of Hippolytus from Seneca's *Phaedra* (see above pp. 189 ff.), with perhaps a glance at Virgil's Mettus (*Aeneid* 8. 642 ff.).

The prayer at *Pe.* 11. 239–45 with its four-fold anaphora might reproduce the similar anaphora using 'sic' at *Carmina minora* 50. 3–14. In this poem, however, Claudian seems to parody by exaggerated repetition the use of 'sic' in prayers. Claudian here might most truly be said to parody the sort of prayer *form* represented by *Pe.* 11. 239 ff., and so does not provide a very solid parallel. It is interesting to note too that Claudian's poem *In Iacobum magistrum equitum* seems to raise a laugh at the expense of the addressee's devotion to the saints:

> Per cineres Pauli, per cani limina Petri,
>   ne laceres uersus, dux Iacobe meos.
> *sic* tua pro clipeo defendat pectora Thomas
>   et comes ad bellum Bartholomaeus eat;
> *sic* ope sanctorum non barbarus inruat Alpes,
>   *sic* tibi det uires sancta Susanna suas;
> *sic* quicumque ferox gelidum transnauerit Histrum
>   mergatur uolucres ceu Pharaonis equi;
> *sic* Geticas ultrix feriat romphaea cateruas
>   Romanasque regat prospera Thecla manus . . .

Pe. 10 provides two passages which raise interesting questions in connection with possible parallels in Claudian. At *Pe.* 10. 346 ff., Prudentius talks of Christ who,

> Aedem sibi ipse mentem hominis condidit
> uiuam, serenam, sensualem, flabilem,
> solui incapacem posse, nec destructilem,
> pulchram, uenustam, praeminentem culmine,
> discriminatis inlitam coloribus.

Lavarenne finds a parallel for this passage in St Paul, 1 Cor. 3: 16: 'Nescitis qua templum Dei estis, et spiritus Dei habitat in uobis'; 1 Cor. 6: 19: 'An nescitis quoniam membra uestra templum spiritus sancti?'; and 2 Cor. 6: 16: 'uos enim estis templum Dei uiui . . .'. Worth comparison too is *Psychomachia*, 822 ff., where the virtues set out to build a temple in the soul. Lavarenne here[68] refers to St Paul, *Eph.* 2: 22, 'uos aedificamini in habitaculum Dei'. At *Contra Symmachum*, 2. 249, God says 'templum mentis amo'. The Christian models for the Prudentian passage at *Pe.* 10, 346 ff. are thus too clear to suppose that Prudentius would have gathered the idea from reading a secular author like Claudian, who at *De consulatu Stilichonis*, 2. 12 speaks of *clementia*:

> haec dea pro templis et ture calentibus aris
> te fruitur posuitque suas hoc pectore sedes.

Claudian's language here is not similar enough to Prudentius' to support the idea of any interdependence, and it seems more likely that Claudian came across the idea in the Pauline epistles, which he is likely to have known through his involvement with the Christian court.

[68] Lavarenne (1963*b*) 132.

At *Pe.* 10. 420, the line 'ductor quietum frenet orbem legibus' picks up a phrase used of Stilicho:

> hactenus armatae laudes: nunc qualibus orbem
> moribus et quanto frenet metuendus amore . . .
>
> *(De cons. Stil.* 2. 1–2)

Although 'frenare' is a verb frequently used of rule or government (cf. Prudentius, *Praef.* 17), it occurs with the noun 'orbem' only in these two contexts. Neither context, however, seems to contribute or derive much from the other. World rule, in both cases, is mentioned in a purely secular context: in Prudentius, in connection with the emperor, in Claudian, with Stilicho.

This review of possible echoes of Claudian in the *Peristephanon* yields rather negative results. There may be said to be a limited number of superficial verbal echoes, perhaps unconsciously included by the poet. Apart from these, there is only one strikingly integrated passage, which in fact is purely descriptive and built into a scene which is otherwise based upon a scene from Seneca's *Phaedra*. This result fits the character of the *Peristephanon*. Community of subject matter provides more opportunity for reference to Claudian in the hexameter poems. Claudian's rather unsympathetic view of the subject of saints is suggested by his poem *In Jacobum* and the matter of martyrdom is likely to have suggested fewer points of contact with his contemporary in Prudentius' mind. Claudian's metrical technique and variety were probably as influential as any aspect of his poetry for Prudentius. This might explain Prudentius' unusual use of the Alcaic hendecasyllable κατὰ στίχον. Claudian is the only other author to use the hendecasyllable in this way, for his *epithalamium* in honour of Honorius and Maria, written in AD 398. Prudentius uses the same metre in *Pe.* 14 for Agnes, a virgin martyr and thereby adapts the joy of a wedding hymn to the Christian joy of martyrdom.[69] A greater joy than that of an earthly wedding awaits Agnes in her role as the 'bride of Christ'. This metrical 'echo' is perhaps Claudian's most significant contribution to the Peristephanon.

Here ends the section on *imitatio* in the *Peristephanon*. The subject has scarcely been exhausted, and if more space were here avail-

---

[69] Cf. Eulalia and the slight evocation of the wedding hymn in *Pe.* 3. See above, pp. 168 ff. On the dactylic metre of *Pe.* 3, see chap. 5, n. 61.

able, it could be devoted to the influence of the Bible and of Christian authors on the collection. An attempt has simply been made here to demonstrate the way in which *imitatio* of mainly Augustan authors works in the *Peristephanon*. It implies a rejection of the methods of earlier Prudentian scholars with their sterile lists of 'verbal parallels', and involves instead an effort to understand the two-way dynamics of *retractatio* of earlier authors. In the *Peristephanon*, wherever the Christian sources are reasonably fluid and exert little pressure on the poet, he is free to draw on earlier secular poetry. In turning in particular to the poets of the Augustan age, he shows an eagerness to relate the ideology and aspirations expressed by the key poets of that time to his own vision of an empire renewed by its wholehearted acceptance of Christianity under its own Christian Augustus, Theodosius. Just as Augustan Rome through the *Aeneid* looked back to its founding heroes and celebrated their virtues, so Prudentius in the *Peristephanon* records the history of the founding heroes of the Christian empire, the martyrs. He draws the parallel by his expression of the martyrs' heroism in terms which draw on the language used by Virgil of his heroes. Prudentius works out, at the literary level, themes which contribute towards his own vision of a Christianized empire, embodying a special continuity with the pagan past: Rome's past splendours (even her poetry) were the preparation and the necessary foundation for the recently achieved climax of her history under Theodosius. As such, they are to be absorbed and assimilated and given new Christian significance. These are the principles behind Prudentius' *imitatio*, which make it far from a purely ornamental or erudite display. Furthermore, Prudentius' confident assimilation of the values as well as the language of earlier authors reflects the contemporary transformation of Roman society:

> ipsa et senatus lumina,
> quondam luperci aut flamines,
> apostolorum et martyrum
> exosculantur limina . . .

> (*Pe.* 2. 517–20)

7

The Martyrdom of Bishop Fructuosus and his Deacons

PRUDENTIUS' originality lies in his translation of his own involvement in martyr cult and its literature into a poetic form which represents both a revivification of the forms and language of the secular poetic tradition, and a new departure in the development of martyr literature. For the Church in the fourth century, the martyrs replace the old heroes of epic and victory ode. They spiritualize and extend the ancient heroic ideal, but also combine features of both soldier and victorious athlete in their battle against persecution.[1] Thus Prudentius moulds for their celebration a new form of poetic panegyric which contains elements of both epic and lyric verse. The martyrs, however, are first and foremost *Christian* champions, and each of Prudentius' poems relies to some extent on Christian accounts of each martyrdom. This aspect of the poems must therefore be given due attention in order that the poet's final synthesis can be fully appreciated.

The surest way of establishing Prudentius' aims and techniques in adapting the material of martyrdom to its poetic setting would be to compare each poem with its Christian source, the corresponding prose account of the martyrdom. In this way, Prudentius' attitude towards historical accuracy as well as his canons of taste for poetic style could be established. Unfortunately, such an exercise is, for the most part, impossible, since in some cases Prudentius supplies our earliest written source for the martyrdoms described (for example in *Pe.* 1, 3, and 9), and in others, the extant prose accounts cannot be dated with certainty to a period earlier than the poet's version (for example, *Pe.* 5 and 7). Some insights

---

[1] For martyrdom as an *agōn* and the martyr as an athlete: St Paul, *1 Cor.* 9: 24–5; *2 Tim.* 2: 5, 4: 7–8; Eusebius, *Hist. eccl.* 5. 1, 11, 19, and 21; *Acta Carpi*, 35; Cyprian, *Ep.* 58. 8. For further references see Delehaye (1966) 153. For martyrdom as the climax of the *militia Christi*: St Paul, *2 Tim.* 2: 3–4; *2 Cor.* 10: 3–6; *Eph.* 6: 10–18; Eusebius, *Hist. eccl.* 5. 1. 155; cf. *2 Macc.* 7: 21–3, 27–9, 41. Also Harnack (1905); Helgeland (1979); Fontaine (1980) and Cattalano (1952). This aspect of the *Peristephanon* is also brought out by Brožek (1954).

into the question can certainly be gained by a study of the general trends and developments in the literary treatment of martyrdoms in the same century.[2] the *Peristephanon*, however, offer two opportunities for a close comparison of the poems with an historical account of the martyrdom. Authentic *Acta*[3] exist for the martyrdom of the Spanish bishop Fructuosus and his deacons, and for St Cyprian of Africa.

The account of the martyrdom of the Spanish saints is generally agreed to have been written either at the time of the martyrdom itself, AD 259,[4] or at latest, soon after the Peace of the Church early in the fourth century.[5] It is thought to represent a genuine account of the facts. Archaeological discoveries at Tarragona indicate that the martyrs' tomb very soon became a cult shrine and centre of pilgrimage,[6] and it is likely that the *Acta* were incorporated in the annual celebration of the *dies natalis* of Fructuosus' martyrdom at an early date. This helps to explain the survival of the essentially original account: Church supervision of the readings for the feast day ensured the preservation of the original text with minimal changes or additions.[7]

It is therefore likely that the *Acta* were very well known in a more or less static form to the inhabitants of Tarragona, and to the regular pilgrims to the shrine. By the end of the fourth century they had also become known in North Africa: Augustine quotes from them in his sermon *In natali martyrum*.[8] The cult, however, does not seem to have spread to Gaul or Italy until after the Visigothic period.[9] Prudentius, therefore, probably wrote *Pe.* 6 primarily for a Spanish audience, either resident in Tarragona, or perhaps in temporary exile from their native town as the result

---

[2] See below, pp. 227 ff. with bibliography, and for example Delehaye (1966).

[3] This term is used to refer to those prose accounts of martyrdom which are based on the official report of the trial. See Musurillo (1972) li–lii; also, Aigrain (1953) 132 ff.

[4] Franchi de' Cavalieri (1935b) esp. 129–30. Also Manjarrés Mangas and Roldán Hervás (1982) 416–17.

[5] Musurillo (1972) xxxii.

[6] García Rodríguez (1966) 316 ff., with bibliography. Also, Serra Vilaró (1946). See below, pp. 268 ff.

[7] Lazzati (1956b) 18–19; Delehaye (1927a) 193 and Mangas and Roldán (1933b) 367.

[8] Augustine, *Serm.* 273, *PL* 38. 1247–9. Manjarrés Mangas and Roldán Hervás (1982: 416 ff.) points out the African influence on the *Acta*, e.g. on vocabulary like *fraternitas* and *refrigerium*.

[9] Moreu-Rey (1971–2). Also García Rodríguez (1966) 317.

of obligations at the imperial court in Milan.[10] He wrote the poem for people who knew the *Acta* by heart. In this situation, an ideal opportunity is offered for examining the ways in which the poet feels at liberty to adapt his original. Some idea may thus be gained of the poet's procedure in other poems where no source survives. Study of *Pe.* 6 should also help to establish the extent to which Prudentius expresses himself by means of classical reminiscences in a case where the Christian tradition is so strong.

It is necessary first to outline and describe the original prose account of the *Acta*.[11] Their authenticity is guaranteed by their simplicity. The account tells of the martyrs' arrest, imprisonment, trial, and execution.[12] 'Only the edifying conclusion (5–7) relating to the appearance of Fructuosus after death, with the eulogistic ending, might have come from a later, more pious hand'.[13] Christian authorship is clear from the development of the narrative beyond the bare bones of the trial and sentence: the writer describes the scene of arrest and Fructuosus' request to put on his sandals before going with the soldiers (1), his silent prayer in the midst of the interrogation (2, 5), and his exchanges with the crowd before execution (3). Authenticity is further confirmed by the conspicuous absence of the miraculous element in the first four and most trustworthy chapters.[14] The author relates the facts in simple language with no extended or unnecessary description or comment.

The account begins by dating the arrest by day and year, naming the two consuls for that year. The arrest is then described in detail: the soldiers (who are named) arrive unexpectedly at Fructuosus' house; the bishop greets them, receives the governor's orders and then requests permission to put on his sandals before leaving with them. As soon as they arrive (the *Acta* do not specify where), they are put in prison: 'Et mox ut uenerunt, recepti sunt in carcerem'. Fructuosus' serenity and his prayers are noted. He baptizes a man called Rogatianus while in prison. After six days,

---

[10] This is speculation based on a reconstruction of Prudentius' probable career at the imperial court, discussed above in chap. 1, pp. 24 ff. Other Spaniards also left their native country for the sake of their commitment to imperial service. See chap. 1, n. 74, with sources and bibliography.

[11] I follow here the text of Musurillo (1972).

[12] Franchi de' Cavalieri (1935*b*) and Musurillo (1972) xxxii.

[13] Musurillo (1972) xxxii. It is a 6th/7th-century addition: Sabbatini (1972) 32–53.

[14] Franchi de' Cavalieri (1935*b*) 163 and Musurillo (1972) xxxii.

the three are taken from prison for trial on Friday, 21 January. The governor asks for them to be brought in, and questions them one by one, starting and finishing with Fructuosus. Finally he asks Fructuosus if he is a bishop: 'Yes, I am', he replies. 'You were', Aemilianus grimly retorts. He then sentences the three to be burnt alive. Their journey to the amphitheatre is described, and the bishop's exchanges with the crowd which accompanies them. He refuses the offer of a drugged drink and also the offer of a man called Augustalis to remove his sandals for him. In reply to the soldier Felix, 'commilito frater noster', who asks him to remember him, the bishop says that he will remember the whole Catholic Church. On arrival at the amphitheatre, Fructuosus addresses the brethen 'with the inspiration and the words of the Holy Spirit' (4. 1). The three then 'enter the way of salvation'. They are briefly compared to the three companions of Daniel, condemned to the furnace. The divine Trinity is visible in them, Father, Son, and Holy Spirit are present to help. When the flames have burnt through their bonds releasing their hands, they joyfully kneel down and pray with arms extended in memory of the Lord's cross. Thus they pray until death.

In *Acta*, 5–7 various 'magnalia' or miracles are described. The Christian servants of Aemilianus see a vision of Fructuosus and his companions rising to heaven. They tell his daughter of this, and also summon the governor himself, but he is not worthy to see the martyrs. The next miracle is the appearance of Fructuosus to the Christians. He asks them to restore any of his ashes which they have taken away as relics to their homes. The last miracle (7) is Fructuosus' appearance to Aemilianus, in which he scolds the governor and mocks him for his belief that he can keep the glorified martyrs on earth.

Although there are details which Prudentius chooses to omit, in general he gives a paraphrase of the prose account of his poem. He does not seem to have known a text of the *Acta* which included the miracle of Chapter 7,[15] which he omits, but otherwise reproduces all the events of the *Acta* in some form. His treatment of the material is, however, markedly different from that of the original. The anonymous author of the *Acta* allows the plainly reported events to speak for themselves, and the courage of the martyrs

---

[15] This is a 5th-century interpolation according to Fernández Alonso (1964) 1297.

emerges from their actions. Prudentius introduces changes and additions which are the result of his new brief. He wants to show the martyrs in the most heroic light possible—this is the natural result of the late fourth-century attitude towards the martyrs as the champions who won for the Church its victory on earth. He wants to do this in poetry, a form which demands more emotional colour and drama than the simple prose account allows. The result of the poet's wish to eulogize the Church's heroes in this form is to make them larger than life. This is achieved by painting their opponents in the blackest colours, by increasing their torments, by attributing bravely defiant speeches to them, and by emphasizing the divine aid which supports them by the record of as many miracles as possible.

By giving this sort of picture of the martyrs, Prudentius not only participates in tendencies at work elsewhere in contemporary martyr literature,[16] but also produces material which is more suitable for the lyric setting of the poem, which needs a more emotionally charged treatment of events. This is clear from the tone and contents of the stanzas which frame the narrative core. The poet begins by addressing Fructuosus directly (1–3) in an oblique thanksgiving for the happiness of Tarragona in being the native city of three such great martyrs. The city is personified and given an unusual and sparkling crown:

> Felix Tarraco, Fructuose, *uestris*
> *attollit caput ignibus coruscum,*
> leuitis geminis procul relucens.
>
> (1–3)

The three jewels in the crown are the three martyrs, and they flash from afar in an image which suggests not only the gleam of gems meant to represent the heavenly glory of the martyrs, but also the very real 'ignes' of the pyre on which they are to suffer death. In the next stanza, the Trinity itself crowns the 'arcem Hiberam' of Tarragona (5), with its three martyrs, 'trino ... martyre' (6). The martyrs reflect the three-fold strength of the Trinity by a piece of word-play achieved through the unusually used distributive 'trino'. This interplay of image and word-play with eulogy and thanksgiving is far from the immediate entry into the narrative

---

[16] See below, pp. 227 ff.

found in the *Acta*, but provides a colourful and arresting introduction to the poem. In these stanzas Prudentius also introduces a strong patriotic note which is absent from the *Acta*, and which must be directed towards his Spanish audience.

By a sudden transition which is well-suited to lyric technique,[17] Prudentius breaks away from his opening section to the narrative. At line 7 he pictures the glorified martyrs proceeding, one by one, 'supernum/Christi ... ad sedile' (8–9): 'Ardens Augurius' goes first, then Eulogius; the whole of the next stanza is devoted to the third and greatest martyr, 'Dux et praeuius et magister illis', that is, Fructuosus. He, too, moves in procession 'ad tantum decus', but the next stanza (13–15) makes it clear that the poet is now no longer describing a picture of imagined heavenly glory, but rather the progress of the martyrs to the forum of Tarragona for judgement before execution. It is only indirectly that they move towards Christ's heavenly seat. Prudentius here unexpectedly moves away from the highly charged picture of triumph in the first two stanzas, to the earthly setting required for the narrative.

In this way, the poet moves smoothly from the introduction to the narrative. He allows the opening scene of the *Acta* to disappear, together with the careful dating of events. He omits the arrival of the soldiers at Fructuosus' house and the bishop's request to put on his sandals. These details, though touching, are too homely and prosaic to provide a suitable opening after the emotive introductory stanzas. He prefers to enter the *Acta* when the action is fully under-way, and at the point when the martyrs' heroic struggle begins in earnest. The opening scene of the *Acta* is too low-keyed: the soldiers are mild in manner, the bishop goes quietly. His quiet courage is not the stuff of heroic grandeur, and it is in these terms that the poet views the martyrs' struggle. He omits the detail of the guards' name from his account. He wants the martyrs' persecutors to play their part as the Christians' enemies to the full and therefore wants to ignore the fact that some of the governor's soldiers may even be Christians.[18] Anybody associated with the persecutor must be portrayed in the

---

[17] Cf. Horace's technique as described by Williams (1969) 16.

[18] Franchi de' Cavalieri (1935b) 152. For Prudentius' caricature of the persecutor, see Opelt (1967); cf. *Acta* and reference to 'commilito frater noster' 3. 3. This may show that the author of the *Acta* was also a soldier and a Christian.

worst possible light in order to highlight the martyrs' courage. Omission of extraneous names also helps to isolate the martyrs at the climactic moments of trial and execution.

The opening scene of the *Acta* is compressed into a single stanza:

> Accitus quia praesidis repente
> iussu uenerat ad forum sacerdos,
> leuitis comitantibus duobus . . .
>
> (13–15)

The first line of the stanza conveys both the orders of the governor and all the suddenness of the arrest (*repente*). Prudentius then pictures the arrival of the prisoners at the city forum, here supplying a detail lost from our version of the *Acta*. He may simply be using his imagination on this point, but the result is a suggestion which is not historically improbable, and which would help to bring the account alive for the inhabitants of Tarragona. However, he allows himself a very free rein in describing the imprisonment of the martyrs. A neutral statement in the *Acta* tells that they were taken to prison. Prudentius regards this as a point ripe for dramatic development. He describes the prison itself in an alliterative circumlocution, 'carceream . . . catenam', which is arranged in such a way that it 'imprisons' the word 'uiros' in its line (16). The poet also exploits the first opportunity for describing the martyrs' enemy, by introducing the figure of the executioner who, in fact, played no part in the *Acta*. In Prudentius' version, the martyrs are 'dragged off' to prison by an executioner who is glutted with blood:

> *pastus sanguine* carnifex trahebat . . .
>
> (17)

Prudentius' next line shows Fructuosus not only undismayed by this treatment, but even rushing joyfully to prison, 'gaudet currere Fructuosus ultro'. Coming directly after the description of the bloody executioner, this statement emphasizes the bishop's bravery even more than the lengthier description of Fructuosus' joy and serenity on imprisonment in *Acta* 1. 4. The poet rejects this peaceful picture in favour of a rousing speech by Fructuosus to his companions on their way to prison. This speech comes entirely from the poet's imagination. In it, the bishop wants to encourage his friends, and exhorts them to stand firm at his side:

> praeceptor uehemens eundo firmat . . .
>
> (20)

He then refers to the 'cruentus . . . coluber' who calls them to their death. This 'bloody serpent' could have a wide range of reference: it is a common Christian image for the forces of evil[19] and could here refer either to the devil himself who plots against the 'Dei ministros' (23) or to his earthly agents, the governor and his servants. 'Cruentus' here recalls the 'pastus sanguine' used to describe the executioner. Perhaps the exact reference is not as important as the rhetorical effect of the line, and the impact of Fructuosus' horrible image in the context of a rousing exhortation. It is balanced by the bishop's more positive reference to the palm of victory which awaits the martyrs after death.

The next stanza of Fructuosus' speech is pure rhetoric, a highly artificial tricolon crescendo which explores the theme of the true value of prison for the Christian. It is his path to heaven:

> *Carcer* christicolis gradus *c*oronae est,
> *carcer* prouehit ad superna *c*aeli,
> *carcer* *c*onciliat Deum beatis.
>
> (25–7)

Anaphora in combination with the alliteration of the 'c' reinforces the vehemence of the bishop's words. Prudentius may have derived the starting point for this tirade from the *Acta*'s reference (1. 4) to Fructuosus' gladness at the prospect of receiving the 'corona domini', but he develops it into a speech which enlivens the martyrs' imprisonment and makes of it a dramatic climax. The bishop no longer passively suffers, but behaves like a general leading his troops into battle. The poet endows him with a more fiery personality than he possesses in the original account.

The *Acta* deal briefly with the incident of the baptism in prison (2. 1). Prudentius devotes most of a stanza to it, omitting the

---

[19] This obviously has its beginning in the story of Adam and Eve (Gen. 3: 1). See Grabar (1969) 19, 33. Also Leclercq (1950). The serpent/devil appears in 2 *Cor.* 11: 3 and *Rev.* 12: 9 (cf. 'serpens' used at *Pe.* 5. 197). For 'pastus sanguine', see chap. 5, n. 38, and n. 44 below.

man's name and describing the sacrament in a solemn and allusive
way:

> His dictis adeunt specum reorum;
> exercent ibi mysticum lauacrum,
> et purgamen aquae stupent tenebrae.

$$(28-30)$$

Prudentius avoids the simple Christian term *baptizare* (a verb not
in fact used anywhere in his poetry), and even the noun *baptisma*,
which he favours elsewhere.[20] Instead he uses the less technical
term *lauacrum*[21] qualified by the Greek adjective *mysticum*.
Baptism becomes a 'mystical cleansing', a 'purification by water'
('purgamen aquae'). These figurative terms elevate the incident of
the baptism above the flat 'baptizavit' of the *Acta* and fit in well
with the introduction here of the miraculous element: the sacra-
ment is so great that even the prison's gloom is dispelled by its
cleansing brightness. The poet here not only indirectly describes
the prison's darkness, but also shows how divine power
channelled through baptism has the strength to dispel it. The
'tenebrae' here serve a double purpose: they represent the literal
shadows of the cell, but also the forces of evil beaten by baptism.
The poet's allusive terms leave interpretation open enough to
allow for both meanings to suggest a miracle. There is nothing
corresponding to this treatment of the baptism in the *Acta*.

The prose account specifies that the martyrs spent six days in
prison. Prudentius too gives the same detail at line 31:

> *sex* hic *continuis* latent *diebus* . . .

This line conveys more of the tedium of the six long days ('con-
tinuis . . . diebus'), and the discomfort of the martyrs' quasi-burial
in their dungeon ('latent'). It is after a long wait ('*tandem*') that
they appear before the governor (32). In the *Acta*, Aemilianus is

---

[20] *Pe.* 2. 375; *Apotheosis*, 697; *Psychomachia*, 103. *Lauacrum* is also better suited to Pru-
dentius' lyric metre at this point (Phalaecian hendecasyllables: $\overset{\smile}{-} \overset{}{-} : -\cup\cup- : \cup-\cup- -$).
Frequently used by Catullus, taken up by later lyric poets, especially Statius and Martial,
Prudentius follows their practice of invariably using a spondaic opening. See Raven (1965)
139–40.

[21] *Cath.* 9. 87; *Pe.* 10. 158; *Apoth.* 679; *Cath.* 7. 76; *Ditt.* 166. Cf. Vulgate, Titus 3: 5:
'lauacrum regenerationis et renouationis Spiritus Sancti'. This might have provided Pru-
dentius with a precedent for his image. Cf. too, the use of this word by Pope Damascus,
Ferrua (1942) 93–4.

simply labelled 'praeses'. Prudentius takes the opportunity of his first appearance to establish *his* characterization of the martyrs' judge. Aemilianus is not only the anonymous 'trux ... hostis' (34), but is threatening in his aspect:

> atrox, turbidus, insolens, profanus,
> aras daemonicas coli iubebat.
>
> (35–6)

The poet thoroughly blackens the governor in this asyndetic crescendo.[22] He wastes no time on the brief enquiries gone through by the Praeses in the *Acta*. He simply orders the martyrs to worship at the altars of the gods, and goes on to reiterate the Emperor's orders[23] in a six-line speech, in which he also outlines Fructuosus' role in causing pagans to abandon the old gods. He refers in particular to the effect of Christianity on 'leues puellae': memories here, perhaps, of Eulalia (*Pe.* 3) and Agnes (*Pe.* 14), since there is no such speech from the Praeses in the *Acta*. His rantings in the poem, however, have little effect on the martyrs. Even before the interrogation, they had received confirmation of their strength from the trembling of the instruments of torture at their approach: 'fratres tergeminos tremunt catastae' (33). The poet here includes a touch of the miraculous which is absent from the prose account. At the moment of the martyrs' trial, the poet wants to give visible and dramatic form to the strength and support which helps them to bear their fate with outstanding courage.

Prudentius reduces the interrogation to one exchange between Fructuosus and the governor. He describes the bishop as 'placidus', an adjective which finds no place in the bare report of the *Acta*, where the bishop's calmness emerges from his series of brief replies to Aemilianus. Prudentius' single exchange is tense and dramatic, with Aemilianus' speech balanced by Fructuosus' reply.

---

[22] Cf. the similar abusive asyndeton in *Pe.* 14. 67–71: 'ut uidit Agnes stare trucem uirum/mucrone nudo, laetior haec ait:/'Exulto, talis quod potius uenit/*uesanus, atrox, turbidus, armiger*/mollisque ephebus tinctus aromate.'

[23] Prudentius probably knows a version of the text in which the Emperor is named—a detail unusual for the *Acta*. Gallienus appears on his own as persecutor in rehandled or unhistorical hagiographical texts, although he was in fact the Emperor who issued an edict of tolerance. The names of both Emperors, however, would have appeared on the edicts of persecution, and Gallienus happens to fit the poet's metre, while Valerianus does not! (Franchi de' Cavalieri (1935*b*) 132.)

The latter in his speech echoes one of Fructuosus' replies from the *Acta* (2. 4): 'Ego unum Deum colo qui fecit caelum et terram et mare et omnia quae in eis sunt.' Prudentius renders this as:

> Aeternum colo principem, dierum
> factorem, dominumque Gallieni,
> et Christum Patre prosatum perenni
> cuius sum famulus gregisque pastor.

(44–7)

Fructuosus here is a little more defiant in his references to God as 'dominumque Gallieni ...' He proudly states his role as bishop without prompting from the governor, and earns the governor's grim joke, which is preserved from the *Acta* as 'Iam fuisti' (48). In *Pe.* 6, however, Aemilianus smiles unpleasantly as he says it. The *Acta* omit this detail and state the sentence briefly: 'et iussit eos uiuos ardere' (2. 9). The sentence represents the climax of the trial, and Prudentius cannot allow such a climactic moment to pass without some reference to the behaviour and reaction of all parties involved. He achieves a striking contrast between the uncontrollable rage of the governor:

> Nec differt furor aut refrenat iram;
> saeuis destinat ignibus cremandos ...

(49–50)

and the rejoicing of the martyrs when they hear the sentence (51):

> exultant prohibentque flere uulgum.

This reaction of the martyrs is recorded in the *Acta* too, but later, when they are already on their way to the amphitheatre. By giving their reaction immediately after that of the governor, Prudentius throws into relief the martyrs' amazing fortitude in the face of death and their spiritual superiority over their enemies.

The poet moves immediately to the incident of the drink which is offered to Fructuosus by members of the crowd. He passes over the fact that the drink is a drugged one (presumably to lessen the pain of death), but develops the bishop's refusal of the draught. In the *Acta*, the bishop refuses on grounds of wanting to keep his fast. Prudentius' bishop begins by giving the same reply, but goes on to explain his decision over another two stanzas in terms which are rather self-righteous, and almost self-congratulatory: 'I will never violate sacred law, and not even death itself will release me from my obligation'. He goes on to compare himself explicitly with Christ thirsting on the cross:

> sic Christus sitiens crucis sub hora
> oblatum sibi poculum recusans
> nec libare uolens sitim peregit,
>
> (58–60)

This parallel might have been more fitting from the spectators or the narrator than from the martyr himself,[24] however valid the parallel. It is very far from the unassuming manner and humble resignation of Fructuosus in the *Acta*. Prudentius wants to give his bishop what he considers to be a more striking and heroic personality. He does this at the cost of introducing a strident and negative note into his characterization.

Next the martyrs reach the amphitheatre. Prudentius diverges completely from the *Acta* at this point, in order to give a vivid picture of the arena as the scene of past violence. The place runs with the blood of wild beasts slain there (62–3). It is ruled by the madness of the crowds which call for blood during 'spectacula . . . cruenta'. Prudentius even refers to the fate of the gladiator as the climax of this horrific description. The poet here uses the excuse of the context to give voice to a criticism common among Christians.[25] He mentions the horror of gladiatorial shows at two other points, in the *Contra Symmachum*,[26] and it may be that these references reflect renewed attempts in his period to ban gladiatorial shows and other blood sports.[27] Here the picture of the dying gladiator as the secular counterpart of the martyrs, and the cruel pleasure which the crowd takes in his end, reinforce the atmo-

---

[24] For example, *The Martyrdom of Polycarp*, where parallels with the Passion of Christ are drawn by the author at 1. 2 and 6. 2. See Delehaye (1927a) 102. I follow here the punctuation given in all editions. It is just possible that this stanza should not be included in the martyr's speech, but be regarded as a comparison made by the poet (cf. the comparison he draws later in the poem at 109 ff.; see p. 220 below).

[25] For example, Tertullian, *Spect.* 12; Cyprian, *ad Donatum*, 7; Arnobius, 2. 41; Lactantius, *Div. inst.* 6. 20, *Epit.* 58. For further references with discussion, see *LRE* 2. 977 and 2. 328 n. 86. Also Solmsen (1965) 239 n. 7.

[26] *Contra Symmachum*, 1. 380 ff. and 2. 1090 ff., esp. 1112–16, a plea to the Emperor to end the abuse.

[27] Theodoret, *Hist. eccl.* 5. 26: Honorius, on coming to the throne in the West, abolished gladiatorial fights. For the role played by the monk Telemachus and the controversy surrounding this abolition, see Delehaye (1914). Cf. chap. 1 above, n. 64.

sphere of horror with which Prudentius surrounds the amphi-
theatre, ready for the death of the martyrs. The *Acta* contain no
such emotive picture, but the poet sees the entry into the place of
death as a further climactic point in the narrative, and accordingly
expands its description to suitably dramatic proportions.

It is in the amphitheatre that the 'niger minister' of the gover-
nor has built the pyre, according to the poet's account (67–9).
This evil servant is not mentioned in the *Acta*, nor indeed is the
pyre itself, but the poet again chooses to give a full and horrifying
picture of the form of execution in anticipation of the martyrs'
deaths. In this way, the cruelty of the judges is also emphasized.
They are presented as the powers of darkness ('niger' (67) perhaps
recalls the symbolic 'tenebrae' of line 30). The pyre, however, is
also to be the means of the martyrs' glorification and victory (70–
2), and Prudentius' second stanza on the subject of the pyre makes
the contrast clear. They pyre will release the souls of the martyrs
not only from the actual prison of the governor, but also from
their bodies, the 'prison' of the flesh.

Having derived maximum effect from the subject of the
amphitheatre and the pyre, Prudentius then changes his tone to
the pathetic. The *Acta* at this point, too, describes the attentions of
the faithful who accompany Fructuosus: first Augustalis, then
Felix approach the bishop with different requests. The pathos here
lies in the emotions implied in these individual encounters. The
author of the prose account conveys the emotions of the moment
by concentrating on two faces from the whole crowd. Prudentius
loses the effectiveness of this technique in his keenness to give a
picture of Fructuosus' overwhelming popularity: in his version
(73) the faithful almost fight for the privilege of serving the
bishop:

> *certant* officiis pii sodales . . .

It is an unnamed 'unus' who wants to loosen Fructuosus' sandals, a
figure who hardly emerges from the blur of the jostling crowd.
Once again, suppression of names is intended to isolate Fructuo-
sus, the better to emphasize his courage. The function of this in-
cident in Prudentius' version seems to be mainly to provide the
starting-point for the bishop's last speech. He says that he wants to
take his shoes off in order not to slow down his steps as he rushes
into the fire (79–81). There is nothing of this grotesque and almost

comic extravagance in Fructuosus' brief reply in the *Acta* (3. 5).[28]
Prudentius then goes on to omit the request of Felix altogether:
the bishop's second reply to the soldier is combined with his first
to Augustalis to form a longer speech. Felix's question becomes an
implied question coming from more than one of the crowd:

> Cur lamenta rigant genas madentes;
> cur vestri memor ut fiam rogatis?

The bishop's answer is to promise 'Cuntis pro populis rogabo
Christum' (84), in words which recall the promise given in the
Acta (3. 6). Prudentius uses this statement to form an impressive
climax to Fructuosus' final words. The emotional level and the
dramatic impact are heightened by the poet's combination and
lengthening of Fructuosus' briefer and separate statements from
the *Acta*.

The poet goes on to compare Fructuosus' removal of his shoes
to Moses' actions by the burning bush (Exod. 3. 2–5). This com-
parison does not exist in the *Acta*. Prudentius uses the picture as a
sort of Christian simile, which not only works at the visual level,
but also at a deeper, typological one. The poet confirms the signi-
ficance of Fructuosus' martyrdom by connecting its details with
an Old Testament incident in which divine interference and
approval is clear. Prudentius shows his interest in this particular
Old Testament scene in the seventh quatrain of his collection the
Dittochaeon, 'Ignis in Rubro', where Moses

> soluit uincla pedum, properat Pharaonis ad arcem.

The removal of Moses' shoes is followed immediately by his
brave return to the house of Pharaoh. There is an obvious parallel
here with Fructuosus, whose removal of his sandals is followed by
his walking to his death. This parallel is left unstated in the poem,
but may have been clear to a Christian reader familiar with the
Old Testament. If the stanzas of the *Dittochaeon* were intended to
accompany paintings of the scene in a Church, then this scene
from Moses' life may have also been one familiar from Church
decoration.[29]

Once Fructuosus has removed his sandals, he is ready for death.

[28] Franchi de' Cavalieri (1935b) 148: the prisoner's shoes have to be removed simply as part of the preparation for the pyre; cf. *The Martyrdom of Polycarp*, 13. 2.
[29] Lavarenne (1963b) 201–2.

In the *Acta*, Fructuosus next delivers a short last speech to encour-
age the faithful. He speaks 'monente pariter ac loquente Spiritu
Sancto', 'with the words and inspiration of the Holy Spirit'. Pru-
dentius either knows a different version here,[30] or chooses
deliberately to reinterpret the text in order to create a miraculous
event. In his poem it is the 'spiritus' itself which speaks:

> ... resultat *ecce*
> *caelo spiritus* et serit loquellam
> quae cunctos tremefecet audientes.
>
> (91–3)

All who hear the miraculous voice tremble. The words them-
selves convey the meaning of Fructuosus' last speech in the *Acta*:
the punishment which they see is only transient; it does not rob
them of life so much as reward them with eternal life. The next
stanza of speech (97–9) expresses what the narrative of the *Acta*
notes after Fructuosus' speech—how 'felices' the three are in their
salvation.

The three then enter the pyre: 'ingressi sunt ad salutem', as the
Acta simply say. Prudentius dramatizes again, painting a vivid
picture. The furnace roars, but even its flames tremble before the
martyrs' steadfast approach. Prudentius again sees the miraculous
where none exists in the *Acta*, and uses it again to emphasize both
the courage of the martyrs and their heavenly support. This is
confirmed in the next two stanzas, where the bonds which tied
the martyrs' hands are burnt away, leaving their skin untouched,
and allowing them to spread their arms in prayer in imitation of
Christ on the cross:

> non ausa est cohibere poena palmas
> in morem crucis ad Patrem leuandas;
> soluit bracchia, quae Deum precentur.
>
> (106–8)

This incident has its starting place in the *Acta*, where the martyrs'
bonds are also burnt through, but without any suggestion of
miraculous intervention—it is simply the result of their being
burnt. The bonds are not loosened by divine aid so that the mar-
tyrs can pray, but the martyrs make use of their hands being freed

[30] Franchi de' Cavalieri (1935*b*). Prudentius may be inspired here by the divine voice of
the *Martyrdom of Polycarp*, 9. 1.

by natural forces to pray until they die (4. 3). This original version is embroidered by Prudentius in order to make the martyrs' deaths more wonderful.

He follows the example of the *Acta* in comparing the three martyrs to the three young men in Daniel (3. 23 ff.) who are condemned to death in the furnace by King Nebuchadnezzar. This Old Testament scene was again one familiar from contemporary Christian art, in which it was used to symbolize God's salvation of man.[31] It may have been the miraculous survival of these biblical young men which inspired Prudentius' insertion of a suggestion of such a miracle in the account of the deaths of the Spanish martyrs. His poetic comparison involves a fuller picture of the biblical scene. He gives a small but lively picture of the three men singing in the Babylonian furnace, and the tyrant's amazement at their courage:

> Priscorum specimen trium putares,
> quos olim Babylonicum per ignem
> cantantes stupuit tremens tyrannus.
>
> (109–11)

Just as the 'pia flamma' spared these young men (for the era of martyrs had not yet begun), so at first the flames spare the Spanish saints, who, however, pray for a speedy death. This is finally granted by the 'exorata Maiestas' (118–19). Prudentius complicates the martyrs' deaths in this way in order to increase tension at the last minute, and to show the martyrs in an heroic light as they pray for death. The same effect is achieved through the development of the biblical comparison. It not only lends Prudentius' version greater narrative richness and variation, but also highlights the Spanish martyrs' outstanding courage: the 'mortis decus' is theirs in a way impossible for the three in the Book of Daniel.

The account of the *Acta* ends with the two miracles described above. Prudentius too records these miracles, but with some changes. He avoids the detail of the names of the governor's servants, and gives the story a clearer point by saying that the governor's daughter was allowed to see the vision although her father

---

[31] Grabar (1969) 10. Prudentius himself gives a fuller and more vivid account of this biblical incident at *Apotheosis*, 128–54.

was not 'ut crimen domini domus timeret' (129). The hint of punishment in store for the governor and his household here is again entirely absent from the *Acta*.

In the next miraculous vision, Prudentius again clarifies motivation. The saint is explicit about the need to restore his ashes to one place ready for final resurrection (136–8). The *Acta* are more vague (6. 3):

oportebat enim Fructuosum martyrem quod in saeculo per misericordiam Dei docendo promiserat in Domino et saluatore nostro in sua postea passione et resurrectione carnis comprobare.

It may be that Prudentius' version refers to a contemporary controversy concerning the relics at a time when their removal from one resting-place to another was at least under discussion. The division and sale of relics was in any case a topical subject at the end of the fourth century in the West.[32]

Prudentius' final sight of the martyrs is more glorious than that of the *Acta*. In his version, all three martyrs appear 'niveis stolis amicti' in a picture which evokes the glorified martyrs of the Apocalypse.[33] Prudentius' intention here is to balance the horror of the martyrs' deaths by the splendour of their glorified state, and the victory which is the true climax of their martyrdom. Their instructions to the faithful are explicit:

> mandant restitui cauoque claudi
> mixtum marmore puluerem sacrandum.

(140–1)

No such statement occurs in the *Acta*. Unless he is working purely from imagination here, Prudentius may be introducing his own knowledge of the contemporary shrine of Fructuosus at Tarragona, since at the time of the persecution itself, the ashes could hardly have been placed immediately in the marble sepulchre which Prudentius' words seem to imply. His words refer either to the later shrine in the necropolis which has now been excavated,[34] or perhaps to the martyrs' final resting-place in a basilica inside

---

[32] Delehaye (1933*b*) 50 ff. At p. 88 he refers to the *CTh* (9. 17. 7, AD 386): 'Humatum corpus nemo ad alternum locum transferat; nemo martyrem distrahat, nemo mercetur'. Also Leclercq (1948).

[33] Rev. 6: 11; 7: 14.

[34] García Rodríguez (1969) 317, and Serra Vilaró (1946). See below pp. 269 ff.

the city itself.[35] Their recent removal to this basilica, or plans for this, might explain the new emphasis given here to keeping the ashes together, since this would have been an ideal moment for the division of the relics. Prudentius' poem may even have been written on the occasion of this translation, although there are, admittedly, no *explicit* references to this in the poem.

Prudentius' reference to the 'cauo ... marmore' supplies the link with the closing section of the poem, which once again congratulates Tarragona on its glorious sons. As Prudentius thinks of the final resting-place of the martyrs, which he surely knows in all its present splendour, his mind naturally turns to the city's celebrations of its 'triplex honor ... triforme culmen'. (Here there *may* be a reference to a special celebration of the feast-day at the time of the translation, for instance.) The poet now enters the poem as choir master and encourages the massed choirs of the faithful to sing of their martyrs. Let the basilica[36] 'in arce' (presumably in the city), and the whole shoreline resound with the hymn:

> Hinc *aurata* sonent in *arce tecta*;
> blandum litoris extet inde murmur,
> et carmen freta feriata pangant.

At the end of the world, Fructuosus will plead on the city's behalf at her judgement. The poet then ends on a more personal note of prayer: he hopes that the saint will intercede for him with Christ after death. All seven final stanzas are without basis in the *Acta* and form part of the lyric frame in which these are set by Prudentius.

At 145–7, Prudentius speaks of the 'praesidium', the protection given to the Pyrenean people by their three 'patroni', the martyrs. The poet here draws on terminology which sets the relationship of faithful and saints in a framework parallel to the secular structure surrounding patrons and clients in Roman society.[37] Just as people in their role of *clientes* applied to their *patronus* for *suffra-*

---

[35] Serra Vilaró (1946). There is no reference to this basilica earlier than the 6th century, unless the lines of Prudentius refer to it with the words 'in arce', which would seem to mean 'in the city itself'. See below p. 272. The terms 'praesidio' (146) and 'in arce' might suggest that the martyrs form a 'heavenly garrison' for the city, as well as a set of *patroni*.

[36] 'aurata ... tecta' surely refers to the Church dedicated to the saint. Cf. *Pe.* 3. 196 ff. for a similar reference to the basilica of Eulalia at Mérida.

[37] See de Ste Croix (1954) esp. 46; also Myres (1960) esp. 28. cf. Homes Dudden (1935) 1. 302 n. 2 and Chadwick (1957) 313–18; also, Brown (1981) 55–6, 59–60, 62–4, and Orselli (1965), reviewed by Fontaine, *Latomus* 26 (1967) 217–20.

gium, their support and the exertion of influence on the client's be-
half, so in a religious context, the martyrs are regarded as
heavenly *patroni*, who can exert influence with God on behalf of
the pious faithful. *Suffragium* comes to mean intercession in con-
nection with the heavenly *patrocinium* of the martyrs. It seems that
Ambrose was the first writer at the end of the fourth century to
coin the vocabulary of patronage in speaking of the martyrs. The
usage was then widely taken up, and appears frequently in the
poems of both Paulinus of Nola and Prudentius.[38] Prudentius'
probable proximity to the Ambrosian circle in Milan and his
direct experience of the cult of the two *patroni* of Milan, Gervasius
and Protasius, may have particularly inspired his adoption of the
terminology.

This detailed comparison makes it clear that Prudentius felt at
liberty to adapt his original in ways which were presumably
acceptable to an audience who knew the *Acta* well. Although the
text of the original *Acta* very clearly forms the basis for the poem,
Prudentius' rendering of them is an interpretation rather than a
transcription into verse. This involves free elaboration and even
additions which grow out of the poet's imagination at work on
the bare facts of the original. The result is a more dramatic and
emotionally charged account, in which persecuted and per-
secutors are painted in vivid colours, and even undergo changes of
personality under the poet's hand. The passive serenity of Fruc-
tuosus in the face of death is exchanged in Prudentius' version for
the rhetorically inclined bishop who rushes defiantly into martyr-
dom. Although Prudentius recognizes the original characteriza-
tion of the bishop by his use of the adjective 'placidus' (43), his
picture goes beyond the bounds of calmness, for instance, in the
bishop's provocative reply to the governor in the course of the in-
terrogation. The poet, however, ignores the discrepancies of his
account in his enthusiasm to give the most strikingly heroic pic-
ture of the martyrs' trial and death. He reads between the lines of
the *Acta* to imagine how such a champion of the Church must
have behaved. His aim is both to elevate the figure of the martyr
and to colour in the rather stark *Acta* with thrilling details.

This, too, is the aim of his emphasis on miracles throughout his

---

[38] Ambrose, *Ep.* 22. 10 and 11. Paulinus of Nola, *Carm*, 13. 27; 14. 105; 18. 5; 23. 99,
202, 214, 318; 26. 232; 27. 147, 198; 22. 1. Cf. 31. 1 (of Felix); Augustine, *De cura gerenda pro
mortuis*, 6. 22. Apart from *Pe.* 6. 145, Prudentius uses the term at *Pe.* 1. 12; 2. 579; 13. 106.

account. These sometimes invented miracles demonstrate the martyrs' superiority over their enemies, as well as adding interest to the narrative. It must be asked how the poem's readers would have reacted to the fairly free play of the poet's imagination over his material. Contemporary standards of historical accuracy were not high in any case,[39] and in the realms of devotional reading, no objection was raised against the addition of unattested material to a saint's life. No matter what the sources, the fuller the picture painted, the happier the reader. Prudentius' unworried attitude towards the changes which he introduces in *Pe.* 6 represents a trend in the literary treatment of martyrs which was general by the end of the fourth century. The simplicity of the original and authentic martyr accounts is almost completely lost amidst the excesses and falsification of so-called 'legendary passions'.[40] The martyr, by this process, becomes a stereotyped hero figure. Prudentius' version of the *Acta* of Fructuosus exemplifies at a fairly low level of development the ways in which the facts of a martyrdom could be distorted with the best of pious intentions in order to produce the picture of the martyr. Useful comparisons of technique can be made with other fourth-century adaptations of authentic *Acta*. Similar dramatizing touches appear, for instance, in Eusebius' 'transcription' of the *Martyrdom of Polycarp*.[41]

The tendency at work in *Pe.* 6 rightly undermines, to some extent, confidence in Prudentius' attitude towards his sources, and his historical sense in general. In *Pe.* 6 he is certainly not as good as his source, and this suggests at least as loose an attitude towards the facts in the other poems. The one other case where authentic *Acta* exist proves this conclusively: in *Pe.* 13, the poet draws on pure legend for his account of Cyprian's early career as a sorcerer who is later converted to Christianity. He does not hesitate to expand on the basis of facts which are well known from a variety of reliable sources.[42] His poems must therefore be regarded in the light of historical novels, loosely based on the fact of martyrdoms, but designed to satisfy the pious curiosity of the faithful who want as rousing a picture as possible of their heroes. In *Pe.* 6, the poet is

---

[39] See chap. 2 above.

[40] This is the term used by Delehaye (1966) in his categorization of martyr literature.

[41] Eusebius, *Hist. eccl.* 4. 15. For a full comparison of Eusebius with the authentic text, see Lazzati (1956a).

[42] Lavarenne (1963b) 181–5; Sabbatini (1972) 47 ff. See below, pp. 235 ff.

relatively restrained in his additions and changes, presumably as
the result of the existence of a well known set of *Acta* which be-
have as a control. It remains only to be guessed how far he relies
on his imagination in poems where there was no such control. His
compositions, however, must have represented a successful mix-
ture of fact and fiction, since in some cases they heavily influenced
the later prose versions.[43] He may not be as good as his sources
where these are reputable, but he is certainly no worse than his
contemporaries in the liberties which he feels free to take.

He is, after all, writing poetry, and not an historical chronicle.
The last point to be derived from *Pe.* 6 concerns the poetry. This
poem is noticeable for its lack of reference to earlier Latin poetry.
A few isolated phrases echo a Virgilian phrase: so 'uix haec edi-
derat' (*Pe.* 6. 85) echoes this introductory formula at *Aeneid*, 5.
693; 'felices animae' (97) recalls the Sibyl's address to the shades at
Aeneid, 6. 669; and the terms used of the gathering of Fructuosus'
remains at 130 ff. recall the scene of Misenus' funeral at *Aeneid*, 6.
227 ff. (the similarity here is a very general one). These echoes are
superficial, and contribute nothing to the context beyond a touch
of epic solemnity and grandeur.[44] In comparison with other
poems in the collection, *Pe.* 6 is remarkably poor in classical allu-
sions. This may be the result of Prudentius' awareness of the *Acta*
behind his poems. He prefers to draw on a more neutral poetic
style here, which still relies to some extent on a poetic diction
with its roots firmly in the classical tradition (see, for instance,
'coluber' (23); 'Tonantis' (98); 'pares Camenas' (153)), but which
draws more on the vocabulary and forms of later Latin: for
example, the adjectives 'carcareus' and 'episcopalis' (16 and 11);
the impersonal 'iussum est' (41); the use of the ablative to express
duration of time (31); the increased use of compound verbs such
as 'conviolare' (56), 'concremare' (70); the use of 'planta' (74), and
the unclassical 'atquin' (79). The result is a lively and vivid narrat-
ive style which gives way naturally to vigorous rhetoric where
speech is introduced, and which has a very different flavour from

---

[43] See the early inclusion of Prudentius' poems in the Mozarabic Hymnal and the poet's influence, for instance, on Gregory of Tours (García Rodríguez (1966) 25 ff.).

[44] Mahoney (1934) 165–6 gives a few more possible parallels, but these, if admissible, remain at the superficial level, and seem to exemplify Prudentius' unconscious involvement in epic diction. The phrase 'pastus sanguine' (17) might contain an Ovidian reference (cf. *Amores*, 3. 10. 8, 'sanguine pasciter eques'), but the new context of martyrdom gives the Ovidian phrase a much more serious force.

the style of the more sophisticated *Pe.* 11, for instance. The strength of Prudentius' Christian source seems to have dictated a more popular style for *Pe.* 6. This might imply less good sources for those poems where Prudentius produces a work of more literary experiment and sophistication (see Chapter 4). It also points to the importance of defining the relation of the *Peristephanon* to contemporary martyr literature.

8

The *Peristephanon* and its Sources

Contemporary martyr-literature: the background[1]

DISTANCE from the actual events of persecution encouraged the tendency to resort to fictional additions in order to provide devotional matter for the faithful, particularly where a surviving authentic account was lacking.[2] In this process, martyrs could become reduced to a stereotype which needed re-surrounding with interesting detail. This tendency was particularly encouraged by the Peace of the Church and the end of persecution at the beginning of the fourth century, when the general attitude towards the role and figure of the martyr and his celebration underwent a change, together with the treatment of the martyrs in contemporary literature. As Raby notes: 'The new conception of the martyr, which was to dominate the whole middle ages, was the creation of the post-Constantinian Church'.[3]

The writings of Eusebius give important insights into this change of attitude and its effects on martyr-literature. For the Church historian, who lived through and beyond the final persecution, the Peace of the Church is, in fact, its victory, the result of a long struggle to defend the divine message against the 'widespread, bitter and recurrent campaigns launched by unbelievers' against it.[4] In this war, the martyrs are the champions who κατὰ καιροὺς τὸν δι᾽ αἵματος καὶ βασάνων ὑπὲρ αὐτοῦ διεξῆλθον ἀγῶνα (*Hist. eccl.* I. 1, 2), men of courage and endurance who triumph over demons and win victories over invisible opponents (5. Praef. 4). This view of the martyrs' instrumental role in bringing about the victory of the Church on earth led in the course of the century to a greatly increased enthusiasm for their cult, accompanied by an ever-growing tendency to present all the martyrs

---

[1] For a full history of martyr literature since the first persecutions see Aigrain (1953); Delehaye (1927*a* and *b*; 1934; 1966); and Lazzati (1956*b*).

[2] Delehaye (1934) 11.

[3] Raby (1953) 51.

[4] Eusebius *Hist. eccl.* I. 1.

according to an heroic stereotype. The martyr's superhuman powers of resistance against the worst tortures that human beings could devise, and the supernatural aid he received from above, were now not only emphasized but exaggerated, to the extent that the simple confession of faith, Χριστιανός εἰμι, which had once formed the climax of the original accounts, was now even sometimes omitted, or at least overshadowed by the lengthy description of the martyr's tortures and execution. The longer and the more heroic a martyr's sufferings and the more numerous and spectacular the occasions of supernatural intervention, the greater appeared the martyr's victory on behalf of the Church.

These elements of the macabre and the miraculous had been given a very limited role in the earliest martyr-literature, but they are used to excess in the later literature, bringing about the inflated heroization of the typical figure which appears so regularly in the later legendary or epic passions. Just as the martyr is himself a stereotype, so events and personalities surrounding him also follow a set pattern. The story is always some combination of the following elements: the martyr's arrest, his trial and interrogation, his tortures, and execution. The martyr may undergo more than one session of tortures and may be sustained by heavenly visions while in prison between bouts. The martyr is always faced with a wicked judge, or even an emperor, who is always described in the blackest terms. The action may be varied by the conversion to Christianity of admiring guards and lengthy speeches in explanation and justification of his faith from the martyr.[5]

Eusebius' rhetorical education and stylistic sensibilities play an important role in his new presentation of the martyrs, and he falls in with Cicero's saying in the *Brutus* (11. 42), where it is deemed possible 'ementiri in historiis, ut aliquid dicere possint argutius'. Eusebius finds further justification for such a course in the religious value, meaning, and message of his Church History. His attitude continues among ecclesiastical writers: Cassian, two centuries later, openly admitted the need for some moulding of the truth for charitable ends.[6] He also anticipated similar develop-

---

[5] Delehaye (1934: 11) deals with these recurrent elements at length. On the figure of the persecutor, see Opelt (1967).

[6] Cassian, *Collationes*, 17. 18: '*sine dubio subeunda est nobis necessitas mentiendi.*

ments among the eastern panegyrists, such as John Chrysostom, the Gregories, and Basil. He may even have influenced their freedom with facts and their stylistic tendencies.

Martyrs and the Liturgy in the Fourth Century

The annual commemoration of a martyr, which is shown to be a recognized practice by the letter about Polycarp's martyrdom, may have included at an early stage a reading of the contemporary account, where one existed. The letter from Smyrna is itself addressed to all the members of the Church of Philomelium, and it seems likely that its directly didactic tone was a feature of its role as a church reading, making it suitable for annual use at the feast of the martyr. The same may have been true for the rest of the earliest martyr-literature at or soon after the time of its composition. For the second and third centuries, it is impossible to tell at which stage in the celebration the Martyr-Acts or Passion were read, or even what form this whole celebration took. In the freer circumstances of the fourth century, the annual celebration clearly involved a vigil and Mass at the martyr's tomb; this practice may have had early precedents.[7]

As enthusiasm for the cult grew, so did the crowds attending feast-day celebrations. Every town was keen to possess its own heavenly *patronus*, whose close relationship with the town was confirmed by the possession of the martyr's remains. What had at first been community feast-days during the actual days of persecution, now became national, if not international, gatherings, so great had become the enthusiasm for pilgrimage.[8] So Paulinus of Nola (itself a cult-centre of St Felix and the scene of colossal annual concourses[9]) travelled to Rome every year on pilgrimage to visit the tombs of the martyrs there. Jerome records the zeal and the number of pilgrims in Rome.[10] Prudentius, too, in *Pe.* 11 and 12 gives a vivid idea of the crowds to be seen in Rome for the celebration of the feast-days of SS Hippolytus and Peter and Paul.

---

[7] Delehaye (1933*b*) 40–1. For Polycarp, see Musurillo (1972).

[8] Bardy (1949).

[9] Paulinus describes these gatherings in his poems, for example, 28. 545 ff.

[10] *Comment. in Epist. ad Galat.* 2. = PL. 26. 355.

The Eastern Fathers were only too conscious of the over-jovial holiday atmosphere which could prevail at such gatherings.[11]

Under these new circumstances, martyr-literature, of necessity, flourished. Once the persecutions were in the past, a need was felt not only to have recourse to contemporary Church records of those days, but also to supply the universal interest with material to satisfy pious curiosity about any martyr celebrated. The very nature of public celebration pressed new needs on the genre. Ambrose formulates the problem in connection with the newly found *patroni* of Milan, the martyrs Gervasius and Protasius:

Morte martyrum religio defensa, cumulata fides, Ecclesia roborata est: uicerunt morti, uicti persecutores sunt. Itaque quorum uitam nescimus, horum mortem celebramus.[12]

The reality of the martyr's victory had to be confirmed by a realistic representatin of his life and martyrdom. Where history failed to supply the facts, imagination supplied the need.

Hagiographic Readings[13]

The simplest way to bring a martyr's victory before a congregation was to include a reading of the accepted martyrdom account in the Mass alongside, or in place of, the usual Scriptural readings from the Old and New Testaments. Within the feast-day Mass, the solemn reading of the *Passio* seems to have held a place in the Mass of the *catechumens* between readings from the Scriptures and the sermon.[14]

This use of non-Scriptural readings was by no means universally accepted. Rome itself, for all its involvement in the celebration of the feasts of its many martyrs, was slow to admit readings from the *Gesta martyrum* into the course of the Mass. The sixth-

---

[11] Delehaye (1933*b*) 42. Basil compares the crowds at the tomb of St Gordius to a swarm of bees (*Or. in S. Gordium = PG* 31. 489). For the feast day of St Mamas, he tells how the whole country is on the move, with the whole town given up to the feast (*Or. in S. Mamantem* 2 = *PG* 31. 592). John Chrysostom struggles to reform customs more worthy of the theatre than of a holy place (*Homil. XXX in Act. Apost. = PG* 60. 225).

[12] Ambrose, *De excessu fratris sui Satyri*, 2 (*De fide resurrectionis*) 45.

[13] de Gaiffier (1954*a*); Raffa (1955); Lazzati (1956*b*) 17–22; Leclercq (1929*b*) esp. 2234.

[14] Urner (1952). See Caesarius of Arles in the sixth century: 'Quando festiuitates martyrum celebrantur, prima missa de euangeliis legatur, reliquae de passionibus martyrum' (Morin (1937 edn.) 2. 122).

century *Decretum Gelasianum* makes this lasting reluctance clear.[15] It is probably significant that the *Liber pontificalis* makes no mention of the practice, when otherwise it tries hard to give the *gesta* the authority of official documents. The *Ordines Romani* of the eighth century make no allusion to the *Acta*, in marked contrast, for example, with *ordines* from Gaul, which mention readings from 'passiones martyrum et uitae patrum Catholicorum' by the same period.[16] This prohibition of formal readings from the *Acta* probably encouraged the proliferation of more fictional passions dedicated to Roman martyrs and the richness of the 'légendier Romain',[17] unrestricted by the Church control which they would have had if used as readings. The Roman Church seems finally to have allowed such readings into the Office in the eighth century, in the time of Pope Hadrian.[18]

The situation was, however, very different outside the Roman Church. As far as can be gathered from the evidence available for Africa, Gaul, and Spain, readings from the *Acta* were allowed as early as the end of the fourth century and the beginning of the fifth. Thus Church councils in Africa in the 390s state 'Liceat enim legi passiones martyrum, cum anniuersarii dies eorum celebrantur'.[19] Many passages in Augustine's *Sermons* confirm the practice of public reading in the basilicas.[20] Augustine is aware of the importance of the *passiones* for boosting popular memory and piety, in a way which he later recognized at Hippo in his institution of the *libelli miraculorum*.[21] He seems, however, to indicate the scarcity of readings recognized as authentic enough for public reading when he notes with some relief of St Stephen, 'Quia cum aliorum martyrum uix gesta inueniamus, quae in solemnitatibus eorum recitare possimus, huius passio in canonico libro est'.[22] It has been suggested that the place in the liturgy given to the martyrs by the

---

[15] On the use of extra-biblical readings, see *Das Decretum Gelasianum de libris recipiendis et non recipiendis*, ed. Dobschütz (1912) 39–41; cf. *Liber pontificalis* I (1886) p. ci.

[16] de Gaiffier (1954) 140.

[17] Delehaye (1927*a*) 192–4 and (1933*a*).

[18] de Gaiffier (1954) 142.

[19] Council of Carthage (AD 393) c. 47, Mansi 3. 891, reiterated in Council of Hippo c. 36, Mansi 3. 924 (AD 397).

[20] de Gaiffier (1954) 144; Lambot (1949); cf. Roetzer (1930), reviewed by Peeters (1931).

[21] *Libelli miraculorum: De ciu. dei*, 22. 8; Delehaye (1925) 74 ff. and 78–9. Also Delehaye (1933*b*) 124–9 and (1910).

[22] *Sermo* 315. I = *PL* 39. 1426.

African Church ensured that these texts escaped destruction in the centuries of turmoil.[23]

An early sixth-century reference for Gaul points to the early inclusion of a reading from the martyr-acts before the homily: 'ex consuetudine sollemni series lectae passionis explicuit'.[24] Caesarius of Arles (d. AD 542) makes reference to the use of over-lengthy readings from Martyr Acts,[25] while the sixth-century rules of St Aurelian (d. AD 551) and St Ferreolus (d. AD 581) prescribe the reading of the acts of the martyrs in public.[26] The Ambrosian Missal, which seems to have been composed essentially in the fifth century, keeps a place for the martyrs in the *Praefationes*,[27] and this may reflect their use, too, as Church readings in this period. They would have replaced the Old Testament prophetic reading on the saint's feast-day.[28]

Direct evidence for the earlier period in Spain is unfortunately lacking, though Braulius of Saragossa gives certain information for the use of hagiographic readings at the beginning of the seventh century. Echoes of *passiones* in the prayers of the Mozarabic rite of the Mass probably reflect earlier acceptance by the Spanish Church of the public use of *Acta* as readings.[29]

Thus, outside Rome at least, the didactic function which was so important and implicit in the earliest forms of martyr-literature, was officially recognized by their inclusion in the rites of the Mass. In this way, another means of familiarization with this genre was provided for an already enthusiastic congregation. The next stage was the composition of highly rhetorical sermons and panegyrics based on the subject matter of the hagiographic reading. The panegyrics were preserved and repeated at a martyr's feast over the years, and encouraged an exaggerated heroization of the martyr at the expense of truth. This process can be seen at work, particularly in the panegyrics of the Eastern Church Fathers. Jerome and Ambrose, to name but two key Church writers in the West,

---

[23]   de Gaiffier (1954) 146.

[24]   St Avitus (AD 515), *MGH Auct. Ant.* 6. 2, 145.

[25]   Morin (1937) I. 309.

[26]   Aurelian, *PL* 68. 396; St Ferreolus, *PL* 66. 965, where the public aspect of the readings is emphasized: 'recenseri in oratorio audientibus cunctis omnino decernimus'.

[27]   Paredi (1937) 67–9.

[28]   de Gaiffier (1954) 152.

[29]   Cagin (1906) 42. Speaking of Prefaces or *Contestationes*, he says that several 'ne sont que des réductions ou des adaptions au genre eucologique exigé par la *contestatio*, des actes ou de la vie du saint dont on célébre la fête'.

had direct experience of the sermons of the Greek Fathers, while Rufinus' translations of Eusebius made the Eastern historians' more rhetorical versions of martyrdoms increasingly available to the West. His translations of the Greek Fathers may also have helped to stimulate interest in them, at least among the educated.[30]

Prudentius shows the influence of these later developments of martyr-literature. Whether or not he knew any of the Eastern Fathers' works on the martyrs at first hand, he was certainly steeped in the sort of contemporary martyr-literature which exemplified the results of their widespread influence. Against this background, it is easy to understand various features of his work: the highly rhetorical eulogy of the martyrs (as in *Pe.* 4), the attribution of fictional speeches to the martyrs, and the extended description of tortures and execution.

Prudentius took the poetical aspects of contemporary rhetoric on the martyrs to its logical conclusion by using prose accounts of martyrdom as the basis for *poems*. Christian poetry had begun to flourish in the course of the fourth century, and poetic treatment of martyrdoms in particular was not wholly without precedent. Ambrose in Milan had included pieces on selected martyrs among his lyrical compositions (see above, pp. 62 ff.), and it is clear from the *Cathemerinon* that these were an important influence for Prudentius in writing his own lyric poetry. He chooses the Ambrosian metre for *Pe.* 2 and 5, for instance.[31] In Rome, his compatriot Pope Damasus helped in the promotion of martyr-cult by his elegantly produced inscriptions for the martyrs' tombs. Each inscription was a verse résumé of the martyr's achievements.[32] It seems likely that Prudentius himself would have read these inscriptions on a visit to the Christian sites of Rome, and he himself seems to confirm this at *Pe.* 11. 7–8:

> Plurima litterulis signata sepulcra loquuntur,
>   martyris aut nomen aut epigramma aliquod . . .

This must surely refer to the recently installed inscriptions, which in fact influenced Prudentius' treatment of the martyrs at a few

[30] Courcelle (1969) 143–4.
[31] Ambrose's hymns on the martyrs: for Agnes, Victor, Nabor and Felix, Protasius and Gervasius, Lawrence, and Peter and Paul.
[32] For Damasus' epigrams, see the editions of Ihm (1895) and Ferrua (1942).

points (see next section).[33] The poet far surpasses his models in the variety of forms he uses and the poems maintain a high level of literary sophistication (see above, Chapters 3, 4, and 5). However, their links with martyr-literature remain clear and important for any assessment of them and certainly ensured their popularity as devotional reading among educated Christians. The next section attempts to analyse the *Peristephanon* in relation to its particular background in Christian writings or traditions about its respective martyrs.

The *Peristephanon*: the sources

Many of these poems provide details about their martyrs which would otherwise be unknown, but it would be a mistake to impose on Prudentius the responsibility of an historian's role. He is primarily a poet, involved in producing interesting and arresting poems, and only in the second place an hagiographer. 'Hagiographer' seems a more suitable title than historian here, since Prudentius is as concerned to give an historically verifiable account as the contemporary hagiographers whose licence has been outlined above. The poet is no better than his sources and sometimes worse. A brief study of the sources of each poem throws into relief the poet's preoccupation with the literary side of his compositions. Hagiographical conventions and audience expectations are, to some extent, influential here, but the poet feels free to rise above the limited demands of his source material. In undertaking a study of Prudentius' sources below, I do not intend to embark upon an exhaustive investigation of the history of each saint, but simply to illustrate Prudentius' attitude as poet towards his source material.

The poems can be divided into several groups according to the nature of the material available to the poet.[34]

I. POEMS FOR MARTYRS WHERE AN AUTHENTIC ACCOUNT EXISTED

This group of poems is the smallest and includes *Pe.* 6 on the Spanish saint Fructuosus and his deacons, *Pe.* 13 on the African bishop Cyprian, and *Pe.* 7 on Bishop Quirinus of Siscia.

---

[33] Particularly on St Agnes in *Pe.* 14 (see below, pp. 250 ff.). Puech (1888) 114–23.
[34] This is the method employed by Sabbatini (1972 and 1973).

Peristephanon 6

I have already carried out a detailed comparison of this poem with the authentic *Acta* in Chapter 7 above, and will only give the conclusions here. Fructuosus was one of the most popular Spanish saints whose cult not only spread rapidly within Spain itself, but also to Gaul and Italy.[35] His *Acta* were probably well known even beyond Spain and Africa, where they were certainly included as one of the readings for the saint's feast-day.[36] Prudentius follows the outline of this well-known text closely, but still feels at liberty to add lengthy speeches and touches of the miraculous which do not exist in the original. These elaborations enrich and enliven the narrative, give scope for a fuller characterization of the protagonists, and bring Prudentius' account into line with preferences at work elsewhere in contemporary martyr-literature, which always chose a longer and less historical account in preference to a simpler, more truthful one. Thus, even where the poet has access to an authentic and well-known account, he chooses to elaborate beyond the given facts.

Peristephanon 13

This tendency becomes even clearer in his account of the martyrdom of Cyprian, whose story was well known from the extant and authentic *Acta*[37] and from his own correspondence written during the 250s under the emperors Decius and Valerian.[38] The *Acta* were certainly known and available in Prudentius' time: Augustine quotes from them in his sermon for St Cyprian's feast-day (*Sermo* 309 = *PL* 38. 1410). Prudentius could easily have written a poem which drew simply on these *Acta*, which deal with the interrogation of Cyprian in AD 257, his arrest and further interrogation in AD 258 and his execution. He chooses, however, to introduce the bishop's death by way of an account of his early life which draws purely on the legend which had grown up around the supposed conversion from magic and sorcery of one Cyprian of Antioch.[39] This legend seems to have been received into the

---

[35] García Rodríguez (1966) 316–20 on Fructuosus, and 77 ff. on Spanish saints in Church Calendars.
[36] Augustine refers to the *Acta* in *Sermo* 273 = *PL* 38. 1247–9.
[37] Musurillo (1972) 168 ff. and Frend (1965) 423–7.
[38] Lavarenne (1963*b*) 181.
[39] Delehaye (1921).

tradition surrounding the African saint as early as AD 379, the date
attributed to a sermon of Gregory of Nazianzus, which includes
this same fiction (*Sermo* 24 = *PG* 35. 1170). Prudentius probably
draws on a common source rather than on the Greek sermon for
his inclusion of this story (*Pe.* 13. 21–8). It has the advantage both
of supplying the bishop with some interesting details for his early
life (about which little was otherwise known), and of highlight-
ing by contrast the Christian achievements of his later years.

Prudentius ends his poem with another legendary episode, that
of the three hundred martyrs who died in the same persecution as
Cyprian (according to the poet only), and whom he calls 'candida
massa' (*Pe.* 13. 76 ff.). They earn this title by their choice of death
in a pit of live coals. The poet's legend here is an attempt to
explain the name of a place near Utica called the 'Massa Candida',
where, however, the word 'Massa' in fact means 'domain'.[40]
Augustine refers to this place where there are indeed a large
number of martyrs buried.[41]. He never, however, refers to Pru-
dentius' story, which must either be the product of his own
imagination or, as seems more likely, the creation of local tradi-
tion. He covers himself perhaps, at line 76, with the phrase 'fama
refert'. There is, in fact, no reason to suppose that the martyrs
buried at Massa Candida were killed in the same persecution as
Cyprian.

Thus, in a poem which could have related nothing more than
the easily available historical facts about Cyprian, Prudentius
gives a version confused by legendary elements. He is not inter-
ested in giving a critical historical account, but in writing a vivid
dramatic account suited to his poetic medium. He is not worried
by the quality of his sources.

Peristephanon 7

For the story of Bishop Quirinus of Siscia, there existed two
possible sources: a set of (probably) early *Acta* in Latin,[42] and
Jerome's translation of the entry for Quirinus in Eusebius' *Chroni-
con*, where the saint's death is put in AD 308:

[40] Delehaye (1933*b*) 387; 'candida' is a suitable adjective for the description of a place of
martyrdom. Franchi de' Cavalieri (1902).
[41] *Sermo* 306 = *PL* 38. 1400–5, 'In natali martyrum Massae Candidae'; cf. *Enarr. in
Psalm.* 49. 9 = *PL* 36. 571 and *Sermo* 311. 10 = *PL* 38. 1417. See Franchi de' Cavalieri (1902).
[42] Sabbatini (1972) 46–7; Simonetti (1955*b*).

Quirinus episcopus Siscianus gloriose pro Christo inficitur. Nam manuali mola ad collum ligata e ponte praecipitatus in flumen diutissime supernatauit, et cum spectantibus conlocutus, ne sui terrerentur exemplo, uix orans, ut mergeretur optinuit.[43]

The *Passio* contains details about Quirinus' arrest, the miraculous light in prison in the middle of the night, and his interrogation, as well as the miracle attending his execution.[44]

The bishop was in fact buried at Sabaria, not at Siscia, as Prudentius affirms.[45] Jerome relates only the final miracle and the martyr's speech, and the poet follows his simplicity of account here. Another detail in Prudentius supports the hypothesis that the poet in fact only had Jerome's account to refer to: although in the passion it is clear that the martyrdom occurred under the emperors Diocletian and Maximianus, the poet puts it explicitly 'sub Galerio duce'. This mistake may have its roots in the absence of an emperor's name in Jerome's entry and the fact that the very next entry concerns the death of Galerius.[45] Also, Prudentius' concentration on Siscia as the burial place of Quirinus may reflect Jerome's description of the bishop as 'Siscianus', and his omission of the actual place of burial. Jerome himself may have known a Latin version of the *Acta*, but whether or not they were generally available by Prudentius' time, the best explanation of his account and its mistaken details seems to be that he depended on Jerome for his information. He thus has only an indirect and imperfect knowledge of the *Acta*. The poet avoids careful research and relies on a secondary source.

II. POEMS WHICH GIVE THE FIRST WRITTEN EVIDENCE FOR THEIR MARTYRS

Peristephanon 1: SS Emeterius and Chelidonius

Prudentius is our first written source for these Spanish soldier saints,[47] and bases his poem on oral tradition. He explains quite

---

[43] *Eusebii chronicorum liber II interprete S. Hieronymo*, ad ann. 308 p. Chr.

[44] *AASS*, Iunii 1. 372–6.

[45] *Hieronymian Martyrology* for 4 June: 'In Sabaria ciuitate Pannoniae Quirini'. See Zeiller (1918) 71–2, and *Passio S. Quirini*, BHL 7035, chap. 5; Gregory of Tours, *Historia Francorum*, 1. 35; *Damasi epigrammata* (ed. Ihm) 76 A.

[46] This is noticed by Simonetti (1955) 242.

[47] Lavarenne (1963*b*) 19 ff.; Sabbatini (1973) 39–41; Amore (1964).

clearly in the course of the poem that all documents concerning the martyrdom were deliberately destroyed by the persecutors in order to deprive future ages of the martyrs' example (73–8). But Prudentius can report that oral tradition omits only the details: the duration of their imprisonment and the sort of tortures which they suffered (79–81). It is tradition again ('ut ferunt' 85–7) which retains an account of the double miracle of the ring and the scarf at the martyrs' death. There is, however, no indication of the date of their death, and the poet refers to their place of execution simply as 'nostro oppido'. In later calendars and martyrologies, the feast of the martyrs is celebrated on 3 March,[48] and the MS title for the poem, albeit probably later than the poet, associates the saints with Calahorra. The year of the martyrdom remains uncertain, although it has been conjectured that the events took place under the persecution of Galerius at the end of the third century.[49]

The only certain facts in Prudentius' account are that the saints were Spanish soldiers who died for a refusal to sacrifice to the idols. Their speech and the miracles may be the result of poetic licence, or at best, oral tradition. Later *Acta*[50] essentially reproduce Prudentius' account, although the detail of the martyrs' final decapitation is added. Gregory of Tours in the sixth century tells of Emeterius and Chelidonius in his *De gloria martyrum* (*c.* 93 = PL 71. 786), but his account too is derived from Prudentius, whom he even quotes directly. He also refers to the martyrs' decapitation—the result perhaps of a rival local tradition—and adds the detail that the martyrs' tomb is to be found in Calagurris (Calahorra). This reference confirms the historical value of the MS title of *Pe.* 1. Gregory could hardly fabricate local tradition.

The martyrs are probably mentioned once more by Prudentius in the short poem in the elegiac metre which is the inscription intended for a baptistery erected on the place of a double martyrdom. Some, though not all, the manuscripts report in the title of the poem that this baptistery is that of Calahorra,[51] and 3–4 would certainly fit the martyrdom of the two soldiers:

---

[48] For instance, in the *Hieronymian Martyrology* and the Roman and Mozarabic calendars.

[49] Amore (1964) 1195.

[50] *AASS*, Martii. 1, 228–34 for 3 March.

[51] Lavarenne (1963*b*) 106–7.

Hic duo purpureum domini pro nomine caesi
martyrium pulchra morte tulere uiri.

Without any earlier source for the history of these soldiers, it is
obviously difficult to judge the licence of the poet's treatment, but
the poem gives the impression of a version which elaborates on
the tradition fairly freely. The fact that Prudentius admits reliance
on oral tradition suggests the possibility of free treatment of a
fluid tradition.

Peristephanon 3: *Eulalia of Mérida*

Once again, Prudentius supplies our first written source for this
saint. He names her native city, Emerita (Mérida), a town in the
south-west of Spain. A reference to Emperor Maximian in line 77
suggests the year AD 303 for Eulalia's execution.[52] The *Hieronymian Martyrology* gives the dates for her feast as 10, 11, and 12
December,[53] and 10 is the date which recurs in the Carthaginian
calendar, the Mozarabic calendars, and the whole tradition.[54]
Later literature on the martyr is scarce, and consists of a sermon
by Augustine,[55] a brief mention by Venantius Fortunatus,[56] a
chapter in Gregory of Tours' *De gloria martyrum*,[57] the *Cantilena
Sanctae Eulaliae*, and an undateable but late prose Passion.[58]
Gregory adds to Eulalia's story the miracle of the three trees
which flower each year by the Church at Mérida on her feast-
day.[59] The *Cantilena* adds the miracle of the pyre which does not
burn, causing the judge to have Eulalia beheaded. It also dates her
execution to the reign of Maximian, although this date may be
untrustworthy, since attributions of martyrs to the 'Great' per-
secution of AD 303 is common in cases where the date is uncertain.
The same caution may be applied to Prudentius' similar dating.

[52] Lavarenne misses this (1963b: 51). The later Cantilena of St Eulalia mentions that
Eulalia was presented to Maximian. Lavarenne writes a note on the emperor's name at line
77.

[53] *Martyrologium hieronymianum* (1894), 151–2. For descriptions of the history and func-
tion of this martyrology and the calendars, see Leclercq (1932a).

[54] Delehaye (1933b) 413.

[55] Morin (1891).

[56] *Miscellanea*, 8. 3 = PL 88. 271.

[57] *De gloria martyrum*, 91 = PL 71. 785.

[58] *AASS*, Februarii 2, 576–80; *BHL* 1. 404–6, nn. 2693–2703. The martyr has two other
hymns (apart from the poem of Prudentius) which appear in the Mozarabic Hymnal. See
Messenger (1944–5).

[59] The flowering of the tree predicts a good year.

The Passion is obviously derived from Prudentius' version, but adds a great number of extra tortures to the martyr's sufferings in a way typical of later passions.

Prudentius' account is, above all, a poem before it is an historical account. Classical reminiscences align the girl-martyr with the young heroes and heroines of the *Aeneid* and with the tender picture of girlhood given by Catullus in his love-poetry.[60] The poem has a strong Christian background for the picture of a virgin martyr in the Ambrosian hymn dedicated to St Agnes[61] and the inscription of Pope Damasus which commemorates the Roman martyr.[62] Both girls are twelve years of age at the time of their death. Both are kept under the surveillance of their parents: for Eulalia

> ... pia cura parentis agit
> uirgo animosa domi ut lateat ...
>
> (3. 36–7)

while in Agnes' case, 'metu parentes territi/claustrum pudoris auxerant' (Ambrose, *Hymn*, 9–10). Both girls manage to escape:

> nocte fores sine teste mouet,
> saeptaque claustra fugax aperit.
>
> (*Pe.* 3. 43–4)

Agnes 'soluit fores custodiae' (*Hymn*, 11). Both display the same proud attitude before the judge (*Pe.* 3. 64; Damasus' epigram, 4). And, finally, the modesty of both girls is shielded by the covering of their hair (*Pe.* 3. 151–4; Damasus, 5–7). Thus, in writing about Eulalia, Prudentius shows himself to be aware of the poetry of Damasus and Ambrose on Agnes. Even if he does not know the poems at first hand, he is aware at least of the same general ideas surrounding the martyrdom of a young virgin. All three poems may derive from a general tradition built around the Christian development of the 'mulier uirilis', who fits in so well with the ideals of martyrdom.[63]

In conclusion, Prudentius' poem draws on local oral tradition

[60] Franchi de' Cavalieri (1908) 134, and see chap. 5 above, esp. p. 168.
[61] In favour of the attribution: Dreves (1893) 69 ff.
[62] Leclercq (1922) and Franchi de' Cavalieri (1962a). For Damasus' inscription, see Ferrua (1942) 176, no. 37, and Ihm (1895) 43–4, no. 40.
[63] Giannarelli (1980); cf. Fontaine (1970).

for Eulalia, but elaborates the story of the 'uirgo animosa' and
brings it into line with a familiar picture of a young virgin mar-
tyr. This treatment is enriched by reference to familiar classical
examples of heroic youth. This poem well illustrates the poet's
priorities: however unhistorical the contents of the poem, as a
poem it is lively and dramatic, and paints a vivid picture of its
heroine.

Peristephanon 4: the Eighteen Martyrs of Saragossa

Prudentius provides the first written evidence for these martyrs of
Saragossa (Caesaraugusta).[64] The martyrs themselves are the cen-
tral subject for celebration in the poem, but the poem unites
eulogy of Saragossa with eulogy of its saints. Local patriotism and
devotion to the local martyrs are here so complementary that
they are identified with each other. Prudentius does not give a
date for the celebration of these martyrs (a sign perhaps of his
writing for a local audience, who would have been familiar with
the feast), but the same eighteen names are found both at 22
January and at 15 April in the *Hieronymian Martyrology*.[65] Since
the latter entry is accompanied by topographical details for the
celebration, which suggest reference to local tradition and know-
ledge of Saragossa, it may be the genuine date for the feast-day.[66]
A seventh-century poem on the basilica of the Eighteen replaces
Prudentius' four Saturnini with the names Cassianus, Januarius,
Matutinus, and Faustus.[67] These names recur in the Mozarabic
Sacramentarium.[68] Among these names appear those of the three
famous martyrs of Cordoba, and it may be that their inclusion
among the Eighteen is the result of some confusion.[69] In his own
account, Prudentius must rely on the local tradition of Saragossa.
The brevity of his list-treatment of the Eighteen probably indi-
cates a dearth of material connected with the martyrs' Passions,
which are left undated. This might explain his lengthier treatment
of other more famous victims of persecution associated with Sara-

---

[64] Lavarenne (1963*b*) 62–3; Sabbatini (1972) 48; García Rodríguez (1966) 324–6.
[65] *Martyrologium hieronymianum* (1894); 20, *AASS*, Novembris 2. 1, 12 and 44. For
commentary see Delehaye (1931). See García Rodríguez (1966) 327–9. The date 22 January
arose from a copyist's error, by which the names of the 17 were added to that of Vincent.
[66] García Rodríguez (1966) 326.
[67] Eugenius Toletanus, *De basilica sanctorum decem et octo martyrum*, 9. 15–16, 19–20.
[68] Férotin (1912) 276.
[69] Delehaye (1933*b*) 364.

gossa (that is, Vincent and Eucratis). In this most lyrical and
hymn-like of the *Peristephanon* poems, it is easy to see how the
poet's technique of composition cleverly disguises a lack of factual
detail. The poem is thus successful as a poem, even if less than
satisfying as an historical source.

Peristephanon 9: St Cassian of Imola

In Prudentius' version of St Cassian's Passion, which is also the
earliest surviving account, the martyr dies most cruelly at the
hands of his own pupils. Later references to the saint do not
supply any more credible historical details,[70] and Prudentius'
poem is the only document which appears in the *Acta Sanctorum*
(for August, 3. p. 22) and in Ruinart (p. 532). The sacristan
through whose description of the shrine-painting the story is told,
refers to the story as 'tradita libris' (19), but lack of such evidence
has led to doubts being raised concerning its authenticity. Legend-
ary status is suggested by the possible models for the martyr's end:
in classical literature, Prudentius may well have known the story
of the treacherous master of the school at Falerii, who was put to
death by the pupils whom he had betrayed to the Romans (Livy,
5. 27).[71] However, the martyr's punishment seems an unlikely
one to come from a Roman judge and this confirms the likelihood
of the story being fictitious. But the poet may still have drawn on
Livy's account in his poem. So at Livy, 5. 27. 9, the master is
'*denudatum* deinde *eum* manibus *post tergum* inligatis', while Pru-
dentius at *Pe.* 9. 43 says of Cassian, '*uincitur post terga* manus
spoliatus amictu ...' The terms used are quite similar, although of
course it is just possible that such a similarity arose from similarity
of circumstances only.

A certain likeness has also been seen to other martyrdom
accounts. So the death of Mark of Arethusa has been suggested as
a model,[72] although this martyr is the victim of a popular up-
rising, not the order of a Roman judge, and the whole population
joins in the execution, not just his pupils. It may also be more than
coincidence that Cassian of Imola's profession is the same as that

[70] Lavarenne (1963b) 10–11; Gordini (1963); Amore (1949) 1004; Lanzoni (1925).
[71] Allard (1885) 399; Franchi de' Cavalieri (1908) 131–2; cf. Suetonius, *Caligula*, 4. 28,
and Tacitus, *Annales*, 8. 49 (Lanzoni 1925: 13).
[72] Delehaye (1966) 156. Lanzoni (1925) 13. This martyr is told of by Gregory of
Nazianzus, *In Iulianum*, 1. 88 = *PG* 35. 620, and Sozomen, *Hist. eccl.* 5. 10.

of Cassian of Tingi, who is a military master of stenography, 'militaris exceptor'. The profession of one may have suggested that of the other. The poet gives no exact indication of the date of his Cassian's death, although his reference to 'uetusti temporis' (20) certainly discounts the likelihood of Cassian having been the victim of the Emperor Julian's edict against Christian school-masters in AD 362.[73]

Whatever the truth of Prudentius' account in detail, it must be true that there was a cult of St Cassian at Imola, and there seems no good reason for denying the possibility of a shrine-painting depicting the martyrdom.[74] Once the existence of such a painting has been admitted, then it follows that the scene it depicted represented local tradition concerning Cassian. In his description, Prudentius may well elaborate the picture which he has seen, but his version must basically represent the facts as accepted by contemporary Christians with a devotion to this saint.

III. MARTYRS FOR WHOM IN PRUDENTIUS' TIME THERE
EXISTED A NUMBER OF SOURCES: EPIGRAMS, HOMILIES,
HYMNS, PICTURES

Peristephanon 2: St Lawrence[75]

St Lawrence was one of the most popular and the earliest-celebrated of the Roman saints[76] and Prudentius tells of his martyrdom in one of the longest poems in his collection (584 lines). The *Acta* for St Lawrence are undatable, but are probably later than Prudentius' account.[77] Ecclesiastical writers and popular tradition agree in dating Lawrence's martyrdom to the persecution of the Emperor Valerian in AD 258. The oldest sources of information about Lawrence are the inscriptions composed by Pope Damasus, and the writings of Bishop Ambrose. In his inscription in the basilica of St Lawrence in Rome, Damasus speaks of a multiplicity of tortures undergone by the martyr:

> uerbera carnifices flammas tormenta catenas
> uincere Laurenti sola fides potuit . . .

---

[73] For this suggestion see *AASS*, Augusti 3, 21.

[74] García Rodríguez (1966) 366. Lanzoni (1925) 9–10. See below, p. 273 ff.

[75] Lavarenne (1963*b*) 28–31. Toschi (1951). Carletti (1966); Delehaye (1933*a*).

[76] Lawrence's feast-day appears in the mid 4th-century *Depositio martyrum* for 10th August: 'III id. aug. Laurenti in Tiburtina' (Duchesne (1886) 1. 11).

[77] *AASS*, Augusti 2, 518–19.

Two other inscriptions concerning Lawrence are attributed to
Damasus,[78] but neither makes detailed reference to the form of
execution suffered by the saint. One even causes further difficul-
ties by referring to Lawrence's miraculous preservation from the
fire. Whatever version of the martyr's death Damasus knew, it
was rejected by Prudentius in favour of the one familiar from
other literature and from iconography.

Ambrose's account bears an obvious relation to Prudentius'. He
gives a fuller account of Lawrence's meeting with Pope Sixtus II
on his way to martyrdom, the order of Valerian's prefect Corne-
lius to hand over all the treasures of the Church, and of
Lawrence's presentation of the poor as the true riches of the
Church. He tells of Lawrence's condemnation to the grill and of
the martyr's ironic reply to the judge: 'Assum est, uersa et man-
duca'.[79] Ambrose also treated Lawrence's martyrdom in a
hymn.[80]

Prudentius' version is essentially the same as that of Ambrose,
and it is likely that the poet was aware of the bishop's treatment,
which he elaborates in the same way as he elaborates the bishop's
ideas in the *Contra Symmachum*. The Ambrosian iambic dimeter
of *Pe.* 2 supports this conjecture. However, where exact verbal
parallels are lacking, it is also possible that Prudentius draws his
more detailed version from a common source in the popular tra-
dition.[81] He may even have known a more ancient version of the
Passio.[82] Prudentius differs from Ambrose, for instance, on the
form of Sixtus' execution, which he holds to have been cruci-
fixion, although Cyprian of Carthage affirms in his correspond-
ence that the Pope was beheaded.[83] It is just possible that the
poet's inaccuracy on this point is the result of a misinterpretation
of a Damasan inscription which refers metaphorically to Sixtus'

[78] Ferrua (1942) 167, no. 33. Ihm (1895) 37–8, no. 32; Ferrua (1942) 168 no. 34, and 212
no. 58; Ihm (1895) no. 55, 57, 101, and 102.
[79] Ambrose, *De officiis ministrorum* 1. 41 = *PL* 16. 92; ibid. 2. 28 = *PL* 16. 149–50.
[80] For the hymn, see *PL* 17. 1216. Its authenticity is maintained by Dreves (1893) 76 ff.,
and figures among the 14 genuine hymns in Blume and Dreves (1909), 1. 14. On the auth-
enticity of Ambrosian hymns, see chap. 3, n. 30.
[81] Leclercq (1929a).
[82] Leclercq (1929a).
[83] Cyprian, *Ep.* 80.

deacons as 'crucis inuictae comites'.[84] Otherwise, his version can only be explained through his ignorance of the facts.

Prudentius also adds the anti-Christian speech of the persecutor, and Lawrence's prayer for Rome, although these are probably the result of poetic imagination rather than adherence to a different tradition. He includes uncritically the controversial death of Lawrence on the grill which was the popular contemporary version of events, whatever its doubtful historical value and whatever its origins.[85]

Once again, Prudentius shows an uncritical attitude towards his material. He is content to accept the most familiar and popular version of the story and to develop this freely into a lengthier and more colourful dramatic narrative, worthy of its poetic form.

Peristephanon 5: *St Vincent*[86]

Prudentius deals with this popular Spanish saint in a poem reminiscent of *Pe.* 2, both by its length (584 lines) and its metre (the Ambrosian iambic dimeter). Vincent thus appears as the Spanish counterpart to Lawrence in importance. Prudentius' account of Vincent's passion also shares certain features with that of Lawrence: both are described as Levite (*Pe.* 2. 39–40: 'leuita sublimis gradu / et ceteris praestantior'; *Pe.* 5. 30: 'leuita de tribu sacra / minister altaris dei / septem ex columnis lacteis'). Vincent also suffers torture on the grill with the same immovable courage (217–32) and he too gives lengthy speeches against the enemy (54–92, 146–72, 186–200).

It cannot be known for certain whether Prudentius in *Pe.* 5 simply gives a verse rendering of the prose passion, which cannot be dated precisely.[87] Augustine may give a *terminus ante quem* when in one of his five sermons in honour of the saint, he speaks of a passion which has just been read out in church. His comments on this passion indicate that it dealt with the same episodes as

---

[84] Ferrua (1942) 154, no. 25, 'Elogium SS Felicissimi et Agapiti', with n. 3 (Ihm (1895) 29, no. 23). Neither Delehaye (1933*a*: 48–9) nor Franchi de' Cavalieri (1920) agree with this explanation of Prudentius' mistake.

[85] Franchi de' Cavalieri (1962*b*) esp. 397. (Also in *Römische Quartalschrift* 14 (1900) 159–70; reviewed by Delehaye, *AB* (1900) 452–3, who sees Eastern origins for the legendary death on the grill.) Cf. Leclercq (1925*a*).

[86] Lavarenne (1963*b*) 71–3; García Rodríguez (1966) 257–79; Moral (1969).

[87] *AASS*, Jan. 3, 7; Ruinart (1713) 364.

those reported by Prudentius, and called the judge by the same name.[88] The *Passio* still in existence displays features typical of legendary passions:[89] the appearance of angels to Vincent while in prison, their cure of the martyr, the exposure of the martyr's body after execution and its miraculous protection by a bird of prey. Prudentius in his poem probably follows an earlier version of this *Passio*.[90]

The saint's feast-day was commonly celebrated on 22 January, but Prudentius does not mention this, or the year of the martyr's death, which has been dated to the persecution of Diocletian at the beginning of the fourth century. Yet again, Prudentius in his poem simply adopts and elaborates the received popular tradition. His poem is no better than the *Passio* from the historical point of view. The only certain facts which emerge are that Vincent was a Spanish deacon martyred for refusal to sacrifice to the idols. More details may be gleaned from Prudentius' brief treatment of Vincent in *Pe.* 4 (77 ff.): he grew up in Saragossa, and was buried 'prope litus altae/forte Sagynti' (99–100), near Valencia.

Peristephanon *10: St Romanus*[91]

The story of Romanus survives in several forms: Eusebius of Caesarea gives two versions, a short one in the Greek text of the *De martyribus Palestinae*, and a longer and fuller version which survives only in the Syriac text. The historian dates the martyrdom to the Diocletianic persecution, and there seems no reason to doubt his evidence for the events of these years which he lived through himself. Romanus is a Palestinian who is a deacon and exorcist in the Church of Caesarea. In the longer version, the scene of the forum is developed. The martyr strengthens the frightened Christians of Antioch in their faith, and exhorts them not to give way before their persecutors. The longer version also adds the miracle of Romanus' speech after the removal of his tongue: he exhorts the Christians to keep their courage in the faith.

---

[88] *Sermo* 276 = *PL* 38. 1255; also 274, 275, 276, and 277 = *PL* 38. 1252 ff.; de Gaiffier (1954*b*) esp. 382.

[89] Delehaye (1927*b*) 86 ff.; also (1966) 236 ff.; Sabbatini (1972) 197.

[90] Josi (1961) 1436–8; Franchi de' Cavalieri (1935*a*).

[91] Lavarenne (1963*b*) 117–19; Sabbatini (1972) 198 ff.; Delehaye (1932); Simonetti (1955*a*).

The story is also preserved in a sermon dealing with the Resurrection which is now attributed to Eusebius of Emesa (d. AD 359).[92] This sermon tells of the saint's visit to Antioch, where he reproves the Christians whom he sees sacrificing to the idols and is arrested and tortured for his interference. A miraculous rain-storm extinguishes the pyre on which Romanus is to meet his death. The emperor orders his release when he hears of this miracle, but Romanus' judge seeks to find a new way to please the tyrant and orders Romanus' tongue to be cut out. A Christian doctor is forced to perform this operation, but Romanus survives and even goes on speaking. The doctor performs another, control operation on a second victim, who proves the miracle by dying immediately.

The same story appears in a panegyric of the saint which has been, in the past, attributed to John Chrysostom.[93] This attribution is now seriously in doubt.[94] It is true that the panegyric contains the new episode of the martyr's request for the judgement of a small child, who professes the Christian faith and is then put to death by the judge. Then Romanus' tongue is removed. Lavarenne thinks that this panegyric may somehow be Prudentius' source, although he admits both the difficulty presented by the Greek language and the impossibility of giving it an exact date. These two factors tend to discredit the panegyric as a source for the poet.

However, an easier solution is available. A Greek passion remains which, although it omits Romanus' country of origin and his Church offices, contains all the elements of the story found in Prudentius' version. A Latin passion also exists which reproduces the Greek with the addition of naming the child picked from the crowd. It seems most likely that Prudentius knew an early Latin version, particularly when certain details are compared. So, for instance, the poet includes the name of the judge, Asclepiades, which appears only in the *Passio*. He refers to Romanus' nobility, again a detail recorded only in the *Passio*, and he tells of the miraculous rain-storm, which is not mentioned at all in the panegyric. The case seems clear, and in this way all the problems surrounding the panegyric are avoided.

[92] *PG* 64. 1097–100.
[93] *Laudatio I sancti martyris Romani* = *PG* 50. 605–12.
[94] Delehaye and Bartolozzi (1933) 125 ff.

As usual, Prudentius goes beyond his sources for his own particular ends in his poem. In this poem, his chief interest seems to be not so much the details of the martyrdom, as Romanus' role as a denouncer of the gentiles and paganism. This side of the poem emerges in the martyr's disproportionately long speeches on these themes. From this point of view, *Pe.* 10 hardly fits in with the scope and purpose of the shorter poems of the collection and may in fact not have been originally intended to form a part of it. This idea is supported by the uncertainty of this poem's position in the MS tradition of the *Peristephanon*, where it often appears either at the beginning or the end of the collection.[95]

In conclusion, it can only be said that Prudentius' poem is only as good as its source, the *Passio*, from the factual point of view. The basic truth of the story can be extracted from the legendary features of the passion by comparison with Eusebius' essentially historical account.

Peristephanon 11: St Hippolytus[96]

The historical background for this saint is extremely confused. His name occurs no less than twelve times in the *Hieronymian Martyrology*. However, it seems likely that all these references point to a single martyr, who is buried on the Via Tiburtina, and whose feast-day was already celebrated on 13 August by the middle of the fourth century.[97] The saint's connection with Portus may be explained by the erection of a basilica there in his honour.[98] The discovery of a probably third-century statue of Hippolytus, with an inscription listing his writings, near the cemetery of Hippolytus at Rome, suggests that the saint of this cemetery and of the Damasan inscription is the Church writer Hippolytus, of the third century.[99] Eusebius, in his *Historia ecclesiastica* (6. 20 and 22), and Jerome in his *De uiris illustribus* (61) also tell of Hippolytus' works. Eusebius calls him 'head of the Church', while Jerome calls him 'bishop of a church the name of

---

[95] Lavarenne (1963*b*) 117; Cunningham, *CCL* 126, xxvi n. 101: 'De ordinibus carminum in libro Peristephanon multa nescimus. Ordo communis etiam si Romanum abstrahes, nihil omnino auctoritatis habet.'

[96] Lavarenne (1963*b*) 159–64. Sabbatini (1972) 206 ff.

[97] Amore (1954) 96–7.

[98] Sabbatini (1972) 207.

[99] The problems of identification are discussed at length by de Rossi, (1881 and 1882). The statue is now preserved in the Lateran Museum.

which I am unable to discover' ('Hippolytus cuiusdam ecclesiae
episcopus—nomen quippe urbis scire non potui').[100] Hippolytus
was, in fact, elected bishop of Rome by an influential minority
and, in opposition to Pope Callistus, became the first 'anti-pope'.
Jerome elsewhere gives Hippolytus the title of martyr, and says
that his writings were read by Ambrose.[101] The *Liber pontificalis*
tells of the deportation of Hippolytus and Pontianus to Sardinia in
AD 235, during the reign of the Emperor Maximinus. Both men
died during their exile. Pontianus' body was brought back to
Rome during the papacy of Fabianus (AD 236–50),[102] and it seems
likely that Hippolytus' body was brought back at the same time.
This explains their shared feast-day on 13 August, which is
recorded in the *Depositio martyrum*.[103]

Prudentius' version of Hippolytus' martyrdom complicates the
picture further. In the earlier part of his poem, he agrees with
Pope Damasus, whose inscription he had no doubt read among
those which he mentions at lines 7–8 (the term 'epigramma' in
particular seems to point to the Damasan compositions). Thus the
poet tells that Hippolytus was a member of the heretical Nova-
tianist sect until his sudden conversion to orthodoxy before mar-
tyrdom (29–34).[104] Unlike Damasus, who says of this
information 'fertur' in his first line (presumably referring to the
common tradition about the martyr), Prudentius states this ver-
sion with no reservations. His lack of caution is ill advised, since
the particular schism of which Damasus speaks only developed
well after Hippolytus' death. Prudentius does not notice this
anachronism and happily reproduces Damasus' mistake.

The centre-piece of the poem is a description of Hippolytus'
martyrdom which Prudentius claims is the subject of a painting in
the saint's catacomb ('picta super tumulum species ...', 125). This
martyrdom is not described by Damasus, and seems to be com-
pletely legendary: Hippolytus is said to have been torn apart by
horses at the mouth of the Tiber. This story recalls the mythical
tale of Hippolytus' classical namesake, the son of Theseus. If a
painting really existed as Prudentius describes (see below, pp.

100 Jerome, *De uiris illustribus*, 61.
101 Jerome, *Ep.* 84. 7. 'Ad Pammachium et Oceanum'.
102 Duchesne (1886) 1. 145, with n. 2, 145–6.
103 Frutaz (1951).
104 Cf. the epigram of Damasus (Ferrua (1942) no. 35, Ihm (1895) no. 37).

273 ff.), then this association of the martyr with the classical hero's
end may have already been generally accepted. Otherwise, the
poet himself may be responsible for a fictional version with liter-
ary precedents. However, it seems unlikely that Prudentius could
dare to fabricate too much about a famous cult-site. Whatever the
origins of this form of martyrdom, this dramatic end suited the
poet's ideas for his poem. His treatment of the subject seems at
points to prove knowledge of Seneca's version of Hippolytus' end
in his *Phaedra*.[105] The death of the classical Hippolytus by the sea,
for instance, may have inspired Prudentius' coastal setting. How-
ever, this setting may also reflect a local devotion to Hippolytus at
Portus, perhaps the result of the saint's passing through it on his
way to exile, or the passing of his remains through the town on
their way to burial at Rome.[106] Or the poet may be confusing the
Hippolytus of Rome with the Hippolytus–Nonnus associated
with Portus in a Greek *Passio* (*PG* 10. 565). The possibilities are
numerous, and no solution seems certainly correct. It is clear,
however, that Prudentius' version is far from an accurate and crit-
ical historical account.

Peristephanon *14: St Agnes*[107]

St Agnes was one of the few saints commemorated in the early
Depositio martyrum: 'XII Kal. Feb. Agnetis in Nomentana'. This
date recurs in the *Hieronymian Martyrology* in the calendars of
Carthage and Naples, in the *Sacramentarium Gelasianum* and
Gregorianum, in the *Capitularia evangeliorum*, and in the Lectionar-
ies. No genuine early *Acta* for this martyr exist, however, and the
first written records of her death occur in the fourth century. Pre-
dating Prudentius' poems are a ten-line hexameter inscription by
Damasus, discovered in the saint's basilica on the Via Nomen-
tana,[108] and two references in the works of Ambrose. The first of
these, dated to AD 377, occurs in his *De uirginibus ad Marcellinam
sororem* (*PL*. 16. 189–90, 192). This is thought to have been based
on three sermons composed in honour of the saint.[109] The second

---

[105] See above, chap. 6, pp. 190 ff.

[106] Lavarenne (1963*b*) 163.

[107] Ibid., 190–5; Allard (1907); Josi (1961); Franchi de' Cavalieri (1962*a*); García Rod-
ríguez (1966) 173–4; Delehaye (1933*b*) 315 ff.; see too, Franchi de' Cavalieri (1962*c*); Allard
(1906); Frutaz (1948).

[108] Ferrua (1942) no. 37 and Ihm (1895) no. 40. Cf. above, p. 240 n. 62.

[109] Lavarenne (1963*b*) 191 n. 2 for the date of *De uirginibus*; also Palanque (1933) 493.

is an incidental reference in the *De officiis ministrorum*, 1 41 (*PL* 16.
90). Ambrose provided another important influence for Pruden-
tius in his hymn in honour of the martyr (*PL* 17. 1210). (For the
authenticity of this hymn, see above, Chapter 3, n. 30.)

Agnes is thought to have died during the Great Persecution of
AD 303–4. Attempts have been made to push the date back to
AD 257 on the basis of information supplied by the *Acta*, in par-
ticular the name of her judge, Aspasius. A man of this name,
Aspasius Paternus, is known to have been *proconsul Africae* in
AD 257/8, and was probably, therefore, a magistrate in Rome the
year before.[110] However, the *Acta* are late (early fifth century at
the earliest) and cannot be used as a reliable historical source.
Additional doubt on Aspasius' role in Agnes' passion is cast by the
appearance of an Aspasius as *proconsul Africae* in the *Passio
Cypriani* (1. 2). The later *Acta* may simply appropriate the name
from this well-known *passio*. In any case, it is unlikely that a
young girl would have died in the earlier persecution, which was
directed chiefly at the heads of the Church. Even so, the date for
her death can only remain conjectural.

Damasus' inscription is based on oral tradition and begins by
admitting this with the words 'fama refert'. He tells of the
attempt of Agnes' parents to protect their daughter at home, of
her escape when persecution breaks out, and of her defiance to-
wards the threats of the Roman authorities. She is burnt to death,
when her 'profusum crinem' (7) covers her body, 'ne domini
templum facies peritura uideret' (8).

The account of Ambrose also seems to be based on oral tradi-
tion. When he mentions her age of twelve years, he says 'traditur'.
He too emphasizes her unusual courage: 'Flere omnes ipsa sine
fletu'.[111] Ambrose seems to use rhetorical expansion to mask
what amounts to a complete lack of historical material, and his
choice of decapitation for the martyr may not represent a version
of the facts so much as his own imagination. In tune with his
overall theme, he makes more than Damasus of Agnes' modesty
and virginity, the triumph of which form part of her martyr's

---

[110] Franchi de' Cavalieri (1962c) 326–7 and *PLRE* 1. 671, 'Paternus 5'. This would date
Agnes' death to the Valerianic persecution. See Frend (1965) 423–7.

[111] *De uirginibus*, 2. 8. Ambrose's treatment of Agnes' death has been compared to
Ovid's treatment of the death of Polymessa in *Metam.* 13. 458 ff., and Lucretia's death at
Fasti, 2. 833–4. See Franchi de' Cavalieri (1962a).

victory. While Damasus only hints at this theme with the picture
of Agnes' modesty being protected by her hair, Ambrose in an
exclamation makes an interesting reference to the number of
suitors who have wanted to marry Agnes: 'Quantorum uota ut
sibi ad nuptias perueniret!'[112] In the *De uirginibus* and the *De
officiis* he talks emphatically of Agnes' preservation of her virgin-
ity, as well as her exchange of life for immortality:

habetis igitur in una hostia duplex martyrium pudoris et religionis: et
uirgo permansit et martyrium obtinuit, quae in duarum maximarum
rerum posita periculo, castitatis et salutis, castitatem protexit, salutem
cum immortalitate commutauit.[113]

The hymn[114] gives a more detailed version of Agnes' end than
the other Ambrosian versions. It tells of Agnes' flight from home
and of her concern for her modesty at the moment of her martyr-
dom (25–32), both of which are missing from the prose accounts.
The danger of Agnes' chastity is hinted at, though not explained
in detail. At 113–16, emphasis is laid on the girl's suitability for
marriage rather than death.

If Prudentius had indeed visited Rome and seen the martyrs' in-
scriptions as he claims in *Pe.* 11, then it is likely that he would
have visited the tomb and basilica of St Agnes on the Via Nomen-
tana. The opening of *Pe.* 14 certainly suggests that he knew at
least the Damasan inscription, whether or not at first hand. His
poem indeed contains certain expressions reminiscent of those of
the inscription. At line 2 he refers to Agnes as 'martyr inclyta'.
Damasus (10) had also spoken of her as 'martyr inclyta'. Pruden-
tius 'trux tyrannus' (21) echoes Damasus' 'trucis ... tyranni' (4);
'haec calcat' (112) recalls Damasus' 'calcasse minas' (4). Pruden-
tius' poem, however, takes little account of the content of the
Damasan epigram. He records no flight of Agnes from her
parents' home, no condemnation to the pyre and no veiling with
her hair. These details may be omitted because of the poet's pre-

---

[112] *De uirginibus*, 1. 2. 9.

[113] Ibid., 1. 2. 8; *De off. min.* 1. 41 = *PL* 16. 84.

[114] For the attribution to Ambrose see *AB* 17 (1898) 465; Dreves (1893) 69 ff.; and Fran-
chi de' Cavalieri (1962a): There are some convincing arguments for an Ambrosian attribu-
tion: the theme is one of Ambrose's favourites and the saint is also the favourite of his sister,
Marcellina. The beginning of the hymn recalls the opening of *De uirginibus*, which com-
memorates St Agnes; and the hymn uses the same genetive, 'Agnes' as the *De uirginibus* (in-
stead of the later form 'Agnetis'). See above, chap. 3, n. 30.

vious use of them in the story of the Spanish virgin-martyr Eulalia
(see above, p. 240), who thus becomes the Spanish answer to
Rome's popular girl saint.

Prudentius seems to keep more closely to Ambrose's version of
events. Thus he, too, as Ambrose in *De uirginibus*, 1. 2. 7, begins
with the girl's age. His omission of the flight from home may
stem from Ambrose's omission of this part of the story. His mar-
tyr, too, is sentenced to death by decapitation rather than by
burning.

The poet's version, however, diverges from both possible
models in Agnes' exposure to shame in a public place and the
double miracle which occurs in connection with the young man
who dares to approach her. This story is not told as such by
Damasus or Ambrose, although Damasus' emphasis on the cover-
ing of the saint by her hair might refer indirectly to a public test to
her modesty, and Ambrose's elliptical references to her suitors and
her 'pudor' might also hint at such a story. Either they know the
story which they choose not to report, or Prudentius himself in-
vents it on the basis of their hints. It is, of course, also possible that
the story reflects a different branch of popular tradition which
could even contain some truth, since condemnation to prostitu-
tion was not completely unknown.[115] The poet himself quite
openly associates the double miracle with oral tradition by his in-
troduction of it with the phrase 'sunt qui rettulerint' (*Pe*. 14. 57).

Thus it is impossible to connect Prudentius' version of the story
too closely with either of the two earlier treatments, which seem
at least incomplete, or perhaps even the products of two slightly
different traditions. Prudentius may represent a third tradition
('aiunt', 10). In this case, variations in the story are not surprising.

All three authors agree on Agnes' extreme youth and her
'double martyrdom', 'pudoris et religionis'. This is the limit of the
facts which can be derived from their evidence. The other ele-
ments of the story found in *Pe*. 14 may or may not be true, but
certainly represent popular tradition. Once again, the poet accepts
this uncritically and elaborates upon it in order to provide some of
the drama of his account.

Two poems remain for discussion: *Pe*. 8, apparently an inscription

---

[115] Tertullian, *Apol.* 50. 12; Frutaz (1948) 468.

destined for a baptistery, and *Pe.* 12, which uses a dramatic frame-
work to tell of the feast-days and basilicas in Rome of the Apostles
Peter and Paul. The probable connection of *Pe.* 8 with two
soldier-martyrs of Calahorra has been discussed above (p. 238).
The dedication of a baptistery at the site of the martyrdom sug-
gests that there was already a basilica there by Prudentius' day.[116]

Peristephanon *12: SS Peter and Paul*

This poem is the briefest of Prudentius' passions, and in fact is less
concerned with a description of the Apostles' martyrdom than
with a vivid account of their feast-day and basilicas. Peter's
inverted crucifixion is dealt with concisely at 11–16:

> Ille tamen ueritus celsae decus aemulando mortis
>   ambire tanti gloriam magistri,
> exigit, ut pedibus mersum caput imprimant supinis,
>   quo spectet imum stipitem cerebro.
>
> (13–16)

The beheading of St Paul occupies another six lines (23–8):

> Nec mora, protrahitur, poenae datur, immoltur ense;
>
> (27)

According to Prudentius, the apostles were martyred on the same
day, but a year apart (21–2). There seems no room for doubt
about the martyrdom of the two Apostles in Rome (it is men-
tioned by several ante-Nicene authors)[118] although the date is less
certain.[119] Official Church propaganda encouraged the idea of
the shared *dies natalis* on 29 June as part of their attempt to eradi-
cate the complications caused by the unofficial cult-centre on the
Via Appia, which was eventually replaced in the third to fourth

---

[116] García Rodríguez (1966) 322.

[117] Lavarenne (1963*b*) 175–7; Sabbatini (1972) 215–16.

[118] Clement of Rome, *Ep. ad Cor.* 5; Irenaeus, *Aduersus haereses*, 3. 3. 2. 3; Tertullian, *De praescriptione haereticorum*, 36; *Adu. gnosticos Scorpiace*, 15; Origen, *Comm. in Genesim iii*, ap. Eusebius, *Hist. eccl.* 3. 1; Eusebius, *Chronicon*, p. 185; and *Hist. eccl.* 2. 25. 6 ff.

[119] Only Dionysios of Corinth mentions that they died κατὰ τὸν αὐτὸν καιρόν. (*Ep. ad Rom.*, ap. Eusebius, *Hist. eccl.* 2. 25. 8). For discussion of the problem see Chadwick (1957) 50–1. See too Piétri (1961). For the ancient evidence see Augustine, *Sermo* 381: 'In natali apostolorum Petri et Pauli' = *PL* 39. 1683 and *Sermo* 295 = *PL* 38. 1352: 'Praecessit Petrus, secutus est Paulus'; Arator *c.* AD 544 in *De actibus apostolorum* 2. 1247–9 = *PL* 68. 246; Gre-gory of Tours, *De gloria martyrum* 29 = *PL* 71. 729 (*c.* AD 580). I follow here the reconstruc-tion of events discussed by Chadwick (1957).

centuries by the separate shrines and then basilicas on the Vatican
and the Via Ostiensis. Prudentius' idea of the same *dies natalis* a
year apart represents a compromise between the more historical
idea of two different days and the propaganda version. Traces of
Prudentius' version can be found in Augustine and in some later
authors. In any case, 29 June was the generally recognized feast-
day for the martyrs by the end of the fourth century. The manner
of the Apostles' martyrdom in *Pe.* 12 reflects early tradition (see
n. 119), in the same way as the Neronian date. Thus, Prudentius
does no more than relay accepted tradition in *Pe.* 12. His main
interest is to describe for Spanish readers the latest constructions in
the martyrs' honour, both of which were associated with com-
patriots: the Spanish Pope Damasus and his fellow countryman,
the Emperor Theodosius (see below, pp. 275 ff.).

In conclusion, it is clear from the analyses above that Prudentius is
not preoccupied in the *Peristephanon* with problems of historical
veracity in the modern scientific sense. All the poems contain ele-
ments of both the historical and the legendary, in proportions
which vary in accordance with the sources available. Popular tra-
dition often provides adequate authority for Prudentius' version,
which is punctuated by phrases like 'fertur', 'memorant', 'fama
refert', and 'aiunt'.[120] The poet is no better or worse than con-
temporary hagiographers and his work is comparable with other
prose examples of the genre from the fourth and fifth centuries.
Realization of this need not involve negative judgement of work
which is first and foremost poetry. It is to the poet's credit that he
had the vision to translate prose hagiography into a poetic form
with so much potential for achieving a variety of effects.

Prudentius and the Spanish Church Calendar

Although the historical value of Prudentius' information for par-
ticular martyrs is often questionable, the value of the poems for an
investigation of the Spanish Church Calendar for the fourth cen-
tury cannot be doubted. The poems constitute, in effect, a versi-
fied Church Calendar, and thus provide the earliest evidence for
the feast-days of the Church's year. In qualification of this, it must

---

[120] *Pe.* 1. 86; 5. 347; 10. 32; 13. 76 and 80; 14. 10 and 57.

be noted that Prudentius does not generally give the date of a martyr's feast-day. Only the feast-day of St Hippolytus is explicitly mentioned to Bishop Valerianus, in a case where the feast is obviously one new to Spain (*Pe.* 11. 232, 'Idibus Augusti mensis'). Prudentius is useful only for an indication of the range of different martyrs celebrated in the Spain of his day. In addition, investigation of each martyr and his or her cult is necessary before the truest picture of martyr-cult in Spain is established. For Prudentius' celebration of foreign saints seems to take him outside the realms of established Spanish cults, and it has to be established whether or not the poet is writing about a martyr hitherto uncelebrated in Spain, or never celebrated in Spain, even after Prudentius' poem. Where Spanish saints are concerned, it is interesting to see how local their cults were in the fourth century: investigation of this aspect of Spanish cult helps to give a clearer picture of the extent of Prudentius' immediate audience for each poem.

Comparison of Prudentius' evidence with other sources gives a more complete view of the poet's interests and achievements in writing each poem. Some inscriptions and a few archaeological remains help in forming an idea of the state of cults in the fourth–fifth centuries. Later evidence for cults and their distribution can be found in Spanish liturgical books and calendars, none of which can be dated to a period earlier than the end of the fifth century or the beginning of the sixth. The earliest Spanish calendar surviving is the unfortunately incomplete *Calendar of Carmona*, which has been dated to the end of the fifth century or the beginning of the sixth.[121] Early liturgical books which give information about the Church Calendar before the Arab invasion are the *Libellus orationum* of Verona, which represents the liturgy of Tarragona,[122] and from which the liturgical calendar for this city at the end of the seventh century can be reconstructed; the *Liber comicus*;[123] the León *Antiphonarium* which represents the seventh-century Calendar of Toledo; and the ninth-century *Liber sacramentorium* of Toledo which is probably based on a seventh-century original.[124]

---

[121] Delehaye (1912) Vives (1941) 46. For the inscription, see Vives (1969) no. 333. On Spanish hagiographical sources, including the liturgical books, see Vives (1966).

[122] García Rodríguez (1966) 50.

[123] Ibid., 55–8.

[124] Ibid., 71.

Outside Spain, reference can be made to the fourth-century *Depositio martyrum* and the *Hieronymian Martyrology*.

   In the case of foreign (that is, Italian, Roman, African, and Eastern) martyrs, lack of evidence for their cult in Spain either before or immediately after Prudentius' time suggests that the poet is introducing new objects of devotion to the Spanish faithful. It is likely that the Spanish churches, like other churches, restricted the celebration of saints to those which were local until the end of the fourth century. So, for instance, the *Depositio martyrum* admits only a few Africans apart from its own Roman martyrs. Even the *Calendar of Carmona*, a century or so later than Prudentius, admits only the famous Milanese saints, Gervasius and Protasius, apart from Spanish saints, although the calendar is admittedly only a fragment. Prudentius' enthusiasm for non-Spanish saints is probably mainly the result of his own wider experience of martyr-cult, both with the imperial court at Milan and in Rome. The poet's personal devotion to the martyrs of whom he tells seems clear, and he is urgent to instil his feelings for these martyrs into those for whom he writes—Spaniards who may have had no such immediate experience of different cults.

   This attitude emerges clearly and explicitly in *Pe.* 11, the letter in which Prudentius tells Bishop Valerianus of his visit to Rome, and his experience there of the cult of Hippolytus. The purpose of his description of the martyr's feast-day and his burial-place is to encourage the adoption of St Hippolytus' feast-day by Valerianus' Church:

> Si bene commemini, colit hunc pulcherrima Roma
>   Idibus Augusti mensis, ut ipsa uocat
> prisco more diem, quem te quoque, sancte magister,
>   annua festa inter dinumerare uelim.

$$(231-4)$$

The only other evidence for the cult of this Roman saint in Spain comes later than Prudentius, in the *Libellus orationum*. This suggests that Prudentius' poem had such a local success in north-eastern Spain, that the feast-day was actually adopted. It is interesting to compare this entry in the early *Orationale* with the *Antiphonarium* of León.[125] Although the latter is two or three centuries later,[126]

---

[125] Porter (1934).   [126] Ibid., 266 n. 3.

its many points of similarity with the *Orationale* suggest that they are based on a common tradition to which each then makes additions based on strictly local tradition. The *Antiphonarium* significantly does *not* include the office of St Hippolytus, which appears in full in the Tarraconensian *Orationale*. Thus it seems that the saint was venerated only in the region of Tarragona. It was a Mass and prayers for St Hippolytus' feast-day which were later composed by Eugenius II of Toledo (d. 657) for Protasius of Tarragona.[127] It seems likely then, that Prudentius' poem was as influential as he wished in the promotion of a new cult in the Tarragona region.[128] The artificiality of the introduction of this martyr and his cult is reflected in its continued restriction to a limited devotion. It cannot be known for certain why Prudentius chooses to introduce this Roman saint to Spain. Apart from the fact that he himself seems to have been struck by his story and his popularity while in Rome, he may have been influenced in his choice by the fact that this is one of the martyrs celebrated in an inscription by his compatriot, Pope Damasus. The devotions of the Spanish faithful may have found extra stimulation in the cult-interests of a Spanish Pope.

The same point could also be made in the case of St Lawrence, whose cult Prudentius also seems to have been instrumental in introducing to Spain, where it seems there was no particular devotion to this martyr before Prudentius' time.[129] The martyr was one of the earliest to be venerated in Rome and also one of the most popular. His name appears in the *Depositio martyrum* and in the early *Calendar of Carthage*. He seems to have acquired equal status with the Apostles of Rome, Peter and Paul, beside whom he appears on an early gold glass.[130] By the end of the fourth century his feast was solemnly celebrated in the basilica of Agro Verano, which was built in his honour under the direction of Pope Damasus.[131] The devotions of the Spanish Pope may once

---

[127] *Ep.* 3 = *PL* 87. 412.

[128] The town where Valerianus was bishop is not known for certain, although Calahorra has been argued for by del Álamo (1939).

[129] García Rodríguez (1966) 176 ff.

[130] Bovini (1950) 18–22; Lawrence also appears *between* the Apostles on a gold glass (Leclercq (1929a), 1925). García Rodríguez (1966) 126; Leclercq, (1923) 1838 no. 217; Arevalo, *PL* 60. 331 and 335.

[131] Delehaye (1930) 8. For Damasus' Spanish nationality, see Duchesne (1886) 212. For a summary of the arguments of the literature on this question, see Ferrua (1942) no. 57 n. 1.

again have influenced Prudentius' choice of subject: informed
Spaniards at home were likely to be well aware of the activities of
their representative at the head of the Western Church in Rome.
In any case, Prudentius' poem was certainly influenced by the
writing of Ambrose (see above, pp. 62 ff.).

The terms of *Pe.* 2 seem to imply that the poem was written in
Spain, probably before a visit by the poet to Rome. This explains
the remarks concerning the separation of Spaniards from the re-
mains of Lawrence at 537–48. Ignorance of Roman sites might
explain the poet's silence about the scale and nature of Lawrence's
feast-day celebrations and the splendours of Damasus' new
basilica. By contrast, in *Pe.* 12, the poet is keen to describe the
Pope's achievements at St Peter's basilica,[132] which he has
obviously visited. However, in *Pe.* 2 the poet is sufficiently open
to cult-interests from outside Spain to choose a foreign saint for
celebration in terms strongly reminiscent of tradition current in
Milan and known to Ambrose. The poem probably reflects Pru-
dentius' early wider interest in martyr-cult outside Spain.

Ambiguity is increased by the very personal terms in which the
poet couches his hopes and prayers at the end of the poem. This,
in fact, is the only point in the whole corpus at which he names
himself:

> Audi benignus supplicem
> Christi reum Prudentium . . .
>
> (581–2)

The intense tone seems to lack the balance provided elsewhere in
similar personalized lyric passages by reference to the whole town
involved in the devotions, as at the end of *Pe.* 3 and 6. This iso-
lated intensity may reflect what is recognized by the poet to be a
more private devotion to the Roman saint. Part of the explana-
tion may lie in the poet's signature at the end of the poem, which
might well indicate its separate conception and publication, apart
from the *Peristephanon* as it finally appeared.[133] The poem's
theme is only secondarily that of Lawrence's martyrdom. Pru-
dentius is more concerned to expound a doctrine of providential
guidance behind the formation of the Roman Empire, which in
this plan was always destined to become ultimately a Christian

[132] Ruysschaert (1966).
[133] Bergman gives this argument in favour of a separate publication (1926: xix).

unity. Hence the final great prayer of Lawrence at 413 ff.: Spain may be geographically remote from Rome, but the saint in heaven looks down on the whole world (545–8). This also emphasizes the unity of a Christian empire. The poem either grows out of the poet's personal preoccupation with this theme, which recurs in the *Contra Symmachum* (2. 577 ff.), or the similar preoccupations of a limited Spanish audience which is also aware of these larger themes and the importance of the Roman saint.

There may also be concealed in the poem a desire to compliment the Spanish imperial family. Lawrence's prediction of the 'futurum principem ... seruum dei' (473–4) who puts an end to paganism in Rome and who closes the temples can refer only to Theodosius and the completion of Christianization which took place under him. *Pe.* 2. 481–4 seem to refer explicitly to this emperor's legislation concerning the preservation of pagan works of art (*CTh.* 16. 10. 8), issued in AD 382. (Another reference to this occurs at *Contra Symmachum*, 1. 501–5.) A compliment to the reigning emperor and a reference to datable legislation make it possible to conclude that *Pe.* 2 was written between AD 382 and 395. This fits in with the poem being an earlier composition than others in the *Peristephanon* collection. Perhaps the Spanish audience of this poem may be narrowed down to a number of Spaniards with court connections, if not to the court itself and the emperor. This would make 536 ff. difficult to explain, but the poet uses the first person plural here simply to express his own sense of separation from the holy places. This fits in with his later humble stance at the end of the poem.

However novel Prudentius' interest in St Lawrence was for the Spaniards, the martyr's cult spread quickly in the years following the poet's death, and the saint's feast-day is commemorated in all the early liturgical books. He seems, however, to have remained less popular than native saints: he merits only one Mass in the *Libellus orationum*, while Vincent, Fructuosus, and Eulalia are allotted more than five each. Prudentius' poem itself influenced later hymns in the martyr's honour.[134] As in the case of Hippolytus, Prudentius' poem may have helped to promote the new cult in its earliest stages.

Agnes is another Roman saint celebrated by the poet, and again

---

[134] García Rodríguez (1966) 68.

one for whose cult there is no evidence in Spain in the period before Prudentius,[135] although Agnes was one of the most popular and earliest-celebrated martyrs in Rome. She too appears in the *Deposito martyrum*, and her image appears in early gold glasses.[136] Her feast-day does not appear in any of the early liturgical books mentioned above, except the *Antiphonarium* of Millán, where she appears with St Emerentiana.[137] This book probably represents local Toledan tradition, so general cult is not attested by this mention. There is no evidence for churches or relics of St Agnes in the Visigothic period. Prudentius' poem was later included in the Office for the saint's day and in this way assisted in the diffusion of the cult.[138]

Once again it must be asked why the poet chooses to celebrate Agnes. The opening of *Pe.* 14 suggests only vague knowledge of the martyr's burial place on the Via Nomentana. There is no mention of the finely decorated basilica. On the other hand, the poem seems at points to echo the Damasan inscription (see above, pp. 250 ff.), although he may have known this at second hand from someone who had visited the martyr's shrine. In any case, the poet was probably strongly influenced by Ambrose's interest in the virgin martyr, which he would certainly have experienced during his time in Milan. The Roman girl-saint must have recalled to Prudentius her Spanish counterpart, Eulalia, to whose poem (*Pe.* 3) the poet in fact transfers some of the details of Agnes' story as recorded by the Pope. Prudentius writes about Agnes as the Roman balance for the Spanish saint. The pairing may be meant to suggest that Spain is as rich in great martyrs as Rome itself, where all acknowledge the greatness of Agnes. A similar patriotic point may be seen at work in the balancing of the poems about Vincent and Lawrence (*Pe.* 5 and 2), where Vincent is portrayed to some extent as the Spanish version of his popular Roman counterpart.

For the Apostles Peter and Paul, Prudentius was dealing with a feast-day already well established in Rome by the end of the fourth century. The feast is mentioned in the *Depositio*

[135] Ibid., 174.
[136] Bovini (1950) 33–5.
[137] García Rodríguez (1966) 174, Férotin (1912) col. 897.
[138] Férotin (1912) col. 897, with García Rodríguez (1966) 173–6.

martyrum.[139] Prudentius' poem is the first reference to the shared feast in Spanish sources, but it seems likely that it was quickly adopted since the Apostles had such obvious universal importance. So a church of Toledo, for instance, was named for the Apostles before the *Acta* of a provincial council in AD 597.[140] Apart from churches named in honour of the Apostles, a particular interest in St Peter is demonstrated in the iconography of Christian sarcophagi in Spain. These bear scenes of the Apostle's denial of Christ and his period in prison, or simply show him next to an orant.[141] These sarcophagi do not prove extensive cult, but demonstrate the Apostles' popularity. The cult is likely to have taken root in the Visigothic period, when pilgrimages to Rome seem to have been undertaken. So, for example, Taio made a visit to Rome before taking up his bishopric at Saragossa. The *Continuatio Isidoriana Hispana* refers to his devotional journey to SS Peter and Paul.[142] The feast-day appears in the fragment of the epigraphic Calendar of Alcalá la Real, which seems to have been exclusively a Calendar of the feasts of the Apostles.[143] It probably figured too in the Calendar of Carmona, which is cut off before the end of June.[144] It later appears in the Mozarabic Calendars. The two Apostles are amply celebrated in all the earliest liturgical books.

Prudentius' poem introduces a new feast-day for the Spaniards for whom he is primarily writing this poem. Its form, the revelation of the meaning of the feast-day to the stranger to Rome, provides a useful way of introducing the reader to a new celebration. The poem may have assisted in the promotion of a more widespread devotion to the Apostles in Spain and obviously grows out of Prudentius' experience of martyr-cult in Rome.

---

[139] *Depositio martyrum* (in *Liber pontificalis* 1. 11: 'III kal. Iul. Petri in Catacumbas et Pauli Ostense, Tusco et Basso cons'. For discussion of this, see Chadwick (1957) and Piétri (1961). See too Chadwick (1982).

[140] For 597 see Sáenz de Aguirre (1693) 3. 116. For later councils in the basilica of the Apostles, see *PL* 84. 411, 467, 487, 509, 527. For other dedications of churches, see García Rodríguez (1966) 148–9, with reference to Vives (1969) no. 198, 116, 171, 512, 119, and 347.

[141] Batlle Huguet (1937–40). Perhaps important here is the influence of Rome and North Italy on Spanish sarcophagi, particularly those produced at the local Tarragona stoneworks in the 4th century; see Manjarrés Mangas and Roldán Hervás (1982: 423–4).

[142] *MGH Auct. Ant.* 11, *Chronica minora* 2, ed. Mommsen (1894) 342–3.

[143] Vives (1969) 114 no. 335.

[144] García Rodríguez (1966) 151.

More puzzling is the inclusion of the poem in honour of Cassian, an Italian saint for whose cult there is no evidence in Spanish sources either before or after the Arab conquest. The saint was certainly increasingly popular in Italy in the fifth century. Pope Symmachus (AD 498–514) dedicated an altar in Cassian's honour in Rome, in the mausoleum to the left of St Peter's basilica, and the saint appears twice in the Ravenna mosaics.[145] The cult seems to have been established in Milan by the middle of the fifth century. This may explain Prudentius' interest in the saint: he may have already been popular with the Milanese at the beginning of the fifth century.

Prudentius may also have been attracted to the subject from the more purely literary point of view. The story may have been inspired by an episode in Livy's history (see above, p. 242), or more recently by Ausonius' treatment of the Crucifixion of Cupid.[146] Or perhaps, as the poem itself suggests, the poet's interest had simply been provoked by a real visit to the shrine, where he was impressed by a painting of Cassian's horrific end. The poem, in any case, is likely to have been written primarily for an audience who either knew of the cult already, or who would be receptive to the idea of devotion to a new Italian saint. This suggests Prudentius' fellow court officials at Milan, compatriots of the poet's own class and experience, who would eventually spread news of the saint in the Spanish homeland (cf. Prudentius' words at line 106: 'domum revertor, Cassianum praedico').

Problems are once more raised by the poet's interest in the eastern saints, Quirinus and Romanus. St Quirinus in particular seems a strange choice. Prudentius' account seems to be based on Jerome's continuation of Eusebius' *Chronicon*, and includes one major mistake which precludes the poet's personal experience of the cult. Although the saint's remains were translated to Rome, this translation must have taken place later than the composition of *Pe.* 7, which is quite clear on the point that the remains are *not* in Rome. The first mention of the relics in fact only appears in connection with Pope Sixtus (AD 432–40).[147] Another explana-

---

[145] Gordini (1963).

[146] Charlet (1980a) 69–70, 122 ff.

[147] Dufourcq (1907) 2. 228: 'Le mouvement légendaire lérinien'. Dufourcq thinks that the translation took place between AD 403/4 and *c.* 440. The Pannonians underwent a period of peace AD 427–40, when the Huns began to invade again. So translation is more likely to have taken place around 440.

tion for *Pe.* 7 might be that Theodosius himself, or at least some members of his retinue, held a special devotion to this saint after eastern campaigns which had taken them to Savia and Siscia.[148] The poem thus obliquely records a successful campaign and is a covert compliment set in devotional form. Such an explanation neatly associates Prudentius once again with the court circle with which he would have had contact at Milan.

The inclusion of St Romanus is less puzzling. A Latin passion was probably in circulation in the West at an early period. As a dealer in words himself, Prudentius is fascinated by a saint who is endowed with miraculous powers of speech. He too is 'mutus' without Christ's help:

> Sum mutus ipse, sed potens facundiae
> mea lingua Christus luculente disseret.

> (*Pe.* 10. 21–2)

He exploits the saint's loquacity to write a poem which, because of its lengthy speeches, is more of an anti-pagan polemic than a simple martyrdom narrative. There is nothing in the poem to suggest a Spanish devotion to this saint in Prudentius' time, and there is no external evidence which shows it. However, this cult seems to have been well established by the seventh century, when the relics are brought to the basilica of Medina Sidonia (AD 630).[149] His Office appears in the *Libellus orationum* of Tarraco and in the Léon *Antiphonarium*. Once again, the poem may have helped to promote Spanish interest in the saint.

In the case of the African bishop, Cyprian, the poet's interest in the martyr reflects contemporary interest. Spain had had close ties with the African Church for a long time, and Prudentius himself refers at the end of *Pe.* 11 to the celebration of Cyprian's feast in Bishop Valerianus' diocese. His name naturally appears in the early Spanish liturgical books.

Spanish Saints

Prudentius' interest in the martyrs of his own country is easier to understand than some of his foreign adoptions. Investigation of

---

[148] Theodosius and Siscia: Piganiol (1972) 280. Pacatus, *Paneg.* 2. 34. 1 (Gallétier (1955) 100).

[149] García Rodríguez (1966) 214; Vives (1946) and (1969) 101 no. 304.

each cult is, however, still worthwhile for the insights which it gives into the probable extent of the first audience for each poem. However much the poetic treatment of each martyr helped to spread knowledge of the different cults throughout Spain and the West, it is likely that poems written for saints only locally venerated in the late fourth century were written originally for residents of that region.

The soldier-martyrs Emeterius and Chelidonius of Calahorra seem to have had only a local cult in Prudentius' time and also in the later Visigothic period. If *Pe.* 8 is truly written for the dedication of a baptistery at their place of martyrdom in Calahorra, then this suggests that the saints were already popular enough locally in Prudentius' day to be honoured with a basilica.[150] The poet does mention visits of foreigners to the shrine (8. 10), but this may refer only to residents of the surrounding regions and neighbouring towns, as opposed to residents of Calahorra itself. The name of Chelidonius is used to indicate the celebration of the martyr's feast either at Saragossa (*Pe.* 11. 237) or Calahorra. The saints were well enough known in Gaul by the fifth century for two bishops to have borne their names,[151] and their story is told by Gregory of Tours in his *De gloria martyrum* (93), although this account is derived from Prudentius' poem. The martyrs' feast-day, 3 March, is indicated in all the Mozarabic calendars and in the *Hieronymian Martyrology*, but not in the earliest (pre–711) Calendar of Carmona. It seems that their cult had probably not spread throughout Spain in the earlier period. There is no record of their relics among Visigothic inscriptions; their feast is not commemorated in the *Orationale* of Tarragona, nor in the later *Liber comicus*. This absence *may* be explained by the falling of the feast in Lent, when it could hardly be celebrated, but otherwise fits in with the picture of a limited local devotion in the period before the Arab conquest. A Mass based largely on Prudentius' poem finally appeared in the Toledan *Liber sacramentorum* of the ninth century. Thus, in this poem, Prudentius probably writes for a limited Spanish audience, natives of Calahorra and the surrounding region.

The same conclusion holds good in the case of the 'Eighteen Martyrs of Saragossa', who went unrecorded before Prudentius'

---

[150] Vives (1969) 322.
[151] Duchesne (1907) I. 114, 275.

poem.[152] The mention of an altar at *Pe.* 4. 189 ff. implies the existence of a basilica in Prudentius' day, which in later references is called 'sancta sanctorum'. The basilica is mentioned in the seventh century,[153] but the saints are not mentioned by Gregory of Tours, although otherwise he often follows Prudentius. The saints do not appear in lists of relics or churches, and are nowhere recorded by writers in the Visigothic period. One votive inscription remains to St Lupercus (*Pe.* 4. 146), but this belongs to a later period.[154] Once again, then, the poet must be writing for a local Saragossan audience, and this is confirmed by the strong note of local patriotism which pervades the whole poem.

The picture is very different for the saints Eulalia, Vincent, and Fructuosus and his deacons. These were, in fact, the only Spanish saints venerated outside Spain before the eighth century.[155] In Spain itself, Eulalia's basilica at Mérida was well established by Prudentius' time, and he describes its beauty at *Pe.* 3. 186–200. Her cult spread quickly within the Peninsula. Her relics were distributed around Spain in the sixth and seventh centuries,[156] and in Prudentius' day, her feast was already celebrated in Calahorra (*Pe.* 11. 237). The cult soon spread beyond Spain to Africa, where Eulalia's name appears in the Carthaginian Calendar, and where Augustine wrote a sermon for her feast-day.[157] Her fame reached Gaul in the fifth century, and a basilica was dedicated to her along with Vincent and Agnes at Béziers in AD 455.[158] In the sixth century, Venantius Fortunatus sings of the martyr in his poem on chastity,[159] and Gregory of Tours tells of her martyrdom in his *De gloria martyrum*, 91 (*PL* 71. 785). His addition of the miraculously flowering trees before her basilica may derive from a misunderstanding of Prudentius' description of the floral decoration of the basilica or, of course, from a tradition unknown to the poet, who was not, after all, probably a native of the region. No evidence exists to prove early devotion to Eulalia in Italy, but she appears between Agnes and Cecilia in the procession of virgin

[152] García Rodríguez (1966) 324–6.
[153] *De uiris illustribus S. Hildefonsi episcopi toletani, PL* 96. 201, 204.
[154] *ILCV* 1. 375, no. 1919.
[155] García Rodríguez (1966) 79.
[156] Vives (1969) 108 no. 316; 102 no. 306; 102–3 no. 307; 110 no. 328.
[157] Morin (1930) 1. 593–5.
[158] *ILCV* 1. 354 no. 1807.
[159] Venantius Fortunatus, 8. 3. 170.

martyrs depicted in the mosaics of S. Apollinare Nuovo in Ravenna. Her feast is included in the ninth-century Neapolitan Calendar, but there is no indication whether or not her inclusion reflects liturgical usage. She does appear in all the earliest Spanish liturgical books, where her popularity in Spain is reflected in the number of masses and prayers composed in her honour. Thus, in this poem, Prudentius is dealing with a devotion which has spread beyond the martyr's native town to the rest of Spain, and even abroad. However, the terms in which the poet encourages the people of Mérida to join with him in celebrating the feast-day at the end of the poem suggests that the poet has chiefly a local audience in mind, even if he is aware that the poem may ultimately have a wider appeal.

Vincent was perhaps the most popular of Spanish martyrs, whose fame very soon spread beyond his own country.[160] He is the only Spanish saint to have his feast-day adopted by the Roman rite for the liturgy of the whole Church and to appear among the very few saints mentioned in the fifth-century calendar of Polemius Silvius.[161] He was originally celebrated both at Valencia, the place of his execution, and at Saragossa, which took pride in its status as his place of birth and education (*Pe.* 4. 97–104). Prudentius' evidence in *Pe.* 5 and *Pe.* 4 indicates parallel cults in these two cities and early efforts to honour the saint with chapels. The cult spread throughout the Peninsula in the fifth century and thence to Gaul, Africa, and Italy. Vincent is mentioned in the Calendar of Carmona and also in the early liturgical books, where he is among the most frequently celebrated saints. I have already mentioned the basilica in Vincent's honour in Béziers in the mid-fifth century; there is however, no other evidence for early cult in Gaul, apart from a funerary chapel dedicated to Vincent at Viennois.[162] In Africa, the saint's *Passion* was known to Augustine, who composed a series of sermons for his yearly celebration.[163] Paulinus of Nola celebrates the martyr as one of the glories of the West in one of his poems (19. 152–6), but the saint seems not to have been widely venerated in Italy until the fifth and sixth centuries. The *Hieronymian Martyrology* notes the dedication dates of

[160] García Rodríguez (1966) 257.
[161] *CIL* 1. 1, 254–79 at 257.
[162] *CIL* 12. 1, 499.
[163] *Sermo* 274–77 = *PL* 38. 1253 ff.

two basilicas in Vincent's honour at Porto and Tivoli, and these entries have been dated to the fifth century.[164] By the seventh century there was a basilica dedicated to Vincent in Rome itself, built by Honorius, 'S. Vincenzo ed Anastasio alle Tre Fontane', which was renovated in the eighth century by Leo III.[165] Vincent is the only other Spanish saint to appear in the mosaics of S. Apollinare Nuovo at Ravenna.

Thus, in writing about Vincent, Prudentius was writing for an audience wider than that of Valencia or Saragossa alone. Nevertheless, it is likely that in the fourth century, Vincent's cult was still best known inside Spain itself, so once again Prudentius may be writing primarily for a Spanish audience. This would fit in with the idea that *Pe.* 5 balances the poem celebrating the Roman martyr Lawrence, in order to make a patriotic point about Spain's richness in martyrs of equal stature to those of Rome.

Early devotion to Fructuosus at Tarragona is confirmed both by the genuine early *Acta* which survive, and by archaeological remains which prove the existence of a fourth–fifth century basilica (see following section). Fructuosus' cult spread fairly quickly: by the early fifth century, his *Acta* were known to Augustine, who used them as the basis for a sermon in his honour (*Sermo* 273 = *PL* 38. 1247–9). The cult only seems to have become popular in Gaul in the later period, particularly in the region of Toulouse. Diffusion of the cult in Italy was later than the Arab invasion.[166] The saint, however, does appear in the *Hieronymian Martyrology* and in all the Spanish liturgical books. Thus, in *Pe.* 6, Prudentius may have been writing for an audience much wider than that of Tarragona, although his exhortations to celebrate the saint at the end of the poem seem restricted to the city itself. The poem would certainly have had the strongest appeal for Spaniards who knew the town and its setting, which enter into the closing lines.

The *Peristephanon Liber* and Archaeological Evidence

Another aspect of the historical value of Prudentius' poems is the occasional insight which they give into the state of particular cult-

---

[164] Delehaye (1931) 270 and 391.
[165] Waal (1907).
[166] García Rodríguez (1966) 319; de Gaiffier (1948).

sites. Prudentius often includes brief glimpses of the contemporary site, which both he and, in some cases, his readers would have visited and known. Poetic licence must be absent from descriptions of places known to contemporaries by direct experience, or at least through hearsay. Thus, Prudentius' information at these points, tantalisingly brief though it is, can be trusted.

Unfortunately, it is nearly always impossible to check Prudentius' pictures against archaeological remains. Spain is very poor in early Christian sites, as the result of barbarian and then Moorish invasions, which necessitated repeated rebuilding of destroyed sites.[167] Only at Mérida and Tarragona can any light be shed on Prudentius' references. In the case of Mérida, the poet's allusion to the basilica and his lyrical if vague description are the earliest mentions of the site buildings, and find confirmation in slightly later literature rather than in excavations. The basilica which Prudentius must have known was in fact sacked and destroyed by the king of the invading Suevi, who suffered death as his punishment (as Hydatius notes with some satisfaction). This was in the year AD 429.[168] The later *Vitae sanctorum patrum emeritensium* makes many allusions to the restored church, which lay on the outskirts of the town.[169] The basilica was reconstructed in the sixth century by Bishop Fidelis, who enlarged it and gave it towers.[170]

By contrast, the site at Tarragona has yielded evidence which is of great interest for comparison with Prudentius' account of the site in his poem about St Fructuosus. Excavations in the 1920s revealed the ancient necropolis dedicated to Fructuosus and hs deacons, complete with a basilica possessing three naves and a baptismal *piscina*. This site is outside the town, on the Via Romana.[171] It is beyond doubt that the necropolis dates from the end of the third century or the beginning of the fourth.[172] The basilica itself, which is later, is found in the midst of more than two thousand tombs, and many of the inscriptions with these can be dated to a period between the end of the fourth and the middle

[167] Grabar (1945–6), I. 424: 'Je ne connais aucun exemple conservé de martyrium paléochrétien en Espagne'; cf. García Rodríguez (1966) 98–100.
[168] Hydatius, *Chronicon*, 90. 5 a. 429; cf. ibid., a. 456. Also Isidore, *Hist. regum Gothicorum*, 32 and *Hist. pseudisidoriana*, 12.
[169] *Vitae*, 5. 11. 2, p. 236; 5. 12. 6–7, p. 246; cf. 1. 1, p. 138 and 5. 11. 17, p. 242.
[170] *Vitae*, 4. 6. 8, p. 178; and 4. 10. 1, p. 186.
[171] García Rodríguez (1966) 317.
[172] Vives (1937–40).

of the fifth centuries. Many allude to burial 'ad sanctos', or say 'sede sanctorum quiesces'.[173] Among the inscriptions in the necropolis itself is one which corresponded to the frieze on the altar dedicated to the saints.[174] This has been convincingly restored to read, according to an African model: 'Memoria sanctorum Fructuosi, Augurii et Eulogii'.

Interpretation of the evidence yielded by this site is not without controversy. It seems that the necropolis was abandoned at the beginning of the sixth century, and there is no sign of its having been used during the Visigothic period. Later references suggest a church dedicated to Fructuosus *inside* the city, where his relics were venerated. In excavations in 1928, the ruins of the *curia* in the city's Roman forum were identified with this church.[175] There are no early written references either to the early basilica by the necropolis, or to the later church in the city. It seems likely, however, that the later basilica was established for the translation of relics implied by the abandoning of the necropolis at the beginning of the sixth century. Translation of relics to the new church then facilitated the wider diffusion of relics.[176]

The main problem surrounding the site of the necropolis is the reason for its abandonment. An early explanation looked to destruction by the troops of Enricus who destroyed Tarragona in AD 475–6.[177] This destruction explains the removal of the relics inside the city. These conclusions have been challenged by Vives (n. 173 above), who shows that there are no real grounds for supposing that the basilica was destroyed by the troops of Enricus. This is implied by the historians of the sixteenth and seventeenth centuries, but in fact finds no confirmation in contemporary writers, nor in later inscriptions, which mention no attempts at the rebuilding and restoration which would have been expected. So the necropolis could quite well have continued in use until the end of the sixth century. Its continued use as the centre of a Christian burial ground confirms this.

Vives sees no reason to suppose a sack of the basilica either by

[173] Vives (1936*b*) also (1969) 109 no. 321.

[174] Vives (1969) 109 no. 321. Also Vives (1933).

[175] This is referred to by the 16th-century historian Pons d'Icart in 'Gradezas de Tarragona'. See Serra Vilaró (1936) 113–20.

[176] Vives (1969) 101 no. 304; 110 no. 326 and 328.

[177] Serra Vilaró (1937).

Enricus in AD 475–6 or by the Franks in AD 540–1. A fire in the basilica could have had the same result, especially in conjunction with the increasingly popular Oriental idea of transferring relics from the original tombs of the martyrs. Perhaps even more likely than fire is the idea of flood.[178] Even if this was the case, the necropolis may not have been completely abandoned even after the translation. Vives's use of the evidence and reconstruction of events seems more convincing than the earlier version.

It remains to examine how Prudentius' references harmonize with this. The poet seems to know the site of the city well: in the first two stanzas of his poem (*Pe.* 6) he plays on Tarraco's lofty position on its limestone coastal cliff.[179] So Tarraco 'attollit caput' in a sense more literal than that implied in its civic pride in its martyrs. The city, literally 'procul relucens' (3), is well described as 'arcem' (5). In fact, both Martial and much later Ausonius had talked of 'Tarraconis arces' and 'arce potens Tarraco'.[180] Paulinus of Nola had described the town's lofty position with the words '*capite insigni* despectat Tarraco pontem'.[181]

The end of *Pe.* 6 (154–7) is even more interesting for the present enquiry. The poet speaks of the praises of the martyrs to be sung in the city:

> Hinc aurata sonent in arce tecta;
> blandum litoris extet inde murmur,
> et carmen freta feriata pangant.

The poet seems here to give a description of the basilica, albeit indirectly and allusively. The 'aurata ... tecta' must stand for the ceiling of the church.[182] It is worth comparing this expression with *Pe.* 3. 196, where the poet describes Eulalia's basilica using the phrase 'tecta corusca'. If Prudentius is indeed referring to Fructuosus' basilica in *Pe.* 6, then the reference not only constitutes the earliest written allusion to the basilica, but also adds a further difficulty to the controversy surrounding the necropolis and the basilica inside the city itself. For although at 39–41 the

---

[178] The site was apparently seriously flooded in 1929 (Vives 1933).

[179] Schulten (1932).

[180] Martial, *Epigr.* 10. 104. 4; Ausonius, *Ordo urbium nobilium*, 13, Tarraco appears at line 84.

[181] Paulinus of Nola, *Carm.* 10. 233.

[182] Lavarenne (1936b) 99; he accepts it as the church in his translation. The Loeb edition, however, refers vaguely to the 'gilded roofs in the city' (Thomson (1953 edn.) 213).

poet seems to refer to the future tomb of the saint (that is, the con-
temporary fourth-century tomb) in a way which must surely re-
fer to the original resting-place in the *necropolis*, his later reference
to the basilica seems to speak of a church *inside* the city. This must
be the meaning of 'in arce', which Lavarenne rightly translates as
'dans la ville'. The hymn is to echo in the town 'hinc' and to be re-
echoed along the shore ('inde', 155). Surely only a hymn sung in
the city itself could be supposed to be echoed directly along the
shore, since the site of the necropolis is inland, along the Via
Romana, and on the far side of the city, a little away from the
coast.[183] This must mean that in Prudentius' time the saint was
already honoured with a basilica in the city itself, as well as at the
place of burial. This need imply nothing for the whereabouts of
the relics, which the reference in the poem suggests were still in-
side the original necropolis. The appearance of the martyrs after
death to ensure the collection of their relics into one place may be
meant to make a topical point for contemporary Tarraco, where
there may already have been some controversy over the possibil-
ity of transferring the martyrs' relics to the new city basilica. This
translation was delayed until the sixth century by conservatives.
Another possible interpretation of the poet's apparent reference to
a basilica *inside* the city might lie in the celebration of the saint's
feast-day, partly in the town basilica, which might not have yet
been dedicated to the saint (this system of dedication to a patron-
saint grew slowly). Such a celebration might begin in the town
basilica and continue in a solemn procession with hymns to the
Via Romana, where the feast would be completed at the necro-
polis itself. Such a practice was common and can be paralleled.[184]
The city basilica would then have been dedicated to the saint later,
at the time of the deposition of the relics.

All interpretations of the final scene and lines of the poem must
ultimately remain conjectural, since Prudentius' words are admit-
tedly vague enough to allow room for doubt. But if a reference to

---

[183] 'Questa necropoli si trova situata alla sinistra del fiume Francoli, il Tulcis dei
Romani, nel luogi in ciu questo fiume e attraversato dalla strada Tarragona–Castellón'
(Serra Vilaró (1936) 244). This must admittedly have been a coast road.

[184] Cf. *Vitae sanctorum patrum emeritensium*, 5. 11. 2, where reference is made to an
Easter procession: 'Hanc uero dispositionem habent ut cum ex more in pascha hic cele-
braueritis missam in ecclesia seniore et post missam, iuxta quod mos est, ad basilicam sanc-
tae Eulaliae psallendo cum omni catholico populo …' Garvin's note on this (p. 501)
discusses (with bibliography), the celebration of Vigils and Mass in different places.

a basilica 'in arce' is admitted here, then it can be explained in the way outlined above, with reference to the archaeological evidence available.

These are the only Spanish sites described in some detail by the poet for which some external evidence also remains. Several other poems give some information about cult-sites in Rome and Italy. In his poem about St Cassian, Prudentius describes a shrine-painting which depicts the martyrdom. In *Pe.* 11 he describes the feast-day and the catacomb at Rome of St Hippolytus. Over this martyr's tomb ('super tumulum', 125), the poet says that he has seen a vivid painting of the martyrdom (127 ff.). *Pe.* 12 involves the description of a new baptistery at St Peter's basilica on the Vatican hill, and also of the recently built basilica of St Paul. None of these descriptions is without problem with regard to the remaining evidence for the sites treated.

Pe. 9 and 11 raise the same problem. Both poems give the first written evidence for their respective martyrdoms, and both use paintings seen at the respective shrines as a means of describing each martyr's end. Even assuming that these versions of the martyrdoms were already a part of the popular tradition concerning the saints before Prudentius composed his poems, the existence of the paintings themselves raises important questions. Doubt has been cast on the existence of such paintings from several points of view. For instance, the Spanish Council of Elvira (AD 303) forbade the use of paintings on church walls in its thirty-sixth canon: 'Placuit picturas in ecclesia esse non debere, ne quod colitur et adoratur in parietibus depingatur.'[185] This prohibition can be explained as a temporary one only, passed as the result of anxieties caused by the Priscillianist trouble in Spain; or it may simply represent a local measure.[186] In any case, it seems unlikely that painted representations were altogether prevented in practice. So Prudentius' own collection, the *Dittochaeon*, for instance, seems to be a set of inscriptions destined for use in connection with Biblical and Gospel scenes painted in a basilica.[187] Such

[185] Hefele (1907) 240; Mansi 2. 13.
[186] García Rodríguez (1966) 370.
[187] On the *Dittochaeon* see Mannelli (1947); cf. Paulinus of Nola, *Ep.* 32, where he refers to texts destined for church paintings; cf. above chap. 4, n. 62.

paintings existed elsewhere in this period, at Nola, for instance.[188] The problem is that almost no examples of paintings of martyrdoms remain from the fourth and fifth centuries.[189] Depiction of martyrdom is a late and relatively rare occurrence, when the martyr's death is only emphasized in connection with its model, the Passion of Christ. In the fourth century, while the theme of martyrdom was still closely tied to funerary art and had not been paralleled with the Eucharistic sacrifice 'il resta fidèle au principe de l'imagerie sépulcrale chrétienne, qui était d'en exclure systématiquement toute représentation, directe ou non, de la mort'.[190] However, the few paintings which do remain may be an indication that there were more which have not survived from the earliest period. This supposition is confirmed by the literature of the fourth–fifth centuries, which contains references to the sort of painting described by Prudentius. Asterius of Amasea, for instance, gives a vivid description of a cycle of paintings depicting the passion and martyrdom of St Euphemia.[191] Grabar comments that Asterius' highly rhetorical description is far more detailed than any of the few remaining examples of such paintings. A similar observation might well hold true for Prudentius' highly coloured poetic descriptions, embellished with all the richness of literary reminiscence. Another reference to a painting in the *memoria* of a martyr occurs in Evodius of Uzali, a contemporary of Augustine, who refers to a votive painting which represents the triumph of the saint over a dragon[192] (this is admittedly not a scene of martyrdom). Pictures of this type on wood or other destructible materials could well have been more common than we can know. Thus a later inscription including the praise of John the Evangelist, refers to a picture of the Apostle.[193] Another inscription[194] refers to the Christobel encountered at the door of the church. This could refer to a painting. These two Spanish examples are not reflected in Spanish literary sources, where Pru-

---

[188] *Natalicia*, 27. 510 ff. See Goldschmidt (1940).

[189] Grabar (1945–6) 2. 16–17.

[190] Ibid., 80; cf. Müntz (1881) 17.

[191] Grabar (1945–6) 2. 72–4. *PG* 40. 334 ff. See Lanzoni (1925). He also mentions descriptions of paintings to be found in Basil (*PG* 31. 434) and Gregory of Nazianzus (*PG* 46. 737).

[192] Evodius, *De miraculis S. Stephani*, 2. 4 = *PL* 41. 851.

[193] Vives (1969) no. 351 (8th century).

[194] Ibid., no. 337.

dentius alone alludes to the Roman and Italian examples under discussion here.

Unfortunately, no evidence survives to confirm either allusion. Excavations carried out in the nineteenth century in the cemetery of St Hippolytus revealed the crypt where the martyr's tomb lies beneath an altar as Prudentius describes, but there was no trace of any painting.[195] This is not conclusive evidence against the existence of such paintings in the poet's time, since the crypt had been considerably restored after destruction at the hands of the Goths in the sixth century.[196] It is also possible that Prudentius alludes here to a depiction of the martyrdom in miniature on glass. Such miniatures of Biblical scenes have been found.[197] The subject-matter of the picture described by the poet is problematical, but could well reflect mistaken popular tradition predating the poet, rather than the imaginative invention of the poet himself. So he is quite likely to be telling of a painting which really existed. There is no reason to suppose that the same conclusion may not also be true of St Cassian's picture at Imola.

Prudentius' final reference to structures standing in his day comes in *Pe.* 12, which seems to demonstrate a greater preoccupation with a description of aspects of the basilicas of SS Peter and Paul, than with the passions of the martyrs themselves, although these are briefly treated. Prudentius' treatment of his subject-matter is impressionistic and poetical, and has caused some controversy. It would, of course, be a mistake to blame the poet for his inexplicit account: he is not, after all, writing an archaeological report. It is, however, possible to extract a great deal of interesting information even from his poetic description, and this has been done most convincingly by Ruysschaert.[198] He points out the imbalance in the way in which the poet describes the whole of St Paul's, but only the fountains which feed the baptistery of St Peter's. The explanation of the latter does not lie in theology or symbolism: this would make little sense in relation to the realistic description of St Paul's. At lines 31–2, the poet pauses at the foot of the Vatican hill, and gives a general view of the north side of the basilica, with its olive grove 'Canens oliua ... *frondem* peren-

[195] de Rossi (1881) and Lanzoni (1925). Also Vives (1944) 199–200.
[196] de Rossi (1881) and Puech (1888) 309.
[197] de Rossi (1881) and Dalton (1901).
[198] Ruysschaert (1966).

nem chrismatis feracem'.[199] The description of this is followed
and balanced by description of the spring. This survey of the land-
scape creates the opening for following the spring down to the
new structures which exploit it (35: 'nunc pretiosa ruit per
marmora . . .'). An inscription once placed on the north wall of
the basilica explains how Pope Damasus was involved in draining
this site of the basilica.[200] The most important part of the work
took place at the top of the hill (6): 'Aggeris immensi deiecit cul-
mina montis', and involved the discovery of a spring (9): 'inuenit
fontem praebet qui dona salutis'. Perhaps the inscription was
originally placed by the spring. As the inscription implies, Dama-
sus seems to have used his discovery in the baptistery which he
had built (72).[201] This explains the details of marble and 'colym-
bus' in Prudentius' account. The 'marble' must have been the
channels which led the water to the artificial pool at the base of
the hill. The poet then takes us into the basilica at its northern end
(37 ff.). He is talking of the Vatican baptistery at the northern ex-
tremity of the transept, which is separated from this by a pair of
columns.[202] Prudentius describes the multicoloured mosaics of
the vault, and their reflections in the baptismal water. These
mosaics also date from the Damasan period, judging by an in-
scription which seems to recall the part taken in the decoration of
the baptistery by a lady called Anastasia. Both Damasus' name
and the 'coelum' of the place are mentioned in the inscription.[203]
A Damasan inscription also connects Damasus with the baptistery
construction: 'Una Petri sedes, unum uerumque lauacrum'.[204] It
seems as though Prudentius has gone out of his way to focus
attention on Damasus' achievements at St Peter's. The anony-
mous 'pastor' of line 43 is probably the Pope, who through his

---

[199] Ibid., 270: the reading 'frondem', instead of 'fontem' as in Bergman and Lavarenne,
makes much more sense. It can be paralleled from *Dittochaeon*, 42 'Mons Oliveti': 'frondi-
bus aeternis praepinguis liquitur umor,/qui probat infusum terris de chrismate donum.'
The association of ideas here is natural for the Christian poet. To read 'fontem' here trans-
ports the reader prematurely into the basilica.

[200] Ferrua (1942) 88–93, n. 4.

[201] Ibid., 90 adn. 2. Ferrua quotes the 6th-century entry in the *Liber pontificalis*, 122–3.

[202] Emminghaus (1962).

[203] Ferrua (1942) 94–6. This inscription is also written in the Philocalian script used in
Damasus' own inscriptions. Chastagnol (1966) also sees Pope Damasus as the inspirer of the
building of the new St Paul's-without-the-walls, begun AD 383–4. *Pe.* 12 would thus celeb-
rate the two cult-sites with Spanish connections.

[204] Ruysschaert (1966) 274–6. For *lavacrum*, see *Pe.* 6. 29 and p. 213 above.

building of the baptistery participates in the baptisms carried out there. Perhaps it is not without significance that the Pope and St Peter figure together on a gold glass of this period.[205]

Prudentius treats St Paul's basilica on the Via Ostia in a more general way, and Ruysschaert shows that once the reader is inside the basilica, the poet concentrates more on praise of the *princeps* than on description of the basilica itself (47 ff.: 'princeps bonus ...'). A problem arises in deciding exactly which *princeps* the poet means here. It is certain that the construction of the basilica was begun under Valentinian II,[206] but an inscription which commemorates the placing of the first column of the basilica bears a date at the end of AD 391, only a few months before Valentinian's death. Since the decoration of the basilica was finished under Theodosius, it seems likely that the *princeps* is Theodosius (although there is, in fact, no internal evidence in the poem to prove this). Prudentius' misattribution of the basilica can be explained on the grounds of a misinterpretation of the late inscription on the pillar base. This mistake may also have led to the later absidal inscription with its reference to Theodosius, as the founder of the basilica. An indirect compliment to Theodosius in Prudentius' poem would certainly fit in with the enthusiasm for this emperor which he demonstrates elsewhere in his poetry (*Pe.* 2 and *Contra Symmachum*). It is not insignificant that the building also took place during Damasus' time as Pope. Enthusiasm for the apparent achievements of a Spanish emperor is thus combined with a special focus on those of a Spanish Pope, and would please both a Spanish audience at court, and one at home in Spain, which would value highly the details of Spanish contributions to the religious life of the exalted but distant capital. It would provide all the extra encouragement needed to promote the celebration in Spain of the feast-day of Peter and Paul (65–6). As far as details about the basilica are concerned, the poet gives a general impression of its richness, and the only hard detail which certainly reflects facts is the 'quaternus ordo' of pillars, which divided the huge basilica.

[205] Bovini (1950) 29.
[206] Ruysschaert (1966) 277–9. On the pillar base inscription, 279–80. Also, Chastagnol (1966) 432–3.

Epilogue

THE *Peristephanon Liber* provides a wealth of detail for the study of martyr-cult in the poet's period. The poet combines written and oral sources, giving us valuable information which might otherwise have been lost, even if, where his literary antecedents are preserved, they remain a better guide to the history of the martyr concerned. Perhaps the most valuable aspect of the collection is its role as a Church calendar in poetic form, which illustrates the extent of each saint's cult in the Spain of Prudentius' day. A picture emerges of strong local loyalties to the 'resident' patron-martyr of each town, which are balanced by a growing interest in foreign martyrs, in particular the famous ones of Rome. Prudentius' enthusiasm for the Roman martyrs, the 'innumeros cineres sanctorum' (*Pe.* 11. 1) and their shrines, grew initially out of his personal experience of martyr-cult in Rome and perhaps found particular stimulus in the activities of the Spanish pope, Damasus. This pope did much to promote martyr-cult at Rome, and it was his elegantly carved inscriptions which contributed to Prudentius' inspiration in the composition of at least some of the *Peristephanon* poems; *Pe.* 2, 11, 12, and 14 all celebrate Roman saints who were treated by Damasus in his epigrams, and whose cult Prudentius was keen to promote in Spain. This is explicitly stated at the end of *Pe.* 11 and 12, while *Pe.* 12 in particular, strikingly records the splendour of two major constructions in honour of the Apostles, which were built under Damasus' papacy. Thus the Spanish interest of those *Peristephanon* poems which have a more local focus (*Pe.* 1. 3–6, 8), is in fact carried further in the apparently more distant enthusiasm for Roman sites. The poet feels free to draw implicit parallels between Vincent and Lawrence, Eulalia and Agnes.

The close Spanish connections in the poems point to their first audience among the educated Spanish Christians discussed in the Introduction. Each poem may have been written at the request of a patron with a special devotion to his local martyr, but, in spite of our considerable acquaintance with Spanish aristocrats of that time, no definite connection can be made with any of them. Prudentius, however, always concentrates on his main theme, the celebration of the martyr, and keeps firmly in mind his express vocation as a Christian poet writing to and for God. The intrusion of worldly patrons would jar with this spiritual dedication of the poetry. In spite of this silence (typical of Prudentius' disinclination to allow worldly particulars to intrude), the *Peristephanon*, by the local and lyrical nature of its contents, gives more information regarding the likely addressees than any other work of the poet. Confirmation of the Spanish destination of these poems is provided by their prominence, in modified form, in the Mozarabic Hymnal. Thus the local popularity of Prudentius' poems spread through the Peninsula within a few generations. It only remains for them now to regain, after long neglect, the recognition and appreciation they deserve.

Bibliography

Editions of sources quoted in the footnotes are listed below under *Principal Ancient Sources*, where ancient authors are listed alphabetically. Editors cited in the footnotes are also listed alphabetically in the main section, *Modern Works*.

PRINCIPAL ANCIENT SOURCES

Acta primorum martyrum sincera et selecta
   Ed. Th. Ruinart (Amsterdam, 1713).
Acts of the Christian Martyrs
   Ed. H. Musurillo (Oxford, 1972).
AFRANIUS
   Comicorum romanorum praeter Plautum et Syri quae feruntur sententiae fragmenta, ed. O. Ribbeck, 2 (Teubner, 1898).
AMBROSE
   De obitu Theodosii, ed. O. Faller (*CSEL* 73, 1955).
   Epistulae, PL 16. 875–1286.
   De uirginibus, ed. O. Faller (*Florilegium Patristicum* 31, 1933).
   De officiis ministrorum, PL 16. 23–184.
   De obitu fratris sui Satyri (*De fide resurrectionis*), ed. P. B. Albers (*Florilegium Patristicum* 15, 1921).
   Hymni S. Ambrosio attributi, PL 17. 1171–222.
AMMIANUS MARCELLINUS
   Rerum gestarum libri qui supersunt, recensuit W. Seyfarth, 2 vols. (Teubner, 1978).
ARATOR
   De actibus apostolorum, PL 68.
ARNOBIUS
   Ed. A Reifferscheid (*CSEL* 4, 1875).
AURELIAN
   PL 68.
AURELIUS VICTOR
   Epitome de Caesaribus, ed. F. Pichlmayr (Teubner, 1911).
AUGUSTINE
   Confessions, ed. P. Knöll (*CSEL* 33, 1896).
   De ciuitate dei, ed. E. Hoffmann (*CSEL*, 40, 1 and 2, 1899).
   Psalmus contra partem Donati, ed. M. Petschenig (*CSEL* 51, 1908: 3–15).

De doctrina christiana, ed. G. M. Green (*CSEL* 80, 1963).
Retractationes, ed. P. Knöll (*CSEL* 36, 1902).
De musica, ed. G. Marzi (Collana di classici della filosofia cristiana 1, 1969).
De cura pro mortuis gerenda, ed. J. Zycha (*CSEL* 41, 1900: 619–60).
De anima, ed. C. F. Urba and J. Zycha (*CSEL* 60, 1913).
Sermones, PL 38 and 39.
De uera religione, PL 34.
De Genesi ad Litteram, PL 34.
Epistulae, ed. A. Goldbacher (*CSEL* 34, 44, 57–8, 1895–1923).
Contra Cresconium, ed. M. Petschenig (*CSEL* 52, 1909).
Miscellanea Agostiniana, Testi e Studi pubblicati a cura dell'Ordine eremitano di S. Agostino nel XV centenario dalla morte del santo dottore, 2 vols. (1930–1).

AUSONIUS
Decimi Magni Ausonii burdigalensis opuscula, ed. S. Prete (Teubner, 1978).

AVITUS
De consolatoria castitatis laude, PL 59.

BASIL
Orationes, PG 31.
Epistulae, PG 32.

CAESARIUS OF ARLES
S. Caesarii opera omnia, ed. G. Morin, 2 vols. (1937).
Carmen ad senatorum ex christiana religione ad idolorum seruitutem conuersum
Ed. R. Peiper (*CSEL* 23, 1881).

CASSIAN
Collationes, ed. M. Petschenig (*CSEL* 13, 1886).

CATULLUS
Catulli carmina, ed. R. A. B. Mynors (Oxford, 1958).

CELESTINUS, POPE
Epistola et decreta, PL 50. 417 ff.

CICERO
De inventione, ed. E. Stroebel (Teubner, 1915).

CLAUDIAN
Claudi Claudiani carmina, recensuit T. Birt (*MGH Auct. Ant.* 10, 1892).

CLEMENT OF ROME:
S. Clementis romani epistula ad Corinthios, ed. C. T. Schaefer (*Florilegium Patristicum* 44, 1941).
Codex Theodosianus
Ed. Th. Mommsen and P. M. Meyer (1905).
Consularia Constantinopolitana
(In *Chronica Minora* 1 ed. Th. Mommsen (*MGH Auct. Ant* 9, 1892).

COMMODIAN
Instructiones and *Carmen apologeticum*, ed. B. Dombart (*CSEL* 15, 1887).

CYPRIAN
Epistulae, ed. G. Hartel (*CSEL* 3, 1871).

DAMASUS
Epigrammata Damasi, ed. M. Ihm, *Anthologiae Latinae Supplementa* 1 (Leipzig, 1895).
Epigrammata Damasiana, ed. A. Ferrua (Rome, 1942).
Depositio Martyrum, in *Liber pontificalis* (see below), (pp. 11–12).

Decretum Gelasianum
Das *Decretum Gelasianum de libris recipiendis et non recipiendis*, in kritischem Text. hrsg. und untersucht von E.v. Dobschütz (*Texte und Untersuchungen*, 3. Reihe, 8. 4, 1912).

DIO CHRYSOSTOM
Orationes, post L. Dindorfium ed. G. de Budé, 2 vols. (Teubner, 1916–19).

EGERIA
Itinerarium Egeriae, ed. P. Geyer (*CSEL* 39, 1898).

EUGENIUS TOLETANUS
Epistulae and *De basilico sanctorum decem et octo martyrum*, ed. F. Vollmer (*MGH Auct. Ant.* 14, 1905).

EUMENIUS
Panégyriques latins, E. Gallétier, 1 (Budé, 1949).

EUNAPIUS
The Fragmentary Classicising Historians of the Later Roman Empire, ed. R. C. Blockley, 2 (Liverpool, 1983), 2–127.

EUSEBIUS
Histoire ecclésiastique, texte grec, traduction et annotation par G. Bardy, 4 vols. (*SC* 31, 41, 55, 73, 1952–60).
Martyrs of Palestine, H. J. Lawlor and J. E. L. Oulton (1927).
Chronicorum lib. II interprete S. Hieronymo, ed. R. Helm (*GCS*, 1956).

EVODIUS
De miraculus S. Stephani, PL 41.

FERREOLUS
PL 66.

GENNADIUS
De uiris illustribus, ed. E. C. Richardson, *Texte und Untersuchungen* 14. 1 (1896) 66 ff.

GREGORY OF NAZIANZUS
PG 35–8.

GREGORY OF NYSSA
PG 44–6.

Gregory of Tours
  De gloria martyrum and *De gloria confessorum*, PL 71.
Hilary of Arles
  Sermo sancti Hilarii de vita sancti Honorati, ed. M. D. Valentin (*SC* 235, 1977).
Hilary of Poitiers
  Hymns, ed. A. J. Feder (*CSEL* 65, 1916: 217–23).
Hildefonsus
  De uiris illustribus, PL 96. 195–206.
Historia Augusta
  Ed. E. Hohl, Ch. Samberger and W. Seyfarth (Leipzig, 1965).
Homer
  Odyssey, ed. T. W. Allen (Oxford, 1916).
Horace
  Q. Horati Flacci opera, ed. E. C. Wickham, H. W. Garrod (Oxford, 1967).
Hydatius
  Chronicon, Chronica minora, 2 ed. Th. Mommsen (*MGH Auct. Ant.* 11, 1894).
Irenaeus
  Aduersus haereses, PG 7. 433 ff.
Isidore of Seville
  Historia Gothorum Wandalorum Sueborum ad a. DCXXIV, Chronica minora 2, ed. Th. Mommsen (*MGH Auct. Ant.* 11, 1894).
  Carmina, PL 83.
Jerome
  Epistulae, ed. I. Hilberg (*CSEL* 54–6, 1910–1918).
  Chronicon, ed. R. Helm (*GCS*, 1956).
  De uiris illustribus, ed. E. C. Richardson, *Texte und Untersuchungen* 14 (1896).
  Vita Pauli, PL 23.
  Praef. in Galat. II, PL 26
  Comment. in Ezechielem prophetam (*CCL* 75, 1964).
John Chrysostom
  PG 47–64.
Julian
  Epistles, ed. W. Wright (Loeb, 1913–23).
Juvenal
  A. Persi Flacci et D. Iuni Iuvenalis saturae, ed. W. V. Clausen (Oxford, 1959).
  Scholia in Juvenalem uetustiora, ed. P. Wessner (Teubner, 1931).
Juvencus
  Euangeliorum libri IV, ed. J. Huemer (*CSEL* 24, 1891).

LACTANTIUS
Diuinae institutiones, ed. S. Brandt and G. Laubmann (*CSEL* 19, 1890).
De mortibus persecutorum, ed. S. Brandt and G. Laubmann (*CSEL* 27, 1897).
Liber pontificalis
Texte, introduction et commentaire par l'Abbé L. Duchesne (Bibl. des écoles françaises d'Athènes et de Rome, tome 1, 1886, tome 2, 1892)
LUCAN
Bellum Ciuile, ed. A. E. Housman (London, 1926).
La Guerre Civile; la Pharsale, texte établi et traduit par A. Bourgery et M. Ponchont, 2 vols. (Budé, 1926–9).
Also ed. C. Hosius (Teubner, 1913), and A. E. Housman (Oxford, 1926).
LUCIAN
Luciani opera, ed. M. D. Macleod, 4 vols. (Oxford, 1972–87).
JOHN LYDUS
De magistratibus populi romani libri tres, ed. R. Wuensch (Teubner, 1903).
MACARIUS
Epistola sancti Macarii monachi ad filios, ed. D. A. Wilmart, *Rev. d'ascétique et de mystique* 1 (1920).
MACROBIUS
Saturnalia and *Commentarium in Somnium Scipionis*, ed. J. Willis, 2 vols. (Teubner, 1963 and 1970).
MARIUS VICTORINUS
Aduersus Arium, ed. P. Henry and P. Hadot (*CSEL* 83, 1971).
MARTIAL
M. Valerii Martialis epigrammaton libri, ed. W. Heraeus (Teubner, 1976).
Martyrologium hieronymianum, ed. G. B. de Rossi and L. Duchesne (*AASS* Nov. 2. 1, 1894, xlviii–l).
MINUCIUS FELIX
Octavius, ed. C. Halm (*CSEL* 2, 1867).
Notitia Dignitatum, ed. O. Seeck (Berlin, 1867).
ORIGEN
Homilies on Jeremiah and Ezekiel, PG 25.
OROSIUS
Historiae aduersus paganos, ed. C. Zangemeister (*CSEL* 5, 1882).
OVID
Metamorphoses, ed. W. S. Anderson (Teubner, 1977).
Fasti, ed. E. H. Alton, D. E. W. Wormell, and E. Courtney (Teubner, 1978).

PACATUS
   Panégyriques latins, ed. É. Gallétier, 3 (Budé, 1955).
PALLADIUS
   Historia Lausiaca, ed. C. Butler (Texts and Studies 6, 1898–1904).
PAULINUS OF MILAN
   Life of St. Ambrose by Paulinus of Milan, ed. M. Pellegrino, *Verba Seniorum*, NS 1 (1961).
PAULINUS OF NOLA
   Carmina and *Epistulae*, ed. G. de Hartel (*CSEL* 29–30, 1894).
PLAUTUS
   T. Macci Plauti comoediae, ed. W. M. Lindsay, 2 vols. (Oxford, 1904).
PLINY THE ELDER
   Naturalis historia, ed. L. Ian and C. Mayhoff, 2 vols. (Teubner, 1967).
PLINY THE YOUNGER
   Epistles, ed. R. A. B. Mynors (Oxford, 1963).
PROPERTIUS
   Sexti Properti carmina, ed. E. A. Barber (Oxford, 1967).
PRUDENTIUS

Editions of the collected works:
F. Arévalo (Rome, 1788–9 = PL 59–60).
Th. Obbarius, *Aurelii Prudentii Clementis carmina* (Tübingen, 1845).
A. Dressel, *Aurelii Prudentii Clementis quae extant carmina* (Leipzig, 1860).
J. Bergman, *Aurelii Prudentii Clementis carmina* (*CSEL* 61, 1926).
M. Lavarenne, *Prudence* (Collection Budé, Paris): vol. i, Cathemerinon liber, 1955); vol. ii, Apotheosis, Hamartigenia (1961); vol. iii, Psychomachia, Contra Symmachum (1963*a*); vol. iv, Peristephanon liber, Dittochaeon, Epilogus (1963*b*).
H. J. Thomson (ed., trans.), *Prudentius* (Loeb Classical Library): vol. i, *Praefatio, Liber cathemerinon, Apotheosis, Hamartigenia, Psychomachia, Contra orationem Symmachi liber I* (1949); vol. ii, *Contra orationem Symmachi liber II, Peristephanon liber, Tituli historiarum, Epilogus* (1953).
J. Guillén (ed. trans.) and I. de Rodríguez (comm.), *Obras completas de Aurelio Prudencio* (Madrid, 1950).
M. P. Cunningham, *Aurelii Prudentii Clementis carmina* (*CCL* 126, 1966).

Separate Texts of the *Peristephanon*:
F. Ermini, *Peristephanon. Studi Prudenziani* (Rome, 1914).
C. Marchesi (trans., comm.), *Le Corone di Prudenzio* (Rome, 1917).
M. Bayo, *Himnos a los mártires* (Madrid, 1946).
V. Paronetto, *Le Corone, inni scelte e commentati* (Turin, 1957).
Querolus,
   Querolus siue Aulularia incerti auctoris comoedia, ed. G. Ranstrand (Göteborg, 1951).

RUFINUS
Historia ecclesiastica, ed. Th. Mommsen (*GCS*, 1908). Also in *PL* 21.
SENECA THE ELDER
Controuersiae, ed. A. Kießling (Teubner, 1872).
SENECA THE YOUNGER
Ad Marciam de consolatione, in L. *Annaei Senecae dialogorum libros XII*,
    ed. E. Hermes (Teubner, 1905) 150–94.
Tragoediae ed. R. Peiper and G. Richter (Teubner, 1902).
SEPTIMIUS SERENUS
    Ed. A. Baehrens, *Fragmenta Poetarum Latinorum* (Leipzig, 1866).
SIDONIUS APOLLINARIS
Poems and Letters 1 and 2. Text and trans. by W. B. Anderson (Loeb,
    · 1936).
SILIUS ITALICUS
Punica, ed. L. Bauer, 2 vols (Teubner, 1890–2).
SIRICIUS
Epistulae, *PL* 13. 1131–96.
SOCRATES
Historia ecclesiastica, ed. R. Hussey (1853). Also in *PG* 67.
SOLINUS
C. *Iulii Solini collectanea rerum memorabilium*, ed. Th. Mommsen
    (Berlin, 1895).
SOPHOCLES
Antigone, ed. A. C. Pearson (Oxford, 1924).
SOZOMEN
Historia ecclesiastica, ed. J. Bidez and G. C. Hansen (*GCS*, 1960). Also
    PG 67.
STATIUS
Silvae, ed. A. Marastoni (Teubner, 1970).
Thebais, ed. A. Klotz (Teubner, 1973).
SULPICIUS SEVERUS
Sulpice Sévère: Vie de saint Martin, texte et traduction, J. Fontaine,
    3 vols. (*SC* 133–5, 1967–9).
SYMMACHUS
Q. *Aurelii Symmachi quae supersunt*, ed. O. Seeck (*MGH Auct. Ant.* 6.
    1, 1883).
TERTULLIAN
Apologeticum, ed. H. Hoppe (*CSEL* 69, 1939).
De praescriptione haereticorum, ed. R. F. Refoule, trad. P. de Labriolle
    (*SC* 46, 1957).
De baptismo, ed. R. F. Refoule (*SC* 35, 1952).
De anima, ed. J. H. Waszink (1947).
Aduersus Gnosticos Scorpiace, *PL* 2. 121–54.

THEMISTIUS
   Orationes, ed. G. Downey, 3 vols. (Teubner, 1965–74).
THEODORET
   Historia ecclesiastica, ed. L. Parmentier and F. Scheidweiler (*GCS* 1954).
VALERIUS FLACCUS
   Argonauticon libri octo, ed. E. Courtney (Teubner, 1970).
VARRO
   Res rusticae, ed. G. Goetz (Teubner, 1912).
VENANTIUS FORTUNATUS
   Carmina, ed. F. Leo (*MGH Auct. Ant.* 4. 1, 1881).
VIRGIL
   P. Vergili Maronis Opera, ed. R. A. B. Mynors (Oxford, 1969).
   Virgil. The Eclogues and Georgics, ed. R. D. Williams (New York, 1979).
Vitae sanctorum patrum Emeritensium, ed. J. N. Garvin (1946).
ZOSIMUS
   Historia nova, ed. F. Paschoud, 4 vols. (Budé, 1971, 1979, and 1986). Vol. 3. 2 has not yet appeared.

MODERN WORKS

AIGRAIN, R. (1931), *La Musique religieuse* (1929), trans. C. Mulcahy (London).
—— (1953), *L'Hagiographie: Ses sources, ses méthodes, son histoire* (Paris).
ÁLAMO, M. DEL (1939), 'Un texte du poète Prudence "Ad Valerianum episcopum" (Peristephanon Hymn XI)', *RHE* 35: 750–6.
ALEXANDER, F. (1936), 'Beziehungen des Prudentius zu Ovid', *WS* 54: 166–73.
ALFONSI, L. (1959), 'Sulla "militia" di Prudenzio', *VChr* 13: 181–3.
ALLARD, P. (1884), 'Prudence historien', *RQH* 35: 345–85.
—— (1885), 'L'Hagiographie au IVe siècle· Martyres de saint Hippolyte, saint Laurent, sainte Agnès, saint Cassien, après les poèmes de Prudence', *RQH* 37: 353–405.
—— (1907), 'Agnes (Sainte)', *DACL* 11: 905–18.
ALTANER, B. (1958), *Patrologie: Leben, Schriften und Lehre der Kirchenväter* (Freiburg im Breisgau; 8th edn. by A. Stuiber, 1978).
AMORE, A. (1949), 'Cassiano d'Imola, santo', *EC* 3: 1004.
—— (1953), 'Romano, santo, martire', *EC* 10: 1310.
—— (1954), 'Note su Ippolito martire', *RAC* 30: 63–97.
—— (1964), 'Emeterio e Chelidonio, santi, martiri di Calahorra', *BSS* 4: 1195–7.
ANGLÈS, H. (1969), 'Latin Chant before St. Gregory', *NOHM* 2, 58–91.
ARÉVALO, F. (1788–9), Prudentius edn., see Principal Ancient Sources.

ARGENIO, R. (1965), 'Il III inno delle "corone" di Prudenzio in onore della martire Eulalia', *RSC* 37: 141–5.

——(1967), 'Prudenzio a Roma visita le basiliche di S. Pietro e S. Paulo', *RSC* 39: 170–5.

ARMSTRONG, H. H. (1901), 'Autobiographical Elements in Latin Inscriptions', *University of Michigan Studies, Latin Philology* 3.

ASSENDELFT, M. M. VAN (1976), *Sol Ecce Surgit Igneus. A Commentary on the Morning and Evening Hymns of Prudentius (Cath. 1, 2, 5 and 6)* (Groningen).

AUER, J. (1980), 'Militia Christi', *Dictionnaire de Spiritualité* 10: 1210–33.

AUERBACH, E. (1953), *Mimesis. The Representation of Reality in Western Literature*, trans. W. R. Trask (Princeton).

——(1965), *Literary Language and its Public in Late Latin Antiquity and in the Middle Ages*, trans. R. Manheim (London).

AUSTIN, R. G. (1955), *P. Vergilii Maronis Aeneidos Liber Quartus* (Oxford).

——(1977), *P. Vergilii Maronis Aeneidos Liber Sextus* (Oxford).

AVENARY, H. (1953), 'Formal Structure of Psalms and Canticles in Early Jewish and Christian Chant', *Musica Disciplina* 7: 1–13.

BAEHRENS, E. (1866), Septimius Serenus edn., see Principal Ancient Sources.

BALDWIN, C. S. (1925), 'St. Augustine and the Rhetoric of Cicero', *PCA* 22: 24–46.

BARB, A. A. (1963), 'The Survival of Magic Arts', in Momigliano (1963a), 100–25.

BARBIERI, G. (1954), 'Mario Massimo', *RFIC*, NS 32: 36–66, 262–76.

BARDENHEWER, O. (1923), *Geschichte der altkirchlichen Literatur* (Freiburg i.B.).

BARDY, G. (1936), 'Faux et fraudes littéraires dans l'antiquité chrétienne', *RHE* 32: 5–23, 275–302.

——(1949), 'Pèlerinage à Rome vers la fin du IVe siècle', *AB* 67: 224–35.

BARNES, T. D. (1968), 'Pre-Decian Acta Martyrum', *JThS* 19: 509–31.

——(1976), 'The Historical Setting of Prudentius' "Contra Symmachum"', *AJPh* 97: 373–86.

——(1981), *Constantine and Eusebius* (Cambridge, Mass.).

BARRY, M. I., and McGUIRE, M. R. P. (1968), *A Concordance of Ovid* (Washington).

——, and CAMPBELL, J. M. (1966), *A Concordance of Prudentius* (Hildesheim).

——, and EAGAN, M. C. (1943), *A Concordance of Statius* (Michigan).

——, and FANNING, M. W (1940), *A Concordance of Lucan* (Washington).

BARSBY, J. (1978), *Ovid* (Oxford).

BARTALUCCI, A. (1973), 'Il "Probus" di Giorgio Valla e il "Commentum Vetustum" a Giovenale', *SIFC* 45: 233–75.

BARTELINK, G. J. M. (1986), *Het Vroege Christendom en de Antieke Cultuur* (Muiderberg).

BATLLE, HUGUET (1937–40), 'Fragmentos de sarcófagos paleocristianos inéditos en Tarragona', *AST* 13: 61–4.

BAUMSTARK, A. (1914), 'Hymns (Greek and Christian)', in *Encyclopedia of Religion and Ethics*, ed. J. Hastings, vol. 8: 5–12 (Edinburgh).

BAYO, M. J. (1946), Prudentius (Peristephanon) edn., see Principal Ancient Sources.

BEARE, W. (1957), *Latin Verse and European Song. A Study in Accent and Rhythm* (London).

BERGMAN, J. (1908), *De codicum Prudentianorum generibus et virtute*, (*SAWW* 157, 5, Vienna).

—— (1912), 'Emendationes Prudentianae', *Eranos* 12: 111–49.

—— (1921), 'Aurelius Prudentius Clemens, der größte christliche Dichter des Altertums. Beiträge zur Erforschung der spätlateinischen Literatur I: Eine Einführung in den heutigen Stand der Prudentius-forschung und eine Studie über die Hymnensammlung "Die Stunden des Tages"', *AUD* 13: Humaniora II 1).

—— (1926), Prudentius edn., see Principal Ancient Sources.

BIRLEY, A. (1967), 'The Augustan History', in Dorey (1967), 113–38.

BIRT, TH. (1882), *Das antike Buchwesen in seinem Verhältnis zur Literatur* (Berlin).

BLOCKLEY, R. C. (1975), *Ammianus Marcellinus; A Study of his Historio-graphy and Political Thought* (*Coll. Latomus* 141, Brussels).

BLUME, CL. and DREVES, G. M. (1897), 'Hymnodia Gotica. Die mozara-bischen Hymnen des altspanischen Ritus', *Analecta Hymnica Medii Aevi* 27 (Leipzig).

—— (1909), *Ein Jahrtausend lateinischer Hymnendichtung. Eine blütenlese aus den Analecta Hymnica*, 2 vols. (Leipzig).

BO, D. (1965), *Lexikon Horatianum*, 2 vols. (Hildesheim).

BOLCHAZY, L. J., SWEENEY, J. A. M., and ANTONETTI, M. G. (1982), *Concordantia in Ausonium* (Hildesheim–New York).

BÖMER, F. (1957–8), *Ovidius Naso. Die Fasten* (Heidelberg).

BONNER, S. F. (1966), 'Lucan and the Declamation Schools', *AJPh* 87: 257–89.

BOVINI, G. (1950), *Monumenti figurati paleocristiani conservati a Firenze nella racolte publiche e negli edifici di culto* (Pontifico Istituto di Archeo-logia cristiana 2. 6, Rome).

BOURGERY, A., and PONCHONT, M. (1926–9), Lucan edn., see Principal Ancient Sources.

BOWRA, M. (1964), *Pindar* (Oxford).

BRAKMAN, C. (1919–20), 'Quae ratio intercedat inter Lucretium et Prudentium', *Mnemosyne* NS 47–8: 434–8.

BREIDT, H. (1887), 'De Aurelio Prudentio Clemente Horatii Imitatore' (diss. Heidelberg).

BRITTAIN, F. (1951), *The Mediaeval Latin and Romance Lyric to A.D. 1300* (Cambridge).

BROCKHAUS, CL. (1872), *Aurelius Prudentius Clemens in seiner Bedeutung für die Kirche seiner Zeit. Nebst einem Anhang: Übersetzung des Gedichtes "Apotheosis"* (Leipzig).

BROOKS, E. W. (1903), *The Sixth Book of the Select Letters of Severus, Patriarch of Antioch, in the Syriac Version of Athanasius of Nisibis*, 2 (London).

BROWN, P. R. L. (1967), *Augustine of Hippo. A Biography* (London).

—— (1972), 'Sorcery, Demons and the Rise of Christianity from Late Antiquity into the Middle Ages', in *Religion and Society in the Age of St. Augustine* (Berkeley) 119–46.

—— (1981), *The Cult of Saints* (Chicago).

BROŽEK, M. (1954), 'De Prudentio—Pindaro Latino I', *EOS* 47: 107–41.

—— (1957–8*a*), 'De Prudentio—Pindaro Latino II', *EOS* 49: 123–50.

—— (1957–8*b*), 'De Prudentii epilogo mutilo', *EOS* 49: 151–4.

—— (1967–8), 'Ad Prudentii praefationem interpretandum', *EOS* 57: 149–56.

—— (1970), 'De Prudentii praefatione carminibus praefixa', in *Forschungen zur römischen Literatur. Festschrift zum 60. Geburtstag von Karl Büchner*, ed. W. Wimmel (Wiesbaden) 31–6.

BRUNT, P. A., and MOORE, J. M. (1975), *Res Gestae Divi Augusti. The Achievements of the Divine Augustus* (London).

BRUYNE, D. de (1913), 'De l'origine de quelques textes liturgiques mozarabes', *R Ben* 30: 423–36.

—— (1922), 'Un système de lectures de la liturgie mozarabe', *R Ben* 34: 147–55.

BRYS, J. B. (1855), *Dissertatio de vita et scriptis Aurelii Clementis Prudentii* (Louvain).

BUCHHEIT, V. (1966), 'Christliche Romideologie im Laurentius-Hymnus des Prudentius', in *Polychronion. Festschrift für Franz Dölger zum 75. Geburtstag*, ed. P. Wirth (Heidelberg) 121–44.

BURN, A. E. (1926), *The Hymn Te Deum and its Author* (London).

BUSA, S. J., and ZAMPOLLI, A. (1975), *Concordantiae Senecanae*, 2 vols. (Hildesheim–New York).

CABROL, F. (1910), 'Cantiques' and 'Cantiques évangéliques', *DACL* 2. 2: 1975–99.

—— (1935), art. 'Mozarabe (la liturgie)' *DACL* 12. 1: 390–441.

CAGIN, P. (1906), '*Te Deum* ou *Illatio?*', *Scriptorium Solesmense* I. I (Abbaye de Solesmes).

CAIRNS, F. (1971), 'Five "Religious" Odes of Horace (I.10; I.21 and IV.6; I.30; I.15)', *AJPh* 92: 433–52.

—— (1979), *Tibullus: A Hellenistic Poet at Rome* (Cambridge).

CAMERON, ALAN (1964*a*), 'Literary Allusions in the *Historia Augusta*', *Hermes* 92: 363–77.

—— (1964*b*), 'The Roman friends of Ammianus Marcellinus', *JRS* 54: 15–28.

—— (1968*a*), 'Theodosius the Great and the Regency of Stilicho', *HSPh* 73: 247–80.

—— (1968*b*), 'Celestial Consulates. A Note on the Pelagian Letter *Humanae referunt*', *JThS*, NS 19: 213–15.

—— (1970), *Claudian: Poetry and Propaganda at the Court of Honorius* (Oxford).

CAMPS, W. (1965), *Propertius. Elegies, Book IV* (Cambridge).

—— (1969), *An Introduction to the Aeneid* (London).

CARLETTI, S. (1966), 'Lorenzo', *BSS* 8: 108–21.

CATTALANO, M. (1952), 'L'Eroe nel mondo classico e nel mondo cristiano con particolare riguardo all'eroe cristiano in Prudenzio', *RSC* 1: 5–23.

CHADWICK, H. (1957), 'St. Peter and St. Paul in Rome: The Problem of the *Memoria Apostolorum ad Catacumbas*', *JThS*, NS 8: 31–52.

—— (1982), 'Pope Damasus and the Peculiar Claim of Rome to St. Peter and St. Paul', in *History and Thought of the Early Church* (London) 313–18.

—— (1967), *The Early Church* (Pelican History of the Church 1, London).

CHADWICK, N. (1955), *Poetry and Letters in Early Christian Gaul* (London).

CHARLET, J.-L. (1975), 'Prudence lecteur de Paulin de Nole. À propos du 23ᵉ quatrain du Dittochaeon', *REAug* 21: 55–62.

—— (1980*a*), *L'Influence d'Ausone sur la poésie de Prudence* (Aix-en-Provence).

—— (1980*b*), 'L'Apport de la poésie latine chrétienne à la mutation de l'épopée antique: Prudence précurseur de l'épopée médiévale', *BAGB* 1980: 207–17.

—— (1982), *La Création poétique dans le Cathémérinon de Prudence* (Paris).

CHASTAGNOL, A. (1965), 'Les Espagnols dans l'aristocratie gouvernmentale à l'époque de Thédose', in *Les Empereurs romains d'Espagne* (Colloque de Madrid–Italica 1964, Paris) 269–92.

—— (1966), 'Sur quelques documents relatifs à la basilique de Saint-Paul-hors-les-murs', in *Mélanges d'archéologie et d'histoire offerts à André Piganiol*, ed. R. Chevallier (Paris) 1, 421–37.

CHAVANNE, P. (1899), 'Le Patriotisme de Prudence', *RHLR* 4: 332–52, 385–413.

CIRAC, E. S. (1951), *Los nuevos argumentos sobre la patria de Prudencio* (Saragossa).

CLARKE, A. K. (1950–1), 'Claudian's Methods of Borrowing in *"De Raptu Proserpinae"'*, *PCPhS* 181: 4–7.

—— (1968), 'Claudian and the Augustinian Circle of Milan', in *Strenas Augustinianas V. Capanaga oblatas* 2 (Madrid) 125–33.

CLARKE, M. L. (1953), *Rhetoric at Rome* (London).

COCHRANE, C. N. (1944), *Christianity and Classical Culture. A Study of Thought and Action from Augustus to Augustine* (London–New York–Toronto).

COMPARETTI, D. (1966), *Virgil in the Middle Ages*, trans. E. F. M. Benecke (London).

CONNELLY, J. (1954), *Hymns of the Roman Liturgy* (London).

COPLEY, F. O. (1972), 'Catullus C.4: the World of the Poem', in Quinn (1972) 9–13.

COSTA, C. D. N. (1974), 'Seneca: the Tragedies', in *Seneca*, ed. C. D. N. Costa (London) 96–115.

COURCELLE, P. (1946), 'Commodien et les invasions du ve siècle', *REL* 24, 227–46.

—— (1950), *Recherches sur les Confessions de S. Augustin* (Paris).

—— (1957), 'Les Exégèses chrétiennes de la quatrième Églogue', *REA* 59: 294–319.

—— (1963), *Les Confessions de St. Augustin dans la tradition littéraire* (Paris).

—— (1969), *Late Latin Writers and their Greek Sources*, trans. H. E. Wedeck (Cambridge, Mass.).

—— (1976), 'Les Lecteurs de l'Énéide devant les grandes invasions germaniques', *Rom Barb* 1: 25–56.

CRACCO RUGGINI, L. (1977), 'The Ecclesiastical Histories and Pagan Historiography: Providence and Miracles', *Athenaeum*, NS 55: 107–26.

—— (1979), *Il paganesimo romano tra religione e politica (384–394 d.C.): per una reinterpretazione del 'Carmen contra paganos'* (MAL 23. 1, Rome).

CUNNINGHAM, M. P. (1955), 'The Place of the Hymns of St. Ambrose in the Latin Poetic Tradition', *SPh* 52: 509–14.

—— (1958), 'Some Facts about the Puteanus MS', *TAPhA* 89: 32–7.

—— (1963), 'The Nature and Purpose of the *Peristephanon*', *SEJG* 14: 40–5.

—— (1966*a*), Prudentius edn., see Principal Ancient Sources.

—— (1966*b*), review of Thraede (1965), *CW* 60: 76–7.

—— (1976), 'The Contexts of Prudentius' Poems', *CPh* 71: 56–66.

CURTIUS, E. R. (1979), *European Literature and the Latin Middle Ages*, trans. W. R. Trask (London).

DALTON, O. M. (1901), 'The Gilded Glasses of the Catacombs', *AJ* 58: 223–53.

DARRE, H. (1968), 'De l'usage des hymnes dans l'église des origines à Saint Grégoire le Grand', *EGr* 9: 25–36.

DAUTREMER, L. (1899), *Ammien Marcellin* (Lille).

DEFERRARI, R. J. (1927), 'Early Ecclesiastical Literature and its Relation to the Literature of Classical and Mediaeval Times', *PhQ* 6: 102–10.

DEGRASSI, A. (1952), *I fasti consolari dell'impero romano dal 30 avanti Cristo al 613 dopo Cristo* (Rome).

DEICHGRÄBER, R. (1967), *Gotteshymnus und Christushymnus in der frühen Christenheit: Untersuchungen zu Form, Sprache und Stil der frühchristlichen Hymnen* (Göttingen).

DELEHAYE, H. (1907), 'Le Témoignage des martyrologies', *AB* 26: 78–99.

—— (1910), 'Les Premiers "Libelli Miraculorum"', *AB* 29: 427–34.

—— (1912), 'Le Calendrier lapidaire de Carmona', *AB* 31: 319–21.

—— (1914), 'Saint Alamachus ou Télémaque', *AB* 33: 421–8.

—— (1921), 'Cyprien d'Antioche et Cyprien de Carthage', *AB* 39: 314–32.

—— (1925), *Les Receuils antiques des miracles des saints* (Brussels).

—— (1927a), *Sanctus: le culte des saints dans l'antiquité* (Brussels).

—— (1927b), *Les Légendes hagiographiques* (Brussels).

—— (1930), 'Loca Sanctorum, *AB* 48: 5–64.

—— (1931), *Commentarius perpetuus in Martyrologium hieronymianum* (*AASS*, Nov. 2. 2).

—— (1932), 'S. Romain, martyr d'Antioche', *AB* 50: 241–83.

—— (1933a), 'Recherches sur le légendier romain', *AB* 51: 34–98.

—— (1933b), *Les Origines du culte des martyrs* (Brussels).

—— (1934), 'Cinq leçons sur la méthode hagiographique' (Brussels) 5–147.

—— (1966), *Les Passions des martyrs et les genres littéraires* (Brussels).

——, and BARTOLOZZI, A. (1933), *Le due omilie crisostomaniane sul martire S. Romano. Studi dedicati alla memoria di Paulo Ubaldi* (Rome).

DEXEL, F. (1907), 'Des Prudentius Verhältnis zu Vergil' (diss. Erlangen).

DIBELIUS, M. (1956), 'The Speeches in the Acts and Ancient Historiography', in *Studies in the Acts of the Apostles*, ed. H. Greeven, trans. M. Ling (London), 138–85.

DILKE, O. A. W. (1963), 'Magnus Achilles and Statian Baroque', *Latomus* 22: 498–503.

DODDS, E. R. (1947), 'Theurgy and its Relation to Neoplatonism', *JRS* 37: 55–69.

——(1985), *The Ancient Concept of Progress* (Oxford).
DÖPP, S. (1968), 'Virgilischer Einfluß im Werk Ovids' (diss. Munich).
DOREY, T. A. (ed.) (1966), *Roman Historians* (London).
——(1967), *Latin Biography* (London).
DRESSEL, A. (1860), Prudentius edn., see Principal Ancient Sources.
DREVES, G. M. (1893), *Aurelius Ambrosius 'der Vater des Kirchengesanges'* (Freiburg i.B.).
DUCHESNE, L. (1886), *Liber Pontificalis*, see Principal Ancient Sources.
——(1907), *Fastes épiscopaux de l'ancienne Gaule* (Paris).
DUFF, J. D. (ed.) (1970), *Juvenal's Satires* (Cambridge).
DUFOURCQ, A. (1907), *Les Gesta martyrum romains* (Paris).
DUNCAN, T. S. (1914), 'The Influence of Art on Description in the Poetry of P. Papinius Statius' (diss. Baltimore).
DU QUESNAY, I. M. (1979), 'From Polyphemus to Corydon. Virgil Eclogue 2 and the Idylls of Theocritus', in West and Woodman (1979) 35–69.
DZIATZKO, C. (1897), 'Buch', *RE* 3. 1: 939–71.
EBERT, A. (1889), *Allgemeine Geschichte der Literatur des Mittelalters im Abendlande bis zum Beginne des XI. Jahrhunderts* (Leipzig).
EDDEN, V. (1974), 'Prudentius' in *Latin Literature of the Fourth Century*, ed. J. W. Binns (London) 160–82.
EMMINGHAUS, J. H. (1962), 'Die Taufanlage *ad sellam Petri Confessionis*', *RQA* 57: 79–103.
ENGEMANN, J. (1974), 'Zu den Apsis-Tituli des Paulinus von Nola', *JAC* 17: 21–46.
ENK, P. J. (1962), *Propertii Elegiarum I* (Leiden).
ENSSLIN, W. (1929), 'Spectabilis', *RE* 3A. 1: 1552–68.
——(1953), 'War Kaiser Theodosius I. zweimal in Rom?', *Hermes* 81: 500–7.
——(1956), 'Praeses', *RE* Suppl. 8: 598–614.
ERMINI, F. (1909), *Il centone di Proba e la poesia centonaria latina* (Rome).
——(1914), Prudentius edn., see Principal Ancient Sources.
FABRE, P. (1948), *Essaie sur la chronologie de l'œuvre de Saint Paulin de Nole* (Strasbourg).
——(1949), *Saint Paulin de Nole et l'amitié chrétienne* (Paris).
FAGUET, E. (1883), 'De A. Prudentii Clementis carminibus lyricis' (diss. Paris).
FAVEZ, C. (1930), 'L'Inspiration chrétienne dans les "Consolations" de S. Ambroise', *REL* 8: 82–91.
——(1937), *La Consolation Latine chrétienne* (Paris).
FEDER, A. J. (1916), Hilary of Poitiers, edn., see Principal Ancient Sources.
FERNÁNDEZ, ALONSO, J. (1964), 'Fruttuoso, Vescovo di Tarragona, Augurio e Eulogio, Diaconi, Santi, Martiri', *BSS* 5: 1296–7.

Férotin, M. (1904), *Le Liber Ordinum en usage dans l'église wisigothique et mozarabe d'Espagne du cinquième au onzième siècle* (Paris).

—— (1912), *Le Liber Mozarabicus Sacramentorum et les manuscrits mozarabes*, (Paris).

Ferrua, A. (1942), Damasus edn., see Principal Ancient Sources.

Flórez, E. (1754), *España Sagrada* I (Madrid).

—— (1757–75), *Medallasde las colonias, municipios y pueblos antiguos de España* (Madrid).

Fontaine, J. (1964*a*), 'Démons et sibylles: la peinture des possédés dans la poésie de Prudence', in *Hommage à Jean Bayet* (*Coll. Latomus* 70, Brussels) 196–213.

—— (1964*b*), 'Le Pèlerinage de Prudence à St. Pierre et la spiritualité des Eaux Vives', *Orpheus* 11: 99–122.

—— (1965), 'Les Chrétiens et le service militaire dans l'Antiquité', *Concilium* 2: 95–105.

—— (1967–9), Sulpicius Severus edn., see Principal Ancient Sources.

—— (1970), 'La Femme dans la poésie de Prudence', *REL* 47 bis (Mél. Durry): 55–83.

—— (1972), 'Valeurs antiques et valeurs chrétiennes dans la spiritualité des grands propriétaires à la fin du IVe siècle occidental', in *Epektasis. Mélanges J. Daniélou* (Paris) 571–95.

—— (1974*a*), 'L'Apport de la tradition poétique romaine à la formation de l'hymnodie latine chrétienne', *REL* 52: 318–55.

—— (1974*b*), 'Société et culture chrétiennes sur l'aire circumpyrénéenne au siècle de Théodose', *BLE* 75: 241–82.

—— (1975*a*), 'Le Mélange des genres dans la poésie de Prudence', in *Forma Futuri. Studi in onore di M. Pellegrino* (Turin) 755–77.

—— (1975*b*), 'Une province inconnue de la littérature chrétienne de l'Espagne: la latinité mozarabe', *REL* 53: 24–6.

—— (1976*a*), 'Unité et diversité du mélange des genres et des tons chez quelques écrivains latins de la fin du IVe siècle. "Ausone, Ambroise, Ammien"', *Entretiens Fondation Hardt* 23, 425–82.

—— (1976*b*), 'Prose et poésie: l'interférence des genres et des styles dans la création littéraire d'Ambroise de Milan', in *Ambrosius Episcopus*, ed. G. Lazzati (Milan) 1, 124–70.

—— (1980), 'Le Culte des martyrs militaires et son expression poétique au IVe siècle: l'idéal évangélique de la non-violence dans le christianisme théodosien', *Ecclesia Orans. Mélanges A. G. Hamman* (*Augustinianum* 20), 141–71.

—— (1981), *La Naissance de la poésie dans l'occident chrétien, esquisse d'une histoire de la poésie latine chrétienne du IIIe au VIe siècle* (Paris).

Fordyce, C. J. (1973), *Catullus. A Commentary* (Oxford).

Fraenkel, E. (1957), *Horace* (Oxford).

—— (1964), 'Lucan als Mittler des antiken Pathos', in *Kleine Beiträge zur klassischen Philologie* 2 (Rome) 233–66.

FRANCHI DE' CAVALIERI, P. (1902), 'I martiri della Massa Candida', *Nuove note agiografiche (Studi e Testi* 9) 39–51.

—— (1908), 'Intorno ad alcune reminiscenze classiche nelle leggende agiografiche del secolo IV', *Hagiographica* (Studi e Testi 19) 123–64.

—— (1920), 'Un Recente Studio sul Luogo del Martirio di S. Sisto II', *Note agiografiche* 4 (Studi e Testi 33) 151–2.

—— (1935*a*), 'A proposito della Passio S. Vincentii Levitae', *Note agiografiche* 8 *(Studi e Testi* 65) 117–25.

—— (1935*b*), 'Gli Atti di S. Fruttuoso di Tarragona', *Note agiografiche* 8 (Studi e Testi 65) 129–99.

—— (1962*a*), 'Sant'Agnese nella tradizione e nella leggenda', *Scritti Agiografici* 1 (1893–1900) (Studi e Testi 221) 293–317.

—— (1962*b*), 'S. Lorenzo e il supplicio della graticola', *Scritti Agiografici 1* (1893–1900) (Studi e Testi 221) 383–99.

—— (1962*c*), 'Santa Agnese', *Scritti Agiografici* 2 (1900–46) (Studi e Testi 222) 337–40.

FREDERIKSEN, P. (1986), 'Paul and Augustine: Conversion Narratives, Orthodox Traditions and the Retrospective Self', *JThS*, NS 37: 3–34.

FREND, W. H. C. (1965), *Martyrdom and Persecution in the Early Church: A Study of Conflict from the Maccabees to Donatus* (Oxford).

FROEBEL, F. (1911), 'Quid veteres de Horatii poematis iudicaverunt' (diss. Jena).

FRUTAZ, A. P. (1948), 'Agnese, santa, martire', *EC* 1: 467–74.

—— (1951), 'Ippolito di Roma, santo martire', *EC* 7: 1538–45.

GAIFFIER, B. de (1937), 'Les Notices hispaniques dans le martyrologe d'Usuard', *AB* 55: 268–83.

—— (1948), 'Hagiographie hispanique', *AB* 66: 289–318.

—— (1949), 'Sermons latins en l'honneur de S. Vincent antérieurs au xe siècle', *AB* 67: 267–86.

—— (1952), 'La Passion de S. Vincent d'Agen', *AB* 70: 160–81.

—— (1954*a*), 'La Lecture des actes des martyrs dans la prière liturgique en occident. A propos du passionaire hispanique', *AB* 72: 134–66.

—— (1954*b*), '*Sub Daciano Praeside*. Étude de quelques passions espagnols', *AB* 72: 378–96.

—— (1967), 'Hagiographie et son public au xie siècle', in *Études critiques d'hagiographie et d'iconologie* (Brussels) 475–00.

—— (1969), 'La Lecture des Passions des martyrs à Rome avant le ixe siècle', *AB* 87: 63–78.

GALINSKY, G. K. (1969), *Aeneas, Sicily and Rome* (Princeton).

GALLÉTIER, E. (1949), Eumenius edn., see Principal Ancient Sources.

—— (1955), Pacatus edn., see Principal Ancient Sources.

GARCÍA RODRÍGUEZ, C. (1966), *El culto de los santos en la España romana y visigoda* (Madrid).

GIANNARELLI, E. (1980), *La tipologia femminile nella biografia e nell' autobiografia cristiana del IVe secolo* (Istituto Storico Italiano per il Medio Evo. Studi Storici 127, Rome).

GIBBON, E. (1909–14), *The History of the Decline and Fall of the Roman Empire*, ed. J. B. Bury (London).

GNILKA, Ch. (1972), *Aetas Spiritalis: die Überwindung der natürlichen Altersstufen als Ideal frühchristlichen Lebens* (Theophaneia 24, Bonn).

GOLDSCHMIDT, R. C. (1940), *Paulinus' Churches at Nola. Texts, Translations and Commentary* (Amsterdam).

GORDINI, G. D. (1963), 'Cassiano d'Imola, santo, martire', *BSS* 3: 909–12.

GOTOFF, H. C. (1971), *The Transmission of the Text of Lucan in the Ninth Century* (Cambridge, Mass.).

GRABAR, A. (1945–6), *Martyrium: Recherche sur le culte des reliques et de l'art chrétien antique*, 2 vols. (Paris).

—— (1969), *Christian Iconography: A Study of its Origins* (London).

GRANSDEN, K. W. (1976), *Virgil, Aeneid Book VIII* (Cambridge).

GRANT, R. M. (1952), *Miracle and Natural Law in Graeco-Roman and Early Christian Thought* (Amsterdam).

—— (1977), 'The Ecclesiastical History and Pagan Historiography, Providence and Miracles', *Athenaeum*, NS 55: 107–26.

—— (1980), *Eusebius as Church Historian* (Oxford).

GREEN, R. P. H. (1977), 'Ausonius' Use of the Classical Poets; Some New Examples and Observations', *CQ*, NS 28: 441–52.

GRIMAL, P. (1959), *Pius Aeneas: A Lecture Delivered to the Virgil Society* (London).

GUDEMAN, A. (1894), 'Literary Frauds Among the Romans', *TAPhA* 25: 140–64.

GUILLÉN, J., and RODRIGUEZ, I. de (1950), Prudentius edn., Principal Ancient Sources.

GWYNN GRIFFITHS, J. (1975), *Apuleius: the Isis Book. Metamorphoses, Book XI* (Leiden).

HAGENDAHL, H. (1958), *The Latin Fathers and the Classics* (Göteborg).

—— (1967), 'Augustine and the Latin Classics' (Göteborg).

HANLEY, S. M. (1959), 'The Classical Sources of Prudentius' (diss. Cornell Univ.).

—— (1962), 'Prudentius and Juvenal', *Phoenix* 16: 41–52.

HARNACK, A. VON (1905), *Militia Christi: Die christliche Religion und der Soldatenstand in den ersten drei Jahrhunderten* (Tübingen, repr. Darmstadt 1963).

HARRIES, J. (1984), 'Prudentius and Theodosius', *Latomus* 43: 69–84.

HARTEL, G. VON (1894), Paulinus of Nola edn., see Principal Ancient Sources.

HEFELE, C. J. (1907), *Histoire des Conciles* I (Paris).

HELGELAND, J. (1979), 'The Christians and the Roman Army from M. Aurelius to Constantine', *ANRW* 23. 1: 724–834.

HELM, R. (1956), Euselius and Jerome edn., see Principal Ancient Sources.

—— (1957), 'Propertius 2', *RE* 23. 1: 758–96.

HENKE, R. (1983), *Studien zum Romanushymnus des Prudentius* (Frankfurt am Main).

HENRIKSSON, K. E. (1956), *Griechische Büchertitel in der römischen Literatur* (Helsinki).

HERTER, H. (1931), 'Kallimachos 6', *RE* Suppl, 5: 386–452.

HIGHET, G. (1954), *Juvenal the Satirist* (Oxford).

HOEFER, O. (1895), *De Prudentii poetae Psychomachia et carminum chronologia* (Marburg).

HOMES DUDDEN, F. (1935), *The Life and Times of St. Ambrose*, 2 vols. (Oxford).

HOPKINS, M. K. (1961), 'Social Mobility in the Later Roman Empire: The Evidence of Ausonius', *CQ*, NS 11: 239–49.

HOSIUS, C. (1932), 'Zum Nachleben des Properz', *PhW* 35–8 (Festschrift Poland): 149–54.

HOUSMAN, A. E. (1926), Lucan edn., see Principal Ancient Sources.

HUBBARD, M. (1974), *Propertius* (London).

HÜBNER, E. (1897a), 'Caesaraugusta', *RE* 3. 1: 1287–8.

—— (1897b), 'Calagurris', *RE* 3. 1: 1327–8.

HUDSON-WILLIAMS, A. (1966), 'Virgil and the Christian Latin Poets', *PVS* 6: 11–21.

HULLEY, K. (1944), Principles of Textual Criticism in Jerome', *HSPh* 55: 108–9.

HUNT, E. D. (1982), *Holy Land Pilgrimage in the Later Roman Empire AD 312–460* (Oxford).

IHM, M. (1895), Damasus edn., see Principal Ancient Sources.

JAEGER, H. (1959), 'L'Examen de conscience dans les religions non-chrétiennes et avant le christianisme', *Numen* 6: 175–233.

JAMES, M. R. (1909–11), *A Descriptive Catalogue of the MSS. in the Library of Corpus Christi College Cambridge* (Cambridge).

JOSI, E. (1961), 'Agnese, santa martire di Roma', *BSS* 1: 382–407.

JUNOD-AMMERBAUER, H. (1975), 'Le Poète chrétien selon Paulin de Nole', *REAug* 21: 13–54.

KEENAN, M. (1940), 'The Terminology of Magic and Witchcraft in the Works of Augustine', *CPh* 35: 294–7.

KELLY, J. N. D. (1975), *Jerome, his Life, Writings and Controversies* (London).

KIESSLING, E. (1929), 'sphragis', *RE* 3A. 2: 1757–8.

KING, A. A. (1930), *Notes on the Catholic Liturgies* (London).

KLINGNER, F. (1930), review of Bergman (1926 edn.), *Gnomon* 6: 39–52.

——(1961), *Römische Geisteswelt* (Munich).

KRANZ, W. (1961), 'Sphragis, Ich-Form und Namensiegel als Eingangs-
und Schlußmotiv antiker Dichtung', *RhM* 104: 3–46.

KRAUS, W. (1942), 'Ovidius Naso 3', *RE* 18. 1: 1910–86.

KROLL, W. (1924), *Studien zum Verständnis der römischen Literatur* (Stutt-
gart).

KÜBLER, B. (1900), 'Consularis', *RE* 4. 1: 1138–42.

KURFESS, A. (1957), 'Prudentius', *RE* 23. 1: 1039–71.

LABHARDT, A. (1960), '*Curiositas*: Notes sur l'histoire d'un mot et d'une
notion', *MH* 17: 206–24.

LABRIOLLE, P. DE (1947), *Histoire de la littérature latine chrétienne* (Paris³).

LACOMBRADE, C. (1951), *Synésios de Cyrène. Héllène et chrétien* (Paris).

LAGARDE, A. (1925), 'La pénitence dans les églises d'Italie au cours des IVᵉ
et Vᵉ siècles', *RHR* 92: 108–47.

LAISTNER, M. L. W. (1957), *The Intellectual Heritage of the Early Middle
Ages* (Ithaca, NY).

LAMBOT, C. (1949), 'Les Sermons de S. Augustin pours les fêtes des
martyrs', *AB* 67: 49–66.

LANA, I. (1962), *Due capitoli Prudenziani. La biografia, la cronologia delle
opere, la poetica* (*Verba Seniorum*, NS 2, Rome).

——(1979), *Analisi del Querolus* (Turin).

LANCEL, S. (1961), '*Curiositas* et préoccupations spirituelles chez Apulée',
RHR 160: 25–46.

LANZONI, F. (1925), 'Le leggende di San Cassiano d'Imola', *ND*, NS 3: 1–
44.

LATTIMORE, R. A. (1942), *Themes in Greek and Latin Epitaphs* (Urbana,
Ill.)

LAVARENNE, M. (1933), *Études sur la langue du poète Prudence* (Paris).

——(1955–63), Prudentius edn., see Principal Ancient Sources.

LAWLOR, H. J., and OULTON, J. E. L. (1927), Eusebius edn., see Principal
Ancient Sources.

LAZZATI, G. (1956a), 'Nota su Eusebio epitomatore di Atti dei martiri',
Studi in onore di A. Calderini e di R. Paribeni I (Milan) 377–84.

——(1956b), *Gli sviluppi della letteratura sui martiri nei primi quattro secoli*
(Turin).

LEASE, E. B. (1895), 'A Syntactic, Stylistic and Metrical Study of Pru-
dentius' (diss. Baltimore).

LECLERCQ, H. (1907), 'Actes des martyres', *DACL* I: 373–446.

——(1922), 'Eulalie de merida et de Barcelone, les saintes', *DACL* 5.1:
705–32.

—— (1923), 'Fonds de coupes', *DACL* 5.2: 1819–59.

—— (1925*a*), 'Gril', *DACL* 6.2: 1827–31.

—— (1925*b*), 'Hymnes', *DACL* 6.2: 2826–928.

—— (1929*a*), 'Laurent', *DACL* 8.2: 1917–61.

—— (1929*b*), 'Leçons', *DACL* 8.2: 2232–5.

—— (1931), 'Magnificat', *DACL* 10.1: 1125–9.

—— (1932*a*), 'Martyrologe', *DACL* 10.2: 2523–619.

—— (1926), 'Polycarpe', *DACL* 10.2: 2359–512.

—— (1948), 'Reliques et reliquaires', *DACL* 14.2: 2294–359.

—— (1950), 'Serpent', *DACL* 15.1: 1353–7.

LE NAIN DE TILLEMONT, L. S. (1705), *Mémoires pour servir à l'histoire ecclésiastique* 10 (Brussels).

LIENHARD, J. T. (1977), *Paulinus of Nola and Early Western Monasticism* (*Theophaneia* 28, Bonn).

LOWE, E. A. (1950), *Codices Latini Antiquiores. A palaeographical guide to Latin Manuscripts Prior to the Ninth Century*, Part 5: France, Paris (Oxford).

LUDWIG, W. (1976), 'Die christliche Dichtung des Prudentius und die Transformation der antiken Gattungen', in *Entretiens Fondation Hardt* 23, 303–64.

McCLURE, J. (1981), 'The Bible Epic and its Audience in Late Antiquity', *Papers of the Liverpool Latin Seminar* 3, 305–22.

MACLEOD, C. (1976), 'Propertius IV.1', *Papers of the Liverpool Latin Seminar* 1–2, 141–53.

—— (1979), 'The Poetry of Ethics: Horace Epistles I', *JRS* 69: 16–27.

MACMULLEN, R. (1962), 'Fourth Century Roman Bureaucratese', *Traditio* 18: 364–78.

—— (1964*a*), 'Some Pictures in Ammianus Marcellinus', *ABull* 46: 435–55.

—— (1964*b*), 'Social Mobility and the Theodosian Code', *JRS* 54: 49–53.

—— (1967), *Enemies of the Roman Order—Treason, Unrest and Alienation in the Empire* (Cambridge, Mass.).

—— (1968), 'Constantine and the Miraculous', *GRBS* 9: 81–96.

MAHONEY, A. (1934), *Vergil in the works of Prudentius* (Washington).

MANELLI, M. G. (1947), 'La personalità prudenziana nel Dittochaeon', *MSLC* 1: 79–126.

MANITIUS, M. (1886), 'Zu spätlateinischen Dichtern', *ZÖG* 37: 81–101, 241–54, 401–11.

—— (1899), 'Beiträge zur Geschichte des Ovidius und anderer römischer Schriftsteller im Mittelalter', *Philologus* Suppl. 7: 723–67.

MANJARRÉS MANGAS, J. and ROLDÁN HERVÁS, J. M. (1982), *España Romana (218 a. de J.C.–414 de J.C.)*, 2: La Sociedad, el Derecho, la Cultura (Madrid).

MARCHESI, C. (1917), Prudentius (*Peristephanon*) edn., see Principal Ancient Sources.

MARIQUE, J. M. F. (1962), (ed.), *Leaders of Iberian Christianity, 50–650 A.D.* (Boston).

MARROU, H.-I. (1953), review of Simonetti (1952), *AC* 22: 271–4.

—— (1958), *S. Augustin et la fin de la culture antique* (Paris).

—— (1965), *Histoire de l'éducation dans l'antiquité* (Paris).

—— (1977), *Décadence romaine ou antiquité tardive IIIe–VIe siècle* (Paris).

MARTIJA, H. (1935), 'Horatii vestigia in Prudentio', in *Palaestra latina, Horatiana* (Cervera) 25–31.

MASON, A. J. (1904), 'The First Latin Christian Poet', *JThS*, NS 5: 413–32.

MATTHEWS, J. F. (1967), 'A Pious Supporter of Theodosius I: Maternus Cynegius and his Family', *JThS*, NS 18: 438–46.

—— (1970), 'The Historical Setting of the "Carmen contra Paganos" (Cod. Par. lat. 8084)', *Historia* 20: 464–79.

—— (1971), 'Gallic Supporters of Theodosius', *Latomus* 30: 1073–99.

—— (1975), *Western Aristocracies and Imperial Court A.D. 364–425* (Oxford).

MEARNS, J. (1914), *The Canticles of the Christian Church Eastern and Western in Early and Mediaeval Times* (Cambridge).

MESLIN, M. (1974), 'Le merveilleux comme language politique chez Ammien Marcellin', in *Mélanges d'histoire ancienne offerts à W. Seston* (Paris), 353–63.

MESSENGER, R. (1944), 'The Mozarabic Hymnal', *TAPhA* 75: 103–26.

—— (1944–5), 'The Legend of St. Eulalia in Mozarabic Hymns', *CW* 38: 12–13.

—— (1946), 'Mozarabic Hymns in Relation to Contemporary Culture', *Traditio* 4: 149–77.

—— (1962), 'Aurelius Prudentius Clemens. A Biographical Study', in Marique (1962) 81–102.

METTE, H. (1956), 'Curiositas', in *Festschrift Bruno Snell* (Munich) 227–35.

METZGER, BRUCE M. (1972), 'Literary Forgeries and Canonical Pseudepigrapha', *JBL* 91: 3–24.

MICHEL, A. (1933), 'Penance', *Dictionnaire de Théologie Catholique*, 12. 1: 722–1127.

MISCH, G. (1973), *A History of Autobiography in Antiquity*, vol. 1, trans. E. W. Dickes (London).

MOHRMANN, CH. (1947), 'La Langue et style de la poésie chrétienne', *REL* 25: 280–97.

—— (1947–8), 'Le Latin commun et le latin des chrétiens', *VChr* 1–2: 1–12.

—— (1949), 'Les Origines de la latinité chrétienne à Rome', *VChr* 3: 63–106.

—— (1955), 'Problèmes stylistiques dans la littérature latine chrétienne', *VChr* 9: 222–46.

—— (1957), *Liturgical Latin, its Origins and Character* (Washington).

—— (1958–77), *Études sur le latin des chrétiens*, 4 vols (Rome).

MOLES, J. L. (1978), 'The Career and Conversion of Dio Chrysostom', *JHS* 98: 79–100.

MOMIGLIANO, A. D. (1963*a*), (ed.) *The Conflict between Paganism and Christianity in the Fourth Century* (Oxford).

—— (1963*b*), 'Christianity and the Decline of the Roman Empire', in Momigliano (1963*a*) 1–16.

—— (1963*c*), 'Pagan and Christian Historiography in the Fourth Century A.D.', in 1963*a*, 79–99.

—— (1966), *Studies in Historiography* (London).

—— (1977), 'Popular Religious Beliefs and Late Roman Historians', in *Essays in Ancient and Modern Historiography* (Oxford) 141–59.

MOMMSEN, TH. (1892), *Consularia Constantinopolitana* edn., see Principal Ancient Sources.

—— (1894), Hydatius and Isidore of Seville edn., see Principal Ancient Sources.

—— (1895), Solinus edn., see Principal Ancient Sources.

—— (1899), *Römisches Strafrecht*. Systematisches Handbuch der deutschen Rechtswissenschaft, Abt. 1. Teil. 4 (Leipzig).

—— (1905), *Codex Theodosianus* edn., see Principal Ancient Sources.

—— (1908), Rufinus edn., see Principal Ancient Sources.

MORAL, T. (1969), 'Vincenzo', *BSS* 12: 1149–55.

MOREU-REY, E. (1973), 'L'antiga devoció a San Fruitós', *BAT Ep. 4 Fasc. 113–20* (Estudis dedicats a la memòria de mossèn Joan Serra i Vilaró): 245–52.

MORIN, G. (1891), 'Une page inédite de saint Augustin', *R Ben* 8: 417–19.

—— (1894), 'Nouvelles recherches sur l'auteur de "Te Deum"', *R Ben* 11: 49–77.

—— (1898), 'Notes d'ancienne littérature chrétienne', *R Ben* 15: 97–108.

—— (1907), 'Le "Te Deum": anaphore préhistorique?' *R Ben* 24: 180–223.

—— (1930), *Miscellanea Agostiniana*, Testi e Studi vol. 1: *Sancti Augustini sermones post Maurinos reperti* (Rome).

—— (1937), Caesarius of Arles edn., see Principal Ancient Sources.

MÜNTZ, E (1881), *Études sur l'histoire de la peinture et de l'iconographie chrétiennes* (Paris).

MUSURILLO, H. (1972), *The Acts of the Christian Martyrs* edn., see Principal Ancient Sources.

MYRES, J. N. L. (1960), 'Pelagius and the End of Roman Rule in Britain', *JRS* 50: 21–36.

NEWMYER, S. T. (1979), *The Silvae of Statius, Structure and Theme (Mnemosyne* Suppl. 53, Leiden).

NEYRAND, L. (1978), 'Le Récit de la passion des martyrs de Lyon dans la traduction de Rufin', *Colloques Internationaux du Centre National de la Recherche Scientifique* 575: Les Martyrs de Lyon 177 [AD], 289–98.

NOCK, A. (1933), *Conversion from Alexander the Great to Augustine of Hippo* (Oxford).

NISBET, R. and HUBBARD, M. (1970), *A Commentary on Horace Odes Book I* (Oxford).

NORBERG, D. (1952), 'L'Origine de la versification latine rythmique', *Eranos* 50: 83–90.

—— (1967), 'Le Début de l'hymnologie latine en l'honneur des saints', *Arctos*, NS 5: 115–25.

—— (1974), 'L'Hymne ambrosien', in *Au seuil de Moyen Age. Études linguistiques, métriques et littéraires* (Padova) 135–49.

NORDEN, E. (1913), *Agnōstos Theos: Untersuchungen zur Formengeschichte religiöser Rede* (Leipzig).

OBBARIUS, TH. (1945), Prudentius edn., see Principal Ancient Sources.

OGILVIE, R. M. (1978), *The Library of Lactantius* (Oxford).

OPELT, I. (1967), 'Der Christenverfolger bei Prudentius', *Philologus* 111: 242–57.

—— (1970), 'Prudentius und Horaz', in *Forschungen zur römischen Literatur: Festschrift zum 60. Geburtstag von K. Büchner*, ed. W. Wimmel (Wiesbaden) 206–13.

ORSELLI, A. M. (1965), *L'idea e il culto del santo patrono cittadino nella letteratura latina cristiana (Studi e Ricerche*, NS 12, Bologna).

OULTON, J. E. L. (1929), 'Rufinus' Translation of the Church History of Eusebius', *JThS* 30: 50–74.

PALANQUE, J.-R. (1933), *Saint Ambroise et l'empire romain* (Paris).

PALLA, R. (1981), *Hamartigenia. Introduzione, traduzione e commento* (Pisa).

PALMER, L. R. (1954), *The Latin Language* (London).

PAREDI, I. (1937), *I prefazi ambrosiani* (Pubblicazioni della Università Cattolica del Sacro Cruore, Ser. 4, col. 25, Milan).

PARIS, M. (1975), '*Troia resurgens*, mito troiano e ideologia de principato', in *AFLB* 18: 65–85.

PARONETTO, V. (1957), Prudentius (*Peristephanon*) edn., see Principal Ancient Sources.

PASCHOUD, F. (1967), *Roma aeterna: Études sur le patriotisme romain dans l'occident latin à l'époque des grandes invasions* (Rome).

—— (1979), Zosimus edn., see Principal Ancient Sources.

PASQUALI, O. (1920), *Orazio lirico* (Florence).

PEASE, A. S. (1935), *P. Vergili Maronis Aeneidos Liber Quartus* (Cambridge, Mass.).

PEEBLES, B. M. (1951), *The Poet Prudentius* (Candlemas Lectures on Christian Literature 2, New York).

PEETERS, P. (1931), review of Roetzer (1930), *AB* 49: 150–2.

PEIPER, R. (1881), *Carmen ad senatorem* edn., see Principal Ancient Sources.

PELLEGRINO, M. (1932), *La poesia di S. Gregorio Nazianzeno* (Milan).

—— (1947), 'La poesia di Sant'Ilario de Poitiers', *VChr* 1: 201–26.

—— (1954), *Inni della Giornata* (*Verba Seniorum* 1, Alba).

—— (1960–1), 'Structure et inspiration des "Peristephanon" de Prudence', *BFS* 39: 437–50.

—— (1961), Paulinus of Milan edn., see Principal Ancient Sources.

—— (1963), *Letteratura latina cristiana* (Universale Studium 48, Rome²).

PHILIP, R. H. (1968), 'The Manuscript Tradition of Seneca's Tragedies', *CQ*, NS 18: 150–79.

PICKMAN, E. (1937), *The Mind of Latin Christendom* (Oxford).

PIÉTRI, CH. (1961), '*Concordia Apostolorum* et *Renovatio Urbis* (culte des martyres et propagande pontificale)', *MEFR* 73: 275–322.

—— (1962), 'Le serment du soldat chrétien: les épisodes de la *militia Christi* sur les sarcophages', *MEFR* 74: 649–664.

PIGANIOL, A. (1972), *L'Empire chrétien* (*A.D. 325–395*), deuxième éd. mise à jour par A. Chastagnol (Paris).

PILLINGER, R. (1980), *Die Tituli Historiarum oder das sogenannte Dittochaeon des Prudentius* (*DAW* 142, Vienna).

POREBOWICZ, E. (1921–2), 'L'"espagnolisme" d'Aurélien Prudence', *EOS* 25: 1–13.

PORTER, A. W. (1933), 'A Note on the Mozarabic Calendar', *JThS* 34: 144–50.

—— (1934), 'Studies in the Mozarabic Office', *JThS* 35: 266–86.

PREMERSTEIN, A. VON (1901), 'Corrector', *RE* 4. 2: 1646–56.

PUECH, A. (1888), *Prudence: Étude sur la poésie latine chrétienne au IVe siècle* (Paris).

QUASTEN, J. (1941), 'The Liturgical Singing of Women in Christian Antiquity', *CHR* 27: 149–65.

—— (1950–60), *Patrology*, 1–3 (Utrecht).

QUINN, K. (1972), (ed.) *Approaches to Catullus* (Cambridge).

RABY, F. J. E. (1953), *A History of Christian Latin Poetry from the Beginnings to the Close of the Middle Ages* (Oxford²).

—— (1957), *A History of Secular Latin Poetry in the Middle Ages* (Oxford²).

RAFFA, V. (1955), 'Lectiones hagiographicae in liturgia occidentali', *Ephemerides Liturgicae* 69: 25–30.

RAND, E. K. (1920), 'Prudentius and Christian Humanism', *TAPhA* 51: 71–83.

RANSTRAND, G. (1951), *Querolus* edn., see Principal Ancient Sources.

RAPISARDA, E. (1948), 'La praefatio di Prudenzio', *ND* 2: 51–61.

—— (1950), 'Influssi lucreziani in Prudenzio. Un suo poema lucreziano e antiepicureo', *VChr* 4: 46–60.

—— (1951), *Introduzione alla lettura di Prudenzio* 1 (Catania).

RAVEN, D. S. (1965), *Latin Metre: An Introduction* (London).

REESE, G. (1940), *Music in the Middle Ages* (London).

RICHARD, G. (1969), 'L'Apport de Virgile à la création épique de Prudence dans le *Peristephanon*', *Caesarodunum* 3: 187–93.

RICHARDSON, E. C. (1896), Gennadius edn., see Principal Ancient Sources.

RIPOSATI, B. (1979), 'La struttura degli inni alle tre vergini martiri di *Peristephanon* di Prudenzio (III; IV, 109–44; XIV)', in *Paradoxos politeia. Studi patristici in onore di Giuseppe Lazzati*, a cura di R. Cantalamessa e L. F. Pizzolato (Milan) 25–41.

RIST, M. (1972), 'Pseudepigraphy and the Early Christians', in *Studies in New Testament and Early Christian Literature. Essays in honour of A. P. Wikgren*, ed. D. E. Arme (Leiden) 75–91.

RODRÍGUEZ-HERRERA, J. (1936), 'Poeta Christianus. Prudentius' Auffassung vom Wesen und von der Aufgabe des christlichen Dichters' (diss. Munich).

RÖSLER, A. (1886), *Der katholische Dichter Aurelius Prudentius Clemens* (Freiburg i.B.).

ROETZER, P. W. (1930), *Des heiligen Augustinus Schriften als liturgiegeschichtliche Quelle* (Munich).

ROSSI, G. B. de (1846–77), *La Roma sotterranea cristiana descritta ed illustrata*, 3 vols. (Rome).

—— (1881), 'Elogio Damasiano del celebre Ippolito, martire sepolto presso la Via Tiburtina', *Bull. di Archeologia cristiana*, 3a serie, 6, 26–55.

—— (1892), 'Il cimiterio di S. Ippolito presso la Via Tiburtina e la sua principale cripta storica ora dissepolta', *Bull. di Archeologia cristiana*, 4a serie, 1: 9–76.

—— (1909), *Descrizione analitica dei monumenti esistenti negli antichi cimiteri suburbani*, 1 (Rome).

——, and DUCHESNE, L. (1894), *Martyrologium hieronymianum* edn., see Principal Ancient Sources.

ROSSI, L. E. (1971), 'I generi letterari e le loro leggi scritte e non scritte nelle letterature classiche', *BICS* 18: 69–94.

ROUSSEAU, P. (1976), 'In Search of Sidonius the Bishop', *Historia* 25: 356–77.

RUSSELL, D. A. (1979), 'De Imitatione', in West and Woodman (1979) 1–16.

RUYSSCHAERT, P. (1966), 'Prudence, l'espagnol poète des deux basiliques romaines de SS Pierre et Paul', *RAC* 42: 267–86.

SABBATINI, P. T. A. (1972), 'Storia e leggenda nel *Peristephanon* di Prudenzio', *RSC* 20: 32–53, 187–221.

——(1973), 'Storia e leggenda nel *Peristephanon* di Prudenzio', *RSC* 21: 39–77.

SÁENZ DE AGUIRRE, G. (1693), *Collectio maxima conciliorum omnium Hispanae et Novi Orbis* (Rome).

STE CROIX, G. E. M. de (1954), 'Suffragium: From Vote to Patronage', *British Journal of Sociology* 5: 33–48.

SALVATORE, A. (1956), 'Qua ratione Prudentius ... Horatium Vergiliumque imitatus sit', *AFLN* 6: 119–40.

——(1958), *Studi prudenziani* (Naples).

——(1959), 'Echi ovidiani nella poesia di Prudenzio', in *Atti del Convegno Internazionale Ovidiano* 2 (Rome) 257–72.

——(1960), 'Appunti sulla cronologia di Commodiano', *Orpheus* 7: 161–87.

——(1977), *Commodiano. Carme Apologetico* (*Corona Patrum* 5, Turin).

SANFORD, E. M. (1931), 'Lucan and his Roman Critics', *CPh* 26: 233–57.

——(1936), 'Were the Hymns of Prudentius Intended to be Sung?', *CPh* 31: 71–2.

SCHANZ, M., HOSIUS, C., and KRÜGER, G. (1914–35), *Geschichte der römischen Literatur bis zum Gesetzgebungswerk des Kaisers Justinian* (*Handbuch der Altertumswissenschaft* 8, Munich).

SCHMEISSER, B. (1972), *A Concordance to the Elegies of Propertius* (Hildesheim).

SCHMITZ, M. (1889), 'Die Gedichte des Prudentius und ihre Entstehungszeit', *Programm des Realgymnasiums zu Aachen für das Schuljahr 1888–9*.

SCHULTEN, A. (1932), 'Tarraco', *RE* 4A. 2: 2398–403.

SCHUMANN, O. (1979–82), *Lateinisches Hexameter-Lexikon. Dichterisches Formelgut von Ennius bis zum Archipoeta*, 5 vols. (Munich).

SCHWEN, CH. (1937), 'Vergil bei Prudentius' (diss. Leipzig).

SEAGER, R. (1983), 'Some Imperial Virtues in the Latin Prose Panegyrics', *Papers of the Liverpool Latin Seminar* 4, 129–66.

SEECK, O. (1876), *Notitia Dignitatum* edn., see Principal Ancient Sources.

——(1883), Symmachus edn., see Principal Ancient Sources.

——(1894), 'Ammianus Marcellinus', *RE* 1. 2: 1845–52.

——(1921), 'Scrinium', *RE* 2A. 1: 893–904.

SERRA VILARÓ, J. (1936), *Fructuós Auguri Eulogi, màrtirs sants de Tarragona* (Tarragona).

——(1937), 'I sepolcri della necropoli di Tarragona', *RAC* 14: 243–80.

SERRA VILARÓ, J. (1946), 'Scavi e ritrovamenti in Spagna', *Orme di Roma nel Mondo* 7 (1946).

SHERWIN-WHITE, A. N. (1985), *The Letters of Pliny. A Historical and Social Commentary* (Oxford³).

SIMONETTI, M. (1952), 'Studi sull'innologia popolare cristiana dei primi secoli', *MAL* ser. 8ª 4. 6: 341–485.

—— (1955a), 'Su Romano d'Antiochia', *RAC* 31: 223–33.

—— (1955b), 'Su S. Quirino di Siscia', *RAC* 31: 234–43.

SIXT, G. (1892), 'Des Prudentius' Abhängigkeit von Seneca und Lucan', *Philologus* 51: 501–6.

—— (1899), *Die lyrischen Gedichte des Aurelius Prudentius Clemens* (Stuttgart).

SMITH, M. (1976), *Prudentius' Psychomachia. A Re-examination* (Princeton).

SOLMSEN, F. (1965), 'The Powers of Darkness in Prudentius' *Contra Symmachum*', *VChr* 19: 237–57.

SOTOMAYOR, M. (1964), 'Eulalia, santa martire in Spagna', *BSS* 5: 204–9.

STEINMANN, F. (1892), *Die Tituli und die kirchliche Wandmalerei im Abendlande vom V. bis zum XI. Jahrhundert* (*Beiträge zur Kunstgeschichte*, NF 19, Berlin).

STEVENSON, J. (1929), *Studies in Eusebius* (Cambridge).

STRZELECKI, L. (1935), 'De Horatio rei metricae Prudentianae auctore', in *Commentationes Horatianae* 1 (Kraków) 36–49.

SUMMERS, W. C. (1894), *A Study of the Argonautica of Valerius Flaccus* (Cambridge).

SÜNDWALL, J. (1915), *Weströmische Studien* (Berlin).

SYME, R. (1968), *Ammianus Marcellinus and the Historia Augusta* (Oxford).

—— (1971), *Emperors and Biography. Studies in the Historia Augusta* (Oxford).

SZÖVÉRFFY, J. (1964), *Die Annalen der lateinischen Hymnendichtung. Ein Handbuch. I: Die lateinischen Hymnen bis zum Ende des 11. Jahrhunderts* (Berlin).

—— (1966), 'Hymnology', *New Catholic Encyclopedia* (Catholic University of America), 287–94.

—— (1970), 'Iberian Hymnody. Preliminary Survey of Mediaeval Spanish and Portuguese Hymnody', *CF* 24: 187–253.

—— (1971), *Iberian Hymnody. Survey and Problems* (Worcester, Mass.).

—— (1985), *A Concise History of Mediaeval Latin Hymnody. Religious Lyrics between Antiquity and Humanism* (Leiden).

THOMSON, H. J. (1928), 'Lucan, Statius and Juvenal in the Early Centuries', *CQ* 22: 24–7.

—— i (1949), ii. (1953), Prudentius edn., see Principal Ancient Sources.

THOMPSON, L. (1973), 'Hymns in Early Christian Worship', *AThR* 55: 458–72.

THORNDIKE, L. (1923), *A History of Magic and Experimental Science*, 1 (New York).

THRAEDE, K. (1965), 'Studien zu Sprache und Stil des Prudentius' (*Hypomnemata* 13, Göttingen).

—— (1973), 'Rom und der Märtyrer in Prudentius, *Peristephanon* II.1–20', *Romanitas et Christianitas*. *Studia Iano Henrico Waszink* (Amsterdam) 317–28.

TOSCHI, P. (1951), 'Lorenzo, santo martire', *EC* 7: 1583–45.

TOWNEND, G. B. (1967), see Dorey (1967).

URNER, H. (1952), *Die außerbiblische Lesung im christliche Gottesdienst. Ihre Vorgeschichte und Geschichte bis zur Zeit Augustins* (Veröffentlichungen der Evangelischen Gesellschaft für Liturgieforschung 6, Göttingen).

VALENTIN, M.-D. (1977), Hilary of Arles edn., see Principal Ancient Sources.

VALMAGGI, L. (1893), 'La fortuna di Stazio nella tradizione letteraria latina e bassolatina', *RFIC* 21: 409–62, 481–554.

VAN DER MEER, F. (1961), *Augustine the Bishop* (London).

VANDERSPOEL, J. (1986), 'Claudian, Christ and the Saints', *CQ*, NS 36: 244–55.

VESSEY, D. (1970), 'Lucan, Statius and the Baroque Epic', *CW* 63: 232–4.

—— (1973), *Statius and the Thebaid* (Cambridge).

VIVES, J. (1933), 'Una inscripció històrica dels màrtirs de Tarragona', *AST* 9: 247–51.

—— (1936a), 'Prudentiana', *AST* 12: 1–18.

—— (1936b), 'Inscripciones cristianas de la necrópolis romano-cristiana de Tarragona', *Annari Inst. Estudis Catalans* 7: 375–400.

—— (1937–40), 'La necrópolis romano cristiana en Tarragona. Su datación', *AST* 13: 47–60.

—— (1941), 'Santoral visigodo en calendarios e inscripciones', *AST* 14: 31–56.

—— (1944), 'Veracidad histórica en Prudencio', *AST* 17: 199–204.

—— (1946), *Oracional visigótico*, Monumenta Hispaniae Sacra I (Barcelona).

—— (1949), 'Un nuevo altar romano-cristiano en la Tarraconense', *AB* 67: 401–6.

—— (1966), 'Tradición y leyenda en la hagiografía hispánica', in *Miscelánea en memoria de Dom Mario Férotin, 1914–64*, 495–508.

—— (1969), *Inscripciones cristianas de la España romana y visigoda* (Barcelona).

—— MARTIN, T., and MARTÍNEZ, G. (1963), *Concilios visigóticos y hispano-romanas* (Barcelona).

VOOGHT, P. de (1938), 'La Notion philosophique du miracle chez saint Augustin dans le "De trinitate" et le "De Genesi ad litteram"', RecTh 10: 317–43.

—— (1939a), 'Les Miracles dans le vie de St. Augustin', RecTh 11: 5–16.

—— (1939b), 'La Théologie du miracle selon Saint Augustin', RecTh 11: 197–222.

VROOM, H. (1933), 'Le Psaume abécédaire de Saint Augustin et la poésie latine rythmique', in Latinitas Christianorum Primaeva (Nijmegen) 5–66.

VULIĆ, N. (1921), 'Savia 3', RE 2A. 1: 258.

WAAL, A. (1907), 'Zum Kult des hl. Vincenz von Saragossa', RQA 21: 135–8.

WADDELL, H. (1930), Mediaeval Latin Lyrics (London³).

WAGNER, P. (1907), Introduction to the Gregorian Melodies. A Handbook of Plainsong, Part 1 (trans. A. Orme and E. G. P. Wyatt, London).

WALPOLE, A. S. (1905), 'Hymns attributed to St. Hilary of Poitiers', JThS, NS 6: 599–603.

—— (1922), Early Latin Hymns (Cambridge, Hildesheim 1966).

WALSH, P. G. (1970), 'Paulinus of Nola and the Conflict of Ideologies in the Fourth Century', in Kyriakon. Festschrift J. Quasten (Münster) 565 ff.

WARD PERKINS, B. (1984), From Classical Antiquity to the Middle Ages. Urban Public Building in Northern and Central Italy, 300–850 (Oxford)

WARWICK, H. H. (1975), A Vergil Concordance (Minneapolis).

WELLEK, R. and AUSTIN, A. (1961), Theory of Literature (London²).

WELLESZ, E. (1945), 'The Earliest Example of Christian Hymnody', CQ 39–41: 34–45.

—— (1947), Eastern Elements in Western Chant (Boston).

—— (1955), 'Early Christian Music', NOHM 2, 1 ff.

—— (1961), A History of Byzantine Music and Hymnography (Oxford).

WESENBERG, G. (1957), 'Provincia', RE 23. 1: 995–1029.

WESSNER, P. (1929), 'Lucan, Statius und Juvenal bei den römischen Grammatikern', PhW 49: 296–303, 328–35.

WEST, D. and WOODMAN T. (1979), (eds.), Creative Imitation and Latin Literature (Cambridge).

WEYMAN, C. (1891), 'Seneca und Prudentius', in Commentationes Woelfflinianae (Leipzig).

—— (1926), Beiträge zur Geschichte der christlich-lateinischen Poesie (Munich, repr. Hildesheim 1975).

WILKINSON, J. D. (1982), Egeria's Travels (Warminster).

WILKINSON, L. P. (1955), Ovid Recalled (Cambridge).

—— (1969), The Georgics of Virgil: a Critical Survey (Cambridge).

WILLEUMIER, P. (1930), 'Virgile et le vieillard de Tarente', *REL* 8: 325–40.

WILLIAMS, G. (1968), *Tradition and Originality in Roman Poetry* (Oxford).

—— (1969), *Horace's Odes, Book 3* (Oxford).

—— (1972), *Horace* (Oxford).

WILLIAMS, R. D. (1973), *Aeneas and the Roman Hero (as reflected in Virgil's Aeneid)* (Basingstoke).

—— (1979), Virgil (*Eclogues* and *Georgics*) edn., see Principal Ancient Sources.

WILMART, D. A. (1920), Macarius edn., see Principal Ancient Sources.

WINSTEDT, E. O. (1903), 'The double recension in the poems of Prudentius', *CR* 17: 206–7.

—— (1904), 'Notes on the MSS. of Prudentius', *JPh* 29: 166–80.

—— (1905), 'The Ambrosian MS. of Prudentius', *CR* 19: 4–7.

WITKE, CH. (1968), 'Prudentius and the Tradition of Latin Poetry', *TAPhA* 99: 509–25.

—— (1971), *Numen Litterarum. The Old and the New in Latin Poetry from Constantine to Gregory the Great* (Leiden).

WÜNSCH, R. (1914), 'Hymnos', *RE* 9. 1: 140–83.

ZAHN, TH. (1901), *Real-Encyclopädie für protestantische Theologie und Kirche* 9 (Leipzig).

ZEILLER, J. (1918), *Les Origines chrétiennes dans les provinces danubiennes de l'empire romain* (Paris).

ZETZEL, J. E. G. (1975), 'On the History of Latin Scholia', *HSPh* 79: 335–54.

General Index

abecedaria form for hymns 60, 71
Abgar, king of Edessa 44
Acilius Severus 13
Actium 129
Acts of martyrs 32, 44, 125, 206–16,
  227–9, 268
aedituus, in *Pe* 9: 114–15
Aemilianus 208, 213–15
Aeneas 140, 160, 169, 172, 178
agentes in rebus 42
Agnes 30, 84, 143, 178–9, 187, 203, 215,
  240, 250–3, 260–1, 266
Alcaic hendecasyllable 74, 203
Alexandrian school under Clement and
  Origen 99
Allecto, fury 155, 164, 195
alliteration 212
Ambrose 23, 57, 62, 79, 102, 180, 223,
  232–3, 243, 249–51
Ambrosian hymns 62–7
Ambrosian Missal 232
amicitia 147
Ammianus Marcellinus 37, 45–9, 55
amphitheatre 216–17
Anacreon 84
anaphora 212
Anastasia 276
Anchises 128, 171, 175
Andromache 179
anima, dove 171
Antioch 246
anti-pagan polemic in *Pe* 93, 264
antiphonal performance of hymns 63, 69
Antiphonarium of León 256–8, 264
Antiphonarium of Millán 261
Apocalypse 221
apocrypha 53
apostles 119, 139, 143 *see also under names*
Apuleius 41–2, 199–200
archaeological evidence, and *Pe* 268–77
aretalogies 49
Arians 59, 62
Ascanius, in *Aeneid* 159, 163–4
Aspasius, Agnes' judge in the *Acta* 251
Aspasius, *proconsul Africae* 251
Asterius of Amasea 274
astrology, belief in 49

Astyanax 192
Augustalis 208
Augustanism 98
Augustine 43, 49–50, 52, 100, 245
Augustus 123, 128, 132, 134, 159, 165,
  204
Aurelian, St 232
Aurelius Victor 38
Ausonius 11, 20, 56, 103, 194, 263, 271
autobiographical information in *Pe* and
  Praef 6–31
autobiography, literary tradition of 10
autopsy in Ovid's *Fasti* and in *Pe* 116

baptistery 29–30, 238, 254, 265, 273,
  275–6
baroque, literary 112, 194
basilica of eighteen martyrs of Saragossa
  265–6; of St Agnes 250, 261, 266; of
  SS Emeterius and Chelidonius 265; of
  St Eulalia 173–4, 266; of St Fructuosus
  221, 268; of St Hippolytus 137, 248;
  of St Lawrence 95, 257; of St Paul 29–
  30, 254, 273, 277; of St Peter 29–30,
  254–5, 259, 263, 273, 275; of St
  Vincent 266–8
beneficia 144
Béziers 266–7
biography, popularity of, in 4th century
  38–9
Braulius of Saragossa 232

Caesar, Julius 128, 131–2
Caesarius of Arles 232
Calahorra (ancient Calagurris) 21, 238,
  265–6
calendar, Christian church 112, 255–64;
  of Carmona 256–7, 262, 265, 267; of
  Carthage 258, 266; of Naples 267; of
  Polemius Silvius 267; *Pe* as versified
  Spanish church calendar 255–64
Callimachus 111, 113
Callistus (pope) 249
Camillus 128, 131–2
Cantilena Sanctae Eulaliae 239
cantus directaneus 73
cantus responsorius 71

capitularia evangeliorum 250
captatio benevolentiae 9, 89
Carmen ad senatorem ex Christiana religione conversum 93
Carmen saeculare 80–1, 139
carmina pro muneribus 10
Cassian of Imola, St 85, 113, 242–3, 263, 273, 275
Cassian of Saragossa 241
Cassian of Tingi 242
catacombs 95, 113, 191, 249
Cato 128
Catullus 17, 84, 104, 115, 168, 240
Cauca (Theodosius' retreat) 26
causa scribendi 9, 11
Cecilia 266
cento nuptialis of Ausonius 103
cento poems 101–2, 104
Chelidonius 122, 143, 146, 148, 152, 237–9, 265
children, in *Pe* 143
choir of boys and girls 174
choirs in classical period 81
chorus 78
Christ in the Roman empire 129, 132
Christian terminology, used by Hilary 62
chronology of Prudentius' poetry 23, 88
church reading, *see* liturgy
Cicero, and Christian attitude to rhetoric 100
classical tradition, poet's involvement in 9; Christian rejection of 20, 99; revival of interest in classical authors in 4th century 37
Claudian 112, 180, 194, 197–203
clerics, in *Pe* 143
clients 222
codex, new form of book 87
Commodian, and statements of conversion 22
compendia, in late period 44
Confessions of St Augustine 9, 13, 14
consistorium 27
Constantine, and the official recognition of the church 99
Constantius, emperor 56
consul, heavenly 133–4
consulere, key word in Ovid's *Fasti* and in *Pe* 114–15
contaminatio 107, 137, 162, 164, 201
Continuatio Isidoriana Hispana 262
Contra Symmachum, dating of 17

controuersia 189
conversion, Christian and non-Christian, personal statement of 11, 19, 22
corona 142
corona civica, and Lawrence 133–4
corrector 25
Cossus 128, 131–2
council of Elvira 273
council of Toledo 58, 68
crucifixion of Cupid in Ausonius 263
cult of martyrs, *see* martyr-cult
cultural continuity in 4th-century society 37, 54
curiositas 32–56, 41–4, 48, 230
curiosus 42
Cyprian, St. 74, 85, 96, 206, 224, 234–5, 264

Damasus (pope) 30, 95, 115, 233, 240, 243–4, 249–50, 255, 258, 276
Daniel 208, 220
De doctrina Christiana, and Christian attitude to rhetoric 100
De viris illustribus, purpose of 101
Decius 128, 235
declamation schools, *see* rhetorical schools
decretum Gelasianum 231
demons 50
depositio martyrum 249–50, 257–8, 261–2
devotional reading 34, 90, 224
Diana 159
diction of earlier Latin poetry, use of 105–6
Dido 160, 173–4; Dido's palace 173
dies natalis 109, 112, 175, 206, 254
diminutives 172–3
Diocletian 237
dirae 156, 164
Dittochaeon 18, 218, 273
divination, belief in 49
doxology, use of, in Mozarabic hymnal 86
Dracontius 194
Drusus 128
dynamic reminiscences 107, 123

Ebro, river (Hiberus) 21
Egeria 43–4, 72
eighteen martyrs of Saragossa 241–3
ekphrasis 199
eloquentia 99

Emerentiana, St 261
Emeterius 122, 143, 146, 148, 152, 237–
9, 265
emperor, as counterpart of God on earth
134; visits to Rome of 123–4
empire, Christian 147, 204
empire, Roman, built under
providential guidance 259
Encratis 155
Enricus 270
epic 101, 124, 200; diction 106; passion
228; values 154
Epilogue 18
epitaphs, Greek and Roman 15, 115, 166
Euander 179
Eucratis 242
Eugenius II, of Toledo 258
Eulalia 30, 143, 147–69, 171–4, 176, 198,
214, 239–41, 260–1
Euphemia, St 274
Euryalus, in *Aeneid* 146, 160, 168
Eusebius of Caesarea 53, 224, 233, 236,
245, 263
Eusebius of Emesa 247
Eutropius 38
Evodius of Uzali 274
execution 211, 233
exorcism 152
exordium, Prudentius' use of topics of
classical 9–10

Fabianus (pope) 249
Fabius Maximus 128
Fabricius 128
fama in Ovid and *Pe* 119–20
Faustus 241
Felix, St 208, 218, 229
Ferreolus, St 232
Festus 38
fiction 225
Fidelis 269
fides 141
flamen, role of, in Ovid's *Fasti* 113
Flavianus 93
flower imagery 168
flowers 174
formulaic phrases, use of, in *imitatio*
105–6
forum as scene of pre-martyrdom debate
246
Frigidus, river 93
Fructuosus 122, 205–26, 234–5, 260, 269
funeral games 171

Galerius 238
genera dicendi, classical 61, 101–2
Gennadius 87, 92
Gentiles denounced by Romans in *Pe* 10:
248
Gervasius 50, 223, 257
gesta martyrum 230
gladiators 216
glyconics *kata stichon* 193
gold glass 257, 261, 277
golden age, Augustan vision reapplied
to Theodosian empire 123
Gospels, as models for Christian writers
99
Goths 275
governor 211, 214, 220
Gracchi 128
grammatici Latini 80
Greek as liturgical language in the West
58
Gregory of Nazianzus 236
Gregory of Tours 239, 266

Hadrian (pope) 231
hagiographic co-ordinates 109
hagiographic readings 230–4
hero, founding 140, 204
heroism, of martyrs 123, 141, 154–5,
177, 204, 232
heroism, non-Christian 153, 177
heterogeneity of *Pe* 97
Hieronymian martyrology 239, 241,
248, 250, 257, 265, 267–8
Hieronymus, *see* Jerome
Hilary of Poitiers, importance for Latin
hymnography 57–61, 63, 73, 79
Hippo 32–3, 231
Hippolytus, St 85, 137–8, 189–91, 201,
229, 248–50, 254, 257–60, 275
Hispania Tarraconensis 21
Historia Augusta 39, 41, 46
Honorius, emperor, and gladiatorial
games 23
Horace 104, 123–4, 144
humility of poet 90, 111
hymnody in the West, origins and
development 58–67
hymns, non-scriptural, in liturgy 68
hymnus 58, 75, 80, 84

iambic dimeter 64, 244–5
iambic senarius 61
iambic trimeter 193

iambic trimeter acatalectic 74
iconography 262
imitatio 98, 102–3, 105, 108, 196, 204
immortality of poet 15
Imola 31, 275
imperium 128–30, 133
ingenium, identification with poet's
    anima 16
inscriptiones 70, 75, 77, 80, 83;
    inscriptions of Damasus 115, 276, *see
    also* index of passages cited
inventio of martyrs 50
Isidore of Seville 58, 98
Iulus 170

Januarius 241
Jerome 100, 197, 232
John Chrysostom 247
Julian 22, 243
Juno 137, 155
Jupiter 124, 134–5, 140
Juvenal 38, 103–4, 180–4
Juvencus 101

lauacrum 213
laudatio funebris 132
laurea and associations in victory 127
Lavinia 169–71
Lawrence, St 21, 30, 84, 95, 102, 122,
    126–38, 154, 243–5, 258–61
lectionaries 250
legendary passions 224, 228
letter form of *Pe* 11: 76, 110
libelli miraculorum of Augustine 50, 231
libellus orationum 256–8, 260, 264–5
liber comicus 256, 265
liber pontificalis 231, 249
liber sacramentorum of Toledo 256, 265
liturgical colours 174
liturgical language 65
liturgy 72, 229–34, 256
lives of saints 54
Livy, abridgements of, 38–9, 103
Lucan 104, 180, 184–8
Lucan, commentary on, available in 4th
    century 184
Lucian 49
Lucretius, in 4th century 104
Lupercus, St 266

Macrobius 44, 103
magic, belief in 49, 235
mannerism 194

manuscripts of Prudentius 18, 87, 104,
    108, 143–4, 167, 248
Marcellus 175
Marius Maximus 38–9, 46
Mark of Arethusa 242
Martial 104, 271
Martianus Capella 44
martyrium 199, 203, 205–26
martyrs: crown of victory 174; cult 30,
    152, 205, 233, 250, 259, 262; literature,
    see acts of martyrs; martyr-soldier
    143, 151; martyr's heroism, *see*
    heroism
martyrs of Saragossa 241–3, 265
Massa Candida 236
Matutinus 241
Maximianus 237, 239
Maximinus 249
Megaera 198–9
melodramatic 194
Memmius 128
Mercury 159
Mérida (ancient Emerita) 173, 198, 239,
    267, 268
Metamorphoses of Ovid 104
metre, importance of, in Hilary's hymns
    60, 71
metrical hymnody, development of 58
Mettus 201
Mezentius 158
Milan, imperial court at 24, 26, 30, 91,
    95, 197, 206, 257, 261
militia in imperial service 27; *militia
    Christi* 140–3, 147–8, 150
miracles 50–3, 153, 208, 213–14, 219–20,
    228, 246
modestia affectata 9
modesty, concern for, in virgin martyrs
    252
mosaics, in St Eulalia's basilica 173; in
    Vatican baptistery 276
Mozarabic hymnal 70, 85; liturgy 67,
    232; *sacramentarium* 241
Mucius Scaevola 133
mulier virilis 240
Muses in Christian poetry 90, 113

narrative 102, 112–13, 225
natalicia poems of Paulinus of Nola,
    number of 109
Naucellius, friend of Symmachus 39
necropolis 221, 269–79, 272
Nicomachus Flavianus the Elder 39

Nisus, in *Aeneid* 146, 160
Nola 274
non-scriptural hymns, *see* hymns
non-scriptural readings, *see*
     hagiographic readings
Novatianist sect 249
Nummius Aemilianus Dexter 26, 101

oral tradition 152, 237, 240, 251–3
orationale, see libellus orationum
ordines Romani 231
orthodox Christian, poet as 8–9
Ovid, in 4th century 104, 111–21, 155,
     159; *Fasti* 104, 110–11, 113, 116, 118,
     121

pagan gods, denunciation of, by martyrs
     163
pagan works of art preserved 260
pageant of heroes 128
painting 115, 243, 249, 263, 273–5
Pallas 179
panegyric 10, 32, 102, 205, 232, 247
paraliturgical aspect of *Pe* 90
parody of cult of saints by Claudian 201
passio 75, 84, 230
patria 141–2, 149
patriotism, local 266
patriotism, Roman and Christianized
     113, 121–3, 125, 140
patrocinium 223
patroni mundi 144
patronus 222–3, 229
Paul, St 85, 123, 126, 135, 139, 229, 254,
     258, 261–2; correspondence with
     Seneca 44
Paulinus of Nola 23, 28, 109, 223, 229,
     267, 271
Peace of the Church 227
periegesis form in the *Pe* 110
Peristephanon, and archaeological
     evidence 268–77; contents 75–86;
     evolution of the collection 87, 108;
     form 70–5; *imitatio* 107–21; purpose
     86–97; sources 234–55
persecution 145, 210, 223, 245;
     persecution of AD 303–4 ('Great
     Persecution') 251
Persius, in 4th century 104
pestis 145
Peter, St 12, 85, 123, 126, 135, 139, 229,
     254, 258, 261–2
pietas 123, 141, 147, 161

piety in Theodosian court 94
pilgrimage 43, 94–5, 111, 116, 123, 229,
     262
piscina 269
Pliny, *Natural History*, in later period 43
Plotinus 49
poet as pilgrim 110–11, 113
poeta doctus 85, 103
poetic licence in *Praef* 16
poetic programme as outlined in *Praef*
     17
polemic 181
Polemius Silvius 267
Polites 195
Pollentia, battle of 23
Polycarp 224, 229
Polyxena 179
Pompey 128, 187
Pontianus 249
popular religious belief, influence of 32
popular tradition, reliance of poet on
     244, 246, 255, 275
Portus 248, 250
praefationes 34; of Ambrosian Missal 232
praeses 214
praetor 154, 163–4, 166
prayer 79, 121, 222
Priscillian 24
private devotion 257, 259
Proba 101
Propertius, in 4th century 104, 110, 113
Protadius, friend of Symmachus 39
Protasius 50, 223, 257–8
provincial governor, Prudentius as 25–6
proximus scriniorum 27, 29
Prudentius, age 19, 22–3; as Christian
     poet 15–19; career 24–8, 91; death,
     date of 31; education 22–3; historical
     sense 224; journey to Rome 29–50,
     117; name 20; origins 20–2
Psalms, model and background for
     Christian literature 14, 58, 59, 65
pseudepigrapha 44–5
Psychomachia in the manuscripts 17–18
puer senilis 157
Pyrenees 21

quaestor palatii 27
quaternus ordo of pillars in St Paul's 277
Querolus 28
Quirinus, St 25, 84, 178, 234, 236–7, 263

Ravenna mosaics 263, 267–8
readings, hagiographic, *see* hagiographic readings
Regulus, as example of pre-Christian martyr-soldier 133, 151
relics 191, 222, 263, 266, 270, 272
Remus 135
Res Gestae of Ammianus Marcellinus 46–8
retractatio 204
rhetoric 233; influence on Prudentius 166; pagan and Christian rejection of 14; rhetorical schools 23, 185, 189
Romanization of culture of empire 55
Romanus, St 102, 186–7, 246–8, 263–4
Rome 31, 124, 126, 138, 140; Christian 198; cult-sites in 273; pilgrimage to 123, 229; poet's journey to 29–31, 117; *Roma caelestis* 134; sack of 17; under Augustus 204; visits of emperor to 123–4; *see also* basilica of St Peter
Romulus 128, 135
Rufinus 44–5, 233

Sabaria 237
sacramentarium Gelasianum 250
sacramentarium Gregorianum 250
Salia, Fl. (*consul ordinarius* AD 348) 22
Sallust, commentary on, available in 4th century 104
Sapphic metre 177
Sapphic stanza 102
Saragossa (ancient Caesaraugusta) 21, 23, 241–3, 246, 262, 267
sarcophagi, Christian 262
Saturnalia 103
Saturnini 241
Savia 25, 264
school curriculum in the 4th century 99, 103, 184
schoolmaster, in *Pe* 143
Scipio 128
scrinia libellorum et memoriae 27, 28
Scriptores Historiae Augustae, see *Historia Augusta*
secular reading in 4th century 37–56
Seneca, correspondence with Paul 44; tragedies 165–6, 180, 188–93, 200, 250
Septimius Serenus 193
sermo humilis in Christian canons of taste 34–5, 91
sermons 232
serpent 212

Servius, commentaries of 44, 103
Sibyl 157–8, 161
Sidonius Apollinaris 33, 91, 94, 98, 194
significant reminiscences in *imitatio* 106
Silvius Aeneas 128
simile 218
Siscia 25, 237, 264
Sixtus II (pope) 244
Sixtus III (pope) 263
social mobility 55–6
sodalitas 146
soldier-martyrs, *see* martyr-soldier
Solinus, effect of *Memorabilia* in later period 43, 47
sorcery 235
sources for poems 88
Spanish church calendar 255–64
Spanish liturgical books 256
Spanish saints 264–8
spectabilis, rank of 28
speeches 86, 103, 154, 217–19, 233, 264
sphragis 121
stanza, use of, in hymns 73–4, 80
Statius, in 4th century 104, 180, 184, 193–7
stereotype 227–8
Stilicho 31, 203
Stoic philosophy 188
Suetonius 39
suffragium 222–3
Sulpicius Severus 54
Symmachus 28, 38–9, 263

Taio 262
Tarragona (ancient Tarraco) 21, 206, 210–11, 221–2, 268–71
Terence, in 4th-century school syllabus 104
Tertullian, attitude towards pagan culture 41, 99
theatre and animal shows, in 4th century 55
Theodosian Code 42
Theodosius I, emperor 25–6, 28, 30, 94, 124, 126, 204, 254, 264, 277
Theseus as classical forerunner of Hippolytus 249
theurgy, Neoplatonist interest in 49
Torquatus 128
torture 151, 189, 214, 233, 245
tragic characters 188
tricolon crescendo 212
trivial reminiscences in *imitatio* 106

trochaic tetrameter catalectic 61
Troy 140
Turnus 155–6, 171
tyrannus 165–6, 247

Ursicinus 47

Valencia 267
Valentinian, emperor 56, 62
Valentinian II, 277
Valerian 235, 243–4, 256–7, 264
variatio as important feature of *Pe* 116
Vatican, *see* basilica of St Peter
Venantius Fortunatus 239, 266
veritas 99
Verona, battle of 23
Vertumnus 113
Vettius Agorius Basilius Mavortius
    (consul AD 527) 92, 104
Via Appia 254

Via Nomentana 250, 261
Via Ostiensis 255
Via Romana 269, 272
Via Tiburtina, burial-place of St
    Hippolytus 248
Vincent, St 122, 177, 242, 245–6, 260–1,
    267
Virgil 103, 123; *Aeneid* and Prudentius
    124–39, 176–9; *Georgics* and Augustan
    patriotism 138
virgin martyr 155, 252, *see also individual
    names*
virgines 143
virtus 141–6, 149, 151–3, 156, 204
vitae sanctorum patrum Emeritensium 269
vocation as Christian poet 13, 19, 89,
    111

wedding hymn 168
Western aristocracy 93–4

Index of Passages Cited

Acta Fructuosi
  1. 4: 211
  2. 1: 212
  2. 4: 215
  2. 9: 215
  3. 5: 218
  3. 6: 218
  4. 1: 208
  4. 3: 220
  6. 3: 221
  7: 208
Ambrose
  De virginibus
    1: 250
    1. 2. 7: 253
    1. 2. 9: 252
  De officiis ministrorum 1. 41: 251 f.
  Hymn 9 f.: 240
Ammianus Marcellinus
  14. 6. 2: 46
  14. 6. 18: 12, 38
  14. 6. 19: 12, 38
  15. 1. 1: 46
  15. 2. 9: 46
  16. 1: 46
  16. 8. 6: 46
  17. 4. 6: 47
  17. 7. 9 ff.: 47
  19. 3. 1 ff.: 47
  19. 12. 19 f.: 49
  20. 3. 1 f.: 47
  20. 11. 26 ff.: 47
  21. 1. 14: 49
  22. 8. 1: 46
  23. 6. 85 ff.: 47
  24. 3. 12 f.: 47
  25. 10, 2 f.: 47
  25. 10. 3: 47
  26. 1. 1: 46
  26. 1. 2: 46
  27. 2. 11: 46
  27. 9. 4: 46
  28. 1. 15: 46
  28. 4. 14: 12, 38
  29. 1. 15: 46
  29. 3. 6: 25

  31. 2. 12: 46
  31. 5. 10: 46
  31. 16. 9: 46
Augustine
  Confessions
    1. 9 ff.: 14
    2. 13: 42
    6. 11: 14
    8. 6: 12
    8. 6: 20
    9. 7: 65
    9. 7. 16: 51
    10. 35: 43
    13. 21: 43
    20. 26: 15
  De anima 4. 7. 9: 103
  De civitate dei
    1. 15: 133
    2. 29: 141
    3. 15: 51
    10. 16: 53
    21. 7: 43, 50
    21. 8: 51
    22. 8: 33, 50
  De doctrina Christiana 2. 40: 100
  De Genesi ad litteram
    6. 14: 50
    9. 17: 50
  De trinitate 3. 8: 50
  Enarr. in Psalm. 49. 9: 120
  Ep.
    72. 2: 51
    137. 11 ff.: 50
  Psalm against the Donatists: 60, 71
  Retractationes 1. 19 ff.: 71
  Sermo
    90. 5: 50
    273: 206, 268
    306: 120
    311: 120
[Aurelius Victor], *Epitome de Caesaribus*
    48. 11: 27
Ausonius, *Ordo urbium nobilium* 13: 271
  Praefatiunculae
    1. 2 ff.: 11
    4: 27

Bible: *see* John, Paul, Wisdom of
Solomon

Callimachus, *fr.* 7. 13 Pf.: 120
Cassian, *Coll.* 17. 18: 238
Catullus, *Carm.* 55. 17: 171
Cicero, *Brutus* 11. 42: 228
Claudian
  Carmina minora
    23. 18: 198
    30. 48: 200
    50. 3 ff.: 200–2
  De raptu Proserpinae 1. 211: 200
  Eutrop. 2. 418: 200
  Gild. 472 ff.: 200–1
  In Ruf.
    1. 123: 198
    1. 135: 199
    2. 5: 200
    2. 245: 200
    2. 340: 200
    2. 382: 200
    2. 431: 200
  Nupt. Hon. 88: 200
  Stil.
    1. 86: 200
    2. 1 f.: 203
    2. 12: 203
Commodian, *Carmen apologeticum* 3 ff.:
  13
  Instructiones 1 f., 4 ff.: 13
Cyprian, *Ep.* 10: 127

Damasus, *Inscr.*
  32 (Ihm pp. 37 f.): 134
  37 (Ihm p. 42): 249
  40 (Ihm pp. 43 f.): 240, 250–2, 261

Eusebius
  Historia eccl.
    5 praef. 1, 4: 141–2, 227
    6. 20: 248
    6. 22: 248
  Martyrs of Palestine 4. 14. 15: 40

Gregory of Nazianzus, *Carm.* 45. 131 ff.:
  15
  Sermo 24: 236
Gregory of Tours, *De gloria martyrum*
  64: 33
  93: 238, 265–6

Hilary of Poitiers, *Hymns* 2. 21 f.:
  35
Historia Augusta
  Aelius 21. 4: 40
  Aurelianus 2. 1: 41
  Aurelius 10. 1: 41
  Avidius Cassius 9. 9: 40
  Carus et Carinus et Numerianus 21. 2:
    41
  Commodus
    15. 5: 40
    18. 2: 39
    18. 2: 40
  Firmus 1. 1: 40
  Hadrian
    2. 10: 40
    20. 3: 40
  Opellius Macrinus 1. 3 ff.: 41
  Pertinax
    2. 8: 39
    15. 8: 40
  Probus 2. 8: 41
Homer, *Odyssey* 11. 39: 166
Horace
  Carmen saeculare
    47: 139
    73 ff.: 81
  Epistles
    1. 20. 19 ff.: 10
    2. 1. 156 f.: 131
  Odes
    1. 1. 29: 12
    1. 1. 35 f.: 15
    1. 2. 13: 116
    1. 8: 146
    1. 12: 134
    2. 11. 9: 200
    3. 2: 145
    3. 2. 1: 149
    3. 2. 13 ff.: 148–50
    3. 2. 17 ff.: 147–8
    3. 2. 21 ff.: 150
    3. 3: 137
    3. 3. 11: 171
    3. 3. 18 ff.: 140
    3. 5. 29: 151
    3. 5. 49: 151
    4. 5. 1: 139
    4. 5. 5: 165
    4. 6: 83
    4. 10. 3: 169
  Satires
    1. 5: 118

Isidore of Seville, C. 9: 98
  De ecclesiasticis officiis 1. 6: 59

Jerome
  De viris illustribus
    61: 248
    91: 13
    100: 59
  Epistles
    21. 13. 4: 100
    108. 10. 2: 34
    108. 15: 14
  In Ezech. 12. 40. 5: 77
  In Mich. 7. 5 ff.: 103
  In Rufinum 1. 16: 104
  Vita Pauli 6: 35
John the Evangelist 17. 1 ff.: 14
Julian, *Ep.* 36: 101
Juvenal, *Sat.*
  2. 149 ff.: 182
  6. 343: 181
  8. 102 ff.: 182
  10. 33 ff.: 183
  11. 68: 183

Livy 5. 27: 242, 271
Lucan, *Pharsalia*
  2. 173 ff.: 186
  2. 177 f.: 186
  2. 181 f.: 187
  3. 572 ff.: 185
  3. 657 f.: 185
  6. 226 f.: 187
  6. 613: 187
  8. 708 ff.: 185–6
  9. 1 ff.: 187
  9. 12 ff.: 187
Lucian, *De conscr. historia* 29: 40

Martial, *Epigr.* 10. 104. 4: 271
Minucius Felix, *Octavius* 37: 133

Ovid
  Fasti
    1. 78 ff.: 119
    2. 4: 117
    2. 203 f.: 120
    2. 237: 120
    3. 168: 120
    3. 525 ff.: 119
    3. 662: 120
    3. 792: 118

    4. 311: 120
    4. 377: 118–19
    4. 685 ff.: 114
    4. 769: 119
    4. 905: 114
    5. 84: 120
    5. 259 f.: 116
    5. 377 ff.: 121
    5. 625: 120
    5. 646: 118
    6. 104: 120
    6. 237: 118
    6. 395 ff.: 119
    6. 557: 120
  Heroides 19. 115: 159
  Metam.
    2. 441: 161
    8. 37: 171
    9. 272: 162
    9. 137: 120
    12. 43 ff.: 120
    15. 492 ff.: 116
    15. 875 f.: 162
  Remedia amoris 752: 173
  Tristia
    4. 10: 10
    4. 10, 129 f.: 15

Paul
  1. Cor.
    1. 19: 15
    3. 16: 202
    6. 19: 202
    9. 5: 127
  Eph.
    2. 22: 202
    4. 22 ff.: 15
    6. 10 ff.: 127
  Hebr. 2. 14: 134
  Rom. 13. 12: 127
Paulinus of Nola
  Carmina
    10. 233: 271
    14. 1: 109
    19. 152 ff.: 267
    19. 266 ff.: 152
  Epistles 40. 11: 15
Propertius, *Elegies*
  2. 10. 5: 9
  2. 34. 67 f.: 118
Prudentius
  Cathemerinon
    3. 26 ff.: 99

4. 75: 69
12. 125 ff.: 168
Contra Symmachum
　1. 35: 130
　1. 380 ff.: 216
　1. 501 ff.: 260
　1. 504 ff.: 124
　1. 513 ff.: 125
　1. 541 ff.: 124
　1. 587: 125
　2. 24 f.: 142
　2. 35 f.: 142
　2. 1112 ff.: 216
　2. 249: 202
Hamartigenia 853: 134
Peristephanon
　1: 237–9
　1. 4 f.: 109, 143
　1. 5: 109
　1. 10 ff.: 122
　1. 10: 144
　1. 11: 120
　1. 13 ff.: 144
　1. 22 ff.: 148
　1. 24: 148
　1. 25 ff.: 144, 149
　1. 28 f.: 150
　1. 31 ff.: 144, 146
　1. 34: 147
　1. 37 ff.: 147
　1. 47: 151
　1. 48: 148
　1. 51: 149–50
　1. 53: 146
　1. 55 ff.: 146–7
　1. 61 ff.: 147
　1. 73 ff.: 238
　1. 74: 120
　1. 79 f.: 152, 195
　1. 79 ff.: 238
　1. 82: 153
　1. 85 ff.: 238
　1. 91 ff.: 151
　1. 97 ff.: 144
　1. 103: 152
　1. 106: 144 f.
　1. 118: 69
　1. 120: 109
　1. 225 f.: 200
　2: 243–5
　2. 5 f.: 126
　2. 6 ff.: 129
　2. 7 f.: 127, 129

　2. 9 ff.: 130
　2. 12: 130
　2. 13 ff.: 131
　2. 19 f.: 134
　2. 21 ff.: 126
　2. 39 f.: 245
　2. 276: 127
　2. 413 ff.: 130, 135
　2. 416: 129
　2. 417 ff.: 126, 129, 135
　2. 431 ff.: 126
　2. 437 ff.: 135
　2. 445: 136
　2. 451: 130
　2. 473: 126
　2. 473 f.: 260
　2. 481 f.: 260
　2. 497 ff.: 125
　2. 514: 181
　2. 515 f.: 69
　2. 516: 83
　2. 517 ff.: 134
　2. 517 ff.: 204
　2. 518 f.: 182
　2. 529: 198
　2. 536 ff.: 260
　2. 537 ff.: 21
　2. 541: 120
　2. 544: 168
　2. 545 ff.: 122
　2. 553 ff.: 133
　2. 575: 116
　2. 581 ff.: 120
　2. 581 f.: 259
　2. 582: 22
　3: 239–41
　3. 6 ff.: 109
　3. 6: 198
　3. 16 f.: 156
　3. 17: 164
　3. 24 f.: 199
　3. 25: 157
　3. 31 ff.: 157–8
　3. 36 f.: 159, 162
　3. 36 f.: 240
　3. 41 f.: 160
　3. 43 f.: 240
　3. 47: 160
　3. 60: 162
　3. 61 f.: 163
　3. 64: 240
　3. 66 ff.: 163
　3. 72: 163

Prudentius (*cont.*)
  Peristephanon (*cont.*)
    3. 109 ff.: 167, 174
    3. 126 ff.: 165
    3. 151 ff.: 240
    3. 152: 169
    3. 154: 177
    3. 156 ff.: 171
    3. 161: 171
    3. 165: 171
    3. 169: 171
    3. 170: 170
    3. 176 ff.: 172
    3. 184 f.: 173
    3. 186 ff.: 266
    3. 188 f.: 173
    3. 199 f.: 174
    3. 203 ff.: 175
    3. 206 ff.: 78, 176
    3. 207: 69, 174
    4. 9: 192
    4. 16 ff.: 86
    4. 20: 127
    4. 22 f.: 127
    4. 31 f.: 22
    4. 53 ff.: 127
    4. 73: 127
    4. 77 ff.: 246
    4. 91: 195
    4. 97 ff.: 122
    4. 97 ff.: 246, 267
    4. 109 ff.: 155
    4. 121: 151
    4. 137 ff.: 117
    4. 146: 266
    4. 148: 69
    4. 153 f.: 78
    4. 164 ff.: 86
    4. 197 ff.: 78
    5: 245–6
    5. 4: 127
    5. 54 ff.: 245
    5. 146 ff.: 245
    5. 186 ff.: 245
    5. 217 ff.: 245
    5. 437: 185
    5. 441 ff.: 185
    5. 561 ff.: 78
    6: 205–21
    6. 1 ff.: 209
    6. 5 f.: 209
    6. 8 f.: 209
    6. 13 ff.: 210–11

6. 16 f.: 211
6. 20: 212
6. 23: 212
6. 25: 127
6. 25 ff.: 212
6. 28 ff.: 213
6. 30: 217
6. 44 ff.: 215
6. 48 ff.: 215
6. 51: 215
6. 58 ff.: 216
6. 67 ff.: 217
6. 70 ff.: 217
6. 73: 217
6. 79 ff.: 217
6. 84: 122
6. 84: 218
6. 91 ff.: 291
6. 97 ff.: 219
6. 106 ff.: 219
6. 108 ff.: 220
6. 118 f.: 220
6. 129: 221
6. 136 ff.: 221
6. 140 f.: 221
6. 145 ff.: 70
6. 148 ff.: 78
6. 151: 69, 78, 83
6. 154 ff.: 271
6. 209: 83
7: 236–7
7. 49: 178
9: 242–4
9. 3 f.: 114, 139, 140
9. 3: 200
9. 6: 140
9. 8: 116
9. 11: 200
9. 85: 178
9. 103: 200
9. 104 f.: 116
9. 106: 263
10: 246–8
10. 9 f.: 186
10. 21 f.: 264
10. 71: 127
10. 142 ff.: 183
10. 189: 120
10. 225: 120
10. 269 ff.: 182
10. 346 ff.: 202
10. 420: 203
10. 675: 182

10. 696 ff.: 192
10. 700: 183
10. 701 f.: 192
10. 906: 187
10. 907 ff.: 192
11: 248–50
11. 1: 110
11. 2: 116
11. 7 f.: 233
11. 7 f.: 249
11. 13 f.: 117
11. 17: 200
11. 18 ff.: 116
11. 29 ff.: 249
11. 43 f.: 137
11. 115 ff.: 200–1
11. 123 ff.: 116
11. 125: 249, 273
11. 127 ff.: 273
11. 127 ff.: 116–17
11. 131 ff.: 190–1
11. 151: 200
11. 179 ff.: 117
11. 211 f.: 200
11. 213 ff.: 257
11. 215 ff.: 137, 215 ff.
11. 216: 200
11. 219: 138
11. 219: 200
11. 220: 196
11. 225: 138
11. 231 f.: 117–18, 138
11. 232: 256
11. 237: 265
11. 237: 266
11. 239 ff.: 200–1
12: 254–5
12. 3 f.: 118
12. 10: 196
12. 11 ff.: 254
12. 23 ff.: 254
12. 31 ff.: 122
12. 54: 174
12. 54: 200
12. 55: 139
12. 56: 130
12. 57 f.: 197
12. 60: 69, 83
12. 65 f.: 277
13: 235–6
13. 2: 96
13. 21 ff.: 236
13. 73: 199

13. 76: 120
13. 76 ff.: 236
13. 102 ff.: 96
14: 250–4
14. 2: 252
14. 10: 253
14. 21: 252
14. 57: 253
14. 63: 155
14. 89: 187
14. 94 ff.: 187
14. 94 ff.: 178–9
14. 112: 252
14. 119: 127
14. 124: 179
14. 132 f.: 84
Praef.
1 ff.: 7–8
7 ff.: 13, 23
10 ff.: 14
23: 14
24: 22
35 ff.: 15–16
37: 69
37 ff.: 17–19
42: 88, 109
43 ff.: 16, 121
Psychomachia 845 ff.: 167

Seneca the Elder, *Controversiae* 2. 5:
    165 ff.
Seneca the Younger, *Oedipus* 999 f.: 192
    Troades
        578 ff.: 165
        582 ff.: 189
        1098 ff.: 192
        1104 ff.: 192
        1114 ff.: 192
Servius, *Comm. ad Aen.* 2. 683: 170
    Comm. ad Georg, 4. 125: 118
Sidonius Apollinaris, *Ep.* 2. 9: 33, 91, 99
Solinus, *Memorabilia* 53. 23 ff.: 47
Sophocles, *Antigone* 813 ff.: 166
Statius, *Silvae* 1. 3. 35: 196
    Thebaid
        1. 186: 196
        5. 580: 200
        5. 590: 196
        5. 598: 196
        8. 493: 195
Sulpicius Severus, *Life of St Martin*
    Praef. 3 ff.: 99

Symmachus, *Ep.*
  3. 11. 3: 39
  4. 18.5: 39

Tertullian, *De praescriptione haereticorum*
  7: 99
Theodoret, *Hist. eccl.* 5. 26: 216

Varro, *Res rusticae* 3. 16. 10: 118
Virgil
  Aeneid
    1. 7: 137
    1. 10: 140, 178
    1. 166: 138
    1. 229: 135
    1. 232: 130
    1. 264: 135
    1. 279 f.: 125
    1. 285: 130
    1. 288: 159
    1. 291 ff.: 135
    1. 292: 134
    1. 294: 136
    1. 403 ff.: 169
    1. 446 ff.: 137
    1. 646: 159
    1. 726: 173
    2. 317: 149
    2. 448: 196
    2. 682 f.: 170
    3. 284 f.: 172
    3. 321: 179
    3. 339: 196
    3. 636: 196
    4. 173: 120
    4. 274 ff.: 149
    4. 666: 120
    4. 693 ff.: 178
    5. 17: 135
    5. 500 ff.: 171
    5. 545 ff.: 160
    5. 672: 163
    6. 45 ff.: 157–8
    6. 100 ff.: 158
    6. 307: 166
    6. 462 ff.: 160
    6. 756 ff.: 125
    6. 765: 128
    6. 782: 128
    6. 789 ff.: 132
    6. 794 ff.: 125

    6. 795: 128
    6. 806: 125
    6. 812: 128
    6. 817 f.: 128–9
    6. 825: 131
    6. 832 ff.: 131
    6. 841: 131
    6. 851 ff.: 128–9
    6. 883 ff.: 175
    6. 890: 125
    7. 72 ff.: 169
    7. 104: 120
    7. 143: 155
    7. 391: 195
    7. 452: 164
    7. 473: 199
    7. 601 ff.: 138
    7. 602: 136, 200
    7. 803 ff.: 157
    8. 25: 138
    8. 642 ff.: 201
    8. 699: 129
    9. 184 ff.: 160
    9. 427: 164
    9. 435 ff.: 168
    9. 641 f.: 160, 162
    10. 116: 135
    10. 711: 158
    11. 24 f.: 141
    11. 252 ff.: 163
    12. 84: 171
    12. 155: 198
    12. 532 ff.: 156
    12. 834: 135
    12. 847: 156
    12. 849: 164
  Eclogues
    5. 56 f.: 178
    10: 176
  Georgics
    1 *ad fin.*: 137
    1. 302: 176
    2. 175: 9
    2. 330 ff.: 176
    2. 399: 198
    2. 534: 138
    4. 54: 174
    4. 125: 118
    4. 182: 174

Wisdom of Solomon 4. 8 ff.: 157